ACCA

Audit and Assurance (AA)

Practice & Revision Kit

For exams in September 2020,
December 2020, March 2021
and June 2021

First edition 2007
Thirteenth edition February 2020

ISBN 9781 5097 8392 2
(previous ISBN 9781 5097 2401 7)

e-ISBN 9781 5097 2929 6
(previous e-ISBN 9781 5097 2428 4)

Cataloguing-in-Publication Data
A catalogue record for this book
is available from the British Library

Published by

BPP Learning Media Ltd
BPP House, Aldine Place
London W12 8AA

www.bpp.com/learningmedia

Printed in the United Kingdom

Your learning materials, published by BPP Learning Media Ltd, are printed on paper obtained from traceable sustainable sources.

We are grateful to the Association of Chartered Certified Accountants for permission to reproduce past examination questions. The suggested solutions in the Practice & Revision Kit have been prepared by BPP Learning Media Ltd, except where otherwise stated.

BPP Learning Media is grateful to the IASB for permission to reproduce extracts from the International Financial Reporting Standards including all International Accounting Standards, SIC and IFRIC Interpretations (the Standards). The Standards together with their accompanying documents are issued by:

The International Accounting Standards Board (IASB) 30 Cannon Street, London, EC4M 6XH, United Kingdom. Email: info@ifrs.org Web: www.ifrs.org

Disclaimer: The IASB, the International Financial Reporting Standards (IFRS) Foundation, the authors and the publishers do not accept responsibility for any loss caused by acting or refraining from acting in reliance on the material in this publication, whether such loss is caused by negligence or otherwise to the maximum extent permitted by law.

Contents

Question index

The headings in this checklist/index indicate the main topics of questions, but questions are expected to cover several different topics.

Questions set under the old syllabus *Audit and Assurance* (F8) and *Audit and Internal Review* (AIR) exams are included because their style and content are similar to those which appear in the Audit and Assurance exam. The questions have been amended to reflect the current exam format.

BPP
LEARNING
MEDIA

	Marks	Time allocation Mins	Page number Question	Page number Answer
Sample questions from the examining team				
Section A Questions				
195-196 March 2017	4	7	106	316
197–198 June 2017	4	7	107	317
199-200 September 2017	4	7	108	318
201-202 December 2017	4	7	109	318
203-204 March 2018	4	7	110	319
205-206 June 2018	4	7	111	319
207-208 September 2018	4	7	112	320
209-210 December 2018	4	7	113	320
211-212 March 2019	4	7	114	321
213-214 June 2019	4	7	115	321
215-216 September 2019	4	7	117	322
217-218 December 2019	4	7	118	323

Mock exam 1 (September 2016 CBE)

Mock exam 2 (Specimen Exam CBE)

Mock exam 3 (December 2016 CBE)

Mock exam 4 (Mar/Jun 2019 Hybrid Exam CBE)

Topic index

Listed below are the key Audit and Assurance syllabus topics and the numbers of the questions in this Kit covering those topics. If you need to concentrate your practice and revision on certain topics or if you want to attempt all available questions that refer to a particular subject, you will find this index useful.

Syllabus topic	Question numbers
Accounting estimates	142
Analytical procedures	73(a), 77(b), 81(a)-(c), 113(c), 154(a), 204
Assurance engagement	1, 3, 4, 74(c), 114(b), 194(a), 206
Audit acceptance, engagement and tendering	5, 56-60, 63-64, 79(a)
Audit evidence	134, 153(a), 202
Audit planning and documentation	36, 79(b), 129, 207
Audit regulation	14, 65
Auditor's report	151(d), 153(c), 156(e), 157(d), 158(d), 163, 169, 172-173, 178, 183, 186, 188, 192, 194(c), 196, 200, 210, 211, 212
Audit risk	41, 52, 53, 55, 71(b), 72(a), 73(a), 74(b), 75(a)-(b), 76(a)-(b), 77(b), 78(a)-(b), 79(c), 80(b)
CAATs	130, 144
Data analytics	10, 150(d)
Cash and bank	111(d), 123, 137-138, 118(b), 158(b), 199, 215
Communicating with management	108(a), 111(a)-(b), 118(a)
Corporate governance	6-9, 16-20, 30-33, 72(d), 213, 217
Directors' emoluments	72(c), 156(d), 157(c)
Documentation	70
Ethics	11-13, 15, 21-29, 61-62, 78(c), 116(a), 152(a), 203
Experts	122, 197
External audit	
Fraud, laws and regulations	2, 44, 74(a), 80(a), 107(c) , 109(c), 128
Going concern	73(b), 158(c)-(d), 174-175, 177-178, 180-183, 189-192, 205, 214, 218
Interim audit	66-67, 110(b)
Internal audit	34-35, 90, 94-95, 108(d), 117(c)
Internal audit – using work	68, 69, 107(e), 132
Internal controls	45, 82-86, 96-98, 105-6, 107(a), 115, 116(b)-(c)
Inventory	40, 72(b), 75(c)-(d), 81(d), 114(a), 124-125, 133, 149, 153(b), 160-161, 194(b)
Materiality and misstatements	37, 78(a), 179, 184, 187

BPP
LEARNING
MEDIA

The exam

Computer-based exams

It has only been possible from exams in June 2019 for candidates to sit Applied Skills exams as a computer-based exam (CBE). Applied Skills exams are all computer-based exams.

Introduction to Audit and Assurance (AA)

Overall aim of the syllabus

This exam requires students to develop knowledge and understanding of the process of carrying out the assurance engagement and its application in the context of the professional regulatory framework.

Brought forward knowledge

The *Audit and Assurance* syllabus assumes prior knowledge and understanding of the accounting topics in *Financial Accounting* (with the exception of group financial statements). A summary of such knowledge is included in the Essential reading relating to chapter 18.

The syllabus

The broad syllabus headings are:

A   Audit framework and regulation
B   Planning and risk assessment
C   Internal control
D   Audit evidence
E   Review and reporting

Main capabilities

On successful completion of this exam, candidates should be able to:

- Explain the concept of audit and assurance and the functions of audit, corporate governance, including ethics and professional conduct.

- Demonstrate how the auditor obtains and accepts audit engagements, obtains an understanding of the entity and its environment, assesses the risk of material misstatement (whether arising from fraud or other irregularities) and plans an audit of financial statements.

- Describe and evaluate internal controls, techniques and audit tests, including IT systems to identify and communicate control risks and their potential consequences, making appropriate recommendations. Describe the scope, role and function of internal audit.

- Identify and describe the work and evidence obtained by the auditor and others required to meet the objectives of audit engagements and the application of the International Standards on Auditing (ISAs).

- Explain how consideration of subsequent events and the going concern principle can inform the conclusions from audit work and are reflected in different types of auditor's report, written representations and the final review and report.

Displaying the right qualities and avoiding weaknesses

In order to pass Audit and Assurance it is important that you get some of the basics right. These include the following:

Read the question

Again this sounds obvious but is absolutely critical. When you are reading the question think about the following:

- Which technical area is being tested?

    This should let you identify the relevant areas of technical knowledge to draw on.

- What am I being asked to do?

    (We will take a more detailed look at the wording of requirements later.)

- Are there any key dates?

    This is important in questions on inventory. If the inventory count takes place at a time other than the year-end you need to be aware of this.

- What is the status of your client?

    For example is it large or small, is it a new or existing client? This might affect issues such as risk.

- What is the nature of the business?

    This is particularly relevant in planning questions as it will have an impact on risk areas.

- How many marks are allocated to each part of the question so approximately how many points do I need to make?

When you think about the number of points you need to achieve you need to consider this in relation to the requirement. If you are asked for explanation it is likely that you will score more marks per point than if you are simply asked for a list of points.

You also need to think about the order in which you read information in the question. Particularly in Section B it is important that you read the requirement first so that as you read through the rest of the information you are aware of the key matters/issues which you are looking out for. For example if you are asked for risks in a scenario you can try to identify as many risk factors as possible as you read the detailed information.

Understand the requirements

It is important that you can understand and differentiate between the requirements and terms that the examining team typically uses. Here are some examples:

Requirement	Meaning
Explain	Make a point clear, justify a point of view
Describe	Give an account of something, including the key features
Define	Give the meaning of
Recommend	Advise the appropriate actions to pursue in terms the recipient will understand
Discuss	Critically examine an issue
List	Normally punchier points than 'explain' or 'discuss'
Illustrate	Explain by using examples
Audit procedures/audit tests	Actions
Enquiries	Questions
Evidence	Source (eg document) and what it proves

Think and plan

No matter how well prepared you are, you are going to have to do some thinking in the exam. Obviously you will be under time pressure but, if used effectively, thinking and planning time should not be seen as a waste of time.

Generating ideas can often be a problem at this stage. Remember that your knowledge of key ISAs can serve as a good starting point.

In audit evidence questions you may think about the financial statement assertions (completeness, accuracy, existence etc). You could also think about the different types of procedures (inspection, observation, inquiry, confirmation, recalculation/reperformance and analytical procedures).

In risk questions it might be helpful to think about the different elements of risk (inherent risk, control risk, detection risk).

Repeating this knowledge will not be sufficient in most cases to pass the question but these ideas can form a very sound basis for developing a good answer.

Keep going back to the requirement and make sure that you really are answering the question. One of the most common errors in auditing exams is identifying the correct point but using it in the wrong way. Make sure that your answer is focused on the requirements. It may be tempting to write everything you know about a particular point but this will not help you to pass the exam. This 'scattergun' approach will attract few, if any, marks.

Producing your answer

Although much of the hard work has been done by the time you get to this stage you need to think carefully about how you put down each point on paper. The way you make the point can make a difference to the number of marks scored. You need to make sure your answers do not suffer from a lack of clarity and precision. This is particularly the case regarding questions on audit evidence. For example, lists of tests stating 'check this' and 'check that' without explaining what is being checked and why is likely to score few marks. If you find it difficult to gauge the right level of detail try to imagine that you are explaining the procedure to a junior member of staff. Would they be able to perform the procedure based on your description?

Think about your style. A well-structured answer with clearly identifiable points is generally preferable to long paragraphs of text. However, do not fall into the trap of producing note-form answers. This is rarely sufficiently detailed to score marks.

Format of the exam

The exam format is the same irrespective of the mode of delivery and will comprise two exam sections:

Section	Style of question type	Description	Proportion of exam (%)
A	Objective test (OT) case	3 questions × 10 marks Each question will contain 5 subparts each worth 2 marks	30
B	Constructed response (long questions)	1 question × 30 marks 2 questions × 20 marks	70
Total			100

Section A questions will be selected from the entire syllabus. The responses to each question or subpart in the case of OT cases are marked automatically as either correct or incorrect by computer.

Section B questions will mainly focus on the following syllabus areas but a minority of marks can be drawn from any other area of the syllabus

- Planning and risk assessment (syllabus area B)
- Internal control (syllabus area C)
- Audit evidence (syllabus area D)

The responses to these questions are human marked.

For exam sittings from September 2019 onwards, questions have used a dating convention whereby the 'current' date is 1 July 20X5.

Additional information

The study guide provides more detailed guidance on the syllabus and can be found by visiting the exam resource finder on the ACCA website: www.accaglobal.com/uk/en/student/exam-support-resources.html

Helping you with your revision

BPP Learning Media – Approved Content Provider

As an ACCA **Approved Content Provider**, BPP Learning Media gives you the **opportunity** to use revision materials reviewed by the ACCA examining team. By incorporating the ACCA examining team's comments and suggestions regarding the depth and breadth of syllabus coverage, the BPP Learning Media Practice & Revision Kit provides excellent **ACCA approved** support for your revision.

These materials are reviewed by the ACCA examining team. The objective of the review is to ensure that the material properly covers the syllabus and study guide outcomes used by the examining team in setting the exams in the appropriate breadth and depth. The review does not ensure that every eventuality, combination or application of examinable topics is addressed by the ACCA Approved Content. Nor does the review comprise a detailed technical check of the content as the Approved Content Provider has its own quality assurance processes in place in this respect.

BPP Learning Media does everything possible to ensure that material is accurate and up to date when sending to print. In the event that any errors are found after the print date, they are uploaded to the following website: www.bpp.com/learningmedia/Errata.

Question practice

Question practice under timed conditions is absolutely vital. We strongly advise you to create a revision study plan which focuses on question practice. This is so that you can get used to the pressures of answering exam questions in limited time, develop proficiency in the Specific AA skills and the Exam success skills. Ideally, you should aim to cover all questions in this Kit, and very importantly, all four mock exams.

To help you plan your revision, we have provided a full topic index which maps the questions to topics in the syllabus (see page ix).

Making the most of question practice

At BPP Learning Media we realise that you need more than just questions and model answers to get the most from your question practice.

- Our **Top tips** included for certain questions provide essential advice on tackling questions, presenting answers and the key points that answers need to include. .

- We include **marking guides** to show you what the examining team rewards.

- We include **comments from the examining team** to show you where students struggled or performed well in the actual exam.

Attempting mock exams

There are four mock exams that provide practice at coping with the pressures of the exam day. We strongly recommend that you attempt them under exam conditions. **Mock exam 1** is the September 2016 exam; **Mock exam 2** is the Specimen exam; **Mock exam 3** is the December 2016 exam and **Mock exam 4** includes the Section B questions from the March/June 2019 Hybrid exam.

Topics to revise

The Audit and Assurance exam assumes knowledge of Financial Accounting. It is important, therefore, that candidates can apply the knowledge they have gained in Financial Accounting to the Audit and Assurance exam.

All questions are compulsory so you must revise the **whole** syllabus. Since the exam includes three 10 mark OT case questions (each comprising five OT questions of 2 marks each) in Section A, you should expect questions to cover a large part of the syllabus. Selective revision **will limit** the number of questions you can answer and hence reduce your chances of passing. It is better to go into the exam knowing a reasonable amount about most of the syllabus rather than concentrating on a few topics to the exclusion of the rest.

In Section B, all questions will require a written response but there may be questions requiring the calculation and interpretation of some basic ratios in the context of audit planning or review.

In short, remember that **all** the questions in this exam are compulsory. Therefore, we **strongly advise** that you do not selectively revise certain topics – any topic from the syllabus could be examined. Selective revision will limit the number of questions you can answer and hence reduce your chances of passing this exam.

Question practice

Practising as many exam-style questions as possible will be the key to passing this exam. You must do questions under **timed conditions** and ensure you write full answers to the discussion parts as well as doing the calculations.

Avoid looking at the answer until you have finished a question. Your biggest problem with Audit and Assurance questions may be knowing how to start, and this needs practice.

Also ensure that you attempt all four mock exams under exam conditions. Gaining the easy marks in this exam tend to fall into two categories.

Objective test questions (OTs) in Section A

Some OTs are easier than others, particularly MCQs. Answer those that you feel fairly confident about as quickly as you can. Come back later to those you find more difficult. This could be a way of making use of the time in the examination most efficiently and effectively.

Make sure that you understand the wording of OTs before selecting your answer.

Discussions in Section B questions

A Section B question may separate discussion requirements from calculations, so that you do not need to do the calculations first in order to answer the discussion part. This means that you should be able to gain marks from making sensible, practical comments without having to complete the calculations.

Discussions that are focused on the specific organisation in the question will gain more marks than regurgitation of knowledge. Read the question carefully and more than once, to ensure you are actually answering the specific requirements.

Pick out key words such as 'describe', 'evaluate' and 'discuss'. These all mean something specific.

- 'Describe' means to communicate the key features
- 'Evaluate' means to assess the value
- 'Discuss' means to examine in detail by argument

Clearly label the points you make in discussions so that the marker can identify them all rather than getting lost in the detail.

Provide answers in the form requested. Use a report format if asked for and give recommendations if required.

Tackling Objective Test Case Questions

You will see a variety of question styles in addition to MCQs, including number entry, multiple response and drag and drop.

First, read the whole case scenario. Make a note of any specific instructions or assumptions, such as key dates.

Then skim through the requirements of the five questions. The questions are independent of each other and can be answered in any order.

Some of the questions will be easier than others. For example, you may be asked to identify risks to independence from a given scenario.

Other questions will be more difficult and/or complex. There are two types of question that may take you longer to answer.

The first more time-consuming question is one where you are asked to consider two related issues. The best approach to adopt here is a step-by-step approach, dealing with each issue in turn. For example you could be asked to consider whether a potential adjustment is material and the impact of this on the audit report based on circumstances set out in the scenario. The first step would be to assess the materiality of the adjustment using your technical knowledge, but also applying any information given to you in the scenario. Having made a decision it should be possible to discount at least one of the distracters. Then think about the impact on the auditor's report. Does the audit opinion need to be modified or not? If it is, is the issue pervasive or not? If possible, try to come to your own conclusion before looking at the options available, then check whether your answer is one of the options listed. (Obviously if you are struggling looking at the remaining available options may help to jog your memory.) Having selected your answer always check the remaining distracters to ensure that you haven't made a common mistake.

The second more time-consuming question is one where you are asked to consider a number of statements and identify which one (or more) of them is correct. Make sure that you read each statement at least twice before making your selection. Be careful to follow the requirements of the question exactly, for example if you are asked to identify **two** correct statements. Make sure that you have spotted any negative questions, eg 'Which **TWO** of the following are **NOT**....'

Analysis of past papers

The table below provides details of when each element of the syllabus has been examined in the most recent sittings.

From December 2016, the ACCA have released a 'sample' exam every two sittings which shows only questions set in Section B of the exam. Only one such sample exam was released in 2019.

Workbook chapter		Mar/ Jun 2019	Sep/ Dec 2018	Mar/ Jun 2018	Sep/ Dec 2017	Mar/ Jun 2017	Dec 2016	Sept 2016	Specimen Paper
	Audit framework and regulation								
1	The concept of audit and other assurance engagements								
2	External audits								\
3	Corporate governance	B Q16d					A Q1, Q2		
5	Professional ethics and ACCA's Code of Ethics and Conduct			B Q16a	B Q16c	B Q16d	A Q11, Q12, Q13, Q14, Q15	A Q1, Q2, Q3, Q5
	Planning and risk assessment								
6	Obtaining and accepting audit engagements						B Q16a	B Q18c	
6	Objective and general principles								
6	Assessing audit risks	B Q17	B Q16c	B Q17b	B Q17c	B Q16a,b	B Q16c	B Q18b	B Q16a, Q16b
6	Understanding the entity and its environment		B Q16a, b				B Q16b		
6	Fraud, laws and regulations			B Q17a					
7	Audit planning and documentation				B Q17a, b			B Q18a	B Q16c, Q16d, Q16e
	Internal control								
9	Internal control systems	B Q16a		B Q16a	B Q16b	B Q18a			

Workbook chapter		Mar/Jun 2019	Sep/Dec 2018	Mar/Jun 2018	Sep/Dec 2017	Mar/Jun 2017	Dec 2016	Sept 2016	Specimen Paper
9	The use and evaluation of internal control systems by auditors							B Q16a	
10	Tests of controls	B Q16b	B Q17b	B Q16a, b	B Q16c	B Q18b	B Q17	B Q16b, Q16c	B Q17a
10	Communication on internal control		B Q17a						
4	Internal audit and governance and the differences between external and internal audit						A Q3		A Q4
4	The scope of the internal audit function, outsourcing and internal audit assignments			B Q16c			A Q4, Q5		
	Audit evidence								
8	Financial statement assertions and audit evidence						A Q11, Q12, Q15		A Q7, Q8
11	Audit procedures						A Q13, Q14		
11	Audit sampling and other means of testing							A Q4	
12-17	The audit of specific items	B Q16c, B Q18a, b, c	B Q16d, e, B Q18a, b	B Q16d, B Q18a, b, c	B Q16d, B Q18a, b, c	B Q17a, c d	B Q18a		A Q6, Q7, Q9, Q10, Q13, Q14 B Q17b, B Q18b (ii)
11	Computer-assisted audit techniques					B Q17b		A Q5	
12	The work of others								B Q18 b (i)
18	Not-for-profit organisations								

Workbook chapter		Mar/Jun 2019	Sep/Dec 2018	Mar/Jun 2018	Sep/Dec 2017	Mar/Jun 2017	Dec 2016	Sept 2016	Specimen Paper
	Review and reporting								
19	Subsequent events	B Q18d					A Q8	A Q6, Q7, Q8	A Q12
19	Going concern		B Q18c				A Q6, Q9, Q10	B Q17b	
19	Written representations								
19	Audit finalisation and the final review						A Q7		
20	Auditor's reports		B Q18d	B Q18d	B Q18d	B Q17e	B Q18b	A Q9, Q10	A Q11, Q15, B Q18c

Essential skills areas to be successful in Audit and Assurance

We think there are three areas you should develop in order to achieve exam success in Audit and Assurance (AA):

(1)   Knowledge application

(2)   Specific AA skills

(3)   Exam success skills

These are shown in the diagram below:

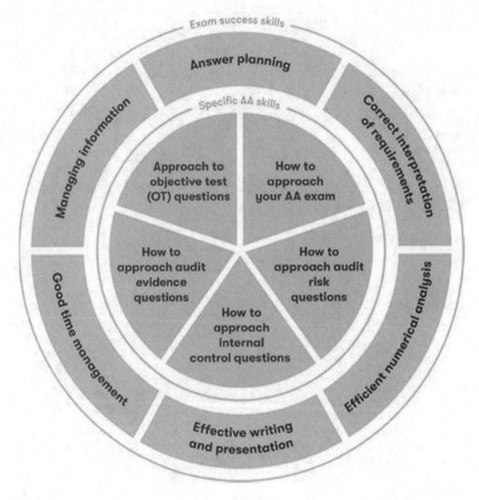

Specific AA skills

These are the skills specific to AA that we think you need to develop in order to pass the exam.

In this Workbook, there are five skills checkpoints which define each skill and show how it is applied in answering a question. A brief summary of each skill is given below:

Skill 1: How to approach your AA exam

Passing AA is much more about exam technique than detailed knowledge. Therefore, it is important that you plan your approach to the exam, and practise this approach, before you sit your exam.

A step-by-step technique for ensuring that you have a **planned approach to your AA exam** is outlined below:

Step 1	Attempt Section A first. Read the requirements to each of the OT questions before reading the OT case scenario. Do not rush through this section of the exam.
Step 2	Then attempt Section B. Skim through all three questions and attempt them in your order of preference. Read all requirements in detail and use the scenario fully.

Skills Checkpoint 1 in the BPP Workbook covers this technique in detail.

Skill 2: How to approach audit risk questions

In the exam, it is highly likely that you will need to attempt a scenario based question on audit risk.

Step 1	Allow some of your allotted time to read the requirement and the scenario. Don't rush into starting to write your answer. Start by analysing the requirements so that you know what you are looking for when you read the scenario.
Step 2	Re-read the scenario and set out an answer plan using the risks you identify as you read through. Use headings. Work through each paragraph of the scenario identifying specific audit risks. Each risk is worth one mark and the auditor's response is also worth one mark, so you would need five properly explained risks and responses to gain ten marks.
Step 3	Where there are more than the required number of audit risks, choose those that you can best explain. Use your headings to write your answer, describe the audit risk in detail explaining the potential impact on the financial statements. Also remember to explain the practical steps the auditor would take and the work they would do. Start each point in a new paragraph.

Skills Checkpoint 2 in the BPP Workbook covers this technique in detail through application to an exam-standard question.

Skill 3: How to approach internal control questions

Similarly, to Skill 2, it is likely that you will need to attempt a scenario based question on internal controls in your exam.

A step-by-step technique for attempting such questions is outlined below.

Step 1	Allow some of your allotted time to read the requirement and the scenario. Don't rush into starting to write your answer.
	Start by analysing the requirements so that you know what you are looking for when you read the scenario.
Step 2	Re-read the scenario and set out an answer plan using the deficiencies you identify as you read through.
	Use headings.
	Work through each paragraph of the scenario identifying specific deficiencies. Each deficiency is worth one mark and the recommendation is also worth one mark, hence why you would need six properly explained deficiencies and recommendations to gain 12 marks.
Step 3	Often there are more than the required number of deficiencies in a scenario, therefore choose the ones for which you can provide a recommended control.
	Use your headings to write your answer, explain the deficiency in terms of its impact on the entity. Also remember to explain the recommendation, what internal control should be implemented and by whom.
	Start each point in a new paragraph.

Skills Checkpoint 3 in the BPP Workbook covers this technique in detail through application to an exam-standard question.

Skill 4: How to approach audit evidence questions

These questions can appear in both sections of the exam. It is very important that you discern exactly what the requirement is asking for and that you use any scenario provided in the exam.

A step-by-step technique for approaching audit evidence questions is outlined below.

Step 1	Identify exactly what you are being asked for in the requirement: audit procedures, tests of controls or substantive procedures.
	Also identify whether the requirement is testing audit procedures that relate to a particular assertion.
Step 2	Now that you have understood what the requirement demands you are much better placed to answer it. Consider the following:
	Is there a scenario you should use?
	Can you remember the accounting treatment for the item? Would that give you a starting point?
	What audit procedures have you learnt/used at work?
	Can you use the mnemonic AEIOU to help you to generate audit procedures?
Step 3	Write out your audit procedure using the **'verb-document-reason'** approach.
	What do you want to be done (eg recalculate, agree, vouch)?
	To which document (eg invoice, physical asset, board minutes)?
	Why (eg to ensure that receivables are recoverable (valuation))? You might choose to link this to an assertion.
	Start each audit procedure on a new line.

Skills Checkpoint 4 in the BPP Workbook covers this technique in detail through application to a sample of exam-standard questions.

Skill 5: Approach to objective test (OT) questions

Section A comprises 30% of the exam and consists of three OT case questions. Candidates can be tempted to rush through this section in order to make up time for Section B however this is a risky approach because there are a lot of marks you could lose.

A step-by-step technique for approaching OT questions is outlined below:

Step 1	**Answer the questions you know first.**
	If you're having difficulty answering a question, move on and come back to tackle it once you've answered all the questions you know. It is often quicker to answer discursive style OT questions first, leaving more time for calculations. The AA exam doesn't have many calculations but you may be asked to calculate financial statement ratios.
Step 2	**Answer all questions.**
	There is no penalty for an incorrect answer in ACCA exams, there is nothing to be gained by leaving an OT question unanswered. If you are stuck on a question, as a last resort, it is worth selecting the option you consider most likely to be correct, and moving on. Make a note of the question, so if you have time after you have answered the rest of the questions, you can revisit it.
Step 3	**Read the requirement first!**
	The requirement will be stated in bold text in the exam. Identify what you are being asked to do, any technical knowledge required and **what type of OT question** you are dealing with. Look for key words in the requirement such as "which TWO of the following," or "which of the following is NOT".

Skills Checkpoint 5 in the BPP Workbook covers this technique in detail through application to an exam-standard question.

Exam success skills

Passing the AA exam requires more than applying syllabus knowledge and demonstrating the specific AA skills. It also requires the development of excellent exam technique through question practice.

We consider the following six skills to be vital for exam success. The skills checkpoints show how each of these skills can be applied in the exam.

Exam success skill 1

Managing information

Questions in the exam will present you with a lot of information. The skill is how you handle this information to make the best use of your time. The key is determining how you will approach the exam and then actively reading the questions.

Advice on developing Managing information

Approach

The exam is three hours long. There is no designated 'reading' time at the start of the exam.

However, one approach that can work well is to start the exam by spending 10–15 minutes carefully reading through all of the questions to familiarise yourself with the exam.

Once you feel familiar with the exam consider the order in which you will attempt the questions; always attempt them in your order of preference. For example, you may want to leave to last the question you consider to be the most difficult.

If you do take this approach, remember to adjust the time available for each question appropriately – see Exam success skill 6: Good time management.

If you find that this approach doesn't work for you, don't worry because you can develop your own technique.

Active reading

You must take an active approach to reading each question. In Section B questions in particular, focus on the requirement first, making a note of key verbs such as 'explain' and 'discuss', to ensure you answer the question properly. Then read the rest of the question, making notes on important and relevant information you think you will need.

Exam success skill 2

Correct interpretation of the requirements

The active verb used often dictates the approach that written answers should take (eg 'explain', 'discuss'). It is important you identify and use the verb to define your approach. The correct interpretation of the **requirements** skill means correctly producing only what is being asked for by a requirement. Anything not required will not earn marks.

Advice on developing the Correct interpretation of the requirements

This skill can be developed by analysing question requirements and applying this process:

Step 1   Read the requirement

Firstly, read the requirement a couple of times slowly and carefully and note the active verbs. Use the active verbs to define what you plan to do. Make sure you identify any sub-requirements.

Step 2   Read the rest of the question

By reading the requirement first, you will have an idea of what you are looking out for as you read through the case overview and exhibits. This is a great time saver and means you don't end up having to read the whole question in full twice. You should do this in an active way – see Exam success skill 1: Managing Information.

Step 3   Read the requirement again

Read the requirement again to remind yourself of the exact wording before starting your written answer. This will capture any misinterpretation of the requirements or any missed requirements entirely. This should become a habit in your approach and, with repeated practice, you will find the focus, relevance and depth of your answer plan will improve.

Exam success skill 3

Answer planning: Priorities, structure and logic

This skill requires the planning of the key aspects of an answer which accurately and completely responds to the requirement.

Advice on developing Answer planning: Priorities, structure and logic

Everyone will have a preferred style for an answer plan. For example, it may be a mind map, bullet pointed lists or simply making some notes. Choose the approach that you feel most comfortable with, or, if you are not sure, try out different approaches for different questions until you have found your preferred style.

Exam success skill 4

Efficient numerical analysis

This skill aims to maximise the marks awarded by making clear to the marker the process of arriving at your answer. This is achieved by laying out an answer such that, even if you make a few errors, you can still score subsequent marks for follow-on calculations. It is vital that you do not lose marks purely because the marker cannot follow what you have done.

Advice on developing Efficient numerical analysis

There are not many marks available for numbers in the AA exam, however you may need to calculate ratios such as the receivables collection period. This skill can be developed by applying the following process:

Step 1	**Use a standard proforma working/formula where relevant**
	If answers can be laid out in a standard proforma or using a standard formula then always plan to do so. This will help the marker to understand your working and allocate the marks easily. It will also help you to work through the figures in a methodical and time-efficient way.
Step 2	**Show your workings**
	Keep your workings as clear and simple as possible and ensure they are cross-referenced to the main part of your answer. Where it helps, provide brief narrative explanations to help the marker understand the steps in the calculation. This means that if a mistake is made you do not lose any subsequent marks for follow-on calculations.
Step 3	**Keep moving!**
	It is important to remember that, in an exam situation, it can sometimes be difficult to get every number 100% correct. The key is therefore ensuring you do not spend too long on any single calculation. If you are struggling with a solution then make a sensible assumption, state it and move on.

Exam success skill 5

Effective writing and presentation

Written answers should be presented so that the marker can clearly see the points you are making, presented in the format specified in the question. The skill is to provide efficient written answers with sufficient breadth of points that answer the question, in the right depth, in the time available.

Advice on developing Effective writing and presentation

Step 1   Use headings.

Using the headings and sub-headings from your answer plan will give your answer structure, order and logic. This will ensure your answer links back to the requirement and is clearly signposted, making it easier for the marker to understand the different points you are making. Making your headings bold will also help the marker.

Step 2   Write your answer in short, but full, sentences.

Use short, punchy sentences with the aim that every sentence should say something

different and generate marks. Write in full sentences, ensuring your style is

professional.

Step 3   Do your calculations first and explanation second.

Questions sometimes ask for a discussion or explanation with suitable calculations. The best approach is to prepare the calculation first then add the explanation.

Performing the calculation first should enable you to explain what you have done.

Exam success skill 6

Good time management

This skill means planning your time across all the requirements so that all tasks have been attempted at the end of the three hours available and actively checking on time during your exam. This is so that you can flex your approach and prioritise requirements which, in your judgement, will generate the maximum marks in the available time remaining.

Advice on developing Good time management

The exam is three hours long, which translates to 1.8 minutes per mark. Therefore a 20-mark requirement should be allocated a maximum of 36 minutes to complete your answer before

you move on to the next task. At the beginning of a question, work out the amount of time you should be spending on each requirement and write the finishing time next to each requirement on your exam. If you take the approach of spending 10–15 minutes reading and planning at the start of the exam, adjust the time allocated to each question accordingly.

Keep an eye on the clock

Aim to attempt all requirements, but be prepared to move on if your answer is not going as planned. The challenge for many is sticking to planned timings. Be aware this is difficult to achieve in the early stages of your studies and be ready to let this skill develop over time. If you find yourself running short on time and know that a full answer is not possible in the time you have, consider recreating your plan in overview form and then add key terms and details as time allows. Remember, some marks may be available, for example, simply stating a conclusion which you don't have time to justify in full.

Question practice

Question practice is a core part of learning new topic areas. When you practise questions, you should focus on improving the Exam success skills – personal to your needs – by obtaining feedback or through a process of self-assessment.

Questions

AUDIT FRAMEWORK AND REGULATION

Questions 1–35 cover Audit framework and regulation, the subject of Part A of the BPP Workbook for Audit and Assurance.

BJM Co   **18 mins**

The following scenario relates to questions 1–5.

You are an audit senior of YHT & Co and have worked on the external audit of BJM Co (BJM), an unlisted company, since your firm was appointed external auditor two years ago.

BJM owns a chain of nine restaurants and is a successful company. BJM has always been subject to national hygiene regulations, especially in relation to the food preparation process. Non-compliance can result in a large fine or closure of the restaurant concerned.

The board of BJM has recently notified you that the national hygiene regulations have been updated and are now much more stringent and onerous than before.

With this in mind, the board has asked your firm to conduct a review of BJM's compliance with hygiene regulations, in order to allow the board to assess whether the appropriate processes have been implemented at each of the nine restaurants. The review is not expected to include the provision of accounting advice or the preparation of figures in the financial statements.

The work is likely to be very lucrative. Your firm has sufficient experience to undertake the above review engagement.

1   Despite running a successful company, BJM's board has often needed to be reminded of some fundamental principles and you often have to explain key concepts.

Which of the following statements best defines the external audit?

☐   The external audit is an exercise carried out by auditors in order to give an opinion on whether the financial statements of a company are fairly presented.

☐   The external audit is an exercise carried out in order to give an opinion on the effectiveness of a company's internal control system.

☐   The purpose of the external audit is to identify areas of deficiency within a company and to make recommendations to mitigate those deficiencies.

☐   The external audit provides negative assurance on the truth and fairness of a company's financial statements.

2   The board has also struggled to differentiate between its responsibilities and those of the external auditor in circumstances such as the prevention and detection of fraud and error, and compliance with regulations.

Which of the following statements best describes YHT & Co's responsibility regarding BJM's compliance with hygiene regulations, in line with ISA 250 (Revised) *Consideration of Laws and Regulations in an Audit of Financial Statements*?

☐ YHT & Co should actively prevent and detect non-compliance with the regulations.

☐ YHT & Co should perform specific audit procedures to identify possible non-compliance.

☐ YHT & Co should obtain sufficient appropriate audit evidence about BJM's compliance with the regulations as they have a direct effect on the financial statements.

☐ YHT & Co does not have any responsibility as the hygiene regulations do not have a direct effect on the financial statements.

3   The partner responsible for the review of hygiene compliance has informed you that the engagement is an assurance engagement.

Which of the following would **NOT** have been relevant to the partner in forming this opinion?

☐ The existence of a three-party relationship

☐ The existence of suitable criteria

☐ The determination of materiality

☐ The subject matter

4   The partner responsible for the review engagement has asked you to tell him what level of assurance you believe YHT & Co should provide, and also what type of opinion the firm should give.

What is the level of assurance and type of opinion that can be provided on this review engagement?

	Level of assurance	Report wording
☐	Reasonable	Positive
☐	Reasonable	Negative
☐	Limited	Positive
☐	Limited	Negative

5   The audit engagement partner has told you that the independence threats arising from YHT & Co performing the review engagement should be monitored carefully.

Which of the following is likely to cause the audit engagement partner most concern?

☐ According to the ACCA *Code of Ethics and Conduct*, YHT & Co is prohibited from providing other assurance services to an audit client.

☐ The review engagement is likely to give rise to a self-review threat, as the outcomes of the review could form the basis of the financial statements which the audit team will audit.

☐ The lucrative nature of the review engagement may make the external audit team less inclined to require management to make adjustments or to issue a modified audit opinion, for fear of losing the review engagement.

☐ If the new review engagement causes YHT & Co's fee income from BJM to exceed 15% of the firm's total fees, the ACCA *Code of Ethics and Conduct* states that the new engagement must be turned down.

(Total = 10 marks)

Conoy   18 mins

The following scenario relates to questions 6–10.

Conoy designs and manufactures luxury motor vehicles. It is not a listed company, but its board has recently decided that it would like to improve its corporate governance in order to apply best practice. Conoy's shares are held equally by six shareholders, four of whom are also executive directors. The remaining two shareholders are not involved with Conoy, other than as shareholders.

Conoy has an internal audit department which is managed by Adrian Muse, the chief internal auditor. Adrian frequently comments that Conoy's board does not understand his reports, and does not provide sufficient support for his department and for the company's internal control systems. RWG & Co, Conoy's external auditors, have also expressed concern in this area.

Adrian has submitted a proposal to the board to establish an audit committee, and this is currently under consideration. The proposed membership of the audit committee is:

- Adrian Muse (chief internal auditor)
- Penny Dinty (existing executive director with some financial expertise)
- Sharon Header (proposed new non-executive director)
- Fredrick Rowe (proposed new non-executive director)

The board is also considering a significant expansion of the company. However, the company's bank is concerned by the standard of financial reporting as Conoy's finance director recently left the company. The board is delaying providing the bank with financial information until a new finance director has been appointed.

As part of its commitment to the effectiveness of the external audit process, the chair of Conoy's audit committee, Leslie Schiff, is keen to ensure that the external audit makes use of the latest auditing techniques. She has heard about data analytics routines, but is unsure exactly what they entail.

6   Conoy's internal audit department is currently not well understood or supported by the board.

Which **TWO** of the following statements describe the main advantages of establishing an audit committee?

- ☐ The position of the internal audit department will be strengthened within the organisation.

- ☐ Corporate governance will be enhanced as the board of directors will report to the audit committee.

- ☐ The effectiveness of the internal audit department will be improved as the audit committee will monitor and review its performance on a regular basis.

- ☐ The workload of the internal audit department will be better managed as the audit committee will be able to minimise the extent to which the external auditors rely on the work of the internal auditors.

---

7   Once established, the audit committee will have many objectives.

Which of the following does **NOT** form part of the audit committee's objectives?

- ☐ Safeguarding the privacy of whistleblowers

- ☐ Appointing the external auditor

- ☐ Monitoring the independence of the external auditor

- ☐ Implementing a policy on the supply of non-audit services by the external auditor

---

8   In relation to the proposed membership of the audit committee, state whether each proposed member should be included or not.

Proposed member	Include in audit committee	Do not include in audit committee
Adrian Muse	☐	☐
Penny Dinty	☐	☐
Sharon Header	☐	☐
Fredrick Rowe	☐	☐

BPP LEARNING MEDIA

9   Which of the following statements best describes why having an audit committee could help Conoy raise additional finance by addressing the concerns of the bank?

☐ The independent non-executive members of the audit committee can provide guarantees to the bank concerning Conoy's financial viability.

☐ The audit committee will have at least one member who has relevant financial experience. This person will be able to stand in as Conoy's finance director before a new finance director is appointed.

☐ The audit committee will have at least one member who has relevant financial experience, so that they can monitor the integrity of the financial statements.

☐ The audit committee will review all the available evidence to substantiate information in financial reporting, thus improving the credibility of the financial statements.

10   The following statements concern the auditor's use of data analytics routines is true. Indicate whether each statement is false?

	True	False
A key drawback of data analytics software is that it is difficult to tailor to each particular audit client	☐	☐
Data analytics routines enable auditors to examine complex data using simple visualisation techniques	☐	☐
Although powerful, data analytics routines must be applied to strictly limited quantities of data so as to extrapolate correctly from a sample	☐	☐

(Total = 10 marks)

Stark   18 mins

The following scenario relates to questions 11–15.

You are an audit manager of Ali & Co and have just been assigned the audit of Stark Co (Stark). Stark, a listed company, provides investment advice to individuals, and is regulated by the relevant financial conduct authority.

Mr Day, a partner in Ali & Co, has been the audit engagement partner for Stark for the previous nine years and has excellent knowledge of the client. Mr Day has informed you that he would like his daughter Zoe to be part of the audit team this year; Zoe is currently studying for her first set of exams for her ACCA qualification.

In an initial meeting with the finance director of Stark, you learn that the audit team will not be entertained on Stark's yacht this year; instead, he has arranged a balloon flight costing less than one-tenth of the expense of using the yacht and hopes this will be acceptable.

Ali & Co has always carried out tax advisory work for Stark. The tax advisory services do not have an impact on the figures reported in the financial statements. The finance director has stated that he feels strongly that the firm that offers taxation services this year should charge a fee which is based on a percentage of tax saved. He also trusts that your firm will accept a fixed fee for representing Stark in a dispute regarding the amount of sales tax payable to the taxation authorities.

11   From a review of the information above, your audit assistant has highlighted some of the potential risks to independence in respect of the audit of Stark.

(1)   Mr Day would like his daughter Zoe to be part of the audit team
(2)   Audit team to be offered a balloon flight
(3)   Tax fee to be based on a percentage of tax saved
(4)   Firm to represent Stark in a dispute with the tax authorities

Which of the following options best identifies the valid threats to independence and allocates the threat to the most appropriate category?

	Advocacy	Intimidation	Self-interest
☐	(3) and (4)	(3) only	(1) and (2)
☐	(4) only	(3) only	(2) and (3)
☐	(3) only	(3) and (4)	(2) only
☐	(3) and (4)	(1) and (4)	(1) and (2)

12   In relation to the audit team being offered a balloon ride:

Which of the following actions should be taken to ensure the firm complies with ACCA's *Code of Ethics and Conduct*?

☐   The gift may be accepted as Stark has taken appropriate measures to reduce the value of the gift compared to previous years.

☐   The value of the gift should be assessed to determine whether it is of material value to the financial statements.

☐   The gift should only be accepted if its value is trivial and inconsequential to the recipients.

☐   Only the audit engagement partner and audit manager should accept the gift.

13   In relation to the audit engagement partner holding the role for nine years:

Which of the following safeguards should be implemented in order to comply with ACCA's *Code of Ethics and Conduct*?

☐   An independent review partner should be appointed to the audit.

☐   The audit engagement partner should be removed from the audit team but may serve as a quality control reviewer.

☐   Ali & Co should not audit Stark for a five-year period.

☐   The audit engagement partner should be removed from the audit team.

14   Mr Day's daughter, Zoe, is currently learning about International Standards on Auditing (ISAs) in her studies. She has asked you for clarification of the following.

Which is the correct order of the following stages involved in the development of an ISA?

(1)   Distribution of exposure draft for public comment

(2)   Consideration of comments received from the public

(3)   Approval by IAASB members

(4)   Establishment of task force to develop draft standard

(5)   Discussion of proposed standard at a public meeting

☐   1, 5, 4, 3, 2

☐   2, 4, 1, 3, 5

☐   4, 5, 1, 2, 3

☐   5, 4, 2, 1, 3

15   Zoe is also concerned that Ali & Co might breach confidentiality were the audit firm to represent Stark in its dispute with the tax authorities.

Which of the following statements best reflects the auditor's duty of confidentiality?

☐   Auditors must never, under any circumstances, disclose any matters of which they become aware during the course of the audit to third parties, without the permission of the client.

☐   Auditors may disclose any matters in relation to criminal activities to the police or taxation authorities, if requested to do so by the police or a tax inspector.

☐   Auditors may disclose matters to third parties without their client's consent if it is in the public interest, and they must do so if there is a statutory duty to do so.

☐   Auditors may only disclose matters to third parties without their client's consent if the public interest or national security is involved.

(Total = 10 marks)

Tangerine Tech Co (Mar/Jun 16) (amended)   18 mins

The following scenario relates to questions 16–20.

You are an audit manager of Satsuma & Co and have been assigned to the audit of Tangerine Tech Co (Tangerine), a company which is planning to list on a stock exchange within six months. The listing rules of the stock exchange require compliance with corporate governance principles, and the directors are unsure whether they are following best practice in relation to this. They have asked the audit engagement partner for their view on this matter.

Tangerine's board is comprised of six executive directors, a non-executive chairman and three other non-executive directors (NEDs). The chairman and one of the NEDs are former directors of Tangerine and on reaching retirement age were asked to take on non-executive roles. The company has established an audit committee, and all NEDs are members including the chairman who chairs the committee. All four members of the audit committee were previously involved in sales or production related roles.

All of the directors have been members of the board for at least four years. As the chairman does not have an executive role, he has sole responsibility for liaising with the shareholders and answering their questions. The company has not established an internal audit function to monitor internal controls.

16   Which of the following features are corporate governance weaknesses which Tangerine Co would need to address prior to their listing?

(1)   The chairman has sole responsibility for liaising with shareholders.

(2)   The company has not established an internal audit function.

(3)   The chairman and one of the NEDs are former executive directors of Tangerine Co.

☐ 1 and 2 only

☐ 1 and 3 only

☐ 2 and 3 only

☐ 1, 2 and 3

---

17   The audit engagement partner's review has identified the following additional corporate governance weaknesses:

(1)   All the directors have been members of the board for at least four years.

(2)   The board is comprised of six executive and four non-executive directors.

Which of the following would the audit engagement partner recommend to address these weaknesses to ensure compliance with corporate governance principles?

	Weakness 1	Weakness 2
☐	The directors should be subject to annual re-election	At least 50% of the board, excluding the Chair, must be comprised of non-executive directors whom the board considers to be independent
☐	The directors must be reappointed annually by the chairman	At least 75% of the board must be comprised of executive directors
☐	The directors should be subject to annual re-election	At least 75% of the board must be comprised of executive directors
☐	The directors must be reappointed annually by the chairman	At least 50% of the board, excluding the Chair, must be comprised of non-executive directors whom the board considers to be independent

18   The audit engagement partner has assessed the make-up of the audit committee.

Which of the following would be valid conclusions from this assessment?

(1)   It is acceptable for the chairman to chair the audit committee.

(2)   A new member of the audit committee with relevant financial experience must be recruited.

☐   1 only

☐   2 only

☐   1 and 2

☐   Neither 1 nor 2

---

19   The directors are aware that in accordance with corporate governance provisions they have responsibilities for internal control but are unclear as to the extent of these responsibilities.

Which of the following correctly describes their responsibilities?

	To review internal controls annually	To report on internal controls to shareholders
☐	No	No
☐	Yes	No
☐	No	Yes
☐	Yes	Yes

---

20   The board of Tangerine is considering establishing an internal audit function.

Which of the following factors would be relevant in making this decision?

(1)   It would help the audit committee to discharge its responsibilities for monitoring internal control.

(2)   The board would no longer need to take responsibility for the prevention and detection of fraud and error.

(3)   The costs of establishing an internal audit function should be considered against the benefits gained.

☐   1 and 2 only

☐   1 and 3 only

☐   2 and 3 only

☐   1, 2 and 3

(Total = 10 marks)

LV Fones (6/10) (amended)

18 mins

The following scenario relates to questions 21–25.

You are the audit manager of Jones & Co and you are planning the audit of LV Fones Co, a listed company, which has been an audit client for four years and specialises in manufacturing luxury mobile phones.

During the planning stage of the audit you have obtained the following information. The employees of LV Fones Co are entitled to purchase smartphones at a discount of 10%. The audit team has in previous years been offered the same level of staff discount.

During the year the financial controller of LV Fones was ill and hence unable to work. The company had no spare staff able to fulfil the role and hence a qualified audit senior of Jones & Co was seconded to the client for three months to cover the work of the financial controller. The audit engagement partner has recommended that the audit senior work on the audit as he has good knowledge of the client. The fee income derived from LV Fones was boosted by this engagement and, along with the audit and tax fee, now accounts for 16% of the firm's total fees (15.7% last year).

From a review of the correspondence files you note 20% of last year's audit fee is still outstanding.

Based on the information above you have summarised some of the potential risks to independence in the audit of LV Fones as follows.

(1)   The audit team has been offered a discount on luxury phones.
(2)   The audit senior was seconded to LV to cover for the financial controller.
(3)   Total fees from LV is over 15% of the total fees of the firm for the second consecutive year.
(4)   Fees are overdue in respect of last year's audit.

21   Which of the following options best identifies the valid potential threats to independence in the audit of LV Fones and allocates the threat to the most appropriate category?

Self-interest	Self-review
☐ 1 and 2 only	3 and 4 only
☐ 3 and 4 only	1 and 2 only
☐ 1, 3 and 4	2 only
☐ 3 only	1, 2 and 4

22   You have also discovered that the audit engagement partner and the finance director have known each other socially for many years, and in fact went on holiday together last summer with their families to the finance director's villa.

Which **TWO** threats to independence are raised by this relationship and what safeguards should be applied?

Threats	Safeguards
☐ Familiarity and self-interest	Jones & Co to resign as auditors
☐ Self-review and intimidation	Rotation of audit engagement partner
☐ Self-review and intimidation	Jones & Co to resign as auditors
☐ Familiarity and self-interest	Rotation of audit engagement partner

23   In relation to the audit team being offered a 10% discount on mobile phones:

Indicate whether the following statements are true or false, in accordance with ACCA's *Code of Ethics and Conduct.*

	True	False
The audit team can accept the discount as it is on the same terms as that offered to staff	☐	☐
Junior members of the audit team are allowed to accept the discount, but the audit manager and audit engagement partner should not	☐	☐
Unless the value of the discount is trivial and inconsequential to the audit team members, the offer should be declined	☐	☐
The audit team is only allowed to accept a discount of up to 5%	☐	☐

24   Which of the following steps must Jones & Co take, as the fees from LV have exceeded 15% for the last two years?

(1)   Resign from the audit
(2)   Disclose the matter to those charged with governance
(3)   Arrange for a pre- or post-issuance review

☐   1 only

☐   2 only

☐   3 only

☐   2 and 3

25   The finance director of LV has made some enquiries about the other services that Jones & Co may be able to assist with.

In the table below indicate whether Jones & Co would or would not be able to provide the other services.

	Service can be provided	Service cannot be provided
Design and implementation of IT systems over financial reporting	☐	☐
Assistance with preparation of tax return	☐	☐
Accounting services	☐	☐
Recruiting service for the position of credit controller	☐	☐

(Total = 10 marks)

Orange (6/12) (amended)   **18 mins**

The following scenario relates to questions 26–30.

You are the audit manager of Currant & Co and you are planning the audit of Orange Financials Co (Orange), which specialises in the provision of loans and financial advice to individuals and companies. Currant & Co has audited Orange for many years.

The directors are planning to list Orange on a stock exchange within the next few months and have asked if the audit engagement partner can attend the meetings with potential investors. In addition, as the finance director of Orange is likely to be quite busy with the listing, he has asked if Currant & Co can produce the financial statements for the current year.

During the year, the assistant finance director of Orange left and joined Currant & Co as a partner. It has been suggested that due to his familiarity with Orange, he should be appointed to provide an independent partner review for the audit.

Once Orange obtains its stock exchange listing it will require several assignments to be undertaken; for example, obtaining advice about corporate governance best practice. Currant & Co is very keen to be appointed to these engagements, however, Orange has implied that in order to gain this work Currant & Co needs to complete the external audit quickly and with minimal questions/issues.

The finance director has informed you that once the stock exchange listing has been completed, he would like the engagement team to attend a weekend away at a luxury hotel with his team, as a thank you for all their hard work. In addition, he has offered a senior member of the engagement team a short-term loan at a significantly reduced interest rate.

Orange is aware that subsequent to the stock exchange listing it will need to establish an audit committee, and has asked for some advice in relation to this.

26 As part of your planning work you have identified a number of potential risks to independence.

Indicate whether each of the following potential risks could give rise to an advocacy threat.

		Yes	No
(1)	The audit engagement partner has been asked to attend meetings with potential investors.	☐	☐
(2)	Currant & Co has been offered the opportunity to provide other services to Orange Financials.	☐	☐
(3)	Currant & Co has been asked to produce the financial statements of Orange Financials.	☐	☐
(4)	There is a suggestion that a partner who previously worked for Orange Financials should be the review partner.	☐	☐

27 Currant & Co has been offered work by Orange Financials. This is dependent on the audit being completed with minimal issues.

Which **TWO** of the following threats does this situation create?

☐ Intimidation

☐ Self-interest

☐ Familiarity

☐ Advocacy

28   The finance director has made two offers to members of the audit team:

(1)   Weekend away

(2)   Loan at reduced rates

Which of the following correctly summarises which of the offers, if any, can be accepted?

	(1)	(2)
☐	Accepted	Accepted
☐	Accepted	Not accepted
☐	Not accepted	Accepted
☐	Not accepted	Not accepted

---

29   In accordance with ACCA's *Code of Ethics and Conduct* you have concluded that if you win the additional work you will need to disclose the proportion of fees obtained from Orange Financials to those charged with governance and conduct a post-issuance review.

Which of the following explains the basis for your conclusion?

☐   Total fees from Orange Financials will make up more than 10% of Currant & Co's total fees for the first time since your appointment.

☐   Total non-audit fees from all Currant & Co's clients make up more than 5% of the total fees of the firm.

☐   Total fees from Orange Financials make up more than 15% of Currant & Co's total fees for the second consecutive year.

☐   The disclosure and review are required in all circumstances where services other than audit are offered, irrespective of the level of fees.

---

30   The board has noted down a number of statements relating to the audit committee and has asked you to confirm whether their understanding is correct.

Indicate whether the following statements are true or false.

	True	False
The audit committee should be made up of independent non-executive directors	☐	☐
The audit committee normally appoints the external auditors at the AGM	☐	☐
The audit committee monitors and reviews the internal audit function	☐	☐
The audit committee sets out the scope of the external auditor's work	☐	☐

(Total = 10 marks)

SGCC

18 mins

The following scenario relates to questions 31–35.

You are an audit manager in HTQ & Co. One of your clients, SGCC, has recently become a listed company and has asked for your advice regarding the changes they should make to achieve appropriate compliance with corporate governance codes.

The board

Mr Sheppard is the Chief Executive Officer and Chairman of the board of SGCC. He appoints and maintains a board of five executive and two non-executive directors. While the board sets performance targets for the senior managers in the company, no formal targets are set for each director and no review of board policies is carried out. Board salaries are therefore set and paid by Mr Sheppard based on his assessment of all the board members, including himself, and not their actual performance.

Internal controls

Internal controls in SGCC are monitored by the senior accountant, although the company assumes that, as external auditors, your firm will carry out a detailed review of internal controls. SGCC does not have an internal audit department or an audit committee.

Annual financial statements are produced, providing detailed information on past performance.

31 From a review of the information above, your audit assistant has highlighted some weaknesses in SGCC's corporate governance arrangements, especially in relation to the composition of the board.

Which of the following actions would be appropriate to improve SGCC's corporate governance compliance?

- ☐ SGCC should appoint an external consultant to review board policies.

- ☐ SGCC should appoint a new chief executive officer or board chairman.

- ☐ SGCC should create a remuneration committee to oversee the appointment of new directors.

- ☐ SGCC should implement a formal and rigorous evaluation of its directors' performance once every two years.

---

32 Which of the following statements is correct with regards to the composition of the board at SGCC?

- ☐ SGCC should appoint three new non-executive directors to the board.

- ☐ SGCC should reappoint two of its executive directors as non-executive directors.

- ☐ SGCC should appoint three new executive directors to the board.

- ☐ SGCC should reappoint three of its executive directors as non-executive directors.

---

33 Your audit assistant does not feel that SGCC's approach to internal controls is sufficiently robust to comply with corporate governance principles and has drawn up a list of recommendations.

Which **TWO** of the following recommendations are valid?

☐ SGCC should establish an audit committee with at least four directors as is required for all listed companies.

☐ SGCC must establish an internal audit department as is required for all listed companies.

☐ Once SGCC has an audit committee and an internal audit department, the head of the internal audit department should report to the audit committee.

☐ SGCC should not rely on the external audit to inform them of deficiencies in internal controls.

34 You are aware that SGCC is considering establishing an internal audit department.

With which of the following activities should the internal audit function **NOT** be involved?

☐ Monitoring of management's performance

☐ Reviewing adequacy of management information for decision-making purposes

☐ Taking responsibility for the implementation of a new sales ledger system

☐ Assessing compliance with regulation relevant to SGCC

35 If SGCC's board decides to establish an internal audit department then it will also need to decide whether it will employ members of staff directly, or will outsource the department to an external firm. You have found a list in your study notes of the advantages of outsourcing as compared to the advantages of employing staff directly. The list includes the following points:

(1) Greater availability of specialist industry skills as required

(2) Flexibility regarding staff numbers in response to changing circumstances

(3) Elimination of direct training costs

(4) Development of skills increasing the human resource strength of the entity

For each consideration, indicate whether it relates to the employment of internal auditors by SGCC, or to the outsourcing of the department.

Consideration	Employed	Outsourced
(1) Greater availability of specialist industry skills as required	☐	☐
(2) Flexibility regarding staff numbers in response to changing circumstances	☐	☐
(3) Elimination of direct training costs	☐	☐
(4) Development of skills increasing the human resource strength of the entity	☐	☐

(Total = 10 marks)

PLANNING AND RISK ASSESSMENT

Questions 36–81 cover Audit planning and risk assessment, the subject of Part B of the BPP Workbook for Audit and Assurance.

Bridgford

18 mins

The following scenario relates to questions 36–40.

You are an audit senior of Ovette & Co and your firm has recently been appointed as the auditor to Bridgford Products (Bridgford), a large company which sells televisions, DVD players and Blu-ray Disc players to electrical retailers.

You are planning the audit for the year ended 31 January 20X9 and your audit manager has asked you to produce both the audit strategy document and the detailed audit plan, including an assessment of materiality.

In order to assist you in your planning work you have visited Bridgford, where you obtained the following information.

Sales have increased during the year ended 31 January 20X9 following a move to attract new customers by offering extended credit. The new credit arrangements allow customers three months' credit, rather than the one-month credit period allowed previously. As a result of this change, you have calculated that the receivables collection period has increased from 49 days to 127 days.

Bridgford installed a new computerised inventory control system, which began operating on 1 June 20X8. Since the inventory control system records both inventory movements and current inventory quantities, Bridgford is proposing to use the inventory quantities on the computer to value the inventory at the year-end rather than carrying out an inventory count.

The production director informed you that in the last month or so there have been reliability problems with the company's products which have resulted in some customers refusing to pay for the products.

As part of the planning process you also undertake a risk assessment. Based on the information you have obtained to date you have identified several audit risks which you feel your team will need to address. The first risk relates to the extended credit terms offered by Bridgford to its customers, and the recent product reliability problems resulting in customers' refusal to pay.

A second audit risk relates to the computerised inventory control system which was implemented on 1 June 20X8. You are concerned about whether data was accurately transferred into the new system, and whether it is sufficiently reliable to determine the quantity of inventory for the year-end financial statements.

36 The audit manager has requested that you cover a number of specified areas in the audit planning documentation.

For each area, indicate whether the information would be included in the audit strategy document or in the detailed audit plan.

Area	Audit strategy document	Detailed audit plan
(1) The availability of the client's data and staff (including internal audit)	☐	☐
(2) The allocation of responsibility for specific audit procedures to audit team members	☐	☐
(3) The audit procedures to be undertaken for each area of the financial statements	☐	☐
(4) The potential for using automated tools and techniques to gather evidence	☐	☐

37   You have set the level of materiality for the financial statements as a whole, and now need to determine performance materiality.

Which of the following statements about performance materiality is **NOT** true?

☐ Performance materiality is used to reduce the risk that the aggregate of uncorrected and undetected misstatements exceeds materiality for the financial statements as a whole to an acceptable level.

☐ Performance materiality refers to the amounts set by the auditor at higher than the materiality level for particular classes of transactions, account balances or disclosures where the materiality level might otherwise mean that such items are not tested.

☐ Once the level of materiality for the financial statements as a whole has been set, a lower level of performance materiality is determined by the auditor using their professional judgement.

☐ The performance materiality level is affected by the auditor's understanding of the entity and the nature and extent of misstatements identified in prior audits.

38   ISA 520 *Analytical Procedures* states that where analytical procedures identify fluctuations or relationships that are inconsistent with other relevant information or that differ significantly from the expected results, the auditor shall investigate the reason for this.

Which of the following auditor responses to the increase in the receivables collection period of Bridgford is the **LEAST** relevant?

☐ Make enquiries of management to understand the likely reason why the receivables collection period exceeds the extended credit period

☐ Perform detailed substantive testing on the aged receivables listing, to determine whether any amounts should be written off

☐ Perform a trend analysis on current year and prior year monthly revenue, to identify whether revenue is overstated as a result of fraud or error

☐ Perform further working capital ratio analysis, to determine the effect of the extended credit on Bridgford's cash position

39   Which of the following statements summarises your key concern regarding the risk relating to the extended credit terms and refusal of certain customers to pay?

☐ That the directors may have prepared Bridgford's financial statements on the going concern basis when this is not applicable

☐ That the financial statements include amounts due from credit customers which are not valid debts

☐ That there are balances due from credit customers which have not been included in the financial statements

☐ That the financial statements include balances due from credit customers which are not recoverable

40   Which **TWO** of the following procedures are relevant responses to the risk that inventory quantities are misstated by the new computerised inventory system?

☐   Review a sample of purchase requisitions to determine whether the quantity of inventory held per the inventory system was verified before the requisition was approved

☐   Determine how often inventory counts are performed and the level of corrections required to the inventory system

☐   Review sales prices of inventory sold after the year end to identify inventory where cost exceeds net realisable value

☐   Test the operation of the inventory system using CAATs

(Total = 10 marks)

EuKaRe (12/08) (amended)   **18 mins**

The following scenario relates to questions 41–45.

You are an audit senior of TEY & Co and are responsible for planning the audit of EuKaRe for the year ended 30 September 20X8.

EuKaRe is a charity which was established over five years ago. The charity's aim is to provide support to children from disadvantaged backgrounds who wish to take part in sports such as tennis, badminton and football.

EuKaRe has a detailed constitution which explains how the charity's income can be spent. The constitution also notes that expenditure relating to the administration of the charity cannot exceed 10% of the charity's income in any year. EuKaRe currently employs 3 permanent members of staff. At present, 100 volunteers work for EuKaRe: some commit up to 3 days a week and others help out on an ad hoc basis. The organisation, including its finance department, is primarily run by volunteers.

The charity's income is derived wholly from voluntary donations. Sources of donations include the public in the form of cash collected in buckets by volunteers in shopping areas, and from generous individuals.

41   Based on your understanding of the nature of EuKaRe, you have identified that income is received primarily in the form of cash and this will affect audit risk.

By clicking on the relevant box indicate whether the following statements regarding the effect on audit risk are true or false.

Detection risk will increase due to the increased risk of cash donations being misappropriated and revenue being overstated	True	False
Inherent risk will increase as the nature of EuKaRe's transactions means that income may be misstated either in error or deliberately.	True	False
Control risk will increase as internal controls may be weak due to the large number of volunteers used by EuKaRe	True	False
Business risk will increase due to the level of volunteers used by EuKaRe	True	False

42   Your audit partner has highlighted to you that it is imperative that TEY & Co acts in line
      with ISA 315 *Identifying and Assessing the Risks of Material Misstatement Through
      Understanding the Entity and its Environment*. This means it must identify and assess the
      risks of material misstatement at both the financial statements level and the assertion level,
      for classes of transactions, events and their related disclosures, and account balances and
      their related disclosures.

      Indicate which of the following statements gives a true explanation of why ISA 315 requires
      a risk assessment to be carried out at the planning stage?

	True	False
The risk assessment will help the audit team gain an understanding of the entity for audit purposes	☐	☐
The risk assessment will enable the audit senior to produce an accurate budget for the audit assignment	☐	☐
The risk assessment will form the basis of the audit strategy and the detailed audit plan	☐	☐
Once the risks have been assessed, TEY & Co can select audit team members with sufficient skill and experience to maximise the chance of those risks being addressed	☐	☐

43   You have identified several audit risks which you feel your team will need to address. One
      such audit risk relates to the risk that income may be understated in the financial
      statements. You are concerned that not all income may be recorded.

      Which of the following statements is **NOT** a valid response to this audit risk?

      ☐   Obtain a breakdown of the income recorded from the cash that was collected in
           buckets, and vouch a sample of entries back to the volunteer in order to determine
           which volunteer collected the relevant donations

      ☐   Perform analytical procedures on the level of donations in shopping areas per
           volunteer

      ☐   Review the internal controls relating to cash collected in buckets to determine
           whether buckets are sealed, sequentially numbered and signed in and out by
           EuKaRe's volunteers

      ☐   Observe the counting and recording of proceeds from collections, to determine
           whether appropriate segregation of duties is in place

44   Another identified audit risk is the susceptibility of EuKaRe's business to fraud due to the
      high levels of cash involved.

      Use the drop down lists to complete the following sentence to correctly describe the
      auditor's responsibilities in accordance with ISA 240 *The Auditor's Responsibilities Relating
      to Fraud in an Audit of Financial Statements*.

      The auditor is not responsible for the [   ] of fraud or error.

      However, they are responsible for obtaining [   ] that the
      financial statements are free from material misstatement whether caused by fraud or error.

Options for drop down list:

First list:

Detection

Prevention

Prevention or detection

Second list:

Absolute assurance

Evidence

Reasonable assurance

45   The audit manager has noted in the detailed audit plan that EuKaRe's control environment may be weak.

Which **TWO** of the following statements are valid reasons as to why EuKaRe may have a weak control environment?

☐   EuKaRe has a detailed constitution which explains how the charity's income can be spent.

☐   EuKaRe's finance department relies on volunteers who may not have accounts experience.

☐   A high proportion of the income of EuKaRe is cash.

☐   Understaffing in the finance department at certain times is due to the ad hoc nature of volunteer working hours.

(Total = 10 marks)

South   18 mins

The following scenario relates to questions 46–50.

You are an audit senior of KLT & Co, and your firm has recently been appointed as the auditor to South, a private company that runs seven supermarkets in the UK. You are currently planning your firm's audit of South and are shortly due to make a preliminary visit to South's head office.

Four months before the year end, the company installed a new till system in all supermarkets. The new till system is linked to the accounting system at head office and automatically posts transactions to the accounting system. Previously journals were made manually based on totals on till rolls. The cost of the new till system which South has capitalised as a non-current asset.

The audit engagement partner has also said that she has is concerned that the new till system may not be reliable, and that consequently not all sales have been recorded, resulting in an understatement of revenue. She is also concerned that staff may not yet be familiar with the system, leading to an increased risk of errors relating to data entry.

Finally, after a number of people living close to one of South's stores became seriously ill, the source of the illness was traced back to meat the customers had purchased from South. Legal proceedings were commenced against South by a number of customers during the financial year, demanding $1m in compensation.

46   Indicate which **TWO** of the following statements describe the objectives of planning the audit of South.

☐   To ensure appropriate attention is devoted to important areas of the audit

☐   To assist in the co-ordination of work done by any auditor's experts

☐   To ensure that the audit engagement is only accepted if this is permissible by the ACCA *Code of ethics and conduct*

☐   To ensure the audit is completed within budget restraints

47   You are about to begin work on the share capital section of the South audit file.

Match each of the following audit procedures to the financial statement assertion to which it is most closely related.

Procedure		Assertion
Recalculate the closing balance on the share capital account		Presentation
Review financial statement notes		Completeness
Review Memorandum and Articles of Association and compare their requirements with issued share capital		Accuracy, valuation and allocation
Read minutes of board meetings for evidence of share issues		Existence

48   In relation to the capitalised costs of the new till system, you are concerned that South may have included within the capitalised costs some items which are revenue in nature, leading to the overstatement of non-current assets.

Which of the following statements is a valid response to this audit risk?

☐   Obtain a copy of the training manual relating to the new till system and discuss with directors the extent of training staff have received on the new system

☐   Agree the capitalised costs from the trial balance back to invoices to confirm their value

☐   Inspect invoices capitalised within the cost of the new till system to determine whether they are directly attributable to the cost of the new till system

☐   Recalculate the depreciation charged on the new till system

49   The audit engagement partner has stated that the new till system may not be reliable. Which **TWO** of the following statements represent valid responses to this audit risk?

☐   Perform analytical procedures by comparing daily/weekly sales by store with both the prior year and with expectations, in order to determine whether any unusual patterns have occurred following the installation of the new system

☐   Vouch the sales revenue per the system to the till receipts to confirm the accuracy of the sales

☐   Obtain a copy of the training manual relating to the new till system and discuss with directors the extent of training staff have received on the new system

☐   Agree sales revenue from till receipts to the cashbook to determine the accuracy of till receipts

50 You plan to review the legal correspondence relating to the claims made by those customers to whom South sold contaminated meat.

Which **TWO** of the following are valid objectives of this audit procedure?

☐ To determine whether South's reputation will have been damaged within the local area

☐ To confirm whether there are deficiencies in South's internal controls relating to food hygiene

☐ To assess whether a provision for customer compensation is required in South's financial statements

☐ To determine whether disclosure of the nature and financial effect of the legal claim is required in South's financial statements

(Total = 10 marks)

Mason   18 mins

The following scenario relates to questions 51–55.

You are an audit senior of IBN & Co and you are planning the audit of Mason Air Services Co (Mason) for the year ended 31 December 20X3.

Mason is a company that provides specialist helicopter support to public services, such as the police force and the ambulance service. Mason has four of these contracts, which contain very similar terms and are equal in value. Mason owns and maintains the helicopter fleet which is held at cost. Each aircraft carries specialist equipment and is operated by a highly skilled specialist pilot. Under the terms of these contracts Mason charges the customer an annual fee to cover the maintenance, storage and testing of the aircraft and equipment. The annual fee is payable in advance each year with the first annual payment being paid on the date the contract commences.

Mason has not purchased any new helicopters during the year to 31 December 20X3; however, there has been a lot of refitting, replacement and adding of specialist equipment to some of the existing aircraft. This has been necessary to keep up with the latest developments in search and rescue, and to maintain the aircraft to the high standard required under the contracts in place.

The original purchase of each aircraft was funded with a secured loan carrying substantial interest charges. The loan is in the process of being renegotiated and the bank has indicated that finance costs will increase further. Furthermore, the directors have told you that Mason's contract with the police force expires in March 20X4, at a time when, in the wake of government cuts, the police are trying to substantially reduce the amount they pay. It is thought that the contract will be put out to tender, and it is possible that another aircraft provider may also bid for the contract.

Mason also holds around $2 million of aircraft spares which are included within inventory. Mason sells the aircraft spares to amateur flying associations. Aircraft spares which are not sold after three years are scrapped.

Approximately one-quarter of this value is made up of specialist equipment taken out of aircraft when it was replaced by newer or more advanced equipment. Such specialist equipment is transferred from non-current assets to inventory without adjustment, and continues to be recognised at amortised cost.

51   In relation to the specialist helicopter support contracts, which of the following statements summarises a key audit risk?

☐   Mason's assets could be undervalued if the market value of the helicopter fleet exceeds its cost.

☐   Mason could breach the terms of its contracts with its customers and be liable to pay penalties, so provisions may be understated.

☐   Revenue may be overstated if it is recognised according to the contract date rather than over the relevant accounting period.

☐   An expert valuer is required to value the helicopters in the financial statements.

52   Given the large amount of refitting of existing aircraft, you are concerned that property, plant and equipment may be overstated in the financial statements.

Indicate which **TWO** of the following statements represent valid responses to this audit risk?

☐   Perform a proof in total calculation of the depreciation charge for the year and investigate any significant differences

☐   Review minutes of training meetings to determine whether the pilots have been trained how to use the specialist equipment

☐   Obtain a breakdown of the capitalised costs and agree a sample of items to invoices to determine the nature of the expenditure

☐   Inspect management's review of whether the value of the aircraft has been impaired

53   In relation to Mason's secured loan, which is the **MOST** important audit risk that should be documented in the detailed audit plan?

☐   Disclosure relating to the secured loan may be omitted from the financial statements.

☐   Mason's going concern status may be at risk if the contract is not renewed.

☐   Interest charges may be understated.

☐   The bank will rely on the audited financial statements when deciding whether to renew the loan.

54   Which **TWO** of the following are valid responses to the fact that Mason's contract with the police force is due for renewal?

☐   Review Mason's contracts with its other three customers to determine whether they contain a break clause, in order to determine the likelihood of losing any further contracts to other aircraft providers

☐   Contact the police force directly and request confirmation as to whether the contract is to be renewed

☐   Review the short-term and long-term funding facilities which are available to Mason

☐   Consider whether the financial statements contain appropriate disclosures in relation to the matter

55 In relation to the aircraft spares held by Mason, indicate which of the following correctly describe areas of audit concern?

	Audit concern	Not audit concern
Non-current assets	☐	☐
Inventory	☐	☐
Completeness	☐	☐
Accuracy, valuation and allocation	☐	☐

(Total = 10 marks)

Severn   18 mins

The following scenario relates to questions 56–60.

You are an audit manager of Rivers & Co. Your firm has been invited to tender for the audit of Severn Co, a listed company. Your firm does not have any other listed clients, and Severn Co will represent the biggest client of your firm (by client annual revenue) if your tender is successful.

A member of the audit committee of Severn Co informed your audit engagement partner that the current auditors were not being invited to stand for re-election as the audit committee felt that the relationship between the firm and the company had begun to lose objectivity due to overfamiliarity. You have reviewed past financial statements of Severn Co and have noted that the company applies IFRS, and that the audit committee reports on its responsibilities with regard to internal control annually. The director confirmed that the board would be happy to confirm their responsibilities in writing with Rivers & Co as they are aware of the relevant audit requirements.

56 The audit engagement partner has asked you to prepare some information ready for the tender.

Identify, by clicking on the relevant box in the table below, if the following items should be included in, or excluded from, the tender for the audit of Severn Co.

The proposed fee for the initial audit of Severn Co	INCLUDE	EXCLUDE
A description of Rivers & Co, including the curriculum vitae of key staff likely to be assigned to the client	INCLUDE	EXCLUDE
Overall level of materiality to be used in the audit	INCLUDE	EXCLUDE
A summary of potential other services Rivers & Co could provide to Severn Co	INCLUDE	EXCLUDE

57 You have identified a number of issues which should be considered prior to tendering for a new client.

Given what you already know of Severn Co, which **TWO** of these are most important to consider further prior to tendering for the audit?

☐ The firm is independent of the potential client

☐ The firm has the appropriate resources to conduct the audit of the potential client

☐ The preconditions of audit will be met

☐ The outgoing auditors will give Rivers & Co access to working papers

Your firm has tendered for the engagement and has been successful. You have been asked to follow through the acceptance procedures for the firm.

58   You are reappraising whether it is appropriate for the firm to accept the engagement.

Which of the following issues arising would cause Rivers & Co to decline the engagement?

☐ The engagement letter not being received by Rivers & Co

☐ Rivers & Co losing a major client meaning Severn's audit fee would represent 20% of annual firm income

☐ A reply from the outgoing auditors stating that they declined to seek reappointment to the audit of Severn Co due to a disagreement over accounting policies

☐ A request from Severn Co that the audit be carried out in March, when Rivers & Co already works at maximum capacity

59   You are drafting an engagement letter in respect of Severn Co, and are aware that ISA 210 *Terms of Audit Engagements* requires certain issues to be included.

Indicate which of the following issues must be included in the engagement letter?

	Include in engagement letter	Do not include in engagement letter
Scope of the audit	☐	☐
Responsibilities of management of Severn Co	☐	☐
Timetable for the provision of accounting information by Severn Co	☐	☐
Fees and billing arrangements	☐	☐

60   Before accepting the audit of Severn Co, Rivers & Co should

[   ] . Once the audit has been accepted, then Rivers & Co

should begin to [   ] .

Options for drop down list:

First list:

Obtain references concerning directors

Submit the letter of engagement

Appoint a quality control reviewer

Second list:

Obtain references concerning directors

Submit the letter of engagement

Determine audit materiality levels

(Total = 10 marks)

Goofy Co (6/11) (amended)

18 mins

The following scenario relates to questions 61–65.

You are an audit manager in NAB & Co, a large audit firm which specialises in the audit of retailers. The firm currently audits Goofy Co (Goofy), a food retailer, but Goofy's main competitor, Mickey Co (Mickey), has approached the audit firm to act as auditors. Both Goofy and Mickey are listed companies. Goofy is concerned that if NAB & Co audits both companies then confidential information could pass across to Mickey.

The audit engagement partner for Goofy has been in place for approximately six years and her daughter, Emma, has just accepted a job offer from Goofy as a warehouse manager. Emma's employment contract states that if a bonus is to be paid it will be awarded as shares in Goofy rather than in cash. Goofy is offering NAB & Co a 5% bonus on top of the audit fee if this year's audit can be completed three weeks earlier than last year. This is to reduce the demands on the finance director's time as he is busy working on other projects.

61   The ACCA *Code of Ethics and Conduct* requires that an external auditor implement appropriate safeguards to ensure that a conflict of interest is properly managed.

Which **TWO** of the following actions should NAB & Co take regarding the potential confidentiality issue?

☐ Inform the audit committees of both Goofy and Mickey of the potential conflict of interest and obtain their consent to act for both parties

☐ Use separate audit teams for each audit with a common independent review partner to determine whether confidentiality has been maintained

☐ Draw up confidentiality agreements to be signed by the board of directors of Goofy and Mickey

☐ Prevent unauthorised physical access to the information relating to both company audits

---

62   From a review of the information above, your audit assistant has highlighted some potential risks to independence in respect of the audit of Goofy.

Indicate the appropriate category to which each of the threats to independence should be allocated.

Threat to independence	Familiarity	Self-interest
(1) Audit engagement partner has been in the position for six years	☐	☐
(2) Audit engagement partner's daughter works for Goofy	☐	☐
(3) Audit engagement partner's daughter's bonus would be in the form of shares	☐	☐
(4) 5% bonus offered if audit is completed three weeks earlier than last year	☐	☐

BPP LEARNING MEDIA

63 NAB & Co has decided that it would like to accept nomination as Mickey's auditors and Mickey's existing auditors have agreed to resign rather than be removed from office. The audit manager in charge of the tender has set out a list of procedures that the firm must undertake before Mickey can be approved as an audit client.

(1) Ensure that the existing auditor's resignation has been properly conducted

(2) Communicate with Mickey's existing auditors

(3) Submit an engagement letter to Mickey's management

(4) Perform client screening procedures, including an assessment of Mickey's risk profile

Drag each of the four options below to the right hand side to show the correct order in which the above procedures should be undertaken.

Procedure   **Order**

(1) Ensure that the existing auditor's resignation has been properly conducted	(1)
(2) Communicate with Mickey's existing auditors	(2)
(3) Submit an engagement letter to Mickey's management	(3)
(4) Perform client screening procedures, including an assessment of Mickey's risk profile	(4)

64 Before NAB & Co can accept appointment as Mickey's auditors it must determine whether the preconditions for an audit are met and obtain management's agreement that it acknowledges and understands its responsibilities.

Which of the following is **NOT** included in the agreement obtained by the auditor?

☐ Management's responsibility for preparing the financial statements

☐ Management's responsibility for internal control to enable the preparation of financial statements which are free from material misstatement

☐ Management's responsibility to provide the auditor with all information relevant to the preparation of the financial statements

☐ Management's responsibility to prevent and detect fraud

65   Indicate which of the following statements are true regarding the regulation of the audit profession?

The auditor has the right of access to the books, records and vouchers of the company	TRUE	FALSE
The auditor has the right to be heard at general meetings on matters relating to the audit	TRUE	FALSE
The auditor is appointed by, and answerable to, those charged with governance of the company	TRUE	FALSE
An auditor can be removed by a simple oral resolution in line with the common law	TRUE	FALSE

(Total = 10 marks)

Carlise   18 mins

The following scenario relates to questions 66–70.

You are an audit senior of UYE & Co and your firm is the external auditor of Carlise, a large private company that runs major sports venues in the UK. Carlise has a year end of 31 December and you are currently planning the interim audit of Carlise for the six months ended 30 June 20X4.

This year you will have another audit senior, James, who has recently joined UYE & Co, working with you. James did not work on any interim audits with his previous audit firm, and your audit manager has asked you to train him to use the different approach used in interim audits.

James has drawn up the following list of audit procedures:

(1)   Update documentation relating to Carlise's accounting systems which has been prepared in prior year audits.

(2)   Obtain third-party confirmations relating to receivables, payables and cash at bank.

(3)   Review the directors' assessment of whether Carlise is a going concern. Consider whether the assumptions made by the directors are reasonable and whether it is appropriate to prepare the accounts on the going concern basis.

(4)   Perform preliminary analytical procedures in order to identify any major changes in the business or unexpected trends.

In July 20X4 Carlise established an internal audit department. The board is still planning the exact responsibilities the internal audit department will have, but it is likely that, among other things, they will be involved in monitoring the internal controls relating to Carlise's online ticket sales system.

It is the policy of UYE & Co that audit files for both interim and final audits are assembled within 60 days of the date when the auditor's report was signed. The files are then locked and cannot be amended after this date, but it is sometimes deemed necessary for further minor procedures to be added to the files after the auditor's report is issued. The files are then retained for 3 years, at which time they are disposed of securely.

66 Indicate whether the procedures identified by James above will be conducted during the interim or the final audit.

Audit procedure		Interim audit	Final audit
(1)	Update documentation relating to Carlise's accounting systems which has been prepared in prior year audits.	☐	☐
(2)	Obtain third-party confirmations relating to receivables, payables and cash at bank.	☐	☐
(3)	Review the directors' assessment of whether Carlise is a going concern. Consider whether the assumptions made by the directors are reasonable and whether it is appropriate to prepare the accounts on the going concern basis.	☐	☐
(4)	Perform preliminary analytical procedures in order to identify any major changes in the business or unexpected trends.	☐	☐

67 During the interim audit, you performed internal controls testing and the results of these indicate that, to date, the control environment is strong and internal controls are operating effectively.

James has asked you to explain the factors that will determine the extent of further work on internal controls that will need to be performed at the final audit.

Which of the following should be taken into account when determining the extent of the additional work needed at the final audit?

(1) The significance of the assessed risks of material misstatement at the assertion level

(2) The specific controls that were tested during the interim period, and significant changes to them since they were tested, including changes in the information system, processes, and personnel

(3) The length of the remaining period

☐ 1 and 2 only

☐ 2 and 3 only

☐ 1 and 3 only

☐ 1, 2 and 3

68 Which of the following considerations is the MOST important when deciding whether or not to rely on the work performed by Carlise's internal audit department?

☐ Whether any members of Carlise's internal audit department hold a professional qualification

☐ Whether the work performed by the internal audit department relates to specific audit assertions over which UYE & Co has concerns

☐ Whether a separate audit committee exists

☐ Whether Carlise's internal audit department has a work plan which schedules the work they should perform to the end of the year

69 Carlise's internal audit team is likely to be involved in monitoring the internal controls relating to Carlise's online ticket sales system.

UYE & Co may use the internal audit department to provide direct assistance to it in the audit of this system. Indicate which of the following statements are true, if direct assistance is used?

	True	False
Carlise's internal auditors would perform audit procedures under the direction, supervision and review of UYE & Co's audit team	☐	☐
UYE & Co should only use direct assistance if the risk of material misstatement in relation to the online ticket sales system is high	☐	☐
UYE & Co's audit team should document its review of the work performed by Carlise's internal auditors	☐	☐
Carlise's internal auditors will be separately liable for any material misstatements in the work they have performed	☐	☐

70 Indicate which of the following are true of UYE & Co's policies regarding the assembly and retention of audit files.

	True	False
UYE & Co's policy of assembling files within 60 days of the auditor's report is stricter than what is required by ISAs	☐	☐
It is incompatible with ISAs for even minor further procedures to be added to the audit files after the 60 day period	☐	☐
It is acceptable to make administrative changes to an audit file after 60 days, so it is not strictly necessary to 'lock' the files to comply with ISAs	☐	☐
It is acceptable for files to be disposed of after 3 years have passed since the date of the auditor's report	☐	☐

(Total = 10 marks)

71 Sleeptight   54 mins

You are an audit senior for Mills & Co. Mills & Co was recently appointed as external auditors of Sleeptight Co for the year ending 31 March 20X0 and you are in the process of planning the audit. The previous auditors issued an unmodified audit opinion last year and access to prior year working papers has been granted.

Sleeptight's principal activity is the manufacture and sale of expensive high quality beds which are largely sold to luxury hotels and owners of holiday apartments. Each bed is crafted by hand in the company's workshop. Construction of each bed only begins once a customer order is received, as each customer will usually want their bed to have a unique feature or to be in a unique style.

The business is family run and all the shares in Sleeptight are owned by the two joint managing directors. The directors are two sisters, Anna and Sophie Jones, and they both have a number of other business interests. As a result they only spend a few days a week working at the company and rely on the small accounts department to keep the finances in order and to keep them informed. There is no finance director but the financial controller is a qualified accountant.

Sleeptight requires customers who place an order to pay a deposit of 40% of the total order value at the time the order is placed. The beds will take 4 to 8 weeks to build, and the remaining 60% of the order value is due within a week of the final delivery. Risks and rewards of ownership of the beds do not pass to the customer until the beds are delivered and signed for. Beds also come with a two-year guarantee and the financial controller has made a provision in respect of the expected costs to be incurred in relation to beds still under guarantee.

Although the company does have some employees working in the workshop, it often uses external subcontractors to help make the beds in order to fulfil all its orders. These subcontractors should invoice Sleeptight at the end of each month for the work they have carried out, but sometimes do not get round to it until the following month.

The company undertakes a full count of raw materials at the year end. The quantities are recorded on inventory sheets and the financial controller assigns the costs based on the cost assigned in the previous year or, if there was no cost last year, using the latest invoice. Most beds are made of oak or other durable woods and the cost of these raw materials is known to fluctuate considerably.

It is expected that work in progress will be insignificant this year, but there will be a material amount of finished goods awaiting dispatch. Anna Jones will estimate the value of these finished goods and has said she will take into account the order value when doing so.

There has been steady growth in sales in recent years and in January 20X0 Sleeptight purchased a building close to its existing workshop. Anna and Sophie plan to turn this into another workshop which should more than double its existing manufacturing capacity. The new workshop is currently undergoing extensive refurbishment in order to make it suitable for bed manufacturing.

The purchase of the new premises was funded by a bank loan repayable in monthly instalments over 12 years and has covenants attached to it. These covenants are largely profit related measures and if they are breached the bank has the option to make the remaining loan balance repayable immediately.

(a)   Auditors are required to plan and perform an audit with professional scepticism, to exercise professional judgement and to comply with ethical standards.

Required

(i)   Explain what is meant by 'professional scepticism' and why it is so important that the auditor maintains professional scepticism throughout the audit.   (3 marks)

(ii)   Define 'professional judgement' and describe TWO areas where professional judgement is applied when planning an audit of financial statements.   (3 marks)

(b)   (i)   Using the information provided, describe EIGHT audit risks, and explain the auditor's response to each risk, in planning the audit of Sleeptight.

Note. Prepare your answer using two columns headed Audit risk and Auditor's response respectively.   (16 marks)

(ii)   Describe Mills & Co's responsibilities in relation to the physical inventory count that will take place at the year end.   (4 marks)

(c)   The workshop currently in use is owned by the company and will be included in the financial statements at its revalued amount rather than at cost. The company has always adopted this policy for land and buildings and the valuation of the workshop is to be brought up to date at 31 March 20X0 by an external valuer.

Required

Describe the procedures the auditor should carry out to gain evidence over the adequacy of the value of the workshop and the related disclosures included in the financial statements.   (4 marks)

(Total = 30 marks)

72 Recorder (6/14) (amended)

36 mins

Recorder Communications Co (Recorder) is a large mobile phone company which operates a network of stores in countries across Europe. The company's year-end is 30 June 20X4. You are the audit senior of Piano & Co. Recorder is a new client and you are currently planning the audit with the audit manager. You have been provided with the following planning notes from the audit engagement partner following his meeting with the finance director.

Recorder purchases goods from a supplier in South Asia and these goods are shipped to the company's central warehouse. The goods are usually in transit for two weeks and the company correctly records the goods when received. Recorder does not undertake a year-end inventory count, but carries out monthly continuous (perpetual) inventory counts and any errors identified are adjusted in the inventory system for that month.

During the year the company introduced a bonus based on sales for its salespeople. The bonus target was based on increasing the number of customers signing up for 24 month phone line contracts. This has been successful and revenue has increased by 15%, especially in the last few months of the year. The level of receivables is considerably higher than last year and there are concerns about the creditworthiness of some customers.

Recorder has a policy of revaluing its land and buildings and this year has updated the valuations of all land buildings.

During the year the directors have each been paid a significant bonus, and they have included this within wages and salaries. Separate disclosure of the bonus is required by local legislation.

Required

(a) Describe **FIVE** audit risks, and explain the auditor's response to each risk, in planning the audit of Recorder Communications Co. **(10 marks)**

(b) Explain the audit procedures you should perform in order to place reliance on the continuous (perpetual) counts for year-end inventory. **(3 marks)**

(c) Describe substantive procedures you should perform to confirm the directors' bonus payments included in the financial statements. **(3 marks)**

Amber Coleman, the finance (executive) director of Recorder, recently attended a course on corporate governance and has now decided that the setup at Recorder needs to be improved, in order to comply voluntarily with the provisions of the UK Corporate Governance Code.

Amber herself provides the main point of contact between Piano & Co and the Board of Directors, and acts as the company's audit committee, on the oral agreement of the Board. Amber is also responsible for the final sign off of Recorder's financial statements.

Required

(d) Describe TWO corporate governance deficiencies faced by Recorder and provide a recommendation to address each deficiency to ensure compliance with corporate governance principles.

Note: Prepare your answer using two columns headed Deficiency and Recommendation respectively. **(4 marks)**

(Total = 20 marks)

73 Walters (2014 Specimen Exam)

36 mins

You are the audit senior of Holtby & Co and are planning the audit of Walters Co (Walters) for the year ended 31 December 20X4. The company produces printers and has been a client of your firm for two years; your audit manager has already had a planning meeting with the finance director. He has provided you with the following notes of his meeting and financial statement extracts.

Walters's management were disappointed with the 20X3 results and so in 20X4 undertook a number of strategies to improve the trading results. This included the introduction of a generous sales-related bonus scheme for their salespeople and a high profile advertising campaign. In addition, as market conditions are difficult for their customers, they have extended the credit period given to them.

The finance director of Walters has reviewed the inventory valuation policy and has included additional overheads incurred this year as he considers them to be production related.

The finance director has calculated a few key ratios for Walters; the gross profit margin has increased from 44.4% to 52.2% and the receivables collection period has increased from 61 days to 71 days. He is happy with the 20X4 results and feels that they are a good reflection of the improved trading levels.

FINANCIAL STATEMENT EXTRACTS FOR YEAR ENDED 31 DECEMBER

	Draft 20X4 $m	Actual 20X3 $m
Revenue	23.0	18.0
Cost of sales	(11.0)	(10.0)
Gross profit	12.0	8.0
Operating expenses	(7.5)	(4.0)
Profit before interest and taxation	4.5	4.0
Inventory	2.1	1.6
Receivables	4.5	3.0
Cash	–	2.3
Trade payables	1.6	1.2
Overdraft	0.9	–

Required

(a)   Using the information above:

(i)   Calculate an additional **THREE** ratios, for **BOTH** years, which would assist the audit senior in planning the audit. **(3 marks)**

(ii)   From a review of the above information and the ratios calculated, describe **SIX** audit risks and explain the auditor's response to each risk in planning the audit of Walters Co. **(12 marks)**

(b)   Describe the procedures that the auditor of Walters Co should perform in assessing whether or not the company is a going concern. **(5 marks)**

(Total = 20 marks)

74 Sycamore (6/15) (amended)   36 mins

You are the audit supervisor of Maple & Co and are currently planning the audit of an existing client, Sycamore Science Co (Sycamore), whose year-end was 30 April 20X5. Sycamore is a pharmaceutical company, which manufactures and supplies a wide range of medical supplies. The draft financial statements show revenue of $35.6 million and profit before tax of $5.9 million.

Sycamore's previous finance director left the company in December 20X4 after it was discovered that he had been claiming fraudulent expenses from the company for a significant period of time. A new finance director was appointed in January 20X5 who was previously a financial controller of a bank, and she has expressed surprise that Maple & Co had not uncovered the fraud during last year's audit.

During the year Sycamore has spent $1.8 million on developing several new products. These projects are at different stages of development and the draft financial statements show the full amount of $1.8 million within intangible assets. In order to fund this development, $2.0 million was borrowed from the bank and is due for repayment over a 10-year period. The bank has attached minimum profit targets as part of the loan covenants.

The new finance director has informed the audit engagement partner that since the year end there has been an increased number of sales returns and that in the month of May over $0.5 million of goods sold (and recognised in revenue) in April were returned.

Maple & Co attended the year-end inventory count at Sycamore's warehouse. The auditor present raised concerns that during the count there were movements of goods in and out of the warehouse and this process did not seem well controlled.

During the year, a review of plant and equipment in the factory was undertaken and surplus plant was sold, resulting in a profit on disposal of $210,000.

Required

(a)   State Maple & Co's responsibilities in relation to the prevention and detection of fraud and error.   (4 marks)

(b)   Describe SIX audit risks, and explain the auditor's response to each risk, in planning the audit of Sycamore Science Co.

       Note. Prepare your answer using two columns headed Audit risk and Auditor's response respectively.   (12 marks)

(c)   Sycamore's new finance director has read about review engagements and is interested in the possibility of Maple & Co undertaking these in the future. However, she is unsure how these engagements differ from an external audit and how much assurance would be gained from this type of engagement.

       ### Required

       (i)   Explain the purpose of review engagements and how these differ from external audits.   (2 marks)

       (ii)   Describe the level of assurance provided by external audits and review engagements.   (2 marks)

                                                                                                   (Total = 20 marks)

75 Smoothbrush (6/10) (amended)   54 mins

Introduction and client background

You are an audit senior in Staple and Co and you are commencing the planning of the audit of Smoothbrush Paints Co (Smoothbrush) for the year ending 31 August 20X0.

Smoothbrush is a paint manufacturer and has been trading for over 50 years. It operates from one central site which includes the production facility, warehouse and administration offices.

Smoothbrush sells all of its goods to large home improvement stores, with 60% being to one large chain store called Homewares. The company has a one-year contract to be the sole supplier of paint to Homewares. It secured the contract through significantly reducing prices and offering a four-month credit period; the company's normal credit period is one month.

Goods in/purchases

In recent years, Smoothbrush has reduced the level of goods directly manufactured and has instead started to import paint from South Asia. Approximately 60% is imported and 40% manufactured. Within the production facility is a large amount of old plant and equipment that is now redundant and has minimal scrap value. Purchase orders for overseas paint are made six months in advance and goods can be in transit for up to two months. Smoothbrush accounts for the inventory when it receives the goods.

To avoid the disruption of a year-end inventory count, Smoothbrush has this year introduced a continuous/perpetual inventory counting system. The warehouse has been divided into 12 areas and these are each to be counted once over the year. The counting team includes a member of the internal audit department and a warehouse staff member. The following procedures have been adopted:

(1)   The team prints the inventory quantities and descriptions from the system and these records are then compared to the inventory physically present.

(2)   Any discrepancies in relation to quantities are noted on the inventory sheets, including any items not listed on the sheets but present in the warehouse area.

(3)   Any damaged or old items are noted and they are removed from the inventory sheets.

(4)   The sheets are then passed to the finance department for adjustments to be made to the records when the count has finished.

(5)   During the counts there will continue to be inventory movements with goods arriving and leaving the warehouse.

At the year-end it is proposed that the inventory will be based on the underlying records. Traditionally Smoothbrush has maintained an inventory provision based on 1% of the inventory value, but management feels that as inventory is being reviewed more regularly it no longer needs this provision.

Finance director

In May 20X0 Smoothbrush had a dispute with its finance director (FD) and he immediately left the company. The company has temporarily asked the financial controller to take over the role while they recruit a permanent replacement. The old FD has notified Smoothbrush that he intends to sue for unfair dismissal. The company is not proposing to make any provision or disclosures for this, as they are confident the claim has no merit.

Required

(a)   Using the information provided, describe **FIVE** audit risks, and explain the auditor's response to each risk in planning the audit of Smoothbrush Paints Co.

        Note. Prepare your answer using two columns headed Audit risk and Auditor's response respectively.   **(10 marks)**

(b)   Discuss the importance of assessing risks at the planning stage of an audit.   **(4 marks)**

(c)   List and explain suitable controls that should operate over the continuous/perpetual inventory counting system, to ensure the completeness and accuracy of the existing inventory records at Smoothbrush Paints Co.   **(10 marks)**

(d)   Describe THREE substantive procedures that the auditor of Smoothbrush Paints Co should perform at the year-end in confirming each of the following:

        (i)   The valuation of inventory   **(3 marks)**

        (ii)   The completeness of provisions or contingent liabilities   **(3 marks)**

                                                                                                         (Total = 30 marks)

76 Aquamarine Co (Mar/Jun 16)   36 mins

You are an audit supervisor of Amethyst & Co and are currently planning the audit of your client, Aquamarine Co (Aquamarine) which manufactures elevators. Its year end is 31 July 20X6 and the forecast profit before tax is $15.2 million.

The company undertakes continuous production in its factory, therefore at the year-end it is anticipated that work in progress will be approximately $950,000. In order to improve the manufacturing process, Aquamarine placed an order in April for $720,000 of new plant and machinery; one-third of this order was received in May with the remainder expected to be delivered by the supplier in late July or early August.

At the beginning of the year, Aquamarine purchased a patent for $1.3 million which gives them the exclusive right to manufacture specialised elevator equipment for 5 years. In order to finance this purchase, Aquamarine borrowed $1.2 million from the bank which is repayable over 5 years.

In January 20X6 Aquamarine outsourced its payroll processing to an external service organisation, Coral Payrolls Co (Coral). Coral handles all elements of the payroll cycle and sends monthly reports to Aquamarine detailing the payroll costs. Aquamarine ran its own payroll until 31 December 20X5, at which point the records were transferred over to Coral.

The company has a policy of revaluing land and buildings and the finance director has announced that all land and buildings will be revalued at the year end. During a review of the management accounts for the month of May 20X6, you have noticed that receivables have increased significantly on the previous year end and against May 20X5.

The finance director has informed you that the company is planning to make approximately 65 employees redundant after the year end. No decision has been made as to when this will be announced, but it is likely to be prior to the year end.

Required

(a)   Define audit risk and the components of audit risk.   (5 marks)

(b)   Describe **SIX** audit risks, and explain the auditor's response to each risk, in planning the audit of Aquamarine Co.   (12 marks)

(c)   Explain the additional factors Amethyst & Co should consider during the audit in relation to Aquamarine Co's use of the payroll service organisation.   (3 marks)

(Total = 20 marks)

77 Kangaroo Construction Co (6/13)   36 mins

You are the audit senior of Rhino & Co and you are planning the audit of Kangaroo Construction Co (Kangaroo) for the year ended 31 March 20X3. Kangaroo specialises in building houses and provides a five-year building warranty to its customers. Your audit manager has held a planning meeting with the finance director. He has provided you with the following notes of his meeting and financial statement extracts.

Kangaroo has had a difficult year; house prices have fallen and, as a result, revenue has dropped. In order to address this, management has offered significantly extended credit terms to their customers. However, demand has fallen such that there are still some completed houses in inventory where the selling price may be below cost. During the year, whilst calculating depreciation, the directors extended the useful lives of plant and machinery from three years to five years. This reduced the annual depreciation charge.

The directors need to meet a target profit before interest and taxation of $0.5 million in order to be paid their annual bonus. In addition, to try to improve profits, Kangaroo changed its main material supplier to a cheaper alternative. This has resulted in some customers claiming on their building warranties for extensive repairs. To help with operating cash flow, the directors borrowed $1 million from the bank during the year. This is due for repayment at the end of 20X3.

FINANCIAL STATEMENT EXTRACTS FOR YEAR ENDED 31 MARCH

	Draft 20X3 $m	Actual 20X2 $m
Revenue	12.5	15.0
Cost of sales	(7.0)	(8.0)
Gross profit	5.5	7.0
Operating expenses	(5.0)	(5.1)
Profit before interest and taxation	0.5	1.9
Inventory	1.9	1.4
Receivables	3.1	2.0
Cash	0.8	1.9
Trade payables	1.6	1.2
Loan	1.0	–

Required

(a)   Explain the concepts of materiality and performance materiality in accordance with ISA 320 *Materiality in Planning and Performing an Audit*.   **(5 marks)**

(b)   Using the information above:

(i)   Calculate **FIVE** ratios, for **BOTH** years, which would assist the audit senior in planning the audit.   **(5 marks)**

(ii)   Using the information provided and the ratios calculated, describe **FIVE** audit risks, and explain the auditor's response to each risk in planning the audit of Kangaroo Construction Co.

Note. Prepare your answer using two columns headed Audit risk and Auditor's response respectively.   **(10 marks)**

(Total = 20 marks)

78 Hurling Co (Mar/Jun 17)   **54 mins**

(a)   Define audit risk and the components of audit risk.   **(4 marks)**

You are an audit supervisor of Caving & Co and you are planning the audit of Hurling Co, a listed company, for the year ending 31 March 20X7. The company manufactures computer components and forecast profit before tax is $33.6m and total assets are $79.3m.

Hurling Co distributes its products through wholesalers as well as via its own website. The website was upgraded during the year at a cost of $1.1m. Additionally, the company entered into a transaction in February to purchase a new warehouse which will cost $3.2m. Hurling Co's legal advisers are working to ensure that the legal process will be completed by the year end. The company issued $5m of irredeemable preference shares to finance the warehouse purchase.

During the year the finance director has increased the useful economic lives of fixtures and fittings from three to four years as he felt this was a more appropriate period. The finance director has informed the audit engagement partner that a revised credit period has been agreed with one of its wholesale customers, as they have been experiencing difficulties with repaying the balance of $1.2m owing to Hurling Co. In January 20X7, Hurling Co introduced a new bonus based on sales targets for its sales staff. This has resulted in a significant number of new wholesale customer accounts being opened by sales staff. The new customers have been given favourable credit terms as an introductory offer, provided goods are purchased within a two-month period. As a result, revenue has increased by 5% on the prior year.

The company has launched several new products this year and all but one of these new launches have been successful. Feedback on product Luge, launched four months ago, has been mixed, and the company has just received notice from one of their customers, Petanque Co, of intended legal action. They are alleging the product sold to them was faulty, resulting in a significant loss of information and an ongoing detrimental impact on profits. As a precaution, sales of the Luge product have been halted and a product recall has been initiated for any Luge products sold in the last four months.

The finance director is keen to announce the company's financial results to the stock market earlier than last year and in order to facilitate this, he has asked if the audit could be completed in a shorter timescale. In addition, the company is intending to propose a final dividend once the financial statements are finalised.

Hurling Co's finance director has informed the audit engagement partner that one of the company's non-executive directors (NEDs) has just resigned, and he has enquired if the partners at Caving & Co can help Hurling Co in recruiting a new NED. Specifically he has requested the engagement quality control reviewer, who was until last year the audit engagement partner on Hurling Co, assist the company in this recruitment. Caving & Co also provides taxation services for Hurling Co in the form of tax return preparation along with some tax planning advice. The finance director has recommended to the audit committee of Hurling Co that this year's audit fee should be based on the company's profit before tax. At today's date, 20% of last year's audit fee is still outstanding and was due to be paid three months ago.

Required

(b)   Describe **EIGHT** audit risks, and explain the auditor's response to each risk, in planning the audit of Hurling Co.

   Note. Prepare your answer using two columns headed Audit risk and Auditor's response respectively.   **(16 marks)**

(c)   (i)   Identify and explain **FIVE** ethical threats which may affect the independence of Caving & Co's audit of Hurling Co; and

   (ii)   For each threat, suggest a safeguard to reduce the risk to an acceptable level.

   Note. The total marks will be split equally between each part. Prepare your answer using two columns headed Ethical threat and Possible Safeguard respectively.   **(10 marks)**

                                                                                                                          (Total = 30 marks)

79 Prancer Construction Co (Sep/Dec 17)   **36 mins**

You are an audit supervisor of Cupid & Co, planning the final audit of a new client, Prancer Construction Co, for the year ending 30 September 20X7. The company specialises in property construction and providing ongoing annual maintenance services for properties previously constructed. Forecast profit before tax is $13.8m and total assets are expected to be $22.3m, both of which are higher than for the year ended 30 September 20X6.

You are required to produce the audit strategy document. The audit manager has met with Prancer Construction Co's finance director and has provided you with the following notes, a copy of the August management accounts and the prior year financial statements.

Meeting notes

The prior year financial statements recognise work in progress of $1.8m, which was comprised of property construction in progress as well as ongoing maintenance services for finished properties. The August 20X7 management accounts recognise $2.1m inventory of completed properties compared to a balance of $1.4m in September 20X6. A full year-end inventory count will be undertaken on 30 September at all of the eleven building sites where construction is in progress. There is not sufficient audit team resource to attend all inventory counts.

In line with industry practice, Prancer Construction Co offers its customers a five-year building warranty, which covers any construction defects. Customers are not required to pay any additional fees to obtain the warranty. The finance director anticipates this provision will be lower than last year as the company has improved its building practices and therefore the quality of the finished properties.

Customers who wish to purchase a property are required to place an order and pay a 5% non-refundable deposit prior to the completion of the building. When the building is complete, customers pay a further 92.5%, with the final 2.5% due to be paid six months later. The finance director has informed you that although an allowance for receivables has historically been maintained, it is anticipated that this can be significantly reduced.

Information from management accounts

Prancer Construction Co's prior year financial statements and August 20X7 management accounts contain a material overdraft balance. The finance director has confirmed that there are minimum profit and net assets covenants attached to the overdraft.

A review of the management accounts shows the payables payment period was 56 days for August 20X7, compared to 87 days for September 20X6. The finance director anticipates that the September 20X7 payables payment period will be even lower than those in August 20X7.

Required

(a) Describe the process Cupid & Co should have undertaken to assess whether the **PRECONDITIONS** for an audit were present when accepting the audit of Prancer Construction Co. **(3 marks)**

(b) Identify **THREE** main areas, other than audit risks, which should be included within the audit strategy document for Prancer Construction Co, and for each area provide an example relevant to the audit. **(3 marks)**

(c) Using all the information provided, describe **SEVEN** audit risks, and explain the auditor's response to each risk, in planning the audit of Prancer Construction Co.

Note. Prepare your answer using two columns headed Audit risk and Auditor's response respectively **(14 marks)**

(Total = 20 marks)

80 Blackberry Co (Mar/Jun 18)   36 mins

You are an audit senior of Loganberry & Co and are planning the audit of Blackberry Co for the year ending 31 March 20X8. The company is a manufacturer of portable music players and your audit manager has already had a planning meeting with the finance director. Forecast revenue is $68.6m and profit before tax is $4.2m.

She has provided you with the following notes of the meeting:

Planning meeting notes

Inventory is valued at the lower of cost and net realisable value. Cost is made up of the purchase price of raw materials and costs of conversion, including labour, production and general overheads. Inventory is held in three warehouses across the country. The company plans to conduct full inventory counts at the warehouses on 2, 3 and 4 April, and any necessary adjustments will be made to reflect post year-end movements of inventory. The internal audit team will attend the counts.

During the year Blackberry Co paid $1.1m to purchase a patent which allows the company the exclusive right for three years to customise their portable music players to gain a competitive edge in their industry. The $1.1m has been expensed in the current year statement of profit or loss. In order to finance this purchase, Blackberry Co raised $1.2m through issuing shares at a premium.

In November 20X7 it was discovered that a significant teeming and lading fraud had been carried out by four members of the sales ledger department who had colluded. They had stolen funds from wholesale customer receipts and then to cover this they allocated later customer receipts against the older receivables. These employees were all reported to the police and subsequently dismissed. As a result of the vacancies in the sales ledger department, Blackberry Co decided to outsource its sales ledger processing to an external service organisation. This service provider handles all elements of the sales ledger cycle, including sales invoicing and chasing of receivables balances and sends monthly reports to Blackberry Co detailing the sales and receivable amounts. Blackberry Co ran its own sales ledger until 31 January 20X8, at which point the records were transferred to the service organisation.

In December 20X7 the financial accountant of Blackberry Co was dismissed. He had been employed by the company for nine years, and he has threatened to sue the company for unfair dismissal. As a result of this dismissal, and until his replacement commences work in April, the financial accountant's responsibilities have been adequately allocated to other members of the finance department. However, for this period no supplier statement reconciliations or purchase ledger control account reconciliations have been performed.

In January 20X7 a receivable balance of $0.9m was written off by Blackberry Co as it was deemed irrecoverable as the customer had declared itself bankrupt. In February 20X8, the liquidators handling the bankruptcy of the company publicly announced that it was likely that most of its creditors would receive a pay-out of 40% of the balance owed. As a result, Blackberry Co has included a current asset of $360,000 within the statement of financial position and other income in the statement of profit or loss.

Required

(a) Describe Loganberry & Co's responsibilities in relation to the prevention and detection of fraud and error. (4 marks)

(b) Describe EIGHT audit risks and explain the auditor's response to each risk in planning the audit of Blackberry Co.

Note. Prepare your answer using two columns headed Audit risk and Auditor's response respectively (16 marks)

(Total = 20 marks)

81 Darjeeling Co (Sep/Dec 18)   54 mins

You are an audit supervisor of Earl & Co and are planning the audit of Darjeeling Co for the year ending 30 September 20X8. The company develops and manufactures specialist paint products and has been a client of your firm for several years. The audit manager has attended a planning meeting with the finance director and has provided you with the following notes of the meeting and financial statement extracts. You have been asked by the audit manager to undertake preliminary analytical procedures using the financial statement extracts.

Planning meeting notes

During the year Darjeeling Co has spent $0.9m, which is included within intangible assets, on the development of new product lines, some of which are in the early stages of their development cycle. Additionally, as the company is looking to expand production, during the year it purchased and installed a new manufacturing line. All costs incurred in the purchase and installation of that asset have been included within property, plant and equipment. These capitalised costs include the purchase price of $2.2m, installation costs of $0.4m and a five-year servicing and maintenance plan costing $0.5m. In order to finance the development projects and the new manufacturing line, the company borrowed $4m from the bank which is to be repaid in instalments over eight years and has an interest rate of 5%. Developing new products and expanding production is important as the company intends to undertake a stock exchange listing in the next 12 months.

The company started a number of initiatives during the year in order to boost revenue. It offered extended credit terms to its customers on the condition that their sales order quantities were increased. In addition, Darjeeling Co made an announcement in October 20X7 of its 'price promise': that it would match the prices of any competitor for similar products purchased. Customers who are able to prove that they could purchase the products cheaper elsewhere are asked to claim the difference from Darjeeling Co, within one month of the date of purchase of goods, via its website. The company intends to include a refund liability of $0.25m, which is based on the monthly level of claims to date, in the draft financial statements.

The finance director informed the audit manager that a problem arose in June 20X8 in relation to the mixing of materials within the production process for one particular product line. A number of these faulty paint products had already been sold and the issue was identified following a number of complaints from customers about the paint consistency being incorrect. As a precaution, further sales have been stopped and a product recall has been initiated for any of these specific paint products sold since June. Management is investigating whether the paint consistency of the faulty products can be rectified and subsequently sold.

Financial statement extracts for year ending 30 September

	Forecast 20X8 $'000	Actual 20X7 $'000
Revenue	19,850	16,990
Cost of sales	(12,440)	(10,800)
Gross profit	7,410	6,190
Inventory	1,850	1,330
Trade receivables	2,750	1,780
Bank	(810)	560
Trade payables	1,970	1,190

Required

(a) Explain why analytical procedures are used during THREE stages of an audit. (3 marks)

(b) Calculate THREE ratios, for BOTH years, which would assist you in planning the audit of Darjeeling Co. (3 marks)

(c) Using the information provided and the ratios calculated, describe EIGHT audit risks and explain the auditor's response to each risk in planning the audit of Darjeeling Co.

Note: Prepare your answer using two columns headed Audit risk and Auditor's response respectively. (16 marks)

(d) Describe substantive procedures the auditor should perform in relation to the faulty paint products held in inventory at the year end. (3 marks)

(e) Describe substantive procedures the auditor should perform to obtain sufficient and appropriate evidence in relation to Darjeeling Co's revenue. (5 marks)

(Total = 30 marks)

INTERNAL CONTROL

Questions 82–118 cover Internal controls, the subject of Part C of the BPP Workbook for Audit and Assurance.

Flowers Anytime (AIR 12/02) (amended)   18 mins

The following scenario relates to questions 82–86.

You are an audit manager in a medium-sized audit firm. You are currently planning the audit of Flowers Anytime (Flowers) for the year ended 31 March 20X7. Flowers, a traditional flower wholesaler, is a new audit client for your firm.

As this is the first year you are auditing Flowers, it is necessary to understand and evaluate the company's system of internal control. The audit firm's policy requires the following steps to be taken when performing first year audits:

(1)   Perform walkthrough tests
(2)   Complete flowcharts and internal control evaluation questionnaires
(3)   Revise the audit strategy and audit plan
(4)   Perform tests of control

You have obtained the following background information about your new client. When customers call the company, their orders are taken by clerks who take details of the flowers to be delivered, the address to which they are to be delivered, and the account details of the customer. The clerks input these details into the company's computer system (whilst the order is being taken) which is integrated with the company's inventory control system.

The audit junior has made the following notes on the system for the receipt, processing and recording of the orders:

•   All orders are recorded on pre-printed, three-part sequentially numbered order forms. One copy is kept by the sales clerk, one copy is forwarded to the warehouse for the dispatch of inventory, and one copy is sent to the customer as evidence of the order.

•   The sales clerk regularly performs reviews of the standing data on the system, matching the price of flowers against an up to date price list.

•   To ensure completeness of orders, a sequence check is performed on the sales invoices manually by the sales clerk and any missing documents are investigated.

•   Sales invoices are posted on a weekly basis to the sales day book and accounts receivable ledger.

82   Drag each of the four options below to the right hand side to show the correct order in which the steps required by the firm's policy for first year audits would take place.

Steps	Order
(1) Perform walkthrough tests	(1)
(2) Complete flowcharts and internal control evaluation questionnaires	(2)
(3) Revise the audit strategy and audit plan	(3)
(4) Perform tests of control	(4)

83 The audit junior has asked you whether internal control questionnaires (ICQs) should be completed as well as internal control evaluation questionnaires (ICEQs).

Which of the following statements is correct in relation to ICQs and ICEQs?

☐ ICEQs determine whether controls exist which meet specific control objectives; ICQs determine whether there are controls which prevent or detect specified errors or omissions.

☐ ICEQs are generally easier to apply to a variety of different systems than ICQs.

☐ ICQs are likely to overlook how internal controls deal with unusual transactions; this will normally have to be recorded using ICEQs.

☐ ICQs can give the impression that all controls are of equal weight; this issue is resolved by using ICEQs.

84 Tick the appropriate box to show whether the internal control activities identified in the audit junior's notes would satisfy the objective of preventing/detecting a material misstatement if it is operating effectively.

Audit junior's notes	Yes	No
All orders are recorded on pre-printed, three-part sequentially numbered order forms. One copy is kept by the sales clerk, one copy is forwarded to the warehouse for the dispatch of inventory, and one copy is sent to the customer as evidence of the order.	☐	☐
The sales clerk regularly performs reviews of the standing data on the system, matching the price of flowers against an up to date price list.	☐	☐
To ensure completeness of orders, a sequence check is performed on the sales invoices manually by the sales clerk and any missing documents are investigated.	☐	☐
Sales invoices are posted on a weekly basis to the sales day book and accounts receivable ledger.	☐	☐

85 You instruct the audit junior to confirm whether the post is opened by more than one individual.

Over which of the following internal control objectives would this provide assurance?

(1) Cash receipts are not misappropriated

(2) All cash receipts that occurred are recorded

(3) Cash receipts are recorded at the correct amounts in the ledger

(4) Cash receipts are posted to the correct receivables accounts and to the general ledger

☐ 1 only

☐ 2 only

☐ 3 and 4

☐ 1 and 4

86   During the course of the audit, the audit team identified numerous deficiencies in internal control relating to the sales system. The amounts exposed to the deficiencies were high and you have concluded that it is likely that the deficiencies would result in material misstatements in the financial statements. A deficiency was also identified in the purchases system but further investigation showed this to be a minor, isolated issue.

Which of the following statements is correct regarding the deficiencies which must be included in the report to management?

☐   The deficiencies identified in the sales system only

☐   The deficiencies identified in the purchases system only

☐   The deficiencies identified in the sales and purchases system

☐   Neither the deficiencies identified in the sales system nor the purchases system

(Total = 10 marks)

KLE Co   **18 mins**

The following scenario relates to questions 87–91.

You are an audit manager in the internal audit department of KLE Co, a listed retail company. The internal audit department is auditing the company's procurement system. The system operates as follows:

Ordering

KLE's ordering department consists of six members of staff: one chief buyer and five purchasing clerks.

All orders are raised on pre-numbered purchase requisition forms, and are sent to the ordering department.

In the ordering department, each requisition form is approved and signed by the chief buyer. A purchasing clerk transfers the order information onto an order form and identifies the appropriate supplier for the goods.

Part one of the two-part order form is sent to the supplier and part two to the accounts department. The requisition is thrown away.

Goods received

When goods are received, the goods inwards department immediately raises a two-part pre-numbered goods received note (GRN).

- Part one is sent to the ordering department, which then forwards the GRN to the accounts department.

- Part two is filed in order of the reference number for the goods being ordered (obtained from the supplier's goods dispatched documentation), in the goods inwards department.

KLE Co's management is concerned that a number of inefficiencies in the procurement system may be having a negative financial impact on the company. As a result, they have requested the internal audit department to carry out a value for money audit focused on the company's procurement practices.

87   Which of the following is **NOT** a likely effect of the deficiencies in the internal control system for ordering described above?

☐   Purchases may be made unnecessarily at unauthorised prices.

☐   Subsequent queries on orders cannot be traced back to the original requisition.

☐   The order forms may contain errors that are not identified.

☐   Goods could be ordered twice in error or deliberately.

88   Which of the following statements are valid recommendations with regards to improving the internal controls for goods received described above?

(1)   The ordering department should match orders to GRNs and mark orders as closed once all goods have been received, to enable any outstanding orders to be chased up.

(2)   The first copy of the GRN should be sent directly to the accounts department, without first going through the ordering department, to prevent delays in recording the purchase.

(3)   The goods inwards department should review the goods for their condition, in order to identify and return any damaged goods.

(4)   GRNs should be filed in date order or by purchase order number, instead of by the supplier's reference number, to ensure that they can be matched easily to orders.

☐   1 and 3

☐   1, 2 and 3

☐   1, 2 and 4

☐   1, 3 and 4

89   As part of your audit of the procurement system, you have recommended that the goods inwards department should ensure that the goods received are valid business purchases, by matching all deliveries to an authorised order form before issuing a GRN.

Which of the following would be an appropriate test of control to confirm that the control is operating effectively?

☐   For a sample of orders, check that there is a matching GRN

☐   Check that the numerical sequence of purchase orders is complete

☐   For a sample of GRNs check that there is an authorised purchase order

☐   Check that the numerical sequence of GRNs is complete

90   KLE Co's management is keen to increase the range of assignments that the company's internal audit undertake.

Which of the following assignments could the internal audit department be asked to perform by management?

☐   Undertake 'mystery shopper' reviews, where they enter the store as a customer, purchase goods and rate the overall shopping experience

☐   Assist the external auditors by requesting bank confirmation letters

☐   Provide advice on the implementation of a new payroll package for the payroll department

☐   Review the company's financial statements on behalf of the board

91   Which of the following best summarises the meaning of 'efficiency' in the context of a Value for Money audit as requested by KLE Co's management?

☐   The lowest cost at which the appropriate quantity and quality of physical, human and financial resources can be achieved

☐   Producing the required goods and services in the shortest time possible

☐   The extent to which an activity is achieving its policy objectives

☐   The relationship between goods and services produced and the resources used to produce them

(Total = 10 marks)

SouthLea (2007 Pilot Paper) (amended)   18 mins

The following scenario relates to questions 92–96.

SouthLea Co, your audit client, is a large unlisted construction company (building houses, offices and hotels) employing a large number of workers on various construction sites.

As part of planning for the audit of the financial statements for the year ended 31 December 20X6, you are reviewing the cash wages systems within the company.

The following information is available concerning the wages systems:

(i)   Hours worked are recorded using a clocking in/out system. On arriving for work and at the end of each day's work, each worker enters their unique employee number on a keypad.

(ii)   Workers on each site are controlled by a foreman. The foreman has a record of all employee numbers and can issue temporary numbers for new employees.

(iii)   Any overtime is calculated by the computerised wages system and added to the standard pay.

(iv)   The two staff in the wages department make amendments to the computerised wages system in respect of employee holidays and illness, as well as setting up and maintaining all employee records.

(v)   The computerised wages system calculates deductions from gross pay, such as employee taxes, and net pay. Every month a wages clerk checks the gross pay and deductions for a sample of employees. Finally a list of net cash payments for each employee is produced.

(vi)   Cash is delivered to the wages office by secure courier.

(vii)   The two staff place cash into wages packets for each employee along with a handwritten note of gross pay, deductions and net pay. The packets are given to the foreman for distribution to the individual employees.

SouthLea's finance director has mentioned to you that an allegation of suspected fraud had been made against a member of the senior management team during the year. This is currently being investigated by the internal audit team and the finance director hopes that the audit may shed further light on the matter.

SouthLea has an internal audit department of six staff. The chief internal auditor appoints staff within the internal audit department, although the chief executive officer is responsible for appointing the chief internal auditor. The chief internal auditor reports directly to the finance director. The chief internal auditor decides on the scope of work of the internal audit department. SouthLea does not currently have an audit committee.

92   In preparation for the audit planning meeting, the audit junior has identified a number of areas requiring audit focus.

Based on the information regarding the wages system, which **TWO** of the following are likely to introduce the highest risk of material misstatement?

- [ ] Completeness of wages

- [ ] Accuracy of deductions from gross pay

- [ ] Cut-off of starters' and leavers' wages

- [ ] Potential fraud risk factors

93   During the previous audit, the audit team had recommended SouthLea's management to ensure that any amendments to standing data on the wages system are reviewed by an authorised manager.

Which of the following is a test of control designed to provide evidence that the recommended internal control is operating effectively?

- [ ] Review overtime lists for evidence of authorisation

- [ ] Review the log of amendments to standing data for evidence of review

- [ ] Perform a proof in total using the number of employees and average wage

- [ ] Obtain printouts of employee wage rates and compare these to HR records

94   Which of the following statements about the responsibilities of external and internal auditors with regards to fraud is **NOT** correct?

- [ ] The external auditor must maintain an attitude of professional scepticism throughout the audit, recognising the possibility that a material misstatement due to fraud could exist.

- [ ] The internal auditor must always consider the potential of management overriding controls and modify their audit procedures accordingly when performing internal audit engagements.

- [ ] It is not the responsibility of the external auditors to detect fraud within a client.

- [ ] The work of internal auditors in reviewing the company's internal control systems helps management to fulfil its responsibility for preventing and detecting fraud.

95   Which of the following recommendations are appropriate in increasing the independence of SouthLea's internal audit department?

(1)   The chief internal auditor should be appointed by the board of directors.

(2)   The chief internal auditor should report to the board of directors.

(3)   The finance director should decide on the scope of the internal audit work.

☐ (1) and (2) only

☐ (1) and (3) only

☐ (2) and (3) only

☐ (1), (2) and (3)

96   You have been told by the finance director that the senior management team is looking to upgrade the company's computerised accounting system in a year's time. This is partly because the senior management team believes that due to the increasing size and complexity of the business, the company will need more robust general IT controls in the future.

Which **TWO** of the following are general IT controls?

☐ Full testing procedures using test data when developing computer applications

☐ One for one checking

☐ Disaster recovery procedures

☐ Hash totals

(Total = 10 marks)

Cherry (6/15) (amended)   18 mins

The following scenario relates to questions 97–101.

Cherry Blossom Co (Cherry) manufactures custom made furniture and its year end is 30 April.

You are the audit supervisor of Poplar & Co and are developing the audit programmes for Cherry's forthcoming interim audit.

You have ascertained that Cherry purchases its raw materials from a wide range of approved suppliers. When production supervisors require raw materials, they complete a requisition form and this is submitted to the purchase ordering department. Requisition forms do not require authorisation and no reference is made to the current inventory levels of the materials being requested.

Cherry has an internal audit department which has provided you with details of the internal controls around the non-current assets cycle. One such control is that upon receipt of a new asset, each asset is assigned a unique serial number and this is recorded on the asset and in the non-current assets register.

97 As part of audit planning, the audit team needs to obtain an understanding of the company's system of internal control. Peter, the audit junior, is unsure what a company's internal control comprises.

Which of the following is **NOT** a component of an entity's internal control?

☐ The control environment

☐ Control activities relevant to the audit

☐ The selection and application of accounting policies

☐ The information system relevant to financial reporting

---

98 Which of the following are the most likely consequences of the internal control deficiency described in the requisition system for raw materials?

(1) Fraudulent purchases may be made, leading to funds being diverted to third parties for illegal purposes.

(2) Stock-outs may occur, resulting in the company being unable to meet orders and lost revenue.

(3) Unnecessary purchases may be made, resulting in excess obsolescent raw materials accumulating in inventory requiring to be written down.

(4) Raw materials of poor quality may be purchased, resulting in low quality products being produced, customer goodwill being lost and going concern risks.

☐ 1 and 3

☐ 2 and 3

☐ 1 and 4

☐ 2 and 4

---

99 While reviewing Cherry's purchases cycle, you identified that goods received notes for raw material purchases are not sequentially numbered.

Which of the following areas would you consider to be most at risk of material misstatement, as a result of this internal control deficiency?

☐ Rights and obligations of inventory

☐ Valuation of payables

☐ Existence of inventory

☐ Completeness of payables

---

100 You now turn your attention to Cherry's non-current assets cycle.

Which of the following statements is correct regarding audit procedures concerning the non-current assets cycle?

☐ If the same ordering documentation is used in the non-current assets cycle as in the purchases cycle, it will not be necessary to produce additional systems documentation.

☐ Because there are likely to be fewer capital purchases than standard purchases in the year, it may not be cost efficient to undertake tests of controls.

☐ Because the control risk around the non-current assets cycle is likely to be high, it is important to perform tests of controls.

☐ The non-current assets cycle is likely to have a lower risk of material misstatement than the purchases cycle.

101 In relation to the control relating to the receipt of a new asset, which **TWO** of the following describe the **MOST RELIABLE** audit procedures which enable the auditor to assess whether this control is operating effectively?

(1) Select a sample of capital additions on site, agree that a serial number is recorded on the asset and confirm it is included in the non-current assets register

(2) Select a sample of assets recorded on the non-current assets register, confirm that it includes a serial number for each asset and agree the number to the physical asset

(3) Inspect the non-current asset register and verify that there are no duplicated serial numbers

(4) Observe the receipt of assets to confirm that serial numbers are assigned and recorded

☐ 1 and 3

☐ 2 and 3

☐ 1 and 4

☐ 2 and 4

(Total = 10 marks)

Swan

The following scenario relates to questions 102–106.

You are the audit senior on the interim audit of Swan Co. The company introduced a new system at the beginning of this financial year. You have discussed the new system with the sales director, and have noted the following two points in particular:

(1)   Existing and new customers input their orders into computerised order forms on Swan Co's website. The order notes the items requested, the billing and sales addresses, and the customer number (if any). The system checks whether goods are in stock and approves the order instantly if so. The order is forwarded automatically to the sales department to be prepared.

(2)   When an order is ready to send out, the sales department inputs the details into their system, and if it matches the order, a goods outward note is produced and the invoicing department is notified automatically. Staff have experienced multiple issues of goods outward notes not matching on the system, and have often resorted to simply printing the order and using it as a goods outward note. The printed order is then taken to the invoicing department for invoicing.

The partner has requested that you document the new system fully during the interim audit. She wants the system notes to be easy to update, and to contain an element of evaluation of the system.

102   In relation to orders received through the website which of the following control objectives is met?

☐   Goods are sold to customers with good credit ratings.

☐   The company is able to fulfil the orders.

☐   Customers do not exceed credit limits.

☐   Changes in customer data are authorised.

---

103   Your audit junior has identified four possible risks arising from the use of the printed order as a goods outward note and subsequent hand delivery to the invoicing department.

Which **TWO** of the below risks arise from the identified system deficiency?

☐   Orders are not fulfilled.

☐   Goods are sent out but not invoiced.

☐   Goods are invoiced but not sent out.

☐   Wrong goods are sent to customers.

---

104   You are reviewing the audit plan for tests of controls over invoicing, which reads:

(1)   Observe the invoicing clerk to ensure that prices are checked to the official price list.

(2)   Review a sample of invoices to ensure their numerical sequence.

(3)   Review a sample of goods out notes to ensure they have been matched to sales invoices.

(4)   Review a sample of sales invoices to verify evidence that the calculations were checked before they were sent to customers.

Which **TWO** of the procedures relate to the completeness assertion?

☐ Observe the invoicing clerk to ensure that prices are checked to the official price list.

☐ Review a sample of invoices to ensure their numerical sequence.

☐ Review a sample of goods out notes to ensure they have been matched to sales invoices.

☐ Review a sample of sales invoices to verify evidence that the calculations were checked before they were sent to customers.

---

105 Your audit junior is seeking to understand when deficiencies in internal control would be judged to be significant and therefore should be reported to those charged with governance.

Which **TWO** of the following factors would influence your judgement of whether the control deficiencies identified at Swan are significant?

☐ The likelihood of material misstatement resulting

☐ The fact that the system is new

☐ The number of deficiencies identified

☐ The fact that the deficiencies are associated with the sales system

---

106 In the light of the partner's request concerning documentation, you are considering different options for recording the system.

Which of the following recording methods most suits her requirements?

☐ A computerised ICEQ

☐ Computerised narrative notes

☐ A flowchart

☐ Copying the company's control manual

(Total = 10 marks)

107 Chuck (12/11) (amended)   54 mins

Introduction and client background

You are the audit senior of Blair & Co and your team has just completed the interim audit of Chuck Industries Co, whose year-end is 31 January 20X2. You are in the process of reviewing the systems testing completed on the payroll cycle, as well as preparing the audit programmes for the final audit.

Chuck Industries Co manufactures lights and the manufacturing process is predominantly automated; however, there is a workforce of 85 employees who monitor the machines, as well as approximately 50 employees who work in sales and administration. The company manufactures 24 hours a day, 7 days a week. The payroll system operates as follows.

Factory workforce

The company operates three shifts every day with employees working eight hours each. They are required to clock in and out using an employee swipe card, which identifies the employee number and links into the hours worked report produced by the computerised payroll system. Employees are paid on an hourly basis for each hour worked. There is no monitoring/supervision of the clocking in/out process.

On a weekly basis, the payroll department calculates the cash wages to be paid to the workforce. This is calculated based on the hours worked report multiplied by the hourly wage rate, with appropriate tax deductions. These calculations are not checked by anyone as they are generated by the payroll system. During the year the hourly wage was increased by the human resources (HR) department and this was notified to the payroll department verbally.

Each Friday, the payroll department prepares the pay packets and physically hands these out to the workforce, who operate the morning and late afternoon shifts, upon production of identification. The pay packets for night shift workers are given to the factory supervisor to distribute. If any night shift employees are absent on pay day then the factory supervisor keeps these wages and returns them to the payroll department on Monday.

Sales and administration staff

The sales and administration staff are paid monthly by bank transfer. Employee numbers do fluctuate and during July two administration staff joined; however, due to staff holidays in the HR department, they delayed informing the payroll department, resulting in incorrect salaries being paid out.

Required

(a)   Identify and explain **SIX DEFICIENCIES** of Chuck Industries Co's payroll system and provide a recommendation to address each of these deficiencies.

Note. Prepare your answer using two columns headed Control deficiency and Control recommendation respectively.   **(12 marks)**

(b)   Describe substantive procedures you should now perform to confirm the accuracy and completeness of Chuck Industries Co's payroll charge.   **(6 marks)**

(c)   Last week the company had a visit from the tax authorities who reviewed the wages calculations and discovered that incorrect levels of tax had been deducted by the payroll system, as the tax rates from the previous year had not been updated. The finance director has queried with the audit team why they did not identify this non-compliance with tax legislation during last year's audit.

Required

Explain the responsibilities of management and auditors of Chuck Industries Co in relation to compliance with law and regulations under ISA 250 (Revised) Consideration of Laws and Regulations in an Audit of Financial Statements.   **(4 marks)**

(d)   Chuck Industries Co has decided to outsource its sales ledger department and as a result it is making 14 employees redundant. A redundancy provision, which is material, will be included in the draft accounts.

Required

Describe substantive procedures you should perform to confirm the redundancy provision at the year end.   **(5 marks)**

(e)   Chuck Industries Co is considering establishing an internal audit (IA) department next year. The finance director has asked whether the work performed by the IA department can be relied upon by Blair & Co.

Required

Explain the factors that should be considered by an external auditor before reliance can be placed on the work performed by a company's internal audit department.   **(3 marks)**

(Total = 30 marks)

108 Greystone (12/10) (amended)   54 mins

Greystone Co is a retailer of ladies' clothing and accessories. It operates in many countries around the world and has expanded steadily from its base in Europe. Its main market is aimed at 15 to 35 year olds and its prices are mid to low range. The company's year end was 30 September 20X0.

In the past the company has bulk ordered its clothing and accessories twice a year. However, if their goods failed to meet the key fashion trends then this resulted in significant inventory write downs. As a result of this the company has recently introduced a just–in-time ordering system. The fashion buyers make an assessment nine months in advance as to what the key trends are likely to be; these goods are sourced from their suppliers but only limited numbers are initially ordered.

Greystone Co has an internal audit department but at present their only role is to perform regular inventory counts at the stores.

Ordering process

Each country has a purchasing manager who decides on the initial inventory levels for each store; this is not done in conjunction with store or sales managers. These quantities are communicated to the central buying department at the head office in Europe. An ordering clerk amalgamates all country orders by specified regions of countries, such as Central Europe and North America, and passes them to the purchasing director to review and authorise.

As the goods are sold, it is the store manager's responsibility to reorder the goods through the purchasing manager; they are prompted weekly to review inventory levels as although the goods are just-in-time, it can still take up to four weeks for goods to be received in store.

It is not possible to order goods from other branches of stores as all ordering must be undertaken through the purchasing manager. If a customer requests an item of clothing, which is unavailable in a particular store, then the customer is provided with other branch telephone numbers or recommended to try the company website.

Goods received and invoicing

To speed up the ordering to receipt of goods cycle, the goods are delivered directly from the suppliers to the individual stores. On receipt of goods the quantities received are checked by a sales assistant against the supplier's delivery note, and then the assistant produces a goods received note (GRN). This is done at quiet times of the day so as to maximise sales. The checked GRNs are sent to head office for matching with purchase invoices.

As purchase invoices are received they are manually matched to GRNs from the stores; this can be a very time-consuming process as some suppliers may have delivered to over 500 stores. Once the invoice has been agreed then it is sent to the purchasing director for authorisation. It is at this stage that the invoice is entered onto the purchase ledger.

(a) Auditors have a responsibility under ISA 265 *Communicating Deficiencies in Internal Control to those Charged with Governance and Management* to communicate deficiencies in internal controls. In particular, **significant** deficiencies in internal controls must be communicated in writing to those charged with governance.

Required

Explain examples of matters the auditor should consider in determining whether a deficiency in internal controls is significant.   (5 marks)

(b) As the external auditors of Greystone Co, write a report to management in respect of the purchasing system which:

(i) Identifies and explains FOUR deficiencies;

(ii) Provides a recommendation to address each of these deficiencies; and

(iii) Describe a test of control Greystone's internal audit department could perform to assess whether each of these controls, if implemented, is operating effectively.

A covering letter is required.

Note. Up to two marks will be awarded within this requirement for presentation.

(14 marks)

(c) Describe substantive procedures the auditor should perform on the year-end trade payables of Greystone Co. (5 marks)

(d) Describe additional assignments that the internal audit department of Greystone Co could be asked to perform by those charged with governance. (6 marks)

(Total = 30 marks)

109 Tinkerbell (6/11) 54 mins

Introduction

Tinkerbell Toys Co (Tinkerbell) is a manufacturer of children's building block toys; they have been trading for over 35 years and they sell to a wide variety of customers including large and small toy retailers across the country. The company's year-end is 31 May 20X1.

The company has a large manufacturing plant, four large warehouses and a head office. Upon manufacture, the toys are stored in one of the warehouses until they are dispatched to customers. The company does not have an internal audit department.

Sales ordering, goods dispatched and invoicing

Each customer has a unique customer account number and this is used to enter sales orders when they are received in writing from customers. The orders are entered by an order clerk and the system automatically checks that the goods are available and that the order will not take the customer over their credit limit. For new customers, a sales manager completes a credit application; this is checked through a credit agency and a credit limit entered into the system by the credit controller. The company has a price list, which is updated twice a year. Larger customers are entitled to a discount; this is agreed by the sales director and set up within the customer master file.

Once the order is entered an acceptance is automatically sent to the customer by mail/email confirming the goods ordered and a likely dispatch date. The order is then sorted by address of customer. The warehouse closest to the customer receives the order electronically and a dispatch list and sequentially numbered goods dispatch notes (GDNs) are automatically generated. The warehouse team packs the goods from the dispatch list and, before they are sent out, a second member of the team double checks the dispatch list to the GDN, which accompanies the goods.

Once dispatched, a copy of the GDN is sent to the accounts team at head office and a sequentially numbered sales invoice is raised and checked to the GDN. Periodically a computer sequence check is performed for any missing sales invoice numbers.

Fraud

During the year a material fraud was uncovered. It involved cash/cheque receipts from customers being diverted into employees' personal accounts. In order to cover up the fraud, receipts from subsequent unrelated customers would then be recorded against the earlier outstanding receivable balances and this cycle of fraud would continue.

The fraud occurred because two members of staff 'who were related' colluded. One processed cash receipts and prepared the weekly bank reconciliation; the other employee recorded customer receipts in the sales ledger. An unrelated sales ledger clerk was supposed to send out monthly customer statements but this was not performed. The bank reconciliations each had a small unreconciled amount but no one reviewed the reconciliations after they were prepared. The fraud was only uncovered when the two employees went on holiday at the same time and it was discovered that cash receipts from different customers were being applied to older receivable balances to hide the earlier sums stolen.

Required

(a) Recommend **SIX** tests of controls the auditor would normally carry out on the sales system of Tinkerbell, and explain the objective for each test. **(12 marks)**

(b) Describe substantive procedures the auditor should perform to confirm Tinkerbell's year-end receivables balance. **(8 marks)**

(c) Identify and explain controls Tinkerbell should implement to reduce the risk of fraud occurring again and, for each control, describe how it would mitigate the risk. **(6 marks)**

(d) Describe substantive procedures the auditor should perform to confirm Tinkerbell's revenue. **(4 marks)**

(Total = 30 marks)

110 Trombone (6/14)   **54 mins**

Trombone Co (Trombone) operates a chain of hotels across the country. Trombone employs in excess of 250 permanent employees and its year end is 31 August 20X4. You are the audit supervisor of Viola & Co and are currently reviewing the documentation of Trombone's payroll system, detailed below, in preparation for the interim audit.

Trombone's payroll system

Permanent employees work a standard number of hours per week as specified in their employment contract. However, when the hotels are busy, staff can be requested by management to work additional shifts as overtime. This can either be paid on a monthly basis or taken as days off.

Employees record any overtime worked and days taken off on weekly overtime sheets which are sent to the payroll department. The standard hours per employee are automatically set up in the system and the overtime sheets are entered by clerks into the payroll package, which automatically calculates the gross and net pay along with relevant deductions. These calculations are not checked at all. Wages are increased by the rate of inflation each year and the clerks are responsible for updating the standing data in the payroll system.

Employees are paid on a monthly basis by bank transfer for their contracted weekly hours and for any overtime worked in the previous month. If employees choose to be paid for overtime, authorisation is required by department heads of any overtime in excess of 30% of standard hours. If employees choose instead to take days off, the payroll clerks should check back to the 'overtime worked' report; however this report is not always checked.

The 'overtime worked' report, which details any overtime recorded by employees, is run by the payroll department weekly and emailed to department heads for authorisation. The payroll department asks department heads to only report if there are any errors recorded. Department heads are required to arrange for overtime sheets to be authorised by an alternative responsible official if they are away on annual leave; however there are instances where this arrangement has not occurred.

The payroll package produces a list of payments per employee; this links into the bank system to produce a list of automatic payments. The finance director reviews the total list of bank transfers and compares this to the total amount to be paid per the payroll records; if any issues arise then the automatic bank transfer can be manually changed by the finance director.

Required

(a)   In respect of the payroll system of Trombone Co:

  (i)   Identify and explain **FIVE** deficiencies;

  (ii)   Recommend a control to address each of these deficiencies; and

  (iii) Describe a test of control Viola & Co should perform to assess if each of these controls is operating effectively.

  Note. The total marks will be split equally between each part. Prepare your answer using three columns headed Control deficiency, Control recommendation and Test of control respectively.   **(15 marks)**

(b)   Explain the difference between an interim and a final audit.   **(5 marks)**

(c)   Describe substantive procedures you should perform at the final audit to confirm the completeness and accuracy of Trombone Co's payroll expense.   **(6 marks)**

Trombone deducts employment taxes from its employees' wages on a monthly basis and pays these to the local taxation authorities in the following month. At the year end the financial statements will contain an accrual for income tax payable on employment income. You will be in charge of auditing this accrual.

Required

(d)   Describe the audit procedures required in respect of the year-end accrual for tax payable on employment income.   **(4 marks)**

                                                                 (Total = 30 marks)

111 Fox Industries Co (6/13) (amended)   54 mins

Introduction

Fox Industries Co manufactures engineering parts. It has one operating site and a customer base spread across Europe. The company's year-end was 31 March 20X6. Below is a description of the purchasing and payments system.

Purchasing system

Whenever production materials are required, the relevant department sends a requisition form to the ordering department. An order clerk raises a purchase order and contacts a number of suppliers to see which can dispatch the goods first. This supplier is then chosen. The order clerk sends out the purchase order. This is not sequentially numbered and only orders above $5,000 require authorisation.

Purchase invoices are input daily by the purchase ledger clerk, who has been in the role for many years and, as an experienced team member, does not apply any application controls over the input process. Every week the purchase day book automatically updates the purchase ledger; the purchase ledger is then posted manually to the general ledger by the purchase ledger clerk.

Payments system

Fox Industries Co maintains a current account and a number of saving (deposit) accounts. The current account is reconciled weekly but the saving (deposit) accounts are only reconciled every two months.

In order to maximise their cash and bank balance, Fox has a policy of delaying payments to all suppliers for as long as possible. Suppliers are paid by a bank transfer. The finance director is given the total amount of the payments list, which he authorises and then processes the bank payments.

(a)   ISA 260 *Communication with Those Charged with Governance* provides guidance to auditors in relation to communicating with those charged with governance on matters arising from the audit of an entity's financial statements.

Required

(i) Explain why it is important that auditors communicate throughout the audit with those charged with governance. **(2 marks)**

(ii) Describe **THREE** examples of matters that the auditors may communicate to those charged with governance. **(3 marks)**

(b) As the external auditors of Fox Industries Co, write a report to management in respect of the purchasing and payments system described above which:

(i) Identifies and explains **SIX** deficiencies in the system and recommends a control to address each of these deficiencies; and

(ii) Includes a covering letter

Note. Up to two marks will be awarded within this requirement for the covering letter.

(14 marks)

(c) Identify and explain **FOUR** application controls that should be adopted by Fox Industries Co to ensure the completeness and accuracy of the input of purchase invoices. **(5 marks)**

(d) Describe substantive procedures the auditor should perform to confirm the bank and cash balance of Fox Industries Co at the year end. **(6 marks)**

(Total = 30 marks)

112 Bluesberry (12/10)   36 mins

Bluesberry Hospital is located in a country where healthcare is free, as the taxpayers fund the hospitals which are owned by the Government. Two years ago management reviewed all aspects of hospital operations and instigated a number of measures aimed at improving overall 'value for money' for the local community. Management have asked that you, an audit manager in the hospital's internal audit department, perform a review over the measures which have been implemented.

Bluesberry has one centralised buying department and all purchase requisition forms for medical supplies must be forwarded here. Upon receipt the buying team will research the lowest price from suppliers and a purchase order is raised. This is then passed to the purchasing director, who authorises all orders. The small buying team receives in excess of 200 forms a day.

The human resources department has had difficulties with recruiting suitably trained staff. Overtime rates have been increased to incentivise permanent staff to fill staffing gaps; this has been popular, and reliance on expensive temporary staff has been reduced. Monitoring of staff hours had been difficult but the hospital has implemented time card clocking in and out procedures and these hours are used for overtime payments as well.

The hospital has invested heavily in new surgical equipment which, although very expensive, has meant that more operations could be performed and patient recovery rates are faster. However, currently there is a shortage of appropriately trained medical staff. A capital expenditure committee has been established, made up of senior managers, and they plan and authorise any significant capital expenditure items.

Required

(a) Explain the purpose of a value for money audit. **(4 marks)**

(b) (i) Identify and explain **FOUR STRENGTHS** within Bluesberry's operating environment. **(6 marks)**

(ii) For each strength identified, describe how Bluesberry might make further improvements to provide best value for money. **(4 marks)**

(c)   Describe **TWO** substantive procedures the external auditor of Bluesberry should adopt to verify **EACH** of the following assertions in relation to an entity's property, plant and equipment:

(i)   Valuation;
(ii)   Completeness; and
(iii)   Rights and obligations.

Note. Assume that the hospital adopts IFRS. **(6 marks)**

(Total = 20 marks)

113 Bronze Industries Co (Sep/Dec 15)   36 mins

You are an audit senior of Scarlet & Co and are in the process of reviewing the systems testing completed on the payroll cycle of Bronze Industries Co (Bronze), as well as preparing the audit programmes for the final audit.

Bronze operates several chemical processing factories across the country; it manufactures 24 hours a day, 7 days a week and employees work a standard shift of 8 hours and are paid for hours worked at an hourly rate. Factory employees are paid weekly, with approximately 80% being paid by bank transfer and 20% in cash; the different payment methods are due to employee preferences and Bronze has no plans to change these methods. The administration and sales teams are paid monthly by bank transfer.

Factory staff are each issued a sequentially numbered clock card which details their employee number and name. Employees swipe their cards at the beginning and end of the eight-hour shift and this process is not supervised. During the shift employees are entitled to a 30-minute paid break and employees do not need to clock out to access the dining area. Clock card data links into the payroll system, which automatically calculates gross and net pay along with any statutory deductions. The payroll supervisor for each payment run checks on a sample basis some of these calculations to ensure the system is operating effectively.

Bronze has a human resources department which is responsible for setting up new permanent employees and leavers. Appointments of temporary staff are made by factory production supervisors. Occasionally overtime is required of factory staff, usually to fill gaps caused by staff holidays. Overtime reports which detail the amount of overtime worked are sent out quarterly by the payroll department to production supervisors for their review.

To encourage staff to attend work on time for all shifts Bronze pays a discretionary bonus every six months to factory staff; the production supervisors determine the amounts to be paid. This is communicated in writing by the production supervisors to the payroll department and the bonus is input by a clerk into the system.

For employees paid by bank transfer, the payroll manager reviews the list of payments and agrees to the payroll records prior to authorising the bank payment. If any changes are required, the payroll manager amends the records. For employees paid in cash, the pay packets are prepared in the payroll department and a clerk distributes them to employees; as she knows most of these individuals she does not require proof of identity.

Required

(a)   Identify and explain **FIVE KEY CONTROLS** which the auditor may seek to place reliance on in Bronze Industries Co's payroll system.   **(5 marks)**

(b)   Identify and explain **SIX** internal control **DEFICIENCIES** in Bronze Industries Co's payroll system and provide a **RECOMMENDATION** to address each of these deficiencies.
                                                                                       (12 marks)

(c)   Describe substantive **ANALYTICAL PROCEDURES** you should perform to confirm Bronze Industries Co's payroll expense.   **(3 marks)**

(Total = 20 marks)

114 Lemon Quartz Co (Mar/Jun 16)   36 mins

You are an audit senior of Hessonite & Co and are in the process of reviewing the inventory system documentation for your audit client, Lemon Quartz Co (Quartz), which manufactures computer equipment. The company's factory and warehouse are based on one large site, and their year-end is 30 June 20X6. Quartz is planning to undertake a full inventory count at the year-end of its raw materials, work in progress and finished goods and you will be attending this count. In preparation you have been reviewing the inventory count instructions for finished goods provided by Quartz.

The count will be undertaken by 15 teams of 2 counters from the warehouse department with Quartz's financial controller providing overall supervision. Each team of two is allocated a number of bays within the warehouse to count and they are provided with sequentially numbered inventory sheets which contain product codes and quantities extracted from the inventory records. The counters move through each allocated bay counting the inventory and confirming that it agrees with the inventory sheets. Where a discrepancy is found, they note this on the sheet.

The warehouse is large and approximately 10% of the bays have been rented out to third parties with similar operations; these are scattered throughout the warehouse. For completeness, the counters have been asked to count the inventory for all bays noting the third-party inventories on separate blank inventory sheets, and the finance department will make any necessary adjustments.

Some of Quartz's finished goods are high in value and are stored in a locked area of the warehouse and all the counting teams will be given the code to access this area. There will be no dispatches of inventory during the count and it is not anticipated that there will be any deliveries from suppliers.

Each area is counted once by the allocated team; the sheets are completed in ink, signed by the team and returned after each bay is counted. As no two teams are allocated the same bays, there will be no need to flag that an area has been counted. On completion of the count, the financial controller will confirm with each team that they have returned their inventory sheets.

Required

(a)   In respect of the inventory count procedures for Lemon Quartz Co:

    (i)   Identify and explain **FIVE** deficiencies;

    (ii)   Recommend a control to address each of these deficiencies; and

    (iii)   Describe a **TEST OF CONTROL** the external auditors would perform to assess if each of these controls, if implemented, is operating effectively.

    Note. The total marks will be split equally between each part. Prepare your answer using three columns headed Control deficiency, Control recommendation and Test of control respectively.   **(15 marks)**

(b)   Quartz's finance director has asked your firm to undertake a non-audit assurance engagement later in the year. The audit junior has not been involved in such an assignment before and has asked you to explain what an assurance engagement involves.

    ## Required

    Explain the five elements of an assurance engagement.   **(5 marks)**

                                                            (Total = 20 marks)

115 Equestrian Co (Mar/Jun 17)

36 mins

(a) ISA 315 *Identifying and Assessing the Risks of Material Misstatement through Understanding the Entity and Its Environment* requires auditors to obtain an understanding of control activities relevant to the audit.

Control activities are the policies and procedures which help ensure that management directives are carried out.

Required

Describe FOUR different types of control activities and, for each type, provide an example control a company may implement. **(4 marks)**

Equestrian Co manufactures smartphones and tablets. Its main customers are retailers who then sell to the general public. The company's manufacturing is spread across five sites and goods are stored in its nine warehouses located across the country. You are an audit supervisor of Baseball & Co and in preparation for the forthcoming audit for the year ending 30 June 20X7, you are reviewing the following notes your audit manager has provided you with in relation to the company's internal controls.

Equestrian Co has a small internal audit (IA) department. During the year, IA started a programme of physically verifying the company's assets and comparing the results to the non-current assets register, as this type of reconciliation had not occurred for some time. To date only 15% of assets have had their existence confirmed as IA has experienced significant staff shortages and several members of the current IA team are new to Equestrian Co.

During the year, Equestrian Co conducted an extensive reorganisation of its manufacturing process to improve efficiency. Due to the significant number of employee changes required, the human resources department (HR) has been very busy and to ease their workload during this period, the payroll department has assisted by setting up any new employees who have joined the company. In January 20X7, the wage rate paid to employees was increased by the HR director and he notified payroll by emailing the payroll supervisor.

A new sales ledger system was introduced in May 20X6 and will continue to be run in parallel with the old system until IA has completed its checks between the two systems. New customers obtained by the sales team are required to undergo a full credit check; on the basis of this, a credit limit is proposed by sales staff and approved by the sales director and these credit limits remain static in the sales system.

Monthly perpetual inventory counts are undertaken at each of the nine warehouses, as a full year-end inventory count is too disruptive for the company. High value items are stored in a secure area in each warehouse. Access is via a four digit code, which for convenience is the same across all sites. Due to the company's reorganisation programme, some of the monthly inventory counts were not performed.

Bank reconciliations are undertaken monthly by an accounts clerk and details of all reconciling items are included. Where the sum of the reconciling items is significant, the reconciliation is sent to the financial controller for review. In order to maximise cash balances, the finance director approves all purchase invoices for payment 75 days after receipt of the invoice.

Required

(b) Identify and explain **EIGHT** deficiencies in Equestrian Co's internal controls and provide a recommendation to address each of these deficiencies.

Note. Prepare your answer using two columns headed Control deficiency and Control recommendation respectively. **(16 marks)**

(Total = 20 marks)

116 Comet Publishing Co (Sep/Dec 17)

54 mins

You are an audit supervisor of Halley & Co and you are reviewing the documentation describing Comet Publishing Co's purchases and payables system in preparation for the interim and final audit for the year ending 30 September 20X7. The company is a retailer of books and has ten stores and a central warehouse, which holds the majority of the company's inventory.

Your firm has audited Comet Publishing Co for a number of years and as such, audit documentation is available from the previous year's file, including internal control flowcharts and detailed purchases and payables system notes. As far as you are aware, Comet Publishing Co's system of internal control has not changed in the last year. The audit manager is keen for the team to utilise existing systems documentation in order to ensure audit efficiency. An extract from the existing systems notes is provided below.

Extract of purchases and payables system

Store managers are responsible for ordering books for their shop. It is not currently possible for store managers to request books from any of the other nine stores. Customers who wish to order books, which are not in stock at the branch visited, are told to contact the other stores directly or visit the company website. As the inventory levels fall in a store, the store manager raises a purchase requisition form, which is sent to the central warehouse. If there is insufficient inventory held, a supplier requisition form is completed and sent to the purchase order clerk, Oliver Dancer, for processing. He sends any orders above $1,000 for authorisation from the purchasing director.

Receipts of goods from suppliers are processed by the warehouse team, who agree the delivery to the purchase order, checking quantity and quality of goods and complete a sequentially numbered goods received note (GRN). The GRNs are sent to the accounts department every two weeks for processing.

On receipt of the purchase invoice from the supplier, an accounts clerk matches it to the GRN. The invoice is then sent to the purchase ordering clerk, Oliver, who processes it for payment. The finance director is given the total amount of the payments list, which she authorises and then processes the bank payments. Due to staff shortages in the accounts department, supplier statement reconciliations are no longer performed.

Other information – conflict of interest

Halley & Co has recently accepted the audit engagement of a new client, Edmond Co, who is the main competitor of Comet Publishing Co. The finance director of Comet Publishing Co has enquired how Halley & Co will keep information obtained during the audit confidential.

Required

(a) Explain the safeguards which Halley & Co should implement to ensure that the identified conflict of interest is properly managed. **(5 marks)**

(b) Explain the steps the auditor should take to confirm the accuracy of the purchases and payables flowcharts and systems notes currently held on file. **(5 marks)**

(c) In respect of the purchases and payables system for Comet Publishing Co:

    (i) Identify and explain **FIVE** deficiencies;

    (ii) Recommend a control to address each of these deficiencies; and

    (iii) Describe a **TEST OF CONTROL** the auditor should perform to assess if each of these controls, if implemented, is operating effectively to reduce the identified deficiency.

    Note. Prepare your answer using three columns headed Control deficiency, Control recommendation, and Test of control respectively. The total marks will be split equally between each part. **(15 marks)**

(d) Describe substantive procedures the auditor should perform to obtain sufficient and appropriate evidence in relation to Comet Publishing Co's purchases and other expenses. **(5 marks)**

(Total = 30 marks)

117 Raspberry Co (Mar/Jun 18)

Raspberry Co operates an electric power station, which produces electricity 24 hours a day, seven days a week. The company's year-end is 30 June 20X8. You are an audit manager of Grapefruit & Co, the auditor of Raspberry Co. The interim audit has been completed and you are reviewing the documentation describing Raspberry Co's payroll system.

Systems notes – payroll

Raspberry Co employs over 250 people and approximately 70% of the employees work in production at the power station. There are three shifts every day with employees working eight hours each. The production employees are paid weekly in cash. The remaining 30% of employees work at the head office in non-production roles and are paid monthly by bank transfer.

The company has a human resources (HR) department, responsible for setting up all new joiners. Pre-printed forms are completed by HR for all new employees and, once verified, a copy is sent to the payroll department for the employee to be set up for payment. This form includes the staff member's employee number and payroll cannot set up new joiners without this information. To encourage staff to attend work on time for all shifts, Raspberry Co introduced a discretionary bonus, paid every three months for production staff. The production supervisors determine the amounts to be paid and notify the payroll department. This quarterly bonus is entered into the system by a clerk and each entry is checked by a senior clerk for input errors prior to processing. The senior clerk signs the bonus listing as evidence of undertaking this review.

Production employees are issued with clock cards and are required to swipe their cards at the beginning and end of their shift. This process is supervised by security staff 24 hours a day. Each card identifies the employee number and links into the hours worked report produced by the payroll system, which automatically calculates the gross and net pay along with relevant deductions. These calculations are not checked.

In addition to tax deductions from pay, some employees' wages are reduced for such items as repayments of student loans owed to the central government. All employers have a statutory obligation to remit funds on a timely basis and to maintain accounting records which reconcile with annual loan statements sent by the government to employers. At Raspberry Co student loan deduction forms are completed by the relevant employee and payments are made directly to the government until the employee notifies HR that the loan has been repaid in full.

On a quarterly basis exception reports relating to changes to the payroll standing data are produced and reviewed by the payroll director. No overtime is worked by employees. Employees are entitled to take 28 holiday days annually. Holiday request forms are required to be completed and authorised by relevant line managers, however this does not always occur.

On a monthly basis, for employees paid by bank transfer, the senior payroll manager reviews the list of bank payments and agrees this to the payroll records prior to authorising the payment. If any errors are noted, the payroll senior manager amends the records.

For production employees paid in cash, the necessary amount of cash is delivered weekly from the bank by a security company. Two members of the payroll department produce the pay packets, one is responsible for preparing them and the other checks the finished pay packets. Both members of staff are required to sign the weekly payroll listing on completion of this task. The pay packets are then delivered to the production supervisors, who distribute them to employees at the end of the employees' shift, as they know each member of their production team.

Monthly management accounts are produced which detail variances between budgeted amounts and actual. Revenue and key production costs are detailed however, as there are no overtime costs, wages and salaries are not analysed.

Required

(a) In respect of the payroll system for Raspberry Co:

    (i) Identify and explain **FIVE KEY CONTROLS** which the auditor may seek to place reliance on; and

    (ii) Describe a **TEST OF CONTROL** the auditor should perform to assess if each of these key controls is operating effectively.

    Note. Prepare your answer using two columns headed Key control and Test of control respectively. The total marks will be split equally between each part. **(10 marks)**

(b) Identify and explain **FIVE DEFICIENCIES** in Raspberry Co's payroll system and provide a recommendation to address each of these deficiencies.

    Note. Prepare your answer using two columns headed Control deficiency and Control recommendation respectively **(10 marks)**

The finance director is interested in establishing an internal audit department (IAD). In the company she previously worked for the IAD carried out inventory counts, however as this is not relevant for Raspberry Co, she has asked for guidance on what other assignments an IAD could be asked to perform.

Required

(c) Describe assignments the internal audit department of Raspberry Co could carry out.

    (5 marks)

Raspberry Co deducts employment taxes from its employees' wages on a weekly/monthly basis and pays these to the local taxation authorities in the following month. At the year end the financial statements will contain an accrual for income tax payable on employment income.

Required

(d) Describe the substantive procedures the auditor should perform to confirm the year-end accrual for tax payable on employment income. **(5 marks)**

    (Total = 30 marks)

118 Camomile Co (Sep/Dec 18)   36 mins

(a) ISA 260 *Communication with Those Charged with Governance* provides guidance to auditors in relation to communicating with those charged with governance on matters arising from the audit of an entity's financial statements.

    Required

    (i) Explain why it is important for auditors to communicate throughout the audit with those charged with governance; and

    (ii) Identify TWO examples of matters which the auditor may communicate to those charged with governance.

    Note: The total marks will be split equally between each part. **(4 marks)**

(b) Camomile Co operates six restaurant and bar venues which are open seven days a week. The company's year-end is 31 December 20X8. You are the audit supervisor reviewing the internal controls documentation in relation to the cash receipts and payments system in preparation for the interim audit, which will involve visiting a number of the venues as well as the head office. The company has a small internal audit (IA) department based at head office.

The purchasing department based at the company's head office is responsible for ordering food and beverages for all six venues. In addition, each venue has a petty cash float of $400, held in the safe, which is used for the purchase of sundry items. When making purchases of sundries, employees are required to obtain the funds from the restaurant manager, purchase the sundries and return any excess money and the receipt to the manager. At any time, the petty cash sum held and receipts should equal the float of $400 but it has been noted by the company's IA department that on some occasions this has not been the case.

Each venue has five cash tills (cash registers) to take payments from customers. Three are located in the bar area and two in the restaurant area. Customers can pay using either cash or a credit card and for any transaction either the credit card vouchers or cash are placed in the till by the employee operating the till. To speed up the payment process, each venue has a specific log on code which can be used to access all five tills and is changed every two weeks.

At each venue at the end of the day, the tills are closed down by the restaurant manager who counts the total cash in all five tills and the sum of the credit card vouchers and these totals are reconciled with the aggregated daily readings of sales taken from each till. Any discrepancies are noted on the daily sales sheet. The daily sales sheet records the sales per the tills, the cash counted and the total credit card vouchers as well as any discrepancies. These sheets are scanned and emailed to the cashier at head office at the end of each week.

Approximately 30% of Camomile Co's customers pay in cash for their restaurant or bar bills. Cash is stored in the safe at each venue on a daily basis after the sales reconciliation has been undertaken. Each safe is accessed via a key which the restaurant manager has responsibility for. Each key is stored in a drawer of the manager's desk when not being used. Cash is transferred to the bank via daily collection by a security company. The security company provides a receipt for the sums collected, and these receipts are immediately forwarded to head office. The credit card company remits the amounts due directly into Camomile Co's bank account within two days of the transaction.

At head office, on receipt of the daily sales sheets and security company receipts, the cashier agrees the cash transferred by the security company has been banked for all venues. She agrees the cash per the daily sales sheets to bank deposit slips and to the bank statements. The cashier updates the cash book with the cash banked and details of the credit card vouchers from the daily sales sheets. On a monthly basis, the credit card company sends a statement of all credit card receipts from the six venues which is filed by the cashier.

Every two months, the cashier reconciles the bank statements to the cash book. The reconciliations are reviewed by the financial controller who evidences her review by signature and these are filed in the accounts department. All purchases of food and beverages for the venues are paid by bank transfer. At the relevant payment dates, the finance director is given the total amount of the payments list which he authorises.

Required

Identify and explain EIGHT DEFICIENCIES in Camomile Co's cash receipts and payments system and provide a recommendation to address each of these deficiencies.

Note: Prepare your answer using two columns headed Control deficiencies and Control recommendation respectively.

(16 marks)

(Total = 20 marks)

AUDIT EVIDENCE

Questions 119–160 cover Audit evidence, the subject of Part D of the BPP Workbook for Audit and Assurance.

Expert (12/08) (amended)   18 mins

The following scenario relates to questions 119–123.

You are the audit manager in the firm of WSD & Co, an audit firm. You are planning the audit of Truse Co, which operates as a high street retailer and has 15 shops.

All of the shops are owned by Truse Co and have always been included in the financial statements at cost less depreciation. The shops are depreciated over 50 years. However, you know from discussions with management that the company intends to include one of the shops, the flagship store, at a revalued amount rather than cost in the current accounting period. The revalued amount is expected to be materially above the carrying value of the shop. The valuation will be based on a management estimate.

Management has explained that the reason for the revaluation is because the flagship store is located in an area where property prices have risen much more quickly compared to other shop locations. They consider the flagship store to be significantly undervalued on the statement of financial position.

Management will not depreciate the revalued amount allocated to the flagship store's building because they maintain the building to a high standard.

119   In his notes for the audit planning meeting, the audit junior made several statements in relation to the valuation of the shops.

Which **TWO** of the below statements are correct?

☐   Truse Co is allowed under IAS 16 Property, Plant and Equipment to revalue the flagship shop while continuing to measure its three other shops at cost less depreciation.

☐   The revaluation constitutes a change in accounting policy, so we will need to consider the adequacy of the disclosures made in respect of this.

☐   The flagship store should be depreciated on its revalued amount.

☐   We must confirm that all repairs and maintenance costs have been capitalised.

120   Indicate whether the following assertions are relevant to the audit of tangible non-current assets.

Assertion	Yes	No
Existence	☐	☐
Occurrence	☐	☐
Classification	☐	☐
Presentation	☐	☐

121 Which of the following procedures will provide appropriate audit evidence in respect of the completeness of non-current assets?

☐ For a sample of assets selected by physical inspection, agree that they are listed on the non-current assets register

☐ For a sample of non-current assets listed on the non-current assets register, physically inspect the asset

☐ For a sample of assets on the assets register, recalculate the carrying amount in accordance with the entity's accounting policies

☐ For a sample of assets on the assets register, inspect relevant purchase invoices or deeds

122 At the planning meeting, it was decided that an auditor's expert should be sought in relation to the valuation of Truse Co's properties as the company has not used an independent valuer.

ISA 620 *Using the Work of an Auditor's Expert* states that the nature, timing and extent of audit procedures to evaluate the work of the auditor's expert depend on the circumstances of the engagement.

Which of the following matters should the audit team **NOT** consider in determining the nature, timing and extent of these audit procedures?

☐ The risk of material misstatement associated with Truse Co's properties

☐ WSD & Co's experience with previous work performed by the expert

☐ Whether the expert is subject to WSD & Co's quality control policies and procedures

☐ The existence of any interests in or relationships with Truse Co that might pose a threat to the expert's objectivity

123 The audit junior has been assigned to the audit of the bank and cash balances of Truse Co. He has noted down the audit evidence he plans to obtain in respect of the bank and cash balances:

(1) Bank reconciliation carried out by the cashier
(2) Bank confirmation report from Truse Co's bank
(3) Verbal confirmation from the directors that the overdraft limit is to be increased
(4) Cash count carried out by the audit junior himself

Drag each of the four options below to the right hand side to show the order of reliability of the audit evidence, starting with the most reliable first.

Audit evidence		Order
(1)	Bank reconciliation carried out by the cashier	(1)
(2)	Bank confirmation report from Truse Co's bank	(2)
(3)	Verbal confirmation from the directors that the overdraft limit is to be increased	(3)
(4)	Cash count carried out by the audit junior himself	(4)

(Total = 10 marks)

Newthorpe   18 mins

The following scenario relates to questions 124–128.

You are an audit manager, auditing the financial statements of Newthorpe Engineering Co, a listed company, for the year ended 30 April 20X7.

Newthorpe's management has provided you with a schedule of the realisable values of the inventories. A full inventory count was carried out at 30 April 20X7.

Audit tests have confirmed that the inventory counts are accurate and there are no purchases or sales cut-off errors.

One of the company's factories was closed on 30 April 20X7. The plant and equipment and inventories were to be sold. By the time the audit work commenced in June 20X7, most of the inventory had been sold.

You have instructed the audit junior to evaluate the valuation of the inventory related to the closing factory at the year end. The audit junior has sent you a list of planned audit procedures.

On 17 March 20X7, Newthorpe's managing director was dismissed for gross misconduct. It was decided that the managing director's salary should stop from that date, and that no redundancy or compensation payments should be made.

The managing director has claimed unfair dismissal and is taking legal action against the company to obtain compensation for loss of his employment. The managing director says he has a service contract with the company which would entitle him to two years' salary at the date of dismissal. The directors believe that there is a 35% chance of the managing director succeeding in his claim.

The financial statements for the year ended 30 April 20X7 record the resignation of the director. However, they do not mention his dismissal and no provision for any damages has been included in the financial statements.

124 Which **TWO** of the following statements are true regarding the auditor's attendance at the inventory count?

☐ It is the auditor's responsibility to organise the inventory count.

☐ The auditor observes client staff to determine whether inventory count procedures are being followed.

☐ The auditor reviews procedures for identifying damaged, obsolete and slow-moving inventory.

☐ If the results of the auditors' test counts are not satisfactory, the auditor should insist that the inventory is recounted.

125 Which of the audit procedures below is **NOT** appropriate in auditing the valuation assertion for Newthorpe's inventory?

☐ Agree the selling prices of inventory sold since the year end to sales invoices and the cash book.

☐ Assess the reasonableness of management's point estimates of realisable value of inventory that has not yet been sold by reviewing sales before the year end, comparing the values with inventory that has been sold since the year end and considering offers made which have not yet been finalised.

☐ For a sample of inventory sold just before and just after the year end, match dates of sales invoices/date posted to ledgers with date on related goods dispatched notes.

☐ For unsold inventory, assess reasonableness of provisions for selling expenses by comparison of selling expenses with inventory sold.

126 Using the drop down lists, complete the sentence below to show the correct accounting treatment for the legal claim made by the managing director for unfair dismissal and the reason for this treatment.

The legal claim should [＿＿＿＿＿＿＿＿＿＿＿＿] because
[＿＿＿＿＿＿＿＿＿＿].

Options for drop down list:

First list:

be recorded as a provision

not be recorded as a provision but disclosed as a contingent liability

Second list:

a present obligation exists, but the outflow of economic resources is not probable

a possible obligation exists, depending on whether or not some uncertain future event occurs

127 Which of the following audit procedures is likely to provide the auditor with the **MOST** reliable audit evidence regarding the legal claim?

☐ Review the minutes of the disciplinary hearing to understand whether the company has acted in accordance with employment legislation and its internal rules

☐ Review correspondence between the company and its lawyers regarding the likely outcome of the case

☐ Request a written representation from management supporting their assertion that the claim will not be successful

☐ Send an enquiry letter to Newthorpe's lawyers to obtain their view as to the probability of the claim being successful

128 The dismissal of Newthorpe's managing director has alerted you to the possibility that the company may not have complied with employment regulations. You therefore need to determine the impact that such non-compliance may have on the audit.

ISA 250 (Revised) *Consideration of Laws and Regulations in an Audit of Financial Statements* sets out the responsibilities of the auditor in relation to the entity's compliance with laws and regulations.

Which of the following responsibilities is **CORRECT** regarding the responsibilities of Newthorpe's auditors in relation to compliance with employment regulations?

☐ To obtain sufficient appropriate evidence regarding compliance, as they have a direct effect on the financial statements

☐ To perform specific audit procedures to identify possible non-compliance

☐ The auditors do not have any responsibility, as the employment regulations do not have a direct effect on the financial statements

☐ To prevent and detect all non-compliance with the regulations

(Total = 10 marks)

Tirrol (6/09) (amended)   18 mins

The following scenario relates to questions 129–133.

Your audit firm Cal & Co has just gained a new audit client, Tirrol Co, in a tender in which Cal & Co offered competitively low audit fees. You are the manager in charge of planning the audit work. Tirrol Co's year end is 30 June 20X9 with a scheduled date to complete the audit of 15 August 20X9. The date now is 3 June 20X9.

Tirrol Co provides repair services to motor vehicles from 25 different locations. All inventory, sales and purchasing systems are computerised, with each location maintaining its own computer system. The software in each location is the same because the programs were written specifically for Tirrol Co by a reputable software house. Data from each location is amalgamated on a monthly basis at Tirrol Co's head office to produce management and financial statements.

You are currently planning your audit approach for Tirrol Co. One option being considered is to rewrite Cal & Co's audit software to interrogate the computerised inventory systems in each location of Tirrol Co (except for head office) as part of inventory valuation testing. The testing will need to take place while the system is live. You are aware that July is a major holiday period for Tirrol Co.

129 The audit junior is concerned about various circumstances of the audit, which are likely to increase audit risk. He has written to you with some suggestions.

Which **TWO** of the following suggestions are valid?

☐ We should budget for the extra time required to document an understanding of the entity, its environment and its systems, and to verify material opening balances.

☐ Given the tight reporting deadline, a combined approach should be adopted on the audit, relying on tests of controls wherever possible.

☐ We must agree a clear timetable with the client for the testing of the computerised inventory systems, setting out availability of access to the system, files and personnel required to complete testing.

☐ As this is our first year of audit, we should agree separate fees with the client for any additional audit procedures required. If the client refuses, we should consider withdrawing from the audit as Cal & Co would be deemed to be lowballing.

130 Which **TWO** of the following are benefits of using audit software in auditing the inventory of Tirrol Co?

☐ The ability to test all 25 of Tirrol Co's locations using the same audit software, resulting in time and cost savings

☐ The ability to test internal controls relating to the input of data, thus giving greater assurance over the existence of inventory

☐ The ability to select and extract a sample of inventory data for testing, thus reducing sampling risk

☐ The ability to calculate the error rate in sample and thus determine whether further audit procedures are required

131 It has been decided that systematic sampling would be applied to the audit of Tirrol Co's inventory.

Which of the following sampling methods correctly describes systematic sampling?

☐ A sampling method which is a type of value-weighted selection in which sample size, selection and evaluation results in a conclusion in monetary amounts

☐ A sampling method which involves having a constant sampling interval; the starting point for testing is determined randomly

☐ A sampling method in which the auditor selects a block(s) of contiguous items from within the population

☐ A sampling method in which the auditor selects a sample without following any particular structured technique

132 Tirrol Co's internal audit department is going to assist with the statutory audit. The chief internal auditor will provide you with documentation on the computerised inventory systems at Tirrol Co. The documentation provides details of the software and shows diagrammatically how transactions are processed through the inventory system. This documentation can be used to significantly decrease the time needed to understand the computer systems and enable audit software to be written for this year's audit.

Which of the following is **NOT** a matter the audit team should consider in determining whether or not the internal auditor's work is adequate for the purposes of the audit?

☐ Whether the work was properly planned, performed, supervised, reviewed and documented

☐ Whether there are any significant threats to the objectivity of the internal auditor

☐ Whether sufficient appropriate evidence was obtained to allow the internal auditors to draw reasonable conclusions

☐ Whether the conclusions reached are appropriate in the circumstances and the reports prepared are consistent with the results of the work done

---

133 The audit junior has obtained the following extract of the aged inventory report:

Inventory code	Days in inventory	Original cost $	Selling price $	Costs to sell $	Carrying amount $
X070003	98	12,000	20,200	2,000	12,000
X079001	127	14,500	16,000	2,500	14,500
X084000	109	18,000	26,000	3,000	23,000

What is the impact on the value of inventory if no adjustments are made to the carrying amounts above?

☐ Inventory should be $44,500, inventory is overstated.

☐ Inventory should be $43,500, inventory is overstated.

☐ Inventory should be $54,700, inventory is understated.

☐ Inventory should be $62,200, inventory is understated.

(Total = 10 marks)

Wright

The following scenario relates to questions 134–138.

You are the audit manager in the firm of Wright & Co, a large accountancy firm with 30 offices.

It is January 20X6, and a new intake of graduates and apprentices has recently started work at the audit department after completing their first ACCA exams. Julie, one of the new recruits, has been allocated to the audit of Wilbur Co, your audit client, for the year ended 31 December 20X5. You are responsible for providing guidance to her and have asked her to assist in the audit of trade payables and cash at bank.

Trade payables

Julie has performed a reconciliation of key trade payables balances as follows and has concluded that no further work is required:

	Balance per purchase ledger $'000	Cash in transit $'000	Goods in transit $'000	Balance per supplier statement $'000
Supplier XX1	400	–	100 (1)	500
Supplier XX2	650	50 (2)	–	700
Supplier XX3	100	–	–	100
	1,150			1,300

Notes

1   Agreed to GRN dated 31 December 20X5

2   Agreed to cheque posted in the cash book 30 December 20X5

Your follow-up work on this identifies that:

* The goods in transit received from supplier XX1 were recognised in inventory at 31 December 20X5

* The cheque payment to supplier XX2 appeared on the bank statement on 2 January 20X6

* There is a nil balance on the purchase accruals account

Cash at bank

In order to gain assurance over the company's bank balance, you asked Julie to arrange for a bank confirmation letter to be sent to Wilbur Co's bank.

Julie has also prepared a bank reconciliation. This shows a significant number of lodgements which were recorded in the cash book on 31 December 20X5. You are concerned that the cash book may have been kept open to include remittances actually received after the year end.

134 Julie has approached you with the following query:

'I know that as auditors, we have to collect audit evidence in order to support our audit opinion. But how can we tell how much audit evidence we need to get?'

Which of the below factors influence the auditor's judgement regarding the sufficiency of the evidence obtained?

(1) The materiality of the account

(2) The size of the account

(3) The source and quality of the evidence available

(4) The amount of time allocated to the audit

☐ 1 and 3

☐ 2 and 4

☐ 2 and 3

☐ 1 and 4

135 Which of the in-transit items included in the supplier statement reconciliations indicate that there is a cut-off problem?

(1) Cash in transit

(2) Goods in transit

☐ 1 only

☐ 2 only

☐ 1 and 2

☐ Neither 1 nor 2

136 What further evidence, if any, is required in relation to the balance due to XX3 to determine if trade payables is understated?

☐ A review of post year end purchase orders from supplier XX3

☐ A confirmation request must be sent to supplier XX3

☐ No further evidence is required

☐ A review of credit notes issued by Wilbur Co should be performed

137 Which of the following summarises the steps Julie should take in preparing the bank confirmation letter you have requested?

☐ Written on the audit firm's headed paper; information requested to be sent directly to the auditor

☐ Written on the client's headed paper; information requested to be sent directly to the auditor

☐ Written on the audit firm's headed paper; information requested to be sent directly to the client

☐ Written on the client's headed paper; information requested to be sent directly to the client

138   Which of the following pieces of audit evidence would provide the most reliable audit
       evidence that the lodgements recorded on 31 December 20X5 do not relate to amounts
       received after the period end?

☐   Bank statement showing the lodgements cleared by the bank

☐   The date on the cheque paid by the supplier

☐   The date on the remittance advice

☐   The bank's date stamp on the paying-in slip

(Total = 10 marks)

Lodestar   **18 mins**

The following scenario relates to questions 139–143.

You are an audit senior of Beacon & Co and are currently conducting the audit of Lodestar Co
(Lodestar) for the year ended 30 September 20X1. You are reviewing the work of your audit
assistant.

Trade receivables

Your audit assistant has carried out a direct confirmation (a receivables circularisation) on trade
receivables at Lodestar. She selected the 10 largest balances, representing 85% of the sales
ledger at year end, including 2 items that were individually material. Seven customers agreed the
sales ledger balance, two replied noting discrepancies which she has followed up and one has not
replied.

The audit working papers contain the following work in respect of the two balances with
discrepancies.

Customer	Balance per sales ledger $	Balance per customer confirmation $	Comments
Polaris Co	23,400	19,250	Balance is payment sent out on 30 September, agreed to cash book 2 October.
Sirius Co	45,000	39,000	Balancing item is credit requested for goods customer claims were defective in February. Production manager confirms no credit will be issued.

Allowance for doubtful accounts

The company has an accounting policy of creating an allowance for doubtful accounts at 2% of year-end sales ledger balance.

139 You are analysing the sample selection with regard to the direct confirmation.

Which of the following statements in relation to the sample selection is **TRUE**?

☐ The sample is appropriate and, at 85% of the balance, gives good assurance about the overall balance.

☐ As 15% of the ledger balance has not been sampled, the sample is inappropriate.

☐ The sample selection does not address the risk of understatement as it has focused on the ten largest balances.

☐ The sample should have been stratified to provide a representative sample.

140 The audit assistant has identified further procedures to be carried out in respect of the customer who has not responded to the circularisation request as follows.

(1) Send out a follow-up request.

(2) Inspect the sales invoices in the customer account at year end.

(3) Ask the credit controller whether the customer exists.

(4) Reconcile cash receipts after date with pre year end invoices in the customer account.

Which of these procedures would provide audit evidence of the **EXISTENCE** of this receivable?

☐ 1, 2 and 3

☐ 1, 2 and 4

☐ 3 and 4

☐ 1 and 2

141 You are reviewing the work carried out on the disputed balances.

What is the misstatement arising from the above issues and the resultant impact on current assets?

☐ Trade receivables should be $10,150 lower, current assets are overstated.

☐ Trade receivables should be $6,000 lower, current assets are overstated.

☐ Trade receivables should be $4,150 lower, no net effect on current assets as balance is in cash.

☐ Trade receivables should be $10,150 higher, current assets are understated.

142 Your audit assistant has heard that auditing accounting estimates can be problematic and
     has asked you to explain why this is the case.

     Which of the following statements concerning auditing accounting estimates is
     INCORRECT?

     ☐   It can be difficult to obtain evidence concerning accounting estimates as
         management use judgement in their estimation.

     ☐   Accounting estimates are high risk as they can be subject to management bias.

     ☐   Auditors can formulate a point estimate to compare to management's estimate.

     ☐   Auditors should use their own estimate in the financial statements, as auditor-
         generated evidence is more conclusive than management-generated evidence.

143 The audit junior has suggested the following tests could be carried out to test the allowance
     for doubtful accounts:

     (1)   Review cash receipts after year end
     (2)   Review an aged debt analysis of the sales ledger
     (3)   Ask the credit controller what debts are considered to be doubtful
     (4)   Review sales invoices relating to overdue accounts

     Which of the following correctly ranks these tests in terms of their appropriateness to the
     VALUATION assertion (most appropriate being listed first)?

     ☐   1, 2, 3, 4

     ☐   2, 4, 3, 1

     ☐   1, 2, 4, 3

     ☐   3, 2, 1, 4

(Total = 10 marks)

Porthos   **18 mins**

The following scenario relates to questions 144–148.

Porthos, a limited liability company, is a retailer of sports equipment, specialising in racquet
sports such as tennis, squash and badminton. The company purchases equipment from a variety
of different suppliers and then resells this online. Customers place their orders directly on the
company website. The ordering/sales software automatically verifies the order details, customer
address and credit card information prior to orders being verified and goods dispatched.

Once the order has been verified the system produces a pre-numbered picking note. The order is
then picked in the warehouse and a goods dispatched note (GDN) is produced. A copy of this is
scanned in to the system and a sequentially numbered invoice is automatically produced and
sent to the customer.

You are the audit senior working on the audit of Porthos for the year ended 31 December 20X7.

As the sales system is highly automated the audit manager has decided that computer-assisted
audit techniques (CAATs) should be used where possible in the audit of the sales account. You
identified the key steps to be taken in planning the application of CAATs, as follows:

(1)   Define the types of transactions to be tested

(2)   Set the objective of the CAAT application

(3)   Define the procedures to be performed on the data

(4)   Determine the content and accessibility of the entity's files

The manager has also decided that test data would be used to test the input of details into the ordering system. You identified the following test data which could be used:

(i)   Orders for unusually large quantities
(ii)   Orders with fields left blank
(iii)   Orders with invalid inventory codes
(iv)   Orders with complete and valid details

In addition to the sales income generated from the sale of sports equipment Porthos earns a small amount of rental income by renting out surplus warehouse space to a local company. The rental agreement shows that the annual rent from 1 March 20X7 was $24,000, increased from $21,600 per annum.

144   Which of the following identifies the correct order in which the steps to be taken in planning the application of CAATs should be performed?

☐   2, 4, 1, 3

☐   1, 4, 2, 3

☐   2, 1, 3, 4

☐   4, 2, 3, 1

145   Which of the test data identified by the audit junior should be used to confirm the completeness and accuracy of input into the sales system?

☐   (ii) only

☐   (ii) and (iii) only

☐   (i), (ii) and (iii) only

☐   (i), (ii), (iii) and (iv)

146   Which of the following procedures would provide evidence that sales cut-off for Porthos has been applied correctly?

☐   For sales invoices issued before 31 December 20X7 use audit software to determine whether there is a matching GDN dated before 31 December 20X7

☐   For sales invoices issued before 31 December 20X7 use audit software to determine whether there is a matching GDN dated after 31 December 20X7

☐   For picking notes issued before 31 December 20X7 use audit software to determine whether there is a matching GDN dated before 31 December 20X7

☐   For picking notes issued before 31 December 20X7 use audit software to determine whether there is a matching GDN dated after 31 December 20X7

147 As part of substantive audit procedures, you perform a sequence check on the sales invoice numbers issued by Porthos over the year.

What is the purpose of the sequence check you have performed on the sales invoice numbers?

☐ To give assurance that cut-off has been applied accurately

☐ To give assurance over the occurrence of the sales transactions recorded

☐ To provide audit evidence over the completeness of the recording of sales

☐ To provide audit evidence that the sales figure has been calculated accurately

---

148 You are using a proof in total calculation to assess the accuracy of the rental income.

Which of the following correctly shows the calculation which would be used?

☐ $24,000 × 12/12

☐ $21,600 × 12/12

☐ (21,600 × 2/12) + (24,000 × 10/12)

☐ (21,600 × 10/12) + (24,000 × 2/12)

(Total = 10 marks)

149 Lily (12/12)   54 mins

Lily Window Glass Co (Lily) is a glass manufacturer, which operates from a large production facility, where it undertakes continuous production 24 hours a day, 7 days a week. Also on this site are two warehouses, where the company's raw materials and finished goods are stored. Lily's year end is 31 December.

Lily is finalising the arrangements for the year-end inventory count, which is to be undertaken on 31 December 20X2. The finished windows are stored within 20 aisles of the first warehouse. The second warehouse is for large piles of raw materials, such as sand, used in the manufacture of glass. The following arrangements have been made for the inventory count.

The warehouse manager will supervise the count as he is most familiar with the inventory. There will be ten teams of counters and each team will contain two members of staff, one from the finance and one from the manufacturing department. None of the warehouse staff, other than the manager, will be involved in the count.

Each team will count an aisle of finished goods by counting up and then down each aisle. As this process is systematic, it is not felt that the team will need to flag areas once counted. Once the team has finished counting an aisle, they will hand in their sheets and be given a set for another aisle of the warehouse. In addition to the above, to assist with the inventory counting, there will be two teams of counters from the internal audit department and they will perform inventory counts.

The count sheets are sequentially numbered, and the product codes and descriptions are printed on them but no quantities. If the counters identify any inventory which is not on their sheets, then they are to enter the item on a separate sheet, which is not numbered. Once all counting is complete, the sequence of the sheets is checked and any additional sheets are also handed in at this stage. All sheets are completed in ink.

Any damaged goods identified by the counters will be too heavy to move to a central location, hence they are to be left where they are but the counter is to make a note on the inventory sheets detailing the level of damage.

BPP
LEARNING
MEDIA

As Lily undertakes continuous production, there will continue to be movements of raw materials and finished goods in and out of the warehouse during the count. These will be kept to a minimum where possible.

The level of work in progress in the manufacturing plant is to be assessed by the warehouse manager. It is likely that this will be an immaterial balance. In addition, the raw materials quantities are to be approximated by measuring the height and width of the raw material piles. In the past this task has been undertaken by a specialist; however, the warehouse manager feels confident that he can perform this task.

Required

(a) For the inventory count arrangements of Lily Window Glass Co:

(i) Identify and explain **SIX** deficiencies; and

(ii) Provide a recommendation to address each deficiency.

The total marks will be split equally between each part. **(12 marks)**

You are the audit senior of Daffodil & Co and are responsible for the audit of inventory for Lily. You will be attending the year-end inventory count on 31 December 20X2.

In addition, your manager wishes to utilise computer-assisted audit techniques for the first time for controls and substantive testing in auditing Lily Window Glass Co's inventory.

Required

(b) Describe the procedures to be undertaken by the auditor **DURING** the inventory count of Lily Window Glass Co in order to gain sufficient appropriate audit evidence. **(6 marks)**

(c) For the audit of the inventory cycle and year-end inventory balance of Lily Window Glass Co:

(i) Describe **FOUR** audit procedures that could be carried out using computer-assisted audit techniques (CAATs);

(ii) Explain the potential advantages of using CAATs; and

(iii) Explain the potential disadvantages of using CAATs.

The total marks will be split equally between each part. **(12 marks)**

(Total = 30 marks)

150 Westra Co   54 mins

Westra Co assembles mobile telephones in a large factory. Each telephone contains up to 100 different parts, with each part being obtained from 1 of 50 authorised suppliers.

Like many companies, Westra Co's accounting systems are partly manual and partly computerised. In overview, the systems include:

(i) Design software

(ii) A computerised database of suppliers (bespoke system written in-house at Westra Co)

(iii) A manual system for recording goods inwards and transferring information to the accounts department

(iv) A computerised payables ledger maintained in the accounts department (purchased off-the-shelf and used with no program amendments)

(v) Online payment to suppliers, also in the accounts department

(vi) A computerised nominal ledger which is updated by the payables ledger

Mobile telephones are assembled in batches of 10,000 to 50,000 telephones. When a batch is scheduled for production, a list of parts is produced by the design software and sent, electronically, to the ordering department. Staff in the ordering department use this list to place orders with authorised suppliers. Orders can only be sent to suppliers on the suppliers' database.

Orders are sent using electronic data interchange and confirmed by each supplier using the same system. The list of parts and orders is retained on the computer in an 'orders placed' file, which is kept in date sequence.

Parts are delivered to the goods inwards department at Westra Co. All deliveries are checked against the orders placed file before being accepted. A handwritten pre-numbered goods received note (GRN) is raised in the goods inwards department showing details of the goods received with a cross-reference to the date of the order. The top copy of the GRN is sent to the accounts department and the second copy retained in the goods inwards department. The orders placed file is updated with the GRN number to show that the parts have been received.

Paper invoices are sent by all suppliers following dispatch of goods. Invoices are sent to the accounts department, where they are stamped with a unique ascending number. Invoice details are matched to the GRN, which is then attached to the invoice. Invoice details are then entered into the computerised payables ledger. The invoice is signed by the accounts clerk to confirm entry into the payables ledger. Invoices are then retained in a temporary file in number order while awaiting payment.

After 30 days, the payables ledger automatically generates a computerised list of payments to be made, which is sent electronically to the chief accountant. The chief accountant compares this list to the invoices, signs each invoice to indicate approval for payment, and then forwards the electronic payments list to the accounts assistant. The assistant uses online banking to pay the suppliers. The electronic payments list is filed in month order on the computer.

Required

(a) Describe the substantive audit procedures you should perform to confirm the assertions of completeness, occurrence and cut-off for purchases in the financial statements of Westra Co. For each procedure, explain the purpose of that procedure. **(12 marks)**

(b) Describe the audit procedures you should perform on the trade payables balance in Westra Co's financial statements. For each procedure, explain the purpose of that procedure. **(8 marks)**

(c) Describe the internal controls that should be in place over the standing data on the trade payables master file in Westra Co's computer system. **(5 marks)**

(d) Discuss the extent to which audit data analytics techniques might be used in your audit of purchases and payables at Westra Co. **(5 marks)**

(Total = 30 marks)

151 Dashing Co (Sep/Dec 17)   36 mins

Dashing Co manufactures women's clothing and its year end was 31 July 20X7. You are an audit supervisor of Jaunty & Co and the year end audit for Dashing Co is due to commence shortly.

The draft financial statements recognise profit before tax of $2.6m and total assets of $18m. You have been given responsibility for auditing receivables, which is a material balance, and as part of the audit approach, a positive receivables circularisation is to be undertaken.

At the planning meeting, the finance director of Dashing Co informed the audit engagement partner that the company was closing one of its smaller production sites and as a result, a number of employees would be made redundant. A redundancy provision of $110,000 is included in the draft financial statements.

Required

(a) Describe the steps the auditor should perform in undertaking a positive receivables circularisation for Dashing Co. **(4 marks)**

(b) Describe substantive procedures, other than a receivables circularisation, the auditor should perform to verify EACH of the following assertions in relation to Dashing Co's receivables:

(i)   Accuracy, valuation and allocation;

(ii)   Completeness; and

(iii)   Rights and obligations

Note. The total marks will be split equally between each part.   **(6 marks)**

(c)   Describe substantive procedures the auditor should perform to confirm the redundancy provision at the year end.   **(5 marks)**

A few months have now passed and the audit team is performing the audit fieldwork including the audit procedures which you recommended over the redundancy provision. The team has calculated that the necessary provision should amount to $305,000. The finance director is not willing to adjust the draft financial statements.

Required

(d)   Discuss the issue and describe the impact on the auditor's report, if any, should this issue remain unresolved.   **(5 marks)**

(Total = 20 marks)

152 Rose (12/12) (amended)   36 mins

Rose Co operates a chain of health and fitness clubs. Its year end was 31 March 20X6. You are the audit manager and the year-end audit is due to commence shortly. The following three matters have been brought to your attention.

Trade payables and accruals

Rose Co's finance director has notified you that an error occurred in the closing of the purchase ledger at the year end. Rather than it closing on 1 April, it accidentally closed one week earlier on 25 March. All purchase invoices received between 25 March and the year-end have been posted to the 20X7 year-end purchase ledger.

Receivables

Rose Co's trade receivables have historically been low as most members pay monthly in advance. However, during the year a number of companies have taken up group memberships at Rose and hence the receivables balance is now material. The audit senior has undertaken a receivables circularisation for the balances at the year-end; however, there are a number who have not responded and a number of responses with differences.

Reorganisation

The company recently announced its plans to reorganise its health and fitness clubs. This will involve closing some clubs for refurbishment, retraining some existing staff and disposing of some surplus assets. These plans were agreed at a board meeting in March and announced to their shareholders on 29 March. Rose is proposing to make a reorganisation provision in the financial statements.

Required

(a)   Describe substantive procedures the auditor should perform to obtain sufficient and appropriate audit evidence in relation to the issues identified with the trade payables and accruals balance.   **(6 marks)**

(b)   Describe substantive procedures the auditor should perform to obtain sufficient appropriate evidence in relation to the year-end receivables balance.   **(5 marks)**

(c)   Describe substantive procedures the auditor should perform in relation to the proposed reorganisation.   **(4 marks)**

(d)   Explain the purpose of, and procedures for, obtaining written representations.   **(5 marks)**

(Total = 20 marks)

153 Andromeda Industries Co (Sep/Dec 15)   36 mins

Andromeda Industries Co (Andromeda) develops and manufactures a wide range of fast moving consumer goods. The company's year-end is 31 December 20X5 and the forecast profit before tax is $8.3 million. You are the audit manager of Neptune & Co and the year-end audit is due to commence in January. The following information has been gathered during the planning process.

Inventory count

Andromeda's raw materials and finished goods inventory are stored in 12 warehouses across the country. Each of these warehouses is expected to contain material levels of inventory at the year end. It is expected that there will be no significant work in progress held at any of the sites. Each count will be supervised by a member of Andromeda's internal audit department and the counts will all take place on 31 December, when all movements of goods in and out of the warehouses will cease.

Research and development

Andromeda spends over $2 million annually on developing new product lines. This year it incurred expenditure on five projects, all of which are at different stages of development. Once they meet the recognition criteria under IAS 38 *Intangible Assets* for development expenditure, Andromeda includes the costs incurred within intangible assets. Once production commences, the intangible assets are amortised on a straight line basis over five years.

Required

(a)   Explain **FOUR** factors which influence the reliability of audit evidence.   **(4 marks)**

(b)   Describe audit procedures you would perform during the audit of Andromeda Industries Co:

    (i)   **BEFORE** and **DURING** the inventory counts; and   **(8 marks)**
    (ii)   In relation to research and development expenditure.   **(4 marks)**

(c)   During the audit, the team discovers that 1 of the 5 development projects, valued at $980,000 and included within intangible assets, does not meet the criteria for capitalisation. The finance director does not intend to change the accounting treatment adopted as she considers this an immaterial amount.

    ### Required

    Discuss the issue and describe the impact on the auditor's report, if any, if the issue remains unresolved.   **(4 marks)**

    (Total = 20 marks)

154 Traffic Lights   36 mins

Traffic Lights (TL) is a small local charity providing play facilities to families coping with disabilities. Your firm, Amber & Co (Amber), has been the auditor of the charity for a number of years. The charity is required to receive audits to qualify for local authority grants, although it is a small charity.

TL operates a number of 'play rooms' in several towns in Wellshire. The play rooms are staffed by volunteers and operates in premises that have been donated to the charity. There is no charge for attending the play rooms, but pre-registered attendees may make a donation per visit should they wish to. The vast majority of the play equipment has also been donated to TL, with some items being purchased by the charity after specific money raising appeals for those particular items.

TL's income comes from the following sources:

- Donations by families for play sessions, which are placed into a locked donations tin at time of play. These donations are counted at the end of business on a Monday, noted in a cash book and banked on a Tuesday morning by a volunteer.

- Donations by local businesses and individuals, which are sent by cheque to the trustees at the registered office or paid directly by bank transfer.

- Legacies, which are usually paid direct to the charity's bank by the legal advisers handling the legator's estate.

- Local authority grants, which the charity reapplies for annually, and which are paid by direct transfer in January if the application is successful.

The charity has limited controls. The operation of the controls is dependent on the volunteers and the trustees (who are also volunteers). In the past your firm has judged the systems to be working effectively, but inherently limited due to the use of volunteers and the fact that cash is only banked weekly. The firm has therefore usually taken a substantive approach to the audit.

Given that most assets have been donated to the charity, TL has an accounting policy to value assets at 'value to the charity', which equates to fair value in accordance with IAS 16 *Property, Plant and Equipment*. Assets are depreciated over their useful lives of:

- Property   50 years
- Play equipment   10 years

Donated assets are recorded in a donated assets register. Purchased assets are recorded in a purchased asset register.

Required

(a)   Discuss the extent to which Amber will be able to use substantive analytical procedures in the audit of TL.   (3 marks)

(b)   Describe substantive procedures the auditor could perform to obtain sufficient and appropriate audit evidence in relation to the valuation of:

(i)   Property   (4 marks)
(ii)   Play equipment   (5 marks)

(c)   Describe substantive procedures the auditor could perform to obtain sufficient and appropriate audit evidence in relation to:

(i)   Legacies   (2 marks)

(ii)   Donations   (6 marks)

(Total = 20 marks)

155 Hawthorn Enterprises Co (6/15)   36 mins

Hawthorn Enterprises Co (Hawthorn) manufactures and distributes fashion clothing to retail stores. Its year end was 31 March 20X5. You are the audit manager and the year-end audit is due to commence shortly. The following three matters have been brought to your attention.

(i)   Supplier statement reconciliations

Hawthorn receives monthly statements from its main suppliers and although these have been retained, none have been reconciled to the payables ledger as at 31 March 20X5. The audit engagement partner has asked the audit senior to recommend the procedures to be performed on supplier statements.   (3 marks)

(ii)   Bank reconciliation

During last year's audit of Hawthorn's bank and cash, significant cut-off errors were discovered with a number of post year end cheques being processed prior to the year end to reduce payables. The finance director has assured the audit engagement partner that this error has not occurred again this year and that the bank reconciliation has been carefully prepared. The audit engagement partner has asked that the bank reconciliation is comprehensively audited.   (4 marks)

(iii)   Receivables

Hawthorn's receivables ledger has increased considerably during the year, and the year-end balance is $2.3 million compared to $1.4 million last year. The finance director of Hawthorn has requested that a receivables circularisation is not carried out as a number of their customers complained last year about the inconvenience involved in responding. The audit engagement partner has agreed to this request, and tasked you with identifying alternative procedures to confirm the existence and valuation of receivables.   **(5 marks)**

Required

(a)   (i)   Identify and explain **FOUR** financial statement assertions relevant to classes of transactions and events for the year under audit; and

(ii)   For each identified assertion, describe a substantive procedure relevant to the audit of **REVENUE**.   **(8 marks)**

(b)   Describe substantive procedures you would perform to obtain sufficient and appropriate audit evidence in relation to the above three matters.

Note. The mark allocation is shown against each of the three matters above.

(Total = 20 marks)

156 Airsoft Co (Mar/Jun 17)   36 mins

Airsoft Co is a listed company which manufactures stationery products. The company's profit before tax for the year ended 31 December 20X6 is $16.3m and total assets as at that date are $66.8m. You are an audit supervisor of Biathlon & Co and you are currently finalising the audit programmes for the year-end audit of your existing client Airsoft Co. You attended a meeting with your audit manager where the following matters were discussed:

Trade payables and accruals

Airsoft Co purchases its raw materials from a large number of suppliers. The company's policy is to close the purchase ledger just after the year end and the financial controller is responsible for identifying goods which were received pre year-end but for which no invoice has yet been received. An accrual is calculated for goods received but not yet invoiced (GRNI) and is included within trade payables and accruals.

The audit strategy has identified a risk over the completeness of trade payables and accruals. The audit team will utilise computer assisted audit techniques (CAATs), in the form of audit software while auditing trade payables and accruals.

Bank overdraft and savings accounts

Airsoft Co's draft financial statements include a bank overdraft of $2.6m, which relates to the company's main current account. In addition Airsoft Co maintains a number of savings accounts. The savings account balances are classified as cash and cash equivalents and are included in current assets. All accounts have been reconciled at the year end.

Directors' remuneration

Airsoft Co's board is comprised of eight directors. Their overall remuneration consists of two elements: an annual salary, paid monthly; and a significant annual discretionary bonus, which is paid in a separate payment run on 20 December. All remuneration paid to directors is included within wages and salaries. Local legislation requires disclosure of the overall total of directors' remuneration broken down by element and by director.

Required

(a)   Describe substantive procedures the auditor should perform to obtain sufficient and appropriate audit evidence in relation to the **COMPLETENESS** of Airsoft Co's trade payables and accruals.   **(4 marks)**

Excluding procedures included in part (a):

(b)   Describe audit software procedures which could be carried out during the audit of Airsoft Co's trade payables and accruals.   (3 marks)

(c)   Describe substantive procedures the auditor should perform to obtain sufficient and appropriate audit evidence in relation to Airsoft Co's year-end bank balances.   (5 marks)

(d)   Describe substantive procedures the auditor should perform to confirm the directors' remuneration included in the financial statements at the year end.   (3 marks)

A member of your audit team has asked for information on ISA 701 *Communicating Key Audit Matters in the Independent Auditor's Report* as she has heard this standard is applicable to listed clients such as Airsoft Co.

Required

(e)   Identify what a key audit matter (KAM) is and explain how the auditor determines and communicates KAM.   (5 marks)

(Total = 20 marks)

157 Gooseberry Co (Mar/Jun 18)   36 mins

You are an audit manager of Cranberry & Co and you are currently responsible for the audit of Gooseberry Co, a company which develops and manufactures health and beauty products and distributes these to wholesale customers. Its draft profit before tax is $6.4m and total assets are $37.2m for the financial year ended 31 January 20X8. The final audit is due to commence shortly and the following matters have been brought to your attention:

Research and development

Gooseberry Co spent $1.9m in the current year developing nine new health and beauty products, all of which are at different stages of development. Once they meet the recognition criteria under IAS 38 *Intangible Assets* for development expenditure, Gooseberry Co includes the costs incurred within intangible assets. Once production commences, the intangible assets are amortised on a straight line basis over three years. Management believe that this amortisation policy is a reasonable approximation of the assets' useful lives, as in this industry there is constant demand for innovative new products.

Depreciation

Gooseberry Co has a large portfolio of property plant and equipment (PPE). In March 20X7, the company carried out a full review of all its PPE and updated the useful lives, residual values, depreciation rates and methods for many categories of asset. The finance director felt the changes were necessary to better reflect the use of the assets. This resulted in the depreciation charge of some assets changing significantly for this year.

Bonus

The company's board is comprised of seven directors. They are each entitled to a bonus based on the draft year-end net assets, excluding intangible assets. Details of the bonus entitlement are included in the directors' service contracts. The bonus, which related to the 20X8 year end, was paid to each director in February 20X8 and the costs were accrued and recognised within wages and salaries for the year ended 31 January 20X8. Separate disclosure of the bonus, by director, is required by local legislation.

Required

(a)   Describe substantive procedures the auditor should perform to obtain sufficient and appropriate audit evidence in relation to Gooseberry Co's research and development expenditure.   (5 marks)

(b)   Describe substantive procedures the auditor should perform to obtain sufficient and appropriate audit evidence in relation to the matters identified regarding depreciation of property, plant and equipment.   (5 marks)

(c)   Describe substantive procedures the auditor should perform to obtain sufficient and appropriate audit evidence in relation to the directors' bonuses.   (5 marks)

During the audit, the team discovers that the intangible assets balance includes $440,000 related to one of the nine new health and beauty products development projects, which does not meet the criteria for capitalisation. As this project is ongoing, the finance director has suggested that no adjustment is made in the 20X8 financial statements. She is confident that the project will meet the criteria for capitalisation in 20X9.

Required

(d)   Discuss the issue and describe the impact on the auditor's report, if any, should this issue remain unresolved. (5 marks)

(Total = 20 marks)

158 Jasmine Co (Sep/Dec 18)   36 mins

Jasmine Co manufactures motor vehicle components and its year end was 30 June 20X8. You are an audit supervisor of Peppermint & Co and the final audit is due to commence shortly. Total assets are $43.2m and profit before tax is $7.2m. The following matters have been brought to your attention:

Trade receivables

Jasmine Co's trade receivables ledger is comprised of a large number of customers. In previous years, the audit team has undertaken a positive trade receivables circularisation to confirm year-end balances. However, the customer response rate has historically been low and so alternative audit procedures have been undertaken. A decision has been made that for the current year audit a circularisation will not be performed. The year-end trade receivables balance is $3.9m (20X7: $2.8m) and the allowance for trade receivables is $410,000 (20X7: $300,000).

Bank balances

The bank and cash figure included in Jasmine Co's draft financial statements is comprised of a number of bank account balances: an overdraft of $5.1m which is the company's main current account and $0.2m relating to several savings accounts. The finance director has informed the audit manager that all accounts have been reconciled as at the year end.

The overdraft of $5.1m has increased significantly since the prior year (20X7: $1.2m). The directors have informed you that the overdraft facility, which the company requires in order to operate on a daily basis, is due for renewal in October 20X8 and that they are confident it will be renewed.

Required

(a)   Describe substantive procedures the auditor should perform to obtain sufficient and appropriate audit evidence in relation to Jasmine Co's trade receivables. (5 marks)

(b)   Describe substantive procedures the auditor should perform to obtain sufficient and appropriate audit evidence in relation to Jasmine Co's bank balances. (5 marks)

(c)   Describe the audit procedures the auditor should perform in assessing whether or not Jasmine Co is a going concern. (5 marks)

During the final audit, the finance director has informed the audit team that Jasmine Co's bankers will not make a decision on the renewal of the overdraft facility until after the auditor's report is signed. The audit engagement partner is satisfied that the use of the going concern basis is appropriate.

The directors have agreed to include some brief going concern disclosures in the draft financial statements and the audit team still have to assess the adequacy of these disclosures.

Required

(d)   Discuss the issue and describe the impact on the auditor's report of Jasmine Co of adequate AND inadequate going concern disclosure. (5 marks)

(Total = 20 marks)

REVIEW AND REPORTING

Questions 159–194 cover Review and reporting, the subject of Part E of the BPP Workbook for Audit and Assurance.

Chestnut (6/15) (amended)　　　　　　　　　　　　18 mins

The following scenario relates to questions 159–163.

You are the audit manager of Chestnut & Co and are reviewing the key issues identified in the files of two audit clients.

The first audit client is Palm Industries Co (Palm), a listed company. Palm's year end was 31 March 20X5 and the draft financial statements show revenue of $28.2m, receivables of $5.6m and profit before tax of $4.8m. The fieldwork stage for this audit has been completed.

A customer of Palm owed an amount of $350,000 at the year end. Testing of receivables in April highlighted that no amounts had been paid to Palm from this customer as they were disputing the quality of certain goods received from Palm. The finance director is confident the issue will be resolved and no allowance for receivables was made with regards to this balance.

The second audit client is Ash Trading Co (Ash). Ash is a new client of Chestnut & Co, its year end was 31 January 20X5 and the firm was only appointed as auditor in February 20X5, as the previous auditor was suddenly unable to undertake the audit. The fieldwork stage for this audit is currently ongoing.

The inventory count at Ash's warehouse was undertaken on 31 January 20X5 and was overseen by the company's internal audit department. Neither Chestnut & Co nor the previous auditors attended the count. Detailed inventory records were maintained but it was not possible to undertake another full inventory count subsequent to the year end.

The draft financial statements show a profit before tax of $2.4 million, revenue of $10.1 million and inventory of $510,000.

159　Which of the following audit procedures should be performed in order to form a conclusion on whether an amendment is required in Palm's 20X5 financial statements in respect of the disputed balance?

Review whether any payments have subsequently been made by this customer since the audit fieldwork was completed	PERFORM	DO NOT PERFORM
Match the total of the aged receivables listing to the sales ledger control account	PERFORM	DO NOT PERFORM
Vouch the balance owed by the customer at the year end to sales invoices	PERFORM	DO NOT PERFORM
Review the latest customer correspondence with regards to an assessment of the likelihood of the customer making payment	PERFORM	DO NOT PERFORM

160 Which of the following correctly summarises the effect of the issue relating to the inventory count of Ash at the year end?

	Material	Financial statement impact
☐	No	Current assets are understated
☐	No	Gross profit may be understated
☐	Yes	Opening inventory may be materially misstated
☐	Yes	Gross profit may be overstated

161 The audit engagement partner for Ash has requested that additional audit procedures be performed in order to conclude on the level of adjustment needed in relation to the above inventory issue.

Which **TWO** of the following audit procedures should be performed in order to form a conclusion as to whether Ash's 20X5 financial statements require amendment?

☐ Obtain a copy of the aged inventory report and use computer-assisted audit techniques to verify the accuracy of the report. Discuss the valuation of slow-moving inventory with the production director.

☐ Review the internal auditors' reports of the inventory count to identify the level of adjustments made to the records, in order to assess the reasonableness of relying on the inventory records for the purpose of the year-end audit.

☐ Perform test counts of inventory in the warehouse and compare these first to the inventory records, and then from inventory records to the warehouse, in order to assess the reasonableness of the inventory records maintained by Ash.

☐ Review Ash's sales order book for February, March and April 20X5 to estimate the level of inventory that will need to be produced in the new accounting period to fulfil customer demand.

162 Following the inability to attend the inventory count of Ash, an engagement quality control reviewer has been appointed to the audit.

Indicate which of the following should be included within the engagement quality control review?

Evaluation of all significant audit judgments	INCLUDE	EXCLUDE
Evaluation of the performance of specific audit procedures performed	INCLUDE	EXCLUDE
Evaluation of the cost-effectiveness of the audit process	INCLUDE	EXCLUDE
Evaluation of conclusions reached in formulating auditor's report	INCLUDE	EXCLUDE

163 Alternative procedures, performed as a result of Chestnut & Co being unable to attend the inventory count of Ash, did not provide sufficient appropriate audit evidence regarding the inventory balance in the statement of financial position.

From the options below indicate the audit opinion which would be given in these circumstances and the appropriate disclosure in the auditor's report.

Audit opinion	Disclosure in the auditor's report
☐ Qualified	☐ Basis for qualified opinion
☐ Disclaimer	☐ Basis for disclaimer of opinion
☐ Qualified	☐ Key audit matters section
☐ Disclaimer	☐ Emphasis of matter

(Total = 10 marks)

Humphries (12/11) (amended)   18 mins

The following scenario relates to questions 164–168.

Humphries Co, your audit client, operates a chain of food wholesalers across the country and its year end was 30 September 20X1. The final audit is nearly complete and it is proposed that the financial statements and auditor's report will be signed on 13 December. Revenue for the year is $78 million and profit before taxation is $7.5 million.

The following information comes to light:

Humphries Co has three warehouses; following extensive rain on 20 November, rain and river water flooded the warehouse located in Bass. All of the inventory in the warehouse was damaged and has been disposed of. The insurance company has been contacted. No amendments or disclosures have been made in the financial statements.

A customer of Humphries Co has been experiencing cash flow problems and its year-end balance is $0.3 million. The company has just become aware that its customer is experiencing significant going concern difficulties. The management of Humphries Co believes that as the company has been trading for many years, they will receive some, if not full, payment from the customer; hence they have not adjusted the receivable balance.

A key supplier of Humphries Co is suing them for breach of contract. The lawsuit was filed prior to the year end, and the sum claimed by them is $1 million. This has been disclosed as a contingent liability in the notes to the financial statements.

Correspondence has just arrived from the supplier indicating that they are willing to settle the case for a payment by Humphries Co of $0.6 million. It is likely that the company will agree to this.

164   Which of the following audit procedures would identify subsequent events occurring up to the date of the auditor's report?

    (1)   Enquire of management whether there have been any unusual accounting adjustments

    (2)   Enquire of management whether there have been any issues of shares/debentures, or changes in business structure

    (3)   Review management procedures for identifying subsequent events to ensure that such events are identified

    (4)   Obtain written representation that all subsequent events requiring adjustment or disclosure have been adjusted or disclosed

    ☐   1 and 2

    ☐   1 and 3

    ☐   1, 3 and 4

    ☐   1, 2, 3 and 4

---

165   Which **TWO** of the following statements correctly describe the likely impact that the flooding of the warehouse will have on Humphries Co's financial statements for the year ended 30 September 20X1?

    ☐   Inventory should be written down, because the flood damage is an adjusting event.

    ☐   Inventory should not be written down, because the damage is not an adjusting event.

    ☐   If a material amount of inventory is uninsured, it may be necessary to disclose the event and an estimate of the financial losses.

    ☐   If insurance proceeds are more likely than not to be received, a contingent asset should be recognised.

---

166   Which **TWO** of the following audit procedures should be performed in order to form a conclusion on the amendment required to Humphries Co's 20X1 financial statements in respect of the $0.3 million owed by the customer experiencing financial difficulties?

    ☐   Reviewing the post year end period for payments received from the customer in respect of the year-end debt

    ☐   Reviewing correspondence with the customer to assess the likelihood of Humphries Co recovering the $0.3 million

    ☐   Writing to the customer to request confirmation of the amount owed to Humphries Co at the year end

    ☐   Ask management to produce a revised cash flow forecast covering at least 12 months after the year end

167 Complete the following sentence regarding the auditor's report by selecting from the options provided.

The lawsuit relating to the breach of contract is considered to be [   ] and therefore if the financial statements are not revised in the light of the new information then the auditor's opinion will be [   ] .

Impact of breach of contract	Auditor's opinion
material	adverse
material and pervasive	disclaimer
not material	qualified 'except for' – due to insufficient appropriate evidence
	qualified 'except for' – due to material misstatement
	unmodified
	unmodified with emphasis of matter

168 It is now 13 December 20X1. The auditor's report has been signed. The financial statements are due to be issued on 25 December 20X1.

Which of the following statements correctly describes the auditor's responsibility in relation to subsequent events occurring between now and 25 December?

☐ The auditor must design procedures to obtain sufficient appropriate audit evidence that all events up to that date that may require adjustment or disclosure have been identified.

☐ The auditor must perform procedures on matters examined during the audit, which may be susceptible to change after the year end.

☐ The auditor has no obligation to perform procedures, or make enquiries regarding the financial statements. Any subsequent events should be noted and considered in the next period's audit.

☐ If the auditor becomes aware of a fact that, had it been known to the auditor at the date of the auditor's report, may have caused the auditor to amend the auditor's report, the auditor shall discuss the need for any adjustments with management.

(Total = 10 marks)

Greenfields (12/10) (amended)

18 mins

The following scenario relates to questions 169–173.

Greenfields Co specialises in manufacturing equipment which can help to reduce toxic emissions in the production of chemicals. The company has grown rapidly over the past eight years and this is due partly to the warranties that the company gives to its customers. It guarantees its products for five years and if problems arise in this period it undertakes to fix them, or to provide a replacement product.

You are the manager responsible for the audit of Greenfields Co. You are performing the final review stage of the audit and have come across the following issues.

Receivable balance owing from Yellowmix Co

Greenfields Co has a material receivable balance owing from its customer, Yellowmix Co. During the year-end audit, your team reviewed the ageing of this balance and found that no payments had been received from Yellowmix Co for over six months, and Greenfields Co would not allow this balance to be circularised. Instead management has assured your team that they will provide a written representation confirming that the balance is recoverable.

Warranty provision

The warranty provision included within the statement of financial position is material. The audit team has performed testing over the calculations and assumptions which are consistent with prior years. The team has requested a written representation from management confirming that the basis and amount of the provision are reasonable. Management has yet to confirm acceptance of this representation.

Other information

You have reviewed a financial summary which is to be included in the annual report and have found that the details are inconsistent with the financial statements. Your investigations have shown that the error is in the summary and not the financial statements.

169 Assuming you received the written representations as described above for both the receivables balance and the warranty provision, in respect of which balances is the auditor most likely to conclude that sufficient appropriate evidence has been obtained?

- [ ] Receivables balance only
- [ ] Warranty provision only
- [ ] Receivables balance and warranty provision
- [ ] Neither the receivables balance nor the warranty provision

170 Which **TWO** of the following audit procedures could the audit team carry out to obtain independent evidence relating to the recoverability of the debt from Yellowmix Co?

- [ ] Review correspondence with Yellowmix Co regarding the late payment
- [ ] Trace a sample of goods dispatched notes for Yellowmix Co to sales invoices
- [ ] Trace the entries in Yellowmix Co's account in the receivables ledger to invoices and remittances
- [ ] Perform a review of post year-end cash receipts

BPP
LEARNING
MEDIA

171 Management has now stated that it is not prepared to confirm that the basis and amount of the warranty provision are reasonable.

Indicate which of the following actions you must perform in accordance with ISA 580 *Written Representations*?

Discuss with management why they have refused to provide the representations requested	PERFORM	DO NOT PERFORM
Reassess the integrity of management and consider the implications for any other representations	PERFORM	DO NOT PERFORM
Seek legal advice	PERFORM	DO NOT PERFORM
Resign as auditor	PERFORM	DO NOT PERFORM

172 You have discussed the matter with management but they are still not prepared to provide the representations you have requested.

What type of modified opinion would be issued and what would be the basis for this modification?

	Audit opinion	Reason
☐	Qualified	Material misstatement
☐	Disclaimer	Inability to obtain sufficient appropriate evidence
☐	Adverse	Material misstatement
☐	Qualified	Inability to obtain sufficient appropriate evidence

173 You have notified the directors of the error in the summary financial statements.

Which of the following correctly summarises the impact on the auditor's report if the directors do not correct this error?

	Audit opinion	Disclosure
☐	Modified	Other Information section stating that there is nothing to report
☐	Modified	Other Information section would not be required as there is nothing to report
☐	Unmodified	Other Information section including a description of the uncorrected misstatement
☐	Unmodified	Other Matter paragraph including a description of the uncorrected misstatement

(Total = 10 marks)

Strawberry (6/12) (amended)

The following scenario relates to questions 174–178.

You are the audit manager of Kiwi & Co. Your client is Strawberry Kitchen Designs Co (Strawberry), which is a kitchen manufacturer. The company's year-end is 30 April 20X2.

Strawberry has had a challenging year. Grape Co, a major customer of Strawberry which owes $0.6m, is experiencing financial difficulties. However, the balance is included within the financial statements. The sales director has recently left Strawberry and has yet to be replaced. As a result Strawberry has struggled to win any new business in the last six months.

The monthly cash flow has shown a net cash outflow for the last two months of the financial year and is forecast as negative for the forthcoming financial year.

You have performed some analytical procedures on the draft financial statements and have calculated the following ratios:

	20X2 Draft	20X1 Actual
Inventory holding period (days)	95	97
Receivables collection period (days)	65	49
Payables payment period (days)	120	86

Due to its poor cash flow, Strawberry missed a loan repayment and, as a result of this breach in the loan covenants, the bank has asked that the loan of $4.8m be repaid in full within 6 months.

174   Which of the following are potential indicators that Strawberry is not a going concern?

    (1)   The breach of the loan covenants

    (2)   The departure of the sales director

    (3)   The fall in the inventory holding period

    (4)   The negative cash flow figures

    ☐ 1, 2 and 3

    ☐ 2, 3 and 4

    ☐ 1, 3 and 4

    ☐ 1, 2 and 4

175   You are reviewing the management's assessment of Strawberry's ability to continue as a going concern.

    What period must management's assessment cover?

    ☐ At least 12 months from the date of the auditor's report

    ☐ At least 12 months from the date of the financial statements

    ☐ A maximum of 12 months from the date of the auditor's report

    ☐ A maximum of 12 months from the date of the financial statements

176 You are concerned that the debt due from Grape Co may not be recoverable and believe that this would have a significant effect on the viability of Strawberry.

Which of the following would provide you with the most reliable evidence regarding the recoverability of this debt?

☐ A management representation confirming its recoverability

☐ The response from the customer to your circularisation performed earlier in the audit confirming the amount owed

☐ Identification during your subsequent events review of a cash receipt for the full amount

☐ Correspondence between Strawberry's lawyer and Grape Co's lawyers confirming that the amount will be paid

177 You have raised your concerns with management regarding the ability of Strawberry to repay the $0.6m loan in 6 months. The directors have assured you that this will be possible as they have a contingency plan.

Which of the following courses of action by the directors would provide you with the most assurance that Strawberry will be able to meet this commitment?

☐ Plans to dispose of a property valued at $5.2m in August 20X2

☐ The reopening of negotiations regarding the terms of the loan with the current provider

☐ Plans to substantially cut production costs by moving production to Asia

☐ Agreement by an alternative financial institution to lend Strawberry $4.8m in September 20X2

178 You have concluded that Strawberry is not a going concern.

If the directors refuse to amend the financial statements which of the following correctly describes the impact on the auditor's report?

	Auditor's opinion	Explanation of circumstances
☐	Adverse opinion	Basis for adverse opinion
☐	Qualified opinion	Basis for qualified opinion
☐	Adverse opinion	Material uncertainty related to going concern
☐	Qualified opinion	Material uncertainty related to going concern

(Total = 10 marks)

Clarinet (6/14) (amended)

18 mins

The following scenario relates to questions 179–183.

Clarinet Co (Clarinet) is a computer hardware specialist and has been trading for over five years. The company is funded partly through overdrafts and loans and also by several large shareholders; the year end is 30 April 20X4.

Clarinet has experienced significant growth in previous years; however, in the current year a new competitor, Drums Design Co (Drums), has entered the market and through competitive pricing has gained considerable market share from Clarinet including one of its largest customers. Clarinet is looking to develop new products to differentiate itself from the rest of its competitors. It has approached its shareholders to finance this development; however, they declined to invest further in Clarinet. Clarinet's loan is long term and it has met all repayments on time. The overdraft has increased significantly over the year and the directors have informed you that the overdraft facility is due for renewal next month and they believe it will be renewed.

The directors have produced a cash flow forecast which shows a significantly strengthening position over the coming 12 months. They are confident with the new products being developed and, in light of their trading history of significant growth, believe it is unnecessary to make any disclosures in the financial statements regarding going concern.

At the year end, Clarinet received notification from one of its customers that the hardware installed by Clarinet for the customers' online ordering system has not been operating correctly. As a result, the customer has lost significant revenue and has informed Clarinet that they intend to take legal action against them for loss of earnings. Clarinet has investigated the problem post year end and discovered that other work in progress is similarly affected and inventory should be written down by $375,000. The finance director believes that as this misstatement was identified after the year end, it can be amended in the 20X5 financial statements. Draft financial statements for the year ended 30 April 20X4 showed profit after tax of $2.5m.

179 Which of the following correctly summarises whether the uncorrected misstatement of inventory is material and its impact on the 20X4 financial statements?

	Material	Adjust in 20X4 financial statements
☐	No	No
☐	No	Yes
☐	Yes	Yes
☐	Yes	No

180 Which of the following factors are indicators that may cast doubt on Clarinet's ability to continue as a going concern?

(1) The entry of the new competitor reducing Clarinet's market share

(2) The significant increase in the overdraft

(3) The company has a long-term loan

(4) The reluctance of the shareholders to provide further investment in Clarinet

☐ 1, 2 and 3

☐ 1, 2 and 4

☐ 1, 3 and 4

☐ 2, 3 and 4

181   As part of your assessment of going concern you have reviewed the cash flow forecast. This is based on the assumption of significant increases in revenue.

Which of the following procedures would provide the most reliable evidence regarding the validity of this assumption?

☐   Email correspondence between the sales director and potential new customers

☐   A review of board minutes showing details of new customers won

☐   A review of post year-end sales and the order book

☐   Discussions with management regarding their plans for obtaining new business

182   You have concluded that circumstances exist which cast significant doubt on Clarinet's ability to continue as a going concern.

Which of the following must you include in your communication with those charged with governance in accordance with ISA 570 *Going Concern*?

(1)   Whether the circumstances you have identified constitute a material uncertainty

(2)   Whether the use of the going concern basis of accounting is appropriate in the preparation and presentation of the financial statements

(3)   The adequacy of the related disclosures

(4)   The period of time your assessment has covered if less than 12 months from the date of the financial statements

☐   1, 2 and 3

☐   1, 2 and 4

☐   1, 3 and 4

☐   2, 3 and 4

183   The auditors have been informed that Clarinet's bankers will not make a decision on the overdraft facility until after the auditor's report is completed. The directors have now agreed to include some going concern disclosures and you believe these disclosures are adequate.

Which of the following correctly summarises the impact on the auditor's report of Clarinet if the auditor believes the company is a going concern but that this is subject to a material uncertainty?

	Opinion	Disclosure
☐	Modified	Key audit matters
☐	Unmodified	Material uncertainty related to going concern
☐	Unmodified	Key audit matters
☐	Modified	Material uncertainty related to going concern

(Total = 10 marks)

Czech & Dawson

The following scenario relates to questions 184–188.

You are the audit manager of Savage & Co. It is a busy time of year for you as you have several ongoing audit clients at the moment and you are in the process of dealing with a number of outstanding issues and queries from members of your audit teams.

Czech Co (Czech)

Czech is a pharmaceutical company. The fieldwork has been completed and you are currently reviewing the audit file. The audit senior is not sure how to deal with the following issue.

Czech has incurred $2.1m and development expenditure of $3.2m during the year, all of which has been capitalised as an intangible asset. Profit before tax is $26.3m.

Dawson Co (Dawson)

The fieldwork on this audit is also complete with the exception of the following issue which the audit senior has been unable to deal with.

Dawson's computerised wages program is backed up daily; however, for a period of two months the wages records and back-ups have been corrupted, and therefore cannot be accessed. Wages and salaries for these 2 months are $1.1m. Profit before tax is $10m.

184   You have just received a phone call from one particular audit senior who is unsure about the steps to take in relation to uncorrected misstatements.

Which of the following statements correctly describe the auditor's responsibility in respect of misstatements?

☐   ISA 450 *Evaluation of Misstatements Identified During the Audit* states that the auditor only has a responsibility to accumulate material misstatements identified during the audit.

☐   Where misstatements are not material the auditor should request that management correct the misstatements in the following accounting period.

☐   If management refuses to correct some or all of the misstatements, the auditor should consider the implications of this for their audit opinion.

☐   A written representation should be requested from management to confirm whether they believe that the effects of the unadjusted misstatements are immaterial, both individually and in aggregate, to the financial statements as a whole.

185   Which **TWO** of the following audit procedures should be performed in order to form a conclusion on whether an amendment is required to Czech's financial statements in respect of the research and development expenditure?

☐   Discuss the requirements of IAS 38 *Intangible Assets* with the directors in order to determine whether they understand the required accounting treatment of research and development expenditure

☐   Obtain a breakdown of the $5.3m capitalised as an intangible asset and agree to supporting documentation to determine the nature of the projects to which the expenditure relates

☐   Review minutes of board meetings to determine whether the expenditure was authorised

☐   Visit the laboratory where the current research is being undertaken and to confirm occurrence of the research expenditure

186 Which of the following options correctly summarises the impact on the auditor's report for Czech if the issue remains unresolved?

☐ Unmodified opinion with key audit matters paragraph

☐ Qualified opinion with key audit matters paragraph explaining the issue

☐ Qualified opinion

☐ Adverse opinion

187 Which of the following correctly summarises the effect of the issue relating to the wages balance in the financial statements of Dawson?

	Material	Financial statement impact
☐	No	Liabilities to tax authorities may be understated
☐	No	Profit may be overstated
☐	Yes	Wages may be materially misstated
☐	Yes	Proper accounting records have not been kept

188 Based on the above information, which of the following options correctly summarises the impact of the wages and salaries issue on the auditor's report for Dawson?

	Audit opinion	Disclosure in the auditor's report
☐	Qualified	Basis for qualified opinion
☐	Disclaimer	Basis for disclaimer of opinion
☐	Qualified	Key audit matters section
☐	Qualified	Emphasis of matter

(Total = 10 marks)

Medimade (6/10) (amended)   **18 mins**

The following scenario relates to questions 189–193.

Medimade Co is an established pharmaceutical company that has for many years generated 90% of its revenue through the sale of two specific cold and flu remedies. Medimade Co has lately seen a real growth in the level of competition that it faces in its market and demand for its products has significantly declined.

You are the audit manager responsible for the audit of Medimade Co's financial statements for the year ended 31 March 20X7.

In addition to recruiting staff, Medimade Co needed to invest $2m in plant and machinery. The company wanted to borrow this sum but was unable to agree suitable terms with the bank; therefore it used its overdraft facility, which carried a higher interest rate. Consequently, some of Medimade Co's suppliers have been paid much later than usual and hence some of them have withdrawn credit terms meaning the company must pay cash on delivery.

189 Which **TWO** of the following statements are correct with regards to the going concern basis of accounting?

☐ The going concern basis of accounting is used when the entity will be able to continue in business for the foreseeable future.

☐ The foreseeable future is defined for accounting purposes as 36 months from the company's reporting date.

☐ The going concern basis of accounting assumes that the entity will be able to realise its assets and discharge its liabilities in the normal course of business.

☐ Financial statements that are prepared on a going concern basis assert that the company intends to liquidate its operations.

190 Which **TWO** of the following statements describe the most direct impact the withdrawal of supplier credit has on Medimade Co's use of the going concern basis of accounting?

☐ Medimade Co now has to pay cash on delivery and this adds further cash flow strain imposed by the overdraft.

☐ Some suppliers may end their relationship with Medimade Co, preventing the company from producing its products, thus further reducing sales.

☐ Medimade Co will have to seek alternative suppliers, who may not meet Medimade Co's quality control standards.

☐ The bank may impose strict covenants on the overdraft, restricting the way Medimade Co can conduct its future operations.

191 It is May 20X7. The directors have informed you that the bank overdraft facility is due for renewal next month, after the auditor's report is signed. They are confident that it will be renewed.

Which of the following audit procedures would be most effective in assessing whether or not Medimade is a going concern?

☐ Agree current overdraft level to bank letter

☐ Obtain confirmation from the bank that the overdraft facility will be renewed

☐ Obtain written representation from management that they consider the going concern assumption to be appropriate

☐ Review board minutes for meetings held after the year end for evidence which indicates further financial difficulties or evidence of alternative sources of finance

192 The directors have now agreed to include going concern disclosures, while continuing to use the going concern basis of accounting.

You agree with Medimade Co's management that the going concern basis of accounting is appropriate under the circumstances. You have reviewed the draft disclosures and believe they are correct and adequate.

Indicate which form of audit opinion would be appropriate and how the going concern issue would be disclosed in the auditor's report.

Audit opinion	Disclosure in the auditor's report
☐ Disclaimer	☐ Describe the nature of the going concern uncertainty in the Material uncertainty related to going concern section
☐ Unmodified opinion	☐ Describe the nature of the going concern uncertainty in the Key audit matters section
☐ Qualified opinion	☐ Describe the nature of the going concern uncertainty in the Basis for adverse opinion section
☐ Adverse opinion	☐ Describe the nature of the going concern uncertainty in the Basis for qualified opinion section

193 The audit is completed. The auditor's report and the financial statements have been signed but not yet issued.

The finance director of Medimade Co has just informed the audit team that he has been informed by the bank that the overdraft facility will not be renewed. Medimade Co currently does not have any other source of finance.

What actions, if any, should you now take in order to meet the auditor's responsibilities under ISA 560 *Subsequent Events*?

☐ No actions required as the auditor's report and financial statements have already been signed.

☐ Discuss with management about their plans for the company and determine whether the 20X7 financial statements should now be prepared on a break-up basis. If yes, request management to adjust the financial statements, audit the adjustments and provide a new auditor's report.

☐ Discuss with management about their plans for the company and determine whether disclosures should be revised in the 20X7 financial statements. If yes, request management to revise the disclosures and redraft the auditor's report to refer to the revised disclosures.

☐ Request that management adjust for this event in the 20X8 financial statements, as it occurred in the year ending 31 March 20X8.

(Total = 10 marks)

194 Panda (6/13)   36 mins

Panda Co manufactures chemicals and has a factory and four offsite storage locations for finished goods. Panda Co's year end was 30 April 20X3. The final audit is almost complete and the financial statements and auditor's report are due to be signed next week. Revenue for the year is $55 million and profit before taxation is $5.6 million.

The following two events have occurred subsequent to the year end. No amendments or disclosures have been made in the financial statements.

Event 1 – Defective chemicals

Panda Co undertakes extensive quality control checks prior to the dispatch of any chemicals. Testing on 3 May 20X3 found that a batch of chemicals produced in April was defective. The cost of this batch was $0.85 million. In its current condition it can be sold at a scrap value of $0.1 million. The costs of correcting the defect are too significant for Panda Co's management to consider this an alternative option.

Event 2 – Explosion

An explosion occurred at the smallest of the four offsite storage locations on 20 May 20X3. This resulted in some damage to inventory and property, plant and equipment. Panda Co's management have investigated the cause of the explosion and believe that they are unlikely to be able to claim on their insurance. Management of Panda Co has estimated that the value of damaged inventory and property, plant and equipment was $0.9 million and it now has no scrap value.

Required

(a)   Explain the five elements of an assurance engagement.   (5 marks)

(b)   For each of the two events above:

     (i)   Explain whether the financial statements require amendment; and

     (ii)   Describe audit procedures that should be performed in order to form a conclusion on any required amendment.

     Note. The total marks will be split equally between each event.   (12 marks)

(c)   The directors do not wish to make any amendments or disclosures to the financial statements for the explosion (Event 2).

     Required

     Explain the impact on the auditor's report should this issue remain unresolved.   (3 marks)

(Total = 20 marks)

SAMPLE QUESTIONS FROM THE EXAMINING TEAM

Questions 195–217 comprise sample Section A questions from the examining team and cover different syllabus areas.

Q195–196 March 2017   7 mins

Comments from the examining team (March 2017)

Section A

The following two questions are reviewed with the aim of giving future candidates an indication of the types of questions asked, guidance on dealing with exam questions and to provide a technical debrief on the topics covered by the specific questions selected.

195   Following discussions with one of your firm's clients, the audit engagement partner has advised that detailed testing will need to be performed on the valuation of inventory due to some concerns over the net realisable value of certain products.

Which of the following matters disclosed by the client is an indicator that net realisable value could be lower than cost?

☐   General market prices for individual gemstones have remained static for the last three years.

☐   Demand for certain items of jewellery has increased marginally over the past year.

☐   Trade discounts given by suppliers have increased in the past year.

☐   There has been an increase in the average time taken to manufacture each individual jewellery piece.

196   You are an audit senior and have been asked to draft the auditor's report.

Which of the following are elements which should be included in an unmodified auditor's report for a listed company as per ISA 700 (Revised) *Forming an Opinion and Reporting on Financial Statements*?

(1)   Basis for opinion paragraph

(2)   Other reporting responsibilities

(3)   Key audit matters

(4)   Other matters paragraph

☐   (1), (3) and (4)

☐   (1), (2) and 4)

☐   (1), (2) and (3)

☐   (2), (3) and (4)

Comments from the examining team (June 2017)

Section A in the June 2017 examination included questions on the following areas:

- Professional ethics and application of ACCA's *Code of Ethics and Conduct*

- Internal audit

- Corporate Governance

- Substantive testing including testing on tangible assets, receivables, bank and cash and using the work of others

- Subsequent events; and

- Auditor's reports

The following two questions are reviewed with the aim of giving future candidates an indication of the types of questions asked, guidance on dealing with exam questions and to provide a technical debrief on the topics covered by the specific questions selected. Candidates are reminded that there will be a mix of application and knowledge questions in section A and it is imperative that they ensure their knowledge of the International

Standards on Auditing (ISAs) and financial reporting is adequate. The following questions have been selected to demonstrate the importance of these key areas.

197   Which **TWO** of the following matters should the auditor consider prior to placing reliance on the work of the expert?

☐   The availability of alternative sources of audit evidence

☐   The technical expertise required to perform the valuation

☐   The availability of audit staff to complete the evaluation of the expert on a timely basis

☐   The extent to which the use of the expert can be referred to in the auditor's report

198   Which of the following procedures should be performed in relation to the revaluation recorded in the year?

(1)   Recalculate the depreciation charge for the year using the updated valuation.

(2)   Verify that all the assets in the same class have been revalued in line with IAS 16 *Property, Plant and Equipment*.

(3)   Agree the value to the expert's report and recalculate the revaluation adjustment recorded by Gates Co.

(4)   Agree that the revaluation surplus has been recorded in the statement of profit or loss.

☐   (1), (2) and (3) only

☐   (1), (2) and (4) only

☐   (3) and (4) only

☐   (1), (2), (3) and (4)

Q199–200 September 2017

7 mins

Comments from the examining team (September 2017)

Section A

Section A in the September 2017 examination included, but was not limited to, questions on the following areas:

- The concept of assurance and other assurance engagements

- Substantive testing including testing on trade payables, bank and cash and share capital

- Going concern

- Audit finalisation and the final review; and

- Auditor's reports

The following two questions are reviewed with the aim of giving future candidates an indication of the types of questions asked, guidance on dealing with exam questions and to provide a technical debrief on the topics covered by the specific questions selected. Candidates are reminded that there will be a mix of application and knowledge questions.

199   Which of the following audit procedures will test for the **EXISTENCE** of bank and cash?

☐   Review all relevant bank statements to verify that the accounts are held under the company name

☐   Attend the cash count at the year end and re-perform the count

☐   Agree a sample of accounts detailed in the bank confirmation letter to the trial balance

☐   Review the disclosure included in the financial statements to verify only bank accounts as per the bank letter are disclosed

200   The company issued 100,000 $1 ordinary shares in August 20X7. This is currently not reflected in the financial statements for the year ended 31 July 20X7.

If no changes are made to the financial statements which of the following audit opinions will be issued?

☐   Unmodified opinion as the share issue occurred after the year end

☐   Qualified opinion as the financial statements are materially misstated

☐   Qualified opinion as the auditor has not gathered sufficient, appropriate evidence in respect of the share issue

☐   Unmodified opinion with an Emphasis of Matter paragraph drawing shareholders' attention to the share issue

Q201–202 December 2017

7 mins

Comments from the examining team (December 2017)

Section A in the December 2017 examination included, but was not limited to, questions on the following areas:

- Professional ethics and application of ACCA's *Code of Ethics and Conduct*
- Substantive testing including testing on wages and salaries, revenue and tangible assets.
- Subsequent events
- Audit finalisation and the final review; and
- Auditor's reports

The following two questions are reviewed with the aim of giving future candidates an indication of the types of questions asked, guidance on dealing with exam questions and to provide a technical debrief on the topics covered by the specific questions selected. Candidates are reminded that there will be a mix of application and knowledge questions in Section A and it is imperative that they ensure their knowledge of the International Standards on Auditing (ISAs), and important areas of the syllabus such as audit procedures is at an appropriate level. The following questions have been selected to demonstrate the importance of these key areas.

201 Which of the following procedures would **NOT** test for **UNDERSTATEMENT** of the wages accrual in Scarborough Co's statement of financial position?

☐ Agree the payment of the final week's wages from post year-end bank statements to the accrual listing

☐ Agree the final week's wage cost from the payroll listing to the accrual listing

☐ Compare the accrual in the financial statements to the prior year and investigate any significant differences

☐ Select a sample of employees from the final week's payroll listing and recalculate deductions

202 One objective of the final overall review is to ensure that the evidence gathered in the course of the audit supports the audit opinion.

Which **TWO** of the following questions, which are answered as part of the final review, support this objective?

☐ Was the audit plan suitably modified to allow for changing circumstances?

☐ Has the audit firm's continued independence been considered?

☐ Is other information published within the annual report consistent with the financial statements?

☐ Has work been performed in accordance with relevant auditing, legal and professional standards?

Comments from the examining team (March 2018)

Section A in the March 2018 examination included but was not limited to, questions on the following areas:

- Professional ethics and application of ACCA's *Code of Ethics and Conduct*
- Substantive testing including testing on non-current assets and inventory
- Written representations
- Audit finalisation and review
- Auditor's reports

The following questions are reviewed with the aim of giving future candidates an indication of the types of questions asked, guidance on dealing with exam questions and to provide a technical debrief on the topics covered by the specific questions selected. Candidates are reminded that there will be a mix of application and knowledge questions in Section A and it is imperative that they ensure their knowledge of the International Standards on Auditing (ISAs), and important areas of the syllabus such as audit procedures is at an appropriate level.

203   Which TWO of the following statements relating to codes of professional ethics are correct?

☐   Codes of professional ethics are prescriptive ethical rules which professional accountants should consider in every situation

☐   A code of professional ethics allows a professional accountant to apply fundamental ethical principles to a given situation

☐   A code of professional ethics encourages professional accountants to think about more than just legal compliance

☐   Compliance with codes of professional ethics is a legal requirement for professional accountants

204   As a starting point for the audit testing of inventory the audit assistant has carried out ratio analysis on the draft financial statements of Well Heeled Co.

Which of the following ratios would be useful in relation to testing inventory?

☐   Gross profit margin

☐   Quick ratio

☐   Current ratio

☐   Return on assets

Q205–206 June 2018   7 mins

Comments from the examining team (June 2018)

Section A in the June 2018 examination included, but was not limited to, questions on the following areas:

- Professional ethics and application of ACCA's *Code of Ethics and Conduct*
- The level of assurance provided by review engagements
- Substantive testing including testing on revenue, trade receivables and tangible assets
- Going concern
- Audit finalisation and the final review; and
- Auditor's reports

The following questions are reviewed with the aim of giving future candidates an indication of the types of questions asked, guidance on dealing with exam questions and to provide a technical debrief on the topics covered by the specific questions selected. Candidates are reminded that there will be a mix of application and knowledge questions in Section A and it is imperative that they ensure their knowledge of the International Standards on Auditing (ISAs), and important areas of the syllabus such as audit procedures and going concern is at an appropriate level.

205   Which of the following statements summarise the auditor's responsibilities in relation to going concern?

    (1)   Evaluate management's assessment of the entity's ability to continue as a going concern

    (2)   Determine whether or not an entity can prepare its financial statements using the going concern basis of accounting

    (3)   Remain alert throughout the audit for events or conditions which may cast significant doubt on the entity's ability to continue as a going concern

    (4)   Obtain evidence to determine whether a material uncertainty exists if events are identified which may cast doubt on the entity's ability to continue as a going concern

    ☐   (1), (3) and (4) only

    ☐   (1), (2) and (4) only

    ☐   (2) and (3) only

    ☐   (1), (2), (3) and (4)

---

206   Which of the following describes the level of assurance, which will be provided by Red & Co following the review of the five-year profit forecast?

    ☐   Limited assurance, positive conclusion

    ☐   Reasonable assurance, negative conclusion

    ☐   Limited assurance, negative conclusion

    ☐   No assurance

Q207–208 September 2018

7 mins

Comments from the examining team (September 2018)

Section A in the September 2018 examinations included, but was not limited to, questions on the following areas:

- Professional ethics and application of ACCA's *Code of Ethics and Conduct*

- Corporate Governance

- Substantive testing including testing on tangible and intangible non-current assets and investments

- Subsequent events

- Audit finalisation and review

- Auditor's reports

The following questions are reviewed with the aim of giving future candidates an indication of the types of questions asked, guidance on dealing with exam questions and to provide a technical debrief on the topics covered by the specific questions selected. Candidates are reminded that there will be a mix of application and knowledge questions in Section A and it is imperative that they ensure their knowledge of the International Standards on Auditing (ISAs), and important areas of the syllabus such as audit procedures is at an appropriate level.

207 Which **TWO** of the following are objectives of the external auditor?

☐ To consider the adequacy of the accounting records which have been maintained

☐ To confirm the company will continue trading for the foreseeable future

☐ To obtain an understanding of the internal control system in place

☐ To access the books and records of the company

---

208 X Co has a year ended 30 June 20X8. At the end of June 20X8 the company's corporate headquarters building was revalued by a reputable firm of surveyors.

Assuming a reliable valuation is obtained, which of the following procedures should be performed to obtain sufficient appropriate substantive evidence about the carrying amount of X Co's corporate headquarters?

(1) Review the board minutes to ensure that the decision to revalue the headquarters was approved by the board.

(2) Agree the revalued amount in the valuation statement to the amount recorded in the non-current asset register.

(3) Recalculate the revaluation adjustment and agree that it is correctly recorded in the revaluation surplus.

(4) Confirm with the directors that all other assets in the same class as the headquarters have been revalued and agree this to the accounting policy disclosure.

☐ 2 and 3 only

☐ 1, 2 and 3

☐ 2, 3 and 4

☐ 1 and 4 only

Q209–210 December 2018

7 mins

Comments from the examining team (December 2018)

Section A in the December 2018 examination included, but was not limited to, questions on the following areas:

- Professional ethics and application of ACCA's *Code of Ethics and Conduct*

- Corporate governance

- Substantive testing including analytical procedures, revenue, bank and cash and trade payables

- Subsequent events

- Audit finalisation and review

- Auditor's reports

The following questions are reviewed with the aim of giving future candidates an indication of the types of questions asked, guidance on dealing with exam questions and to provide a technical debrief on the topics covered by the specific questions selected. Candidates are reminded that there will be a mix of application and knowledge questions in Section A and it is imperative that they ensure their knowledge of the International Standards on Auditing (ISAs), relevant financial accounting and important areas of the syllabus such as audit procedures is at an appropriate level.

209 Which of the following details should be disclosed in respect of the revaluation of the head office if the auditor is to conclude that the disclosures are adequate?

    (1)   Effective date of the revaluation

    (2)   Name of the valuer

    (3)   The amount of the revaluation increase

    (4)   Carrying amount of the head office under the cost model

    ☐   1, 2 and 3 only

    ☐   1, 3 and 4 only

    ☐   2, 3 and 4 only

    ☐   1, 2, 3 and 4

---

210 All adjustments required by the auditors of X Co have been made to the financial statements with the exception of an adjustment relating to faulty goods held in inventory at the year end. The audit work concluded that the cost of this inventory exceeded its net realisable value by $2.9m. The directors dispute the audit team's figures and believe that the realisable value of the inventory still exceeds its cost. Profit before tax for the year was $131.4m.

Which of the following correctly describes the effect of this matter on the auditor's report?

    ☐   Unmodified opinion with no further disclosure

    ☐   Unmodified opinion with disclosure in an emphasis of matter paragraph

    ☐   Qualified opinion due to material misstatement

    ☐   Qualified opinion due to inability to obtain sufficient appropriate audit evidence

Q211–212 March 2019

7 mins

Comments from the examining team (March 2019)

Section A in the March 2019 examination included, but was not limited to, questions on the following areas:

- Concepts of assurance
- Professional ethics and application of ACCA's *Code of Ethics and Conduct*
- Substantive testing including analytical procedures, revenue, expenses, PPE and estimates
- Written representations
- Auditor's reports

The following questions are reviewed with the aim of giving future candidates an indication of the types of questions asked, guidance on dealing with exam questions and to provide a technical debrief on the topics covered by the specific questions selected. Candidates are reminded that there will be a mix of application and knowledge questions in Section A and it is imperative that they ensure their knowledge of the International Standards on Auditing (ISAs), relevant financial accounting and important areas of the syllabus such as auditor's reports is at an appropriate level. Recent Examiner's reports have noted that performance on knowledge questions was poor and this continued to be the case in March 2019. Questions may test specific details of an ISA, therefore candidates must ensure that they have studied the ISAs in sufficient depth.

211   Identify, by clicking on the relevant box in the table below, whether each of the following statements is true or false.

An unmodified auditor's report includes a statement that the auditor believes the audit evidence obtained is sufficient and appropriate	TRUE	FALSE
Only an auditor's report with a modified opinion includes a statement indicating the report is that of the independent auditor	TRUE	FALSE
Only an auditor's report with a modified opinion includes a description of the meaning of materiality	TRUE	FALSE
An unmodified auditor's report includes a statement that the auditor is independent of the entity and has fulfilled their ethical responsibilities	TRUE	FALSE

212   The auditors have discovered that the chairman's report of XYZ Co, a listed company, is inconsistent with the financial statements and it has been determined that the material inconsistency is in the chairman's report.

Complete the following sentence by dragging and dropping the appropriate audit opinion and type of communication in the auditor's report.

If the directors refuse to amend the inconsistency, then the auditor's opinion will be [   ] and the inconsistency will be explained in a [   ]

Auditor's opinion	Inconsistency explained in
Unmodified	Other matters paragraph
Qualified on the grounds of a material misstatement	Other information section
Qualified on the grounds of an inability to obtain sufficient appropriate audit evidence	Emphasis of matter paragraph
Adverse	Key audit matters section
Disclaimer of opinion	

Q213–214 June 2019   7 mins

Comments from the examining team (June 2019)

Section A in the June 2019 examination included, but was not limited to, questions on the following areas:

- Corporate governance
- Substantive procedures including analytical procedures, revenue, expenses, bank and cash and share capital
- Written representations
- Going concern
- Subsequent events
- Auditor's reports

The following questions are reviewed with the aim of giving future candidates an indication of the types of questions asked, guidance on dealing with exam questions and to provide a technical debrief on the topics covered by the specific questions selected. Candidates are reminded that there will be a mix of application and knowledge questions in Section A and it is imperative that they ensure their knowledge of the International Standards on Auditing (ISAs), relevant financial accounting and important areas of the syllabus such as auditor's reports is at an appropriate level. Recent Examiner's reports have noted that performance on knowledge questions was poor and this continued to be the case in June 2019. Questions may test specific details of examinable documents including ISAs, ACCA's *Code of Ethics and Conduct* and the Corporate Governance Code, therefore candidates must ensure that they have studied these in sufficient depth.

213 X Co is a listed company and has an audit committee.

Identify, by clicking on the relevant box in the table below, whether each of the following statements is true or false.

The audit committee's terms of reference should include reviewing and monitoring the external auditor's independence and objectivity	TRUE	FALSE
The audit committee's terms of reference should include appointing and removing the external auditors	TRUE	FALSE
The audit committee's terms of reference should include evaluating and monitoring the effectiveness of the internal audit function	TRUE	FALSE

214 A & Co is the auditor of Z Co for the year ended 31 December 20X8. The detailed audit work is due to be completed by 30 June 20X9. The directors are planning to approve the financial statements on 31 July 20X9 and then issue them to the shareholders on 15 August 20X9. The management of Z Co has performed an assessment of the company's ability to continue as a going concern based on a cash flow forecast prepared to 31 December 20X9.

Complete the following sentence by dragging and dropping the appropriate date.

A & Co's evaluation of management's assessment of Z Co's ability to continue as a going concern must cover the period up to [   ].

Dates
30 June 20X9
31 July 20X9
15 August 20X9
31 December 20X9

Q215–216 September 2019

7 mins

Comments from the examining team (September 2019)

It was very pleasing to see that once again almost all candidates attempted all 15 questions, across the three OT cases. Candidates preparing for future sessions are advised to work through the past exams which are available and to carefully review how each of the correct answers were derived. Section A questions aim to provide a broad coverage of the syllabus, and future candidates should aim to revise all areas of the Audit and Assurance syllabus, rather than attempting to question spot.

Section A in the September 2019 examination included, but was not limited to, questions on the following areas:

- Professional ethics and application of ACCA's Code of Ethics and Conduct
- Substantive procedures including bank and cash, share capital and inventory
- Audit finalisation and review
- Auditor's reports

The following questions are reviewed with the aim of giving future candidates an indication of the types of questions asked, guidance on dealing with exam questions and to provide a technical debrief on the topics covered by the specific questions selected. Candidates are reminded that there will be a mix of application and knowledge questions in Section A and it is imperative that they ensure their knowledge of the International Standards on Auditing (ISAs), relevant financial accounting and important areas of the syllabus such as auditors' reports is at an appropriate level. Questions may test specific details of examinable documents including ISAs, ACCA's *Code of Ethics and Conduct* and the Corporate Governance Code, therefore candidates must ensure that they have studied these in sufficient depth. Candidates must also ensure that they have studied all areas of the syllabus. The syllabus includes audit evidence learning outcomes relating to a wide range of specific items, any of which may be examined.

215 You have been assigned to the audit of bank and cash for X Co. X Co has a number of bank accounts and due to the nature of its business will hold a significant amount of cash at head office at the year end.

Which of the following audit procedures included in the audit programme will test for EXISTENCE of bank and cash?

☐ Agree a sample of accounts detailed on the bank confirmation letters to the trial balance

☐ Review all relevant bank statements to verify that the accounts are held under X Co

☐ Attend the cash count at the year end and reperform the count

☐ Review the disclosure included in the financial statements to verify only bank accounts per the bank letters are disclosed

216 One objective of the final overall review stage of the audit is to ensure that the evidence gathered in the course of the audit supports the audit opinion.

Which of the following questions, which are answered as part of the final review, support this objective?

(1) Was the audit plan suitably modified to allow for changing circumstances?

(2) Has the audit firm's continued independence been considered?

(3) Have all deficiencies in internal control been communicated to management?

(4) Has work been performed in accordance with relevant auditing, legal and professional standards?

☐ 1 and 4

☐ 1 and 2

☐ 2 and 3

☐ 3 and 4

Q217–218 December 2019   7 mins

Comments from the examining team (December 2019)

Section A It was very pleasing to see that once again almost all candidates attempted all 15 questions, across the three OT cases. Candidates preparing for future sessions are advised to work through the past exams which are available and to carefully review how each of the correct answers were derived. Section A questions aim to provide a broad coverage of the syllabus, and future candidates should aim to revise all areas of the Audit and Assurance syllabus, rather than attempting to question spot. Section A in the December 2019 examination included, but was not limited to, questions on the following areas:

- Principles of assurance
- Corporate Governance
- Substantive procedures including non-current assets
- Audit finalisation and review

217 You are an audit manager working for W & Co which has audited X Co for the last seven years. The board has decided that X Co should be listed on a stock exchange and the board has asked W & Co to advise the company on how to become compliant with corporate governance guidelines.

Which of the following are typical requirements contained within best practice corporate governance guidelines?

(1) The remuneration committee should only consist of independent non-executive directors

(2) The chief executive officer should be responsible for leadership of the board and ensuring its effectiveness

(3) The non-executive directors should provide constructive challenge and strategic guidance

(4) The audit committee's key role is appointing and liaising with the external auditor

A 1 and 3 only

B 2 and 4 only

C 1, 3 and 4

D 2, 3 and 4

218   It is 1 July 20X5. You are an audit supervisor of Y & Co and have been assigned
       responsibility for completing the detailed going concern testing for Z Co for the year ended
       30 April 20X5. Z Co's audit should be finalised and the financial statements signed by 30
       September 20X5. Management's assessment of Z Co's ability to continue as a going
       concern covers the period to 30 November 20X5.

       Which of the following actions should Y & Co take in relation to Z Co's going concern
       assessment?

       A   Request that management extends the assessment period to 30 September 20X6

       B   Request that management extends the assessment period to 30 April 20X6

       C   Perform additional audit procedures to confirm Z Co's going concern status

       D   Review management's assessment to 30 November 20X5 and only request that it is
              extended if it raises doubt that Z Co is a going concern

Answers

BJM Co

1   The correct answer is: The external audit is an exercise carried out by auditors in order to give an opinion on whether the financial statements of a company are fairly presented.

The external audit is carried out by external auditors, who are independent of the company so that they can provide an independent opinion on whether the company's financial statements are prepared, in all material respects, in accordance with an applicable financial reporting framework. The principal aim of the audit is not in relation to the control system in place or to identify other areas of deficiency, although deficiencies and recommendations may be suggested by the external auditors as a by-product of the external audit in a report to management at the conclusion of the audit.

2   The correct answer is: YHT & Co should perform specific audit procedures to identify possible non-compliance.

ISA 250 (Revised) distinguishes between regulations which have a direct effect on the financial statements (in the sense of directly affecting the determination of balances) and those which do not have a direct effect but can still have a material effect (such as an operating licence).

The hygiene regulations do not have a direct effect but they may have a material effect. The external auditor must therefore perform audit procedures to help identify any non-compliance which might have a material effect on the financial statements, ie any breaches of the hygiene regulations that could result in material fines or restaurant closures.

3   The correct answer is: The determination of materiality

This review engagement is an example of an assurance engagement. There are five elements to an assurance engagement: criteria, report, evidence, subject matter and three-party relationship (CREST) (IFAC, 2016).

4   The correct answer is: Limited; Negative.

A review engagement, such as a review of compliance with hygiene regulations, is an assurance engagement where the practitioner carries out limited procedures on BJM's internal controls relating to hygiene compliance.

As the procedures are limited, the practitioner will gain only enough evidence to provide a negative expression of opinion. This means the practitioner gives assurance that nothing has come to their attention which indicates that BJM's internal controls relating to hygiene compliance are not, in all material respects, compliant with national regulation.

5   The correct answer is: The lucrative nature of the review engagement may make the external audit team less inclined to require management to make adjustments or to issue a modified audit opinion, for fear of losing the review engagement.

The fees from the review engagement are likely to be very lucrative, so there is a risk that YHT & Co will not seek adjustments during the external audit process for fear of upsetting the board of BJM and losing the review engagement work.

The provision of non-audit services to unlisted audit clients is not specifically prohibited. While YHT & Co should be alert to self-review threats, in this case it seems unlikely: the scenario states that the review engagement does not include the provision of accounting advice or the preparation of figures in the financial statements. A firm is not required to turn down work when a 15% limit is exceeded. Where fee income from a listed audit client is expected to exceed 15% of the audit firm's total fee revenue, this fact should be disclosed to those charged with governance and a separate review may be required (ACCA *Code of Ethics and Conduct:* para. R410.4-6). However, the 15% fee cap is not a major concern to YHT & Co in this instance because BJM is unlisted.

Conoy

6   The correct answers are:

The position of the internal audit department will be strengthened within the organisation.

The effectiveness of the internal audit department will be improved as the audit committee will monitor and review its performance on a regular basis.

Conoy's internal audit department is currently poorly supported and reports directly to the board, which does not understand its reports. Establishing an audit committee will strengthen the position of the internal audit department by providing a greater degree of independence from management. The audit committee will also monitor and review the effectiveness of internal audit. The audit committee should report to the board as it undertakes tasks on behalf of the board, as opposed to the board reporting to the audit committee. Although the audit committee provides an independent channel of communication between the external auditor and the board, it is not involved in planning the external audit in any way.

7   The correct answer is:

Appointing the external auditor

The audit committee will make recommendations regarding whether the external auditor is reappointed or whether an alternative audit firm should be used. However, the external auditor is actually appointed by the shareholders at a general meeting of the company.

8   The correct answer is:

Proposed member	Include in audit committee	Do not include in audit committee
Adrian Muse		X
Penny Dinty		X
Sharon Header	X	
Fredrick Rowe	X	

The audit committee has a monitoring role and should therefore comprise at least three independent
non-executive directors, one of whom should have relevant financial expertise.

Adrian Muse is the chief internal auditor and so should not be part of the audit committee because he manages the team that will report to the audit committee.

Whilst Penny Dinty has some financial experience, she is already an executive director and so should not be a member of the audit committee as well.

The two new non-executive directors should be appointed to the audit committee provided that they are sufficiently independent and have the relevant skills.

9   The correct answer is: The audit committee will have at least one member who has relevant financial experience, so that they can monitor the integrity of the financial statements.

Conoy's finance director has left and had not yet been replaced. It appears that no one else has appropriate financial reporting knowledge required by Conoy. The audit committee should contain at least one member who has financial experience so that they can monitor the integrity of the financial statements. This may give the bank the confidence it needs before it lends Conoy the money.

Guaranteeing the loan or standing in as interim finance director are not acceptable options, as that will impair the independence of the audit committee.

Substantiating evidence for information used in financial reporting is a function of internal audit, not the audit committee.

10   The correct answer is:

	True	False
A key drawback of data analytics software is that it is difficult to tailor to each particular audit client		✓
Data analytics routines enable auditors to examine complex data using simple visualisation techniques	✓	
Although powerful, data analytics routines must be applied to strictly limited quantities of data so as to extrapolate correctly from a sample		✓

A key advantage of data analytics routines over the older CAATs is precisely that they do not require significant tailoring time – they are standardised and may be applied quickly.

Another advantage of data analytics is that they can be applied to large quantities of data – there is no need to restrict the amount of data they are applied to.

Stark

11   The correct answer is:

Advocacy	Intimidation	Self-interest
(4) only	(3) only	(2) and (3)

Including Mr Day's daughter, Zoe, is unusual but should not raise any significant risks to the audit.

The gift of the balloon flight represents a self-interest threat.

The tax fee represents a self-interest threat as Ali & Co will want to save as much tax as possible in order to charge as high a tax fee as possible. There is also an intimidation threat created by the request as the finance director may make Ali & Co feel that it has to accept the method of calculating tax fees in order to keep Stark as a tax client.

The fact that Stark expects Ali & Co to represent it in a dispute with the tax authorities creates an advocacy threat to audit independence.

12   The correct answer is: The gift should only be accepted if its value is trivial and inconsequential to the recipients

Gifts and hospitality should only be accepted where the value is trivial and inconsequential. In this case it is likely that the value of the gift is too high, so the balloon flight should be declined.

13   The correct answer is: The audit engagement partner should be removed from the audit team.

Stark is a public interest entity, so the audit engagement partner should only remain on the audit team for a maximum of seven years before being rotated. It would also be beneficial for an independent review partner to be appointed but Mr Day should not take on this role as, following rotation, he should have no involvement with the audit client for a 'cooling off' period of five years (ACCA *Code of Ethics and Conduct*: para. R540.11).

14   The correct answer is: 4, 5, 1, 2, 3

This is the process by which the IAASB develops new standards.

15   The correct answer is: Auditors may disclose matters to third parties without their client's consent if it is in the public interest, and they must do so if there is a statutory duty to do so.

There is no blanket prohibition on disclosure, nor is there any general right of the police or taxation authorities to demand information. Auditors have an implied contractual duty of confidentiality. There is no statutory duty of confidentiality.

Tangerine Tech Co

16 The correct answer is: 1 and 3 only

The board as a whole should take on the responsibility for liaising with shareholders, not just the chairman. (The board should state in the annual report the steps it has taken to ensure that the members of the board, and in particular the non-executive directors, develop an understanding of the views of the major shareholders about the company) (FRC *UK Corporate Governance Code*: Introduction).

As the chairman and one of the NEDs are former executive directors they were previously employed by the company and as a result this raises questions about their independence. Independent non-executive directors should be appointed to the board of Tangerine.

Tangerine is not required to have an internal audit function (however, where there is no internal audit function, the audit committee is required annually to consider the need for one).

17 The correct answer is:

Weakness 1	Weakness 2
The directors should be subject to annual re-election	At least 50% of the board, excluding the Chair, must be comprised of non-executive directors whom the board considers to be independent

The directors should be subject to annual re-election by the shareholders (FRC *UK Corporate Governance Code*: para. 18). They are re-elected by the shareholders, not the chairman.

There should be an appropriate balance of executives and NEDs to ensure that the board makes the correct objective decisions. At least half of the board, excluding the Chair, should be comprised of NEDs whom the board considers to be independent (FRC *UK Corporate Governance Code*: para. 11).

18 The correct answer is: 2 only

The audit committee is supposed to be made up of independent NEDs. The chairman should not be a member of the audit committee (FRC *UK Corporate Governance Code*: para. 24).

All four members of the audit committee were previously involved in sales and production related roles. At least one member of the audit committee should have recent and relevant financial experience. (FRC *UK Corporate Governance Code*: para. 24)

19 The correct answer is:

To review internal controls annually	To report on internal controls to shareholders
Yes	Yes

The directors are responsible for implementing and monitoring the company's system of internal control. An annual assessment of internal control should be conducted to confirm that the board has considered all significant aspects of internal control. The directors should report on its review as part of the annual report. (FRC *UK Corporate Governance Code*: para. 29)

20 The correct answer is: 1 and 3 only

The board is responsible for a company's internal control. The establishment of an internal audit function is one of the practical ways in which the board can meet its responsibility to monitor and review internal controls. However, as with all key decisions, costs versus benefits will be assessed too.

The directors are responsible for the prevention and detection of fraud. Whilst the internal audit function may assist the directors in this, the directors retain the ultimate responsibility.

LV Fones

21 The correct answer is:

Self-interest: 1, 3 and 4

Self-review: 2 only

The audit team have previously been offered a 10% discount on luxury phones from LV Fones (LV) which will potentially have a high value. As only goods with a trivial and inconsequential value can be received, if the same discount is again offered, it will constitute a self-interest threat.

The fee income from LV is 16% of Jones & Co's total fees. If, after accounting for non-recurring fees such as the secondment, it remains at this percentage of total fees on a recurring basis there is likely to be a self- interest threat because of undue dependence on this client.

The overdue fees (20% of the total fee) may be perceived as a loan which is prohibited, but may also create a self-interest threat. This is because Jones & Co may be less robust than it should be when it disagrees with management out of fear it may not recover the fees.

The audit senior probably prepared a significant proportion of the records to be audited; this creates a self-review threat as he will review his own work during the audit.

22 The correct answer is:

Threats: Familiarity and self-interest

Safeguards: Rotation of audit partner

The partner and finance director of LV have been on holiday together and appear to have a longstanding close relationship. This results in a familiarity and self-interest threat. Both are senior in their respective organisation and any onlooker would perceive independence to be threatened. The audit firm does not need to resign but the partner should no longer be involved in the audit.

23 The correct answer is: Unless the value of the discount is trivial and inconsequential to the audit team members, the offer should be declined.

	True	False
The audit team can accept the discount as it is on the same terms as that offered to staff		✔
Junior members of the audit team are allowed to accept the discount, but the audit manager and audit partner should not		✔
Unless the value of the discount is trivial and inconsequential to the audit team members, the offer should be declined	✔	
The audit team is only allowed to accept a discount of up to 5%		✔

The ACCA *Code of Ethics and Conduct* states that unless the value of a gift is trivial and inconsequential it should be declined. 10% of the value of a smartphone is unlikely to be trivial and inconsequential. (ACCA *Code of Ethics and Conduct*: para. R420.3)

24   The correct answer is: 2 and 3

For the audit of a public interest entity (which includes listed companies), where total fees from the client exceed more than 15% of the firm's total fees for 2 consecutive years, the auditor must disclose this to those charged with governance and arrange for a review to be conducted (either pre-issuance or post-issuance). Provided these mandatory safeguards are applied the firm is not required to resign from the audit (ACCA *Code of Ethics and Conduct*: para. R410.4-6).

25   The correct answer is:

	Service can be provided	Service cannot be provided
Design and implementation of IT systems over financial reporting		X
Assistance with preparation of tax return	X	
Accounting services		X
Recruiting service for the position of credit controller	X	

In general terms audit firms can provide other services provided that the firm does not assume a management responsibility. The provision of certain services is deemed to create such a threat to independence that safeguards will not be adequate to reduce this to an acceptable level. Additional restrictions will apply to LV as it is a public interest entity. The provision of IT services re accounting systems and accounting services cannot be made to LV, as these services have a direct impact on the financial statements that would be audited. Assistance with preparation of a tax return would be allowed as it is generally based on historical information. Provision of the recruitment service would be possible in this instance as the role is for a credit controller. The recruitment of senior management would be prohibited.

Orange

26   The correct answer is:

		Yes	No
(1)	The engagement partner has been asked to attend meetings with potential investors.	X	
(2)	Currant & Co has been offered the opportunity to provide other services to Orange Financials.		X
(3)	Currant & Co has been asked to produce the financial statements of Orange Financials.		X
(4)	There is a suggestion that a partner who previously worked for Orange Financials should be the review partner.		X

Risk (1) represents an advocacy threat as this may be interpreted as the audit firm promoting investment in Orange Financials Co.

Risk (2) Currant & Co would like to conduct other assignments for Orange Financials Co.

This gives rise to a potential self-interest threat as the total fees generated from this client may form a substantial proportion of the fees of the firm which may have an impact on the firm's objectivity.

Risk (3) Currant & Co have been asked to produce the financial statements of Orange Financials Co.

This represents a possible self-review threat as Currant & Co would be both preparing and auditing the same information.

Risk (4) The assistant finance director of Orange Financials Co has joined Currant & Co as a partner and it has been suggested that he should be the independent review partner.

This represents a self-review threat as the same individual would be responsible for reviewing the audit of financial statements which he has been involved in preparing.

27   The correct answers are: Intimidation and self-interest

This gives rise to an intimidation threat as the audit team may feel under pressure not to perform a thorough audit in order to comply with this request. There is also a self-interest threat as Currant & Co will be keen to win the additional work.

28   The correct answers are: (1) Not accepted (2) Not accepted

As the value of the hospitality is unlikely to be inconsequential no safeguards would be adequate to reduce the threat to an acceptable level. The offer of the weekend away should be declined politely.

If the loan had been made at normal commercial rates then the senior would be able to accept without any consequences for independence.

In this case as the terms are preferential the loan must be declined.

29   The correct answer is: Total fees from Orange Financials Co makes up more than 15% of Currant & Co's total fees for the second consecutive year.

The mandatory safeguards apply to public interest entity audits therefore would be applied to the audit of Orange Financials Co when it is listed.

30   The correct answer is:

	True	False
The audit committee should be made up of independent non-executive directors	X	
The audit committee normally appoints the external auditors at the AGM		X
The audit committee monitors and reviews the internal audit function	X	
The audit committee sets out the scope of the external auditor's work		X

The audit committee makes recommendations about the appointment of external auditors but the shareholders are responsible for appointing them at the AGM.

The scope of the external auditor's work is determined by the audit engagement partner on the basis of the requirements of auditing standards. The scope of the audit may be discussed with the audit committee but the audit committee does not set out the scope of the work as the audit must be an independent exercise.

SGCC

31 The correct answer is:

SGCC should appoint a new chief executive officer or board chairman.

Corporate governance codes indicate that there should be a clear division of responsibilities between running the board of directors and running the company's business so that no individual has unfettered powers of decision (FRC *UK Corporate Governance Code*: Principle G).

32 The correct answer is:

SGCC should appoint three new non-executive directors to the board.

Corporate governance codes indicate that the board should have a balance of executive and non-executive directors. SGCC currently has five executive and two non-executive directors and should therefore appoint a further three non-executive directors in order to balance the board. This is so that at least half the board, excluding the Chair, will be non-executive directors whom the board considers to be independent (FRC *UK Corporate Governance Code*: para. 11).

33 The correct answers are:

Once SGCC has an audit committee and an internal audit department, the head of the internal audit department should report to the audit committee.

SGCC should not rely on the external audit to inform them of deficiencies in internal controls.

SGCC should establish an audit committee with at least three independent non-executive directors (FRC *UK Corporate Governance Code*: para. 24).

Listed companies should review the need for an internal audit department at least annually. They are not automatically required to have an internal audit department (FRC *UK Corporate Governance Code*: para. 25).

34 The correct answer is:

Taking responsibility for the implementation of a new sales ledger system

The internal audit function is a review and monitoring function. It should not take operational responsibility for any part of the accounting or information systems.

35 The correct answer is:

Consideration		Employed	Outsourced
(1)	Greater availability of specialist industry skills as required		X
(2)	Flexibility regarding staff numbers in response to changing circumstances		X
(3)	Elimination of direct training costs		X
(4)	Development of skills increasing the human resource strength of the entity	X	

Where the internal audit department is outsourced to an external firm, SGCC is likely to benefit from specialist industry skills and will benefit from the greater flexibility in staffing numbers as the team can be modified depending on the workload at a particular point in time. SGCC will also be shielded from the direct costs of training staff. However, if the staff are employed by SGCC, this increases the skills held within the business and therefore increases the value of the workforce which is a strength of the company.

Bridgford

36 The correct answer is:

Area		Audit strategy document	Detailed audit plan
(1)	The availability of the client's data and staff (including internal audit)	X	
(2)	The allocation of responsibility for specific audit procedures to audit team members		X
(3)	The audit procedures to be undertaken for each area of the financial statements		X
(4)	The potential for using automated tools and techniques to gather evidence	X	

The audit strategy includes areas such as identifying the characteristics of the engagement, the reporting objectives, timing and nature of communications, knowledge gained from previous audits and during the preliminary risk assessments and the nature, timing and extent of resources in terms of using appropriate personnel.

The availability of the client's data and staff (including internal audit) and the potential for using CAATs are included in the characteristics of the engagement.

The auditor will take the overall audit strategy and convert it into a more detailed audit plan. This will include the allocation of work to audit team members and the audit procedures to be undertaken for each area of the financial statements.

37 The correct answer is:

Performance materiality refers to the amounts set by the auditor at higher than the materiality level for particular classes of transactions, account balances or disclosures where the materiality level might otherwise mean that such items are not tested.

The auditor sets performance materiality at an amount which is lower than the materiality level for the financial statements as a whole. This is so that the impact of misstatements for particular classes of transactions, account balances or disclosures will be considered even if they are not material to the financial statements as a whole (ISA 320).

38 The correct answer is:

Perform a trend analysis on current year and prior year monthly revenue, to identify whether revenue is overstated as a result of fraud or error

An overstatement of revenue would result in a reduction, not an increase in the receivables collection period.

39 The correct answer is:

That the financial statements include balances due from credit customers which are not recoverable

The audit risk relates to the concern about receivables taking 127 days to settle their invoices rather than the permitted 90 days (3-month credit terms), and that some customers are refusing to pay for products due to the reliability issues encountered. This means that the financial statements may include balances from receivables that are not recoverable. This would result in an overstatement of assets, and gives rise to concerns about the valuation of receivables.

Despite the worsening working capital position indicated by the increase in the receivables collection period, on its own it is unlikely to give rise to doubts over Bridgford's going concern status.

40   The correct answers are:

Determine how often inventory counts are performed and the level of corrections required to the inventory system

Test the operation of the inventory system using CAATs

The risk which has been identified relates to inventory quantities. Testing the operation of the inventory system using CAATs and reviewing the level of corrections required to the system would provide evidence regarding the operation of the system used to record the number of units of inventory held.

Reviewing purchase requisitions is a test to determine whether authorisation controls are in place to prevent orders of unnecessary items. The comparison of cost and net realisable value is a valid audit procedure; however it provides evidence regarding the valuation of inventory rather than quantity.

EuKaRe

41   The correct answer is:

Detection risk will increase due to the increased risk of cash donations being misappropriated and revenue being overstated		X
Inherent risk will increase as the nature of EuKaRe's transactions means that income may be misstated either in error or deliberately.	X	
Control risk will increase as internal controls may be weak due to the large number of volunteers used by EuKaRe		X
Business risk will increase due to the level of volunteers used by EuKaRe		X

Inherent risk is the risk that an item will be misstated due to the characteristics of that item. High levels of income in the form of cash increase the risk that income may be misstated either in error or deliberately. In addition, there may be no other independent source to show what the income should be. For example in this instance there would not be any formal record to support the majority of the takings (eg invoice or receipt) collected in the buckets.

Detection risk is the risk that the auditor's substantive procedures will not detect material misstatements. This is likely to increase but the principal risk is of revenue being understated (since some of it may be stolen / misappropriated).

Control risk is the risk that EuKaRe's internal controls will not prevent or detect misstatements. However the explanation states that this will be high due to the reliance on volunteers rather than due to transactions being in the form of cash.

Business risk is the risk that the business will not achieve its objectives and is not an element of audit risk.

42   The correct answer is:

	True	False
The risk assessment will help the audit team gain an understanding of the entity for audit purposes	✔	☐
The risk assessment will enable the audit senior to produce an accurate budget for the audit assignment	☐	✔
The risk assessment will form the basis of the audit strategy and the detailed audit plan	✔	☐
Once the risks have been assessed, TEY & Co can select audit team members with sufficient skill and experience to maximise the chance of those risks being addressed	✔	☐

Whilst an audit firm is a commercial and profit-making organisation, ISA 315 is not concerned with the auditor's budget but rather with ensuring that the auditor has a sufficient understanding of the business. This is so that they can select appropriate audit procedures in order to minimise the risk of undetected material misstatements.

43   The correct answer is:

Obtain a breakdown of the income recorded from the cash that was collected in buckets, and vouch a sample of entries back to the volunteer in order to determine which volunteer collected the relevant donations

This will provide evidence of the occurrence of income, but the key risk here is completeness of income.

44   The correct answer is:

The auditor is not responsible for the **prevention** of fraud or error. However, they are responsible for obtaining **reasonable assurance** that the financial statements are free from material misstatement whether caused by fraud or error. (ISA 240).

The directors, or rather here the trustees, are ultimately responsible for the prevention and detection of fraud and error within EuKaRe. The auditor needs to obtain reasonable assurance that the financial statements are not materially misstated due to fraud or error.

45   The correct answers are:

EuKaRe's finance department relies on volunteers who may not have accounts experience.

Understaffing in the finance department at certain times is due to the ad hoc nature of volunteer working hours.

The fact that EuKaRe has a detailed constitution which explains how the charity's income can be spent is a positive influence on the control environment, as it indicates that there is a benchmark in place against which the suitability of EuKaRe's expenditure can be measured.

The fact that the income of EuKaRe is primarily cash increases inherent risk but does not automatically mean that the control environment is weak.

South

46   The correct answers are: To ensure appropriate attention is devoted to important areas of the audit; To assist in the co-ordination of work done by any auditor's experts.

The main aim of planning is not to ensure the audit is completed within budget restraints, but to ensure that it is carried out in an effective manner as described by the other statements (ISA 300).

The determination of whether the audit engagement is ethically acceptable should have been done before the planning stage, and is not therefore an objective of planning.

47   The correct answer is:

Procedure	Assertion

	Review financial statement notes	Presentation
	Read minutes of board meetings for evidence of share issues	Completeness
	Recalculate the closing balance on the share capital account	Accuracy, valuation and allocation
	Review Memorandum and Articles of Association and compare their requirements with issued share capital	Existence

Comparing issued share capital with the Memorandum and Articles of Association relates to existence because 'equity' that is not issued pursuant to those documents does not legally exist.

48   The correct answer is: Inspect invoices capitalised within the cost of the new till system to determine whether they are directly attributable to the cost of the new till system

The audit risk relates to the concern that South may have capitalised costs which are revenue in nature. As such the appropriate response is to review the invoices which have been capitalised not just for their amount but also to determine the nature of the expense to which the invoice relates.

49   The correct answers are: Perform analytical procedures by comparing daily/weekly sales by store with both the prior year and with expectations, in order to determine whether any unusual patterns have occurred following the installation of the new system; Obtain a copy of the training manual relating to the new till system and discuss with directors the extent of training staff have received on the new system.

The audit risk relates to the concern that the system may not be reliable, that not all invoices have been recorded and that staff may not be familiar with the system.

Vouching the revenue per the system back to till receipts is not a valid response to the audit risk. Given that one concern is that revenue is understated, testing should be from the till receipts to the system to ensure that all sales have been recorded. Similarly, agreeing revenue from till receipts to the cashbook is also the wrong way around – this test should begin with the cashbook in order to test for completeness.

50   The correct answers are: To assess whether a provision for customer compensation is required in South's financial statements; To determine whether disclosure of the nature and financial effect of the legal claim is required in South's financial statements.

The concern over deficiencies in South's internal controls is a valid concern, but the review of legal correspondence is unlikely to be an appropriate response to this as the auditor would need to review internal controls. The impact on the reputation of South is also a valid concern as it could have implications for the viability of the company but again it is unlikely that information specifically relating to this would be available in the legal correspondence reviewed.

Mason

51   The correct answer is: Revenue may be overstated if it is recognised according to the contract date rather than over the relevant accounting period.

There is a risk that the revenue for the annual fees is not properly recognised in the period to which it relates, leading to revenue (and deferred income) being materially misstated in the financial statements. Revenue should be recognised according to the accounting period in which the related performance obligations of the contract are met.

52   The correct answers are: Obtain a breakdown of the capitalised costs and agree a sample of items to invoices to determine the nature of the expenditure; Inspect management's review of whether the value of the aircraft has been impaired.

The auditor should obtain a breakdown of the capitalised costs and vouch them back to invoices to determine whether they relate to a capital or revenue expense. They can then determine whether they have been recognised appropriately in accordance with IAS 16 *Property, Plant and Equipment*.

The large amount of refitting work could also indicate that something is wrong with the aircraft and that their value has become impaired.

53   The correct answer is: Mason's going concern status may be at risk if the contract is not renewed.

The key risk here is going concern. It is possible that the company will lose one of only four customers. In addition, a bank loan is being renegotiated and it is expected that costs will increase. This may threaten Mason's ability to continue as a going concern.

54   The correct answers are: Review Mason's contracts with its other three customers to determine whether they contain a break clause, in order to determine the likelihood of losing any further contracts to other aircraft providers; Review the short-term and long-term funding facilities which are available to Mason.

The main risk here is to the going concern assumption, if Mason loses other key sources of revenue. The auditor would therefore want to consider whether this is likely, by reviewing the other contracts. If, as appears likely, they do, then Mason would need a source of funding to survive.

It would not be appropriate to contact an audit client's customer directly in relation to a matter such as this.

The issue of disclosure would only need to be considered once the going concern status of Mason had been determined.

55   The correct answer is:

	Audit concern	Not audit concern
Non-current assets	☐	✔
Inventory	✔	☐
Completeness	☐	✔
Accuracy, valuation and allocation	✔	☐

Specialist equipment has been removed from the aircraft and is now included in inventory. Inventory should be valued at the lower of cost and net realisable value, not at amortised cost. The fact that the equipment has been replaced suggests that its net realisable value is lower than its cost. This may mean that inventory is overstated in the financial statements.

Severn

56   The correct answer is:

The proposed fee for the initial audit of Severn Co	INCLUDE	
A description of Rivers & Co, including the curriculum vitae of key staff likely to be assigned to the client	INCLUDE	
Overall level of materiality to be used in the audit		EXCLUDE
A summary of potential other services Rivers & Co could provide to Severn Co	INCLUDE	

The materiality level used is included in the audit plan, not the audit tender document. The proposed fee is a critical part of the tender, as is a description of the firm and the key personnel to be associated with Severn.

While there will be limits associated with what other services can be offered to Severn (as it is a listed entity), it would still be appropriate for the firm to list the services it offers, tailored to areas where it might be possible to offer services, as this might be a critical factor for Severn.

57   The firm is independent of the potential client; The firm has the appropriate resources to conduct the audit of the potential client.

These two issues are important when tendering for any audit, but particularly in this case, where Severn Co would represent a major client, and therefore self-interest issues might apply (for instance, the firm might consider it would become over reliant on the fee).

In addition, given the significance of Severn Co to Rivers & Co, it is particularly important to consider whether the firm has the resources (eg number of audit staff available at the appropriate time of year) to provide this audit service.

While the existence of preconditions of audit is an essential part of accepting an audit, in this instance, the firm has already identified that the company applies an applicable financial reporting framework, acknowledges its responsibilities and is prepared to confirm this in writing, so this is of less significance to consider prior to tendering in this circumstance.

While the issue of access to working papers might influence the audit approach in the first year and hence impact on budgeting and fee setting, it is not a reason not to tender, so again, less important to consider than items 1 and 2.

58   The correct answer is: A reply from the outgoing auditors stating that they declined to seek reappoinment to the audit of Severn Co due to a disagreement over accounting policies.

A reply from the outgoing auditors stating that they declined to seek reappoinment to the audit of Severn Co due to a disagreement over accounting policies

This would imply a lack of integrity on the part of the director who asserted the firm had not been
re-elected due to familiarity issues. Disagreement over accounting policies suggests the opposite of familiarity risk, which was the reason the company gave the firm for the change in auditors. It also raises the threat of possible future intimidation, if there may be disagreements concerning accounting policy. It is even possible that the company has deliberately asked a relatively small firm to tender in order to have more sway over them.

It is not necessary to have an engagement letter set up prior to acceptance, although this should be dealt with soon after acceptance.

Although the ACCA *Code of Ethics and Conduct* contains a 15% benchmark in relation to fees from one audit client, it recommends safeguards which could be implemented to mitigate the threat, and the firm could actively seek other clients to replace the lost client and hence lower the proportion represented by Severn Co (ACCA *Code of Ethics and Conduct*: para. 410.A3).

Similarly, although the apparent lack of resources in March is an issue, it is an issue that the firm may be able to work around, by negotiating different audit timetables with other clients, or by coming to a different arrangement with Severn Co. It is not a reason to automatically decline.

59   The correct answer is:

	Include in engagement letter	Do not include in engagement letter
Scope of the audit	✔	☐
Responsibilities of management of Severn Co	✔	☐
Timetable for the provision of accounting information by Severn Co	☐	✔
Fees and billing arrangements	☐	✔

The scope of the audit and the responsibilities of Severn Co's management must be included in the engagement letter. The remaining options may be included, but they are not mandatory elements according to ISA 210 (ISA 210).

60   The correct answers are: Before accepting the audit of Severn Co, Rivers & Co should **obtain references concerning the directors**. Once the audit has been accepted, then Rivers & Co should begin to **submit the letter of engagement**.

References concerning the directors should be obtained before the engagement is accepted. The letter of engagement is then submitted after acceptance but before beginning to perform procedures.

BPP
LEARNING
MEDIA

Goofy Co

61 The correct answers are:

Inform the audit committees of both Goofy and Mickey of the potential conflict of interest and obtain their consent to act for both parties

Prevent unauthorised physical access to the information relating to both company audits

The management of both Goofy and Mickey should be informed and their consent obtained.

Separate audit teams should be used including audit partners and independent review partners.

Confidentiality agreements should be signed by NAB & Co's staff, not by the client.

62 The correct answer is:

Threat to independence	Familiarity	Self-interest
(1) Audit engagement partner has been in the position for six years	X	
(2) Audit engagement partner's daughter works for Goofy	X	
(3) Audit engagement partner's daughter's bonus would be in the form of shares		X
(4) 5% bonus offered if audit is completed three weeks earlier than last year		X

The long association of the audit engagement partner with Goofy represents a familiarity threat as she may not maintain professional scepticism and objectivity. Similarly the audit engagement partner's daughter being employed by Goofy is also a familiarity threat, although there would not be a need for additional safeguards as a warehouse manager is unlikely to influence the financial statements.

A self-interest threat arises from the financial interest in Goofy which the audit engagement partner's daughter will receive if she is awarded a bonus. As an immediate family member of the partner this creates an indirect interest in a client which is not permitted by the ACCA (ACCA *Code of Ethics and Conduct:* para. R510.4).

A bonus relating to the audit being completed three weeks earlier than last year creates a self-interest threat, as there is a danger NAB & Co will be less thorough in order to achieve the deadline and not risk losing the client as a result of not meeting it.

63 The correct answer is:

(1) Communicate with Mickey's existing auditors
(2) Perform client screening procedures, including an assessment of Mickey's risk profile
(3) Ensure that the existing auditor's resignation has been properly conducted
(4) Submit an engagement letter to Mickey's management

NAB & Co should contact the existing auditor before accepting nomination, in order to find out whether there are any reasons behind Mickey's decision to change its auditors about which NAB & Co should be aware. Once this is done, client screening must be performed.

Ensuring that the existing auditor's resignation has been properly conducted and issuing an engagement letter are procedures which should be taken after accepting nomination.

64 The correct answer is:

Management's responsibility to prevent and detect fraud

Although management is responsible for the prevention and detection of fraud, this is not one of the matters included in the agreement obtained by the auditors to establish that the preconditions of an audit exist.

65   The correct answer is:

The auditor has the right of access to the books, records and vouchers of the company	**TRUE**	FALSE
The auditor has the right to be heard at general meetings on matters relating to the audit	**TRUE**	FALSE
The auditor is appointed by, and answerable to, those charged with governance of the company	TRUE	**FALSE**
An auditor can be removed by a simple oral resolution in line with the common law	TRUE	**FALSE**

Carlise

66   The correct answer is:

Audit procedures		Interim audit	Final audit
(1)	Update documentation relating to Carlise's accounting systems which has been prepared in prior year audits.	X	
(2)	Obtain third-party confirmations relating to receivables, payables and cash at bank.		X
(3)	Review the directors' assessment of whether Carlise is a going concern. Consider whether the assumptions made by the directors are reasonable and whether it is appropriate to prepare the accounts on the going concern basis.		X
(4)	Perform preliminary analytical procedures in order to identify any major changes in the business or unexpected trends.	X	

Audit procedures performed during an interim audit are likely to include analytical procedures, tests of controls, updating risk assessments and substantive testing of transactions which have occurred during the first part of the year.

When it comes to the final audit a trial balance or draft set of financial statements will be available, so detailed substantive testing of year-end balances will be conducted. This is in addition to completing the tests of controls and substantive procedures started during the interim audit.

67   The correct answer is:

1, 2 and 3

All of the factors should be taken into account.

68   The correct answer is:

Whether the work performed by the internal audit department relates to specific audit assertions over which UYE & Co have concerns

Where the external auditor plans to rely on the work of the internal audit department, they must ensure that the internal auditors' work has been performed to a good standard. However, most important is the requirement that the work performed by the internal audit department must be relevant to the evidence the external auditor is trying to gather.

69   The correct answers are:

	True	False
Carlise's internal auditors would perform audit procedures under the direction, supervision and review of UYE & Co's audit team	✔	
UYE & Co should only use direct assistance if the risk of material misstatement in relation to the online ticket sales system is high		✔
UYE & Co's audit team should document its review of the work performed by Carlise's internal auditors	✔	
Carlise's internal auditors will be separately liable for any material misstatements in the work they have performed		✔

Direct assistance describes the use of internal auditors to perform audit procedures under the direction, supervision and review of the external auditor (ISA 620).

The external auditor should document their review of the work performed by the internal auditors.

The external auditor is likely to be less inclined to use direct assistance where the assessed risk of material misstatement is high, as this increases audit risk. The auditor must take full responsibility for their audit opinion regardless of whether they rely on the work of others.

70   The correct answers are:

	True	False
UYE & Co's policy of assembling files within 60 days of the auditor's report is stricter than what is required by ISAs		✔
It is incompatible with ISAs for even minor further procedures to be added to the audit files after the 60 day period	✔	
It is acceptable to make administrative changes to an audit file after 60 days, so it is not strictly necessary to 'lock' the files to comply with ISAs	✔	
It is acceptable for files to be disposed of after 3 years have passed since the date of the auditor's report		✔

ISA 230 *Audit documentation* requires the assembly of the final audit file within 60 days of the auditor's report, so UYE & Co's policy is in line with this (and is not therefore stricter than required).

Once this time has passed, it is acceptable for changes can be made where they are administrative in nature – but further procedures would not be administrative and would thus not be acceptable. The files do not necessarily have to be 'locked'.

It is not acceptable to dispose of audit files after just 3 years – ISA 230 requires audit files to be kept for 5 years from the date of the auditor's report.

71 Sleeptight

> **Workbook references.** Chapters 6 and 13.
>
> **Top tips.** This 30-mark case study style question contains a mixture of knowledge-based questions and questions requiring application to a long scenario.
>
> Part (a) requires you to recall your knowledge of professional scepticism and judgement. In part (ii), notice that your examples of areas to apply professional judgement should be limited to the planning stage.

BPP
LEARNING
MEDIA

Part (b)(i) worth 16 marks contains a common requirement where you are asked to explain audit risks and then suggest appropriate responses. Audit risks will be related to potential material misstatements of the financial statements and this should be in the forefront of your mind throughout when you are answering this part of the question. When you are explaining your risk you should therefore state how the financial statements are affected.

Responses are the auditor's responses, not management responses. These will therefore be procedures or actions the auditor will carry out to mitigate the risks.

In part (b)(ii) you should have realised that the auditor must attend the inventory count and is required to perform certain procedures specified by ISA 501.

In part (d), although you would assess the reliability of the expert, don't forget there are also other important procedures such as reviewing the disclosures and the revaluation adjustments.

Easy marks. In part (a), easy marks are available for explaining professional scepticism and defining professional judgement.

Marking scheme

			Marks
(a)	(i)	Professional scepticism 1 mark per valid point up to a maximum of	3
	(ii)	Professional judgement 1 mark per valid point up to a maximum of	3
(b)	(i)	Risks and responses 1 mark per well-explained risk (maximum of 8) and 1 mark for each valid response (maximum of 8) up to a total maximum of	16
	(ii)	Inventory count attendance 1 mark per valid point up to a maximum of	4
(c)		Audit procedures for value of property and disclosure Up to 1 mark per procedure to a maximum of	4
		Maximum marks	**30**

(a)   (i)   **Professional scepticism**

Professional scepticism is an attitude that includes having a questioning mind, being alert to conditions which may indicate possible misstatement due to error or fraud, and subjecting audit evidence to a critical assessment rather than just taking it at face value (ISA 200).

It is important that professional scepticism is maintained throughout the audit to reduce the risks of overlooking unusual transactions, of overgeneralising when drawing conclusions, and of using inappropriate assumptions in determining the nature, timing and extent of audit procedures and evaluating the results of them.

Professional scepticism is necessary to the critical assessment of audit evidence. This includes questioning contradictory audit evidence and the reliability of documents and responses from management and those charged with governance.

(ii)   **Professional judgement**

Professional judgement is the application of relevant training, knowledge and experience in making informed decisions about the appropriate courses of action in the circumstances of the audit engagement. The auditor must exercise professional judgement when planning an audit of financial statements (ISA 200).

Professional judgement will be required in many areas when planning. For example, the determination of materiality for the financial statements as a whole and performance materiality levels will require professional judgement.

Professional judgement will also be required when deciding on the nature, timing and extent of audit procedures.

(b) (i)

Audit risk	Auditor's response
The firm has recently been appointed as auditor. There is a lack of cumulative knowledge and understanding of the business, which may result in a failure to identify events and transactions which impact on the financial statements. Furthermore, opening balances may be misstated.	Adopt procedures to ensure opening balances are properly brought forward and corresponding amounts are correctly classified and disclosed. Review previous auditor's working papers and consider performing additional substantive procedures on opening balances.
The directors only work part time at Sleeptight and there is no finance director. This may promote a weak control environment, resulting in undetected errors or frauds.	The controls will need to be documented and evaluated. If these are weak the level of substantive testing will need to be increased accordingly.
The requirement for customers to pay 40% on ordering and the remainder following delivery could result in revenue recorded before it should be, if the deposit is recorded as a sale and not deferred until delivery. This would result in revenue being overstated. Alternatively, revenue could be understated if the final payment were only recognised when it is received, rather than on delivery of the bed.	Enquire of management the point at which revenue is actually recognised, and review the system of accounting for deposits to ensure they are not included in revenue until goods are delivered and signed for. For a sample of transactions within eight weeks of the year end, ensure the revenue recorded is only in respect of beds delivered to customers in the same period and ensure they have been signed for.
The two-year guarantee on the beds gives rise to a provision, the measurement of which involves a high degree of judgement, and therefore carries a risk of misstatement. This risk is increased by the fact the loan covenants are profit related and there is an incentive to manipulate areas of the financial statements based on judgements.	Establish the basis of the amount provided for and assumptions made by the financial controller. Reperform any calculations and establish the level of warranty costs in the year, and compare with the previous provision. Review the level of repair costs incurred post year end and use these to assess the reasonableness of the provision.
Contractors are required to invoice at the end of each month but often there is a delay in receiving these. There is therefore a risk the company will not accrue for costs, resulting in incomplete liabilities and understatement of expenses.	Review invoices and payments to contractors after the year end and, if they relate to work undertaken before the year end, ensure they are included as accruals.
The current year raw materials costs for materials also in inventory last year are based on prices at least a year old. They should be based on the actual cost or reasonable average cost. Given that prices fluctuate the value of year-end raw materials may be over- or undervalued due to price rises/decreases occurring during the year.	For a sample of materials to include the cost of wood, compare material costs to actual prices on invoices. Investigate and resolve any significant differences and evaluate the potential impact on the inventory value in the financial statements.

Audit risk	Auditor's response
The finished goods value is to be estimated by Anna Jones, who appears to be basing her estimate on order value rather than applying the IAS 2 rule that goods should be valued at the lower of cost and net realisable value (NRV) (IAS 2). This could result in inventory being overstated in the financial statements.	For beds awaiting dispatch, establish the lower of cost and NRV and compare with the figures provided by Anna Jones. Investigate any differences and evaluate the potential impact on the inventory value in the financial statements.
The new workshop is undergoing refurbishment that could result in inappropriate treatment of capital or non-capital items, potentially misstating non-current assets, or repair costs in the statement of profit or loss. Again, this risk is increased by the fact the loan covenants are profit related and there is an incentive to manipulate areas of the financial statements based on judgements.	Obtain a breakdown of the related costs and establish which are included as non-current assets and which are treated as repair costs. Review the nature of items included in non-current assets to ensure only capital items are included and review repairs to ensure no capital items are included.
The new premises purchase was funded by a bank loan which may not be classified correctly between current and non-current liabilities, or may not be properly presented or disclosed as required by IFRSs.	Reperform the calculation of the split between current and non-current liabilities and ensure the loan is properly presented and terms are disclosed as required by IFRSs.
There is a risk the company may fail to comply with the loan covenants, resulting in the loan being recalled. This could then possibly lead to going concern issues.	Obtain and review (or reperform) covenant calculations to identify any breaches. If there are any, the likelihood of the bank demanding repayment will need to be assessed, along with the potential impact on the company. The need to avoid breaching the covenants reinforces the audit team's need to maintain professional scepticism in areas that could be manipulated.

Note. Only 8 risks and 8 related responses were needed to gain 16 marks.

(ii)   ISA 501 *Audit Evidence – Specific Considerations for Selected Items* sets out the responsibilities of auditors in relation to the physical inventory count. It states that where inventory is material, auditors shall obtain sufficient appropriate audit evidence regarding its existence and condition by attending the physical inventory count (ISA 501).

At the count attendance, Mills & Co will need to evaluate management's instructions and procedures for recording and controlling the result of the physical inventory count.

It must also observe the performance of the count procedures to assess whether they are properly carried out.

In addition, Mills & Co should inspect the inventory to verify that it exists and look for evidence of damaged or obsolete inventory. It will also perform test counts to assess the accuracy of the counts carried out by the company.

Mills & Co is also required by ISA 501 to perform audit procedures over the entity's final inventory records to determine whether they accurately reflect the count results (ISA 501).

(c)   Procedures in relation to property valuation and related disclosures

Obtain a copy of the valuer's report and consider the reliability of the valuation after taking account of:

- The basis of valuation
- Independence/objectivity
- Qualifications
- Experience
- Reputation of the valuer

Compare the valuation with the value of other similar properties in the locality and investigate any significant difference.

Reperform the calculation of the revaluation adjustments and ensure the correct accounting treatment has been applied.

Inspect notes to the financial statements to ensure appropriate disclosures have been made in accordance with IFRSs.

72 Recorder

Workbook references. Chapters 3, 6, 7 and 17.

Top tips. This question is packed with several requirements, both scenario based and knowledge based. In part (b), you must link your answer to audit risk in order to score marks. Be as specific as possible in describing the impact each fact would have on the financial statements and on the audit. Likewise, when describing auditors' responses, be as specific as possible: whenever you can, use the audit procedures that you would have memorised using the 'AEIOU' mnemonic.

Easy marks. You should have found part (d) straightforward.

Examining team's comments. As in previous exam sittings, in part (b) some candidates tended to only identify facts from the scenario such as 'Recorder purchases goods from a supplier in South Asia and the goods are in transit for two weeks' but failed to describe how this could impact audit risk; this would only have scored half marks. To gain one mark the point needed to be developed to also explain that this could result in issues over the completeness of inventory.

More so than in previous exam sittings, candidates disappointingly provided business risks rather than audit risks with answers such as stock-outs due to the two-week transit period and possible damage to inventory during transit. As a result these candidates then provided responses related to how management should address these business risks rather than how the auditor should respond. This meant that out of a potential two marks per point, candidates would only score half marks for the identification of the issue from the scenario.

Additionally, many candidates performed poorly with regards to the auditor's responses. Many candidates gave business advice, such as changing the salespeople's bonus structure, or provided vague responses such as perform detailed substantive testing or maintain professional scepticism. Responses which start with 'ensure that...' are unlikely to score marks as they usually fail to explain exactly how the auditor will address the audit risk. Audit responses need to be practical and should relate to the approach (ie what testing) the auditor will adopt to assess whether the balance is materially misstated or not.

Part (c) for three marks required substantive procedures for confirming the directors' bonus payment made during the year. Candidates' performance was disappointing.

Unfortunately, many candidates focused on the authorisation of the bonus; this is not a substantive procedure and would not have scored any marks. A significant minority thought that the directors' bonus was based on sales which was not the case. The scenario stated that salespeople's bonuses were based on sales, hence candidates either confused these two items or failed to read the scenario properly. They then looked to recalculate the bonus based on sales levels which was not appropriate in the circumstances.

A number of vague procedures were suggested such as obtaining written representations or reading board minutes without explaining what for. Analytical procedures were suggested; however, they were unlikely to be valid procedures as bonuses by their very nature tend to vary each year.

Marking scheme

		Marks

(a)   Up to 1 mark per well-described risk and up to 1 mark for each well-explained response. Overall maximum of 5 marks for risks and 5 marks for responses.

New client leading to increased detection risk
Cut-off of goods in transit
Continuous (perpetual) inventory counts
Sales cut-off
Overstatement of receivables
Valuation of land and buildings
Directors' bonus remuneration   10

(b)   Up to 1 mark per well-explained procedure.
Attend one of the continuous (perpetual) inventory counts to review whether the controls are adequate
Review the schedule of counts to confirm completeness of all inventory lines
Review the adjustments made to the inventory records to gain an understanding of the level of differences arising
If significant differences, discuss with management how they will ensure that year-end inventory will not be under- or overstated
Attend the inventory count at the year end to undertake test counts to confirm the completeness and existence of inventory   3

(c)   Up to 1 mark per well-described procedure.
Cast schedule of directors' remuneration including the bonus paid
Agree the individual bonus payments to the payroll records
Confirm the amount of each bonus paid by agreeing to the cash book and bank statements
Review the board minutes to confirm whether any additional bonus payments relating to this year have been agreed
Obtain written representation from management
Review disclosures and assess whether these are in compliance with local   3
legislation

(d)   Corporate governance weakness and recommendations (2 issues required)
Executive director is main point of contact with external auditor – audit committee must be non-exec
Audit committee only has one member – should be at least two
Audit committee has no written terms of reference
Amber is responsible for signing off financial statements and for audit   <u>4</u>
committee

<u><u>20</u></u>

ANSWERS

(a) Auditrisks and auditor's response to each risk

Audit risk	Auditor's response
Increased **detection risk** due to the fact that Recorder is a new client.	Ensure that the audit team is made up of suitably **experienced staff**. Ensure that **sufficient time** is allocated to obtain an understanding of Recorder's business and assess the entity's risks of material misstatement.
Increased risk of material misstatement around **cut-off of inventory, purchases and payables** as a result of purchased goods taking two weeks to arrive at the company's central warehouse.	Perform detailed cut-off testing of goods in transit around the year end to ensure that cut-off has been correctly applied.
Increased risk of material misstatement related to the **completeness, existence and valuation of inventory** under the perpetual inventory system, if all inventory is not counted at least once a year.	Review the inventory count instructions and perform audit procedures to determine whether all inventory is counted at least once a year. Assess the adequacy of internal controls around inventory records to determine whether the inventory records can be relied upon.
Increased risk of material misstatements due to **sales cut-off**, as a result of the sales-based bonus scheme encouraging sales staff to maximise their current year bonus.	Increase sales cut-off testing, and perform additional audit procedures on post year end cancellations to identify cut-off errors.
Increased risk of **overvaluation of receivables**, highlighted by the considerable increase in the receivables balance compared to the prior year, and concerns about the creditworthiness of some customers.	Perform extended testing of post year end cash payments and review the aged receivables ledger. Consider the adequacy of the allowance for receivables.
Risk of material misstatements relating to the **valuation of land and buildings**, if recent revaluations do not comply with IAS 16 *Property, Plant and Equipment*.	Obtain an understanding of the revaluation process through discussions with management, and review the process for compliance with IAS 16. Review the disclosures of the revaluation in the financial statements for compliance with IAS 16.
Non-compliance with local legislation concerning the **disclosure of directors' remuneration**, currently included within wages and salaries.	Discuss the matter with management. Review disclosures required by local legislation in the financial statements to gain assurance over compliance.

(b) Audit procedures where continuous (perpetual) counts for year-end inventory is used

(i) Agree the total on the inventory listing to the continuous inventory records, using computer-assisted audit techniques (CAATs), to check for accuracy

(ii) Attend at least one of the continuous inventory counts: observe the count and review the inventory count instructions to confirm that the procedures are as rigorous as those for a year-end inventory count.

(iii) Review the schedule of counts undertaken/to be undertaken during the year to confirm whether all inventory lines have been counted (or are due to be counted).

(iv) Review corrections to the inventory records to determine the amount of corrections made and the reason for the corrections. Confirm whether the corrections have been authorised by a manager.

(v) Where significant differences arise, enquire of management the actions they will take to ensure that the valuation of inventory is accurate.

(c) **Substantive procedures for directors' bonus payments**

(i) Cast the addition of the schedule of director's bonus payments and ensure the totals are in agreement with the disclosure in the financial statements.

(ii) Compare the bonuses with both the previous year's bonuses and expectations, taking into account the knowledge obtained during the audit (for example, whether the performance targets, if any, have been met).

(iii) Agree the bonus payments to payroll records for the individual directors and agree the amounts paid on the bank statements to the payroll records.

(iv) Review board meeting minutes and meetings of any remuneration committee for evidence of any bonuses not disclosed.

(v) Review the cash book for any unusual transactions which suggest undisclosed directors' emoluments.

(vi) Review the disclosure of directors' bonuses and consider whether they are in accordance with applicable accounting standards and local legislation.

(d) **Corporate governance deficiencies**

Deficiency	Recommendation
Amber Coleman, the finance director and an executive director, is the main point of contact with the auditor. An executive director should not be the main point of contact – this is properly the role of the audit committee.	An independent audit committee should be established, made up of non-executive directors. Amber Coleman could only continue as a member of the audit committee if she stepped down from her role as an executive director.
The audit committee has only one member.	The audit committee must have three members, or two in the case of small companies. Since Recorder is complying with the UK Corporate Governance Code voluntarily, it is likely that an audit committee of two members would be sufficient.
The audit committee (Amber) does not appear to have any official written terms of reference.	The audit committee must be established with clear written terms of reference from the Board.
Amber is responsible for signing off the financial statements, and yet is part of the audit committee. Part of the audit committee's role is to monitor the integrity of the financial statements – Amber would not be able to do this when she herself is responsible for their preparation,	Two further non-executive directors should be appointed to the audit committee – Amber cannot be on the audit committee and retain responsibility for the financial statements. If Amber stands down from the committee, then at least one of these non-executives would need to have financial reporting knowledge and experience.

73 Walters

Marking scheme

			Marks
(a)	(i)	½ mark per ratio calculation per year.	
		Operating margin	
		Inventory holding period	
		Payables payment period	
		Current ratio	
		Quick ratio	3
	(ii)	Up to 1 mark per well-explained audit risk, maximum of 6 marks for risks and up to 1 mark per audit response, maximum of 6 marks for responses.	
		Management manipulation of results	
		Sales cut-off	
		Revenue growth	
		Misclassification of costs between cost of sales and operating	
		Inventory valuation	
		Receivables valuation	
		Going concern risk	12
(b)		1 mark per well-explained point – if the procedure does not clearly explain how this will help the auditor to consider going concern then a ½ mark only should be awarded.	
		Review cash flow forecasts	
		Review bank agreements, breach of key ratios	
		Review post year end sales and order book	
		Review supplier's correspondence	
		Inquire of lawyers for any litigation	
		Subsequent events	
		Board minutes	
		Management accounts	
		Consider additional disclosures under IAS 1	
		Written representation	5
			20

(a)   (i)   Additional ratios

		20X4	20X3
Operating margin	PBT/Revenue	4.5/23 = 19.6%	4/18 = 22.2%
Inventory holding period	Inventories/COS × 365 days	2.1/11 × 365 = 70 days	1.6/10 × 365 = 58 days
Payables payment period	Payables/COS × 365 days	1.6/11 × 365 = 53 days	1.2/10 × 365 = 44 days
Current ratio	Current assets/Current liabilities	6.6/2.5 = 2.6	6.9/1.2 = 5.8
Quick ratio	(Current assets – inventories)/Current liabilities	(6.6 – 2.1)/2.5 = 1.8	(6.9 – 1.6)/1.2 = 4.4

(*Note.* Only three ratios were required.)

(ii)   Audit risks and responses

Audit risk	Audit response
Management were disappointed with the 20X3 results and are under pressure to improve the trading results in 20X4. There is a risk that management have a greater incentive to manipulate the results by adopting a more aggressive approach in relation to accounting estimates (ie provisions).	The audit team will need to remain alert to the risk of creative accounting throughout the audit. It is important that they exercise professional scepticism and evaluate any assumptions made by management in auditing accounting estimates. Current year balances should be compared to the prior year to highlight any unusual trends.
A generous sales-related bonus scheme has been introduced for the company's salespeople. This increases the risk of misstatements arising from sales cut-off as the sales staff seek to maximise their bonus.	Increased sales cut-off testing will be required. Post year end sales returns should be reviewed, as they may provide evidence of incorrect cut-off.
Revenue has grown by 28%, while cost of sales has only increased by 10%. The gross profit margin has increased significantly. Although the bonus scheme and the advertising campaign may explain the growth in revenue, the fact that the cost of sales has seen a corresponding increase needs to be investigated.	Inquiries should be made of management regarding the reason why cost of sales has not increased in line with sales. Substantive procedures should be performed on an increased sample of costs, with an aim to identify any costs omitted or misclassified.

Audit risk	Audit response
Although the gross margin has increased from 44.4% to 52.2%, the operating margin has decreased from 22.2% to 19.6%. This trend is unusual. While the bonus scheme and advertising campaign could account for some of the increase in operating expenses, there is a possibility that costs may have been misclassified from cost of sales to operating expenses.	The classification of costs between cost of sales and operating expenses will be compared with the prior year to ensure consistency. A detailed breakdown of operating expenses and cost of sales should be reviewed for evidence of misclassification. The main components of costs of sales and operating expenses should be identified and compared to the prior year. Any unusual trends (for example, significant costs in the prior year not present in the current year, and vice versa) should be discussed with management.
The inventory valuation policy has been changed, with additional overheads to be included within inventory. The inventory holding period has increased from 58 to 70 days. There is a risk that inventory is overvalued.	The change in the inventory valuation policy should be discussed with management. The additional overheads included should be reviewed, to confirm that they are related to production. Detailed cost and net realisable value testing should be performed and the aged inventory report should be reviewed to assess whether a write down is required.
The receivables collection period has increased from 61 to 71 days and management have extended the credit period given to customers. This leads to an increased risk of unrecoverable receivables.	Extended post year end cash receipts testing and a review of the aged receivables ledger should be performed to assess the need for any write-offs or provision.
The current ratio and quick ratio have both decreased significantly. In addition, the company's positive cash balance of $2.3m in 20X3 has become an overdraft of $0.9m. Taken together with the growth in revenue and the increase in operating expenses, this may indicate overtrading. A going concern risk should be considered.	Detailed going concern testing to be performed during the audit. Cash flow forecasts covering at least 12 months from the year end should be reviewed, and the assumptions discussed with management.

(b)   Going concern procedures

(i)   Obtain Walters' cash flow forecast and review the cash payments and receipts. Assess the assumptions for reasonableness and discuss the findings with management to understand if the company will have sufficient cash flows.

(ii)   Review any current agreements with the bank to determine whether any covenants in relation to the overdraft have been breached.

(iii)   Read minutes of the meetings of shareholders, the board of directors and important committees for reference to financing difficulties and for evidence of any future financing plans.

(iv)   Review the company's post year end sales and order book to assess the levels of trade. Evaluate whether the revenue figures in the cash flow forecast are reasonable.

(v)   Review post year end correspondence with suppliers to identify any restriction in credit that may not be reflected in the cash flow forecasts.

(vi)   Inquire of the lawyers of Walters as to the existence of litigation and claims.

(vii)   Perform audit tests in relation to subsequent events to identify any items that might indicate or mitigate the risk of going concern not being appropriate.

(viii)   Review post year end management accounts to assess if it is in line with cash flow forecast.

(ix)   Consider whether any additional disclosures as required by IAS 1 *Presentation of Financial Statements* in relation to material uncertainties over going concern should be made in the financial statements.

(x)   Confirm the existence, legality and enforceability of arrangements to provide or maintain financial support with related and third parties and assess the financial ability of such parties to provide additional funds.

(xi)   Consider Walters' position concerning any unfulfilled customer orders.

(xii)   Obtain a written representation confirming the director's view that Walters is a going concern.

Note. Only five procedures were required.

74 Sycamore

Workbook references. Chapters 1 and 6.

Top tips. In part (b), make sure that you explain both the audit risk and the auditor's response to the risk. Make sure that you discuss audit risks – the risks which have an impact on the financial statements – only. Talking about business risks in general will not get you marks!

Easy marks. Parts (a) and (c) both offer easy marks. If you know the material well, you should score good marks there.

Marking scheme

Marks

(a)   Up to 1 mark per point.

- Per ISA 240 – obtain reasonable assurance that the financial statements are free from material misstatement, whether caused by fraud or error
- Identify and assess the risks of material misstatement due to fraud
- Obtain sufficient appropriate audit evidence
- Respond appropriately to fraud or suspected fraud identified during the audit
- Maintain professional scepticism throughout the audit
- Discussion within the engagement team   4

(b)   Up to 1 mark per well described risk and up to 1 mark for each well-explained response. Overall max of 6 marks for risks and 6 marks for responses.
- Fraud of previous finance director
- Competence of new finance director
- Treatment of capitalised development expenditure
- New loan finance obtained
- Completeness of finance costs
- Loan covenants
- Post year end sales returns
- Goods in and out during the inventory count
- Profit on disposal of plant and equipment   12

BPP
LEARNING
MEDIA

(c)   (i)   Up to 1 mark per well-explained valid point.
- Description of review engagements
- Difference to external audit

2

(ii)   Up to 1 mark per well-described valid point.
- Level of assurance of external audit
- Level of assurance of review engagements

2
___
20
___

(a) **Fraud responsibility**

Maple & Co must conduct an audit in accordance with ISA 240 *The Auditor's Responsibilities Relating to Fraud in an Audit of Financial Statements* and is responsible for obtaining reasonable assurance that the financial statements taken as a whole are free from material misstatement, whether caused by fraud or error (ISA 240).

In order to fulfil this responsibility, Maple & Co is required to identify and assess the risks of material misstatement of the financial statements due to fraud (ISA 240).

It needs to obtain sufficient appropriate audit evidence regarding the assessed risks of material misstatement due to fraud, through designing and implementing appropriate responses. In addition, Maple & Co must respond appropriately to fraud or suspected fraud identified during the audit (ISA 240).

When obtaining reasonable assurance, Maple & Co is responsible for maintaining professional scepticism throughout the audit, considering the potential for management override of controls and recognising the fact that audit procedures which are effective in detecting error may not be effective in detecting fraud (ISA 240).

To ensure that the whole engagement team is aware of the risks and responsibilities for fraud and error, ISAs require that a discussion is held within the team. For members not present at the meeting, Sycamore's audit engagement partner should determine which matters are to be communicated to them (ISA 240).

(b) **Audit risks and auditors' responses**

Audit risk	Auditor's response
Sycamore's previous finance director left in December after it was discovered that he had been committing fraud with regards to expenses claimed. There is a risk that he may have undertaken other fraudulent transactions; these would need to be written off in the statement of profit or loss. If these have not been uncovered, the financial statements could include errors.	Discuss with the new finance director what procedures they have adopted to identify any further frauds by the previous finance director. In addition, the team should maintain their professional scepticism and be alert to the risk of further fraud and errors.
The new finance director was appointed in January 20X5 and was previously a financial controller of a bank. Sycamore is a pharmaceutical company which is very different to a bank; there is a risk that the new finance director is not sufficiently competent to prepare the financial statements, leading to errors.	During the audit, careful attention should be applied to any changes in accounting policies and in particular any key judgemental decisions made by the finance director.

Audit risk	Auditor's response
During the year, Sycamore has spent $1.8 million on developing new products; these are at different stages and the total amount has been capitalised as an intangible asset However, in order to be capitalised it must meet all of the criteria under IAS 38 *Intangible Assets*. There is a risk that some projects may not reach final development stage and hence should be expensed rather than capitalised. Intangible assets and profit could be overstated.	A breakdown of the development expenditure should be reviewed and tested in detail to ensure that only projects which meet the capitalisation criteria are included as an intangible asset, with the balance being expensed.
Sycamore has borrowed $2.0 million from the bank via a 10-year loan. This loan needs to be correctly split between current and non-current liabilities in order to ensure correct disclosure. Also, as the level of debt has increased, there should be additional finance costs. There is a risk that this has been omitted from the statement of profit or loss, leading to understated finance costs and overstated profit.	During the audit, the team would need to confirm that the $2 million loan finance was received. In addition, the split between current and non-current liabilities and the disclosures for this loan should be reviewed in detail to ensure compliance with relevant accounting standards. The finance costs should be recalculated and any increase agreed to the loan documentation, for confirmation of interest rates, and to cash book and bank statements to confirm the amount was paid and is not therefore a year-end payable.
The loan has a minimum profit target covenant. If this is breached, the loan would be instantly repayable and would be classified as a current liability.	Review the covenant calculations prepared by Sycamore and identify whether any defaults have occurred; if so, determine the effect on the company.
If the company does not have sufficient cash flow to meet this loan repayment, then there could be going concern implications. In addition, there is a risk of manipulation of profit to ensure that covenants are met.	The team should maintain their professional scepticism and be alert to the risk that profit has been overstated to ensure compliance with the covenant.
There have been a significant number of sales returns made subsequent to the year end. As these relate to pre year end sales, they should be removed from revenue in the draft financial statements and the inventory reinstated. If the sales returns have not been correctly recorded, then revenue will be overstated and inventory understated.	Review a sample of the post year end sales returns and confirm if they relate to pre year end sales that were recognised in revenue, that the revenue has been reversed and the inventory included in the year-end ledgers. In addition, the reason for the increased level of returns should be discussed with management. This will help to assess if there are underlying issues with the net realisable value of inventory.
During Sycamore's year-end inventory count there were movements of goods in and out. If these goods in transit were not carefully controlled, then goods could have been omitted or counted twice. This would result in inventory being under- or overstated.	During the final audit, the goods received notes and goods dispatched notes received during the inventory count should be reviewed and followed through into the inventory count records as correctly included or not.

Audit risk	Auditor's response
Surplus plant and equipment was sold during the year, resulting in a profit on disposal of $210,000. As there is a minimum profit loan covenant, there is a risk that this profit on disposal may not have been correctly calculated, resulting in overstated profits.	Recalculate the profit and loss on disposal calculations and agree all items to supporting documentation.
In addition, significant profits or losses on disposal are an indication that the depreciation policy of plant and equipment may not be appropriate. Therefore depreciation may be overstated.	Discuss the depreciation policy for plant and equipment with the finance director to assess its reasonableness.

(c) (i) Review engagements

Review engagements are often undertaken as an alternative to an audit, and involve a practitioner reviewing financial data, such as six-monthly figures. This would involve the practitioner undertaking procedures to state whether anything has come to their attention which causes the practitioner to believe that the financial data is not in accordance with the financial reporting framework.

A review engagement differs to an external audit in that the procedures undertaken are not nearly as comprehensive as those in an audit, with procedures such as analytical review and enquiry used extensively. In addition, the practitioner does not need to comply with ISAs as these only relate to external audits.

(ii) Levels of assurance

The level of assurance provided by audit and review engagements is as follows (ISAE 3000):

External audit – A high but not absolute level of assurance is provided; this is known as reasonable assurance. This provides comfort that the financial statements present fairly in all material respects (or are true and fair) and are free of material misstatements.

Review engagements – Where an opinion is being provided, the practitioner gathers sufficient evidence to be satisfied that the subject matter is plausible; in this case limited assurance is given whereby the practitioner confirms that nothing has come to their attention which indicates that the subject matter contains material misstatements.

75 Smoothbrush

Workbook references. Chapters 6, 13 and 17.

Top tips. Maintaining focus is essential on a long 30-mark question such as this one. A common theme throughout this question is the risk of answering the question you hoped would come up, rather than the question actually being asked.

In part (a), just because you see the words 'audit risks' it doesn't mean you should straight away start describing the audit risk model. You are asked to **describe the audit risk and the auditor's response to the risk** (two mini-requirements) for the actual audit client described in the question. Therefore you need to work methodically through the scenario, pick out a five risks and explain each of them and give an auditor's response to gain as many of the ten marks as you can.

For example, new systems such as the new inventory system in the scenario always carry the risk they may have not been properly implemented and could impact on year end inventory balances. Limit your answer to audit risks only; that is, only those that relate to the audit of the financial statements. Then describe what the auditor would do in response to this (for example, review the method used to transfer information between the two systems and the level of errors found).

Part (b) is a discussion question. You should know why assessing risks at the planning stage is important, in order to focus audit work on important areas and help ensure the audit is performed efficiently and effectively.

Part (c) has two mini-requirements: first to list and secondly to explain suitable controls. Make sure you do both. Also limit your answer to controls over the assertions specified in the question. Commit to memory the fact you want controls over completeness and accuracy only, otherwise you may find yourself listing and explaining controls over all assertions, many of which will be gaining no marks.

In part (d), even though you have just answered a question on controls, you need to switch your mindset to substantive procedures, and be careful not to mix these up with tests of control. Also, you are now looking at valuation of inventory only in part (i), so substantive tests will be concentrated on looking at the different aspects of valuation. Inventory is valued at the lower of cost and NRV, so you need to make sure NRV is above cost by reviewing post year end sales and test that unit costs are in agreement with supporting documents such as purchase invoices. You also need to ensure any damaged items are correctly valued. These thought processes should help you identify appropriate tests. Part (ii) focuses on provisions/contingent liabilities and a different assertion, completeness. You should have picked up on the possible need for a provision as a result of the FD's dismissal and suggested specific procedures in respect of this matter.

Easy marks. Part (b) is a relatively straightforward requirement that does not require application to the scenario. A good knowledge of the importance of risk assessment will enable you to gain the majority of the marks on this part. In part (d) you should be familiar with the standard tests over valuation of inventory.

Examining team's comments. Many candidates performed inadequately on part (a) of the question. Audit risk is a key element of the Audit and Assurance syllabus and candidates must understand audit risk. A number of candidates wasted valuable time by describing the audit risk model. This generated no marks as it was not part of the requirement. Candidates are reminded that they must answer the question asked as opposed to the one they wish had been asked. The main area where candidates lost marks is that they did not actually understand what audit risk relates to. Hence they provided answers which considered the risks the business would face, or 'business risks', which are outside the scope of the syllabus.

Part (b) for four marks required a discussion of the importance of assessing risk at the planning stage of an audit. This was well answered by the majority of candidates, with many identifying that assessing risk would lead to an effective audit with the focus of testing being on high risk areas only.

Part (c) for ten marks required an identification and explanation of controls over the continuous/perpetual inventory counting system in order to ensure completeness and accuracy of the inventory records. This question proved to be challenging for a number of candidates and there were some unsatisfactory answers. Many identified controls, such as 'the inventory team should be independent of the warehouse staff', but then failed to explain these controls; this would have restricted their marks to ½ mark per control as opposed to the 1½ marks available for an identification and explanation.

Part (d) for six marks required three substantive procedures each to confirm the valuation of inventory and the completeness of provisions or contingent liabilities. Performance was mixed for this question; candidates were generally able to provide adequate substantive procedures for provisions or contingent liabilities. The requirement to consider valuation of inventory, a topic which is regularly examined, was on the whole inadequately answered. Candidates seemed to ignore the requirement to consider valuation and often structured their answers with headings such as existence or rights and obligations. Clearly many failed to read the question properly.

(a)   Up to 1 mark per well-described risk and up to 1 mark for each well-explained response. Overall maximum of 5 marks for risks and 5 marks for responses.
- Extended credit terms to Homewares
- NRV of inventory
- Valuation of redundant plant and equipment
- Cut-off
- New system
- Inventory provision
- Provision/contingent liability
        10

(b)   Up to 1 mark per valid point.
- ISA 315 requirement (½ mark only for ISA ref)
- Early identification of material errors
- Understand entity
- Identification of unusual transactions/balances
- Develop strategy
- Efficient audit
- Most appropriate team
- Reduce risk incorrect opinion
- Understanding fraud, money laundering
- Assess risk going concern
        4

(c)   ½ mark for each identification of a control and up to 1 mark per well-explained description of the control.
- Team independent of warehouse
- Timetable of counts
- Inventory movements stopped
- No pre-printed quantities on count sheets
- Second independent team
- Direction of counting floor to records
- Damaged/obsolete goods to specific area
- Records updated by authorised person
        10

(d)   Up to 1 mark per substantive procedure.
   (i)   Inventory:
- Cost to purchase invoice
- NRV to sales invoice
- Manufactured items to invoices/time sheets/production overheads
- Review aged inventory reports
- Compare aged items to 1% provision
- Total level of adjustment over year
- Follow up items noted at inventory count
- Inventory holding period
- Gross margin
        Max 3

(ii) Provisions:
- Discuss with management
- Review correspondence with FD
- Write to lawyers
- Review board minutes
- Obtain written representation

Marks awarded for tests for additional provisions and contingent liabilities

Total marks

(a) **Audit risk and auditor's response**

Audit risk	Auditor's response
In order to win the Homewares contract Smoothbrush has extended their credit period from one month to four months which may result in cash flow problems which could impact Smoothbrush's going concern status.	Review cash flow forecasts to determine how Smoothbrush is intending to finance the increased level of working capital. Review any overdraft limits in place to determine whether limits will be breached and discuss with directors whether they have any alternative sources of funding available to them. Review any bank correspondence relating to the above matters.
The selling prices of goods sold to Homewares are heavily discounted and this may mean that inventory is overstated if the net realisable value of goods has fallen below their cost.	Obtain a breakdown of the cost of a range of inventory items from the Production Director and compare these to the sales prices achieved for such items to determine whether the selling price is above cost.
Smoothbrush has a large amount of old, redundant plant and equipment which is no longer used. It is possible that the recoverable amount (scrap value) of such items is below their carrying amount and the assets are impaired, leading to an overstatement of plant and equipment in the financial statements.	Obtain a breakdown of the carrying amount and estimated scrap value of the redundant plant and equipment. Where an item appears to be impaired (because the scrap value is less than the carrying amount) discuss the asset's valuation with the directors and request that the carrying amount be adjusted accordingly.
Smoothbrush records its inventory when received for goods imported from South Asia but the fact that paint can be in transit for up to two months means it is possible that the purchase, payable and inventory are not recognised at the same time. This may mean that the cut-off of purchases, payables and inventory may be inaccurate leading to an over or understated of purchases, payables and inventory depending on when each part of the transaction is recognised.	Review the agreement with the South Asia importer to determine when title of the goods being shipped passes to Smoothbrush. Extend the amount of cut-off testing performed at the year end in relation to imported goods.

Audit risk	Auditor's response
During the year Smoothbrush introduced a continuous/perpetual inventory counting system and this will provide the year end inventory quantities. Any errors in the implementation or operation of the new system could lead to inaccurate information in the year end inventory quantity which may cause the inventory balance in the financial statements to be materially misstated.	Document the new system and review the results of the periodic counting to determine the level of errors experienced in the new system in order to conclude whether is operating effectively. Attend a sample of the periodic counts to determine whether they are being carried out in a reliable way.
Previously Smoothbrush maintained an inventory provision of 1% however there is no such provision this year. There is a risk that inventory is overvalued if there are items of slow moving inventory which are no longer provided against.	Obtain a schedule of the inventory items which were provided for in the prior year and discuss with directors whether any of these items are still held at the year end and why no provision has been made. Calculate inventory holding period for each major inventory line and discuss the saleability of any slow moving lines with directors.
The company's finance director intends to sue Smoothbrush for unfair dismissal following his pre-year end departure. Smoothbrush does not intend to make any provision/disclosures in respect of this. There is a risk that provisions in the financial statements are understated or that a contingent liability disclosure has been omitted.	Review any legal correspondence from the finance director to obtain an understanding of the claim and also any correspondence from Smoothbrush' lawyer to determine their opinion on the likely outcome of the matter. Review the cash book post year end to determine whether any payments are made to the finance director.

> **Top tip.** There are other audit risks you could have described and provided an auditor's response for, such as the risk arising from a potential lack of information/personnel following the finance director's dismissal, but only five were needed to gain full marks.

(b) **Importance of assessing risks at the planning stage**

ISA 315 *Identifying and Assessing the Risks of Material Misstatement Through Understanding the Entity and its Environment* says that the auditor 'shall identify and assess the risks of material misstatement at the financial statement level and at the assertion level for classes of transactions and related disclosures, and account balances and related disclosures'. (ISA 315)

It is very important that auditors carry out this risk assessment at the planning stage because:

- It helps the auditor gain an understanding of the entity for audit purposes

- It helps the auditor focus on the most important areas of the financial statements (where material misstatements are more likely), therefore increasing efficiency

- The risk assessment will form the basis of the audit strategy and the more detailed audit plan

- Once the risks have been assessed, audit team members of sufficient skill and experience can be allocated to maximise the chance of those risks being addressed

> **Top tip.** Other valid points could have been made here, such as risk assessment as aiding in assessing going concern and the assessment of fraud risks. However, stating the ISA 315 requirement along with four valid points relating to the importance of risk assessment would have gained full marks on this question.

(c) Controls over inventory system: Completeness and accuracy

Suitable controls	Explanation
An inventory count team independent of the warehouse team is used.	There should be segregation of duties between those who have day to day responsibility for inventory and those who are checking it to help prevent fraud and error. The current team including a member of warehouse staff is inadequate and two internal auditors should be used if possible.
Pre-printed inventory sheets are used stating code/descriptions, but without quantities.	Using sheets with quantities already filled in means counters could potentially agree the current quantities to avoid counting and save time. The lack of quantities forces a count to be undertaken in each case.
Damaged/obsolete goods are moved to a designated area for inspection, but left on the sheets. They are provided against if necessary.	Rather than removing damaged/obsolete items from the sheet (and losing the audit trail), they should be written down or provided against to ensure that they are included at the lower of cost and NRV. A member of the finance team should make the assessment as to what needs writing down.
Movements of inventory are not allowed into or out of the area being counted during inventory counts.	Allowing movements in and out of inventory during counts could result in double counting, or inventory not being counted at all. Therefore such movements should be stopped during the count.
A sample of independent checks of the counts is carried out by a separate team. Items to be checked are determined after the first count has been completed.	Counting a sample of inventory lines should again help to ensure completeness and accuracy of the counts, and act as an incentive for the first team to carry out counts more accurately initially.
As a separate exercise after the counts of items on the sheets, teams check that a sample of items which are physically present are correctly included on the sheets.	A count performed from the records to the warehouse will only test for existence or overstatement of inventory line quantities. Testing for completeness requires a different approach where inventory in the warehouse is compared to the records to identify goods physically present but not recorded.
Inventory count sheets are compared to the inventory records after the count. Where adjustments are needed, the reason for them is investigated and they are processed on a timely basis by appropriate personnel.	Only authorised individuals should be able to amend the records in which year-end inventory will be based. On a periodic basis, senior finance team members should review the types and levels of adjustments for indications of fraud.

Top tip. You may have come up with other valid controls here. As long as they meet the control objective for the assertions specified in the question, and are adequately explained, you will have gained marks for these. Other valid controls include the monitoring of timetabling of the counts to ensure all areas are covered at least once a year.

(d)   Substantive procedures to confirm:

(i)   Valuation of inventory

Verify the cost of imported paint and materials to produce manufactured paint to supplier invoice costs (for a statistical sample).

Confirm that the recorded inventory costs do not exceed the NRV by comparing the costs with the value of paint sales made after the year end.

Review aged inventory reports and investigate older items to ensure they are valued at the lower of NRV or are already provided against.

(ii) Completeness of provisions/contingent liabilities

Discuss with management the reason for not providing for or disclosing a potential payment to the director for unfair dismissal and corroborate the responses with documentary evidence where possible.

Review correspondence with the old finance director and the company's lawyers to help assess the likelihood of a claim being successful and to try to assess whether a reliable estimate of any potential payment is possible.

Obtain written representations from directors confirming that they believe a potential liability is only a remote probability, and that is the reason for including no provision or disclosure on the matter.

Top tips. There are a number of other procedures you may have come up with for (d)(i) and (ii), but only three of each were required.

For (i) other procedures include following up on damaged items identified at inventory counts, verifying labour costs for manufactured items against time sheets, confirming production overhead allocation is appropriate, and analytical procedures such as reviewing inventory holding period against the previous year's or comparing gross margin with that of the previous year.

In (ii) you may have suggested writing to the company's lawyers in respect of the unfair dismissal claim and reviewing board minutes for details to support management's assessment of the claim.

---

76 Aquamarine Co

Workbook references. Chapters 6 and 11.

Top tips. For part (b) of the question it is important that you describe the audit risks clearly. A common mistake in this type of question is to simply identify a risk factor from the question eg the company carries out continuous production. This is a risk factor ie something about the way in which the business operates that increases audit risk. The risk itself is the potential issue that this causes. For example in this case the risk would be the difficulty this would create for establishing the cut-off point for WIP which could result in under- or overstatement of inventory. Notice that to score well you must both identify the risk factor and then explain the associated risk. The examining team's comments below give helpful advice about the way in which the audit risk should be explained. Part (b) then asks for the auditor's response at the planning stage. Essentially you are being asked what you would plan to do to address the risks identified. This is probably the more demanding part of the question as you have to tailor your points to the risks you have identified. Think carefully about how you respond, though, as general statements will score few marks and check that the action you are suggesting links to the risk. For example, if you have identified that cut-off is an issue make sure that the procedures you have suggested would provide evidence regarding this assertion.

Take care with timing. Part (c) is for only three marks but it is important that you attempt all parts of the question. Although you may be able to use your knowledge of ISA 402 to help you, you must tailor your answer to the scenario.

Easy marks. Part (a) should represent easy marks as you should be familiar with the concept of audit risk and its components.

The scenario contained more issues than were required to be discussed; a significant minority identified more issues than necessary, often combining risks into one point. This approach sometimes resulted in a lack of detail in the risk and also led to unfocused auditor responses. In addition, a large number of candidates did not explain how each issue could result in an audit risk or impact on the financial statements and therefore were not awarded the explanation ½ mark. To explain audit risk candidates need to state the area of the financial statements impacted with an assertion (eg cut-off, valuation), a reference to under/over/misstated, or a reference to inherent, control or detection risk. Misstated was only awarded if it was clear that the balance could be either over- or understated. In addition, many candidates misunderstood the implication of payroll being outsourced, failing to understand that there was increased detection risk with regards to access to outsourced records and the risk of data being incorrectly transferred to the service organisation.

The provision of relevant auditors' responses continues to be a poorly attempted area and candidates are once again reminded to ensure that this area of the syllabus is adequately studied and practised. While an auditor's response does not have to be a detailed audit procedure, rather an approach the audit team will take to address the identified risk, the responses given were sometimes either too weak eg 'discuss with management' or did not address the issue due to a failure to understand the risk (eg in response to a risk detailing that a provision might be understated, an incorrect response was to 'undertake going concern testing').

In comparison to recent exam sessions, it was disappointing that a significant minority of candidates discussed business risks and therefore concentrated their responses on what management should do rather than the auditor (eg in relation to the plant and machinery ordered pre year end, an inappropriate response was that the auditor should contact the supplier to ensure the delivery was on time).

However, it was pleasing to note that many candidates presented their answers well using a two-column approach with audit risk in one column and the related response in the other column.

Marking scheme

Marks

(a) Up to 1 mark for each definition of audit risk and its components (if just a component is given without an explanation then just give ½ marks).
- Audit risk (max of 2 marks)
- Inherent risk
- Control risk
- Detection risk

5

(b) Up to 1 mark per well-described risk and up to 1 mark for each well-explained response. Overall maximum of 6 marks for risks and 6 marks for responses.
- Work in progress
- Existence of plant and machinery ordered
- Valuation of intangible asset
- New loan finance obtained
- Completeness of finance costs
- Use of service organisation
- Transfer of data to service organisation
- Valuation of land and buildings
- Overvaluation of receivables
- Redundancy provision

12

(c)   Up to 1 mark per well-explained point.
- Gain an understanding of the services being provided
- Assess the design and implementation of internal controls over Aquamarine's payroll at Coral
- Visit Coral and undertake tests of controls
- Contact Coral's auditors to request either a type 1 or type 2 report
- No reference in auditor's report of use of information from Coral's auditors

3
20

(a)   **Audit risk and its components**

Audit risk is the risk that the auditor expresses an inappropriate audit opinion when the financial statements are materially misstated. Audit risk is a function of two main components, being the risk of material misstatement and detection risk. Risk of material misstatement is made up of a further two components, inherent risk and control risk.

Inherent risk is the susceptibility of an assertion about a class of transaction, account balance or disclosure to a misstatement which could be material, either individually or when aggregated with other misstatements, before consideration of any related controls.

Control risk is the risk that a misstatement which could occur in an assertion about a class of transaction, account balance or disclosure and which could be material, either individually or when aggregated with other misstatements, will not be prevented, or detected and corrected, on a timely basis by the entity's internal control.

Detection risk is the risk that the procedures performed by the auditor to reduce audit risk to an acceptably low level will not detect a misstatement which exists and which could be material, either individually or when aggregated with other misstatements. Detection risk is affected by sampling and non-sampling risk.

(b)   **Audit risks and auditors' response**

Audit risks	Auditors' response
Aquamarine Co (Aquamarine) undertakes continuous production and the work in progress balance at the year end is likely to be material. As production will not cease, the exact cut-off of the work in progress will need to be assessed. If the cut-off is not correctly calculated, the inventory valuation may be under- or overstated.	The auditor should discuss with management the process they will undertake to assess the cut-off point for work in progress at the year end. This process should be reviewed by the auditor while attending the year-end inventory count. In addition, consideration should be given as to whether an independent expert is required to value the work in progress. If so, this will need to be arranged with consent from management and in time for the year-end count.
Aquamarine has ordered $720,000 of plant and machinery, two-thirds of which may not have been received by the year end. Only assets which physically exist at the year end should be included in property, plant and equipment. If items not yet delivered have been capitalised, PPE will be overstated. Consideration will also need to be given to depreciation and when this should commence. If depreciation is not appropriately charged when the asset is available for use, this may result in assets and profit being over- or understated.	Discuss with management as to whether the remaining plant and machinery ordered have arrived; if so, physically verify a sample of these assets to ensure existence and ensure only appropriate assets are recorded in the non-current asset register at the year end. Determine if the asset received is in use at the year end by physical observation and, if so, if depreciation has commenced at an appropriate point.

Audit risks	Auditors' response
A patent has been purchased for $1.3 million, and this enables Aquamarine to manufacture specialised elevator equipment for the next five years. In accordance with IAS 38 *Intangible Assets*, this should be included as an intangible asset and amortised over its five-year life. If management has not correctly accounted for the patent, intangible assets and profits could be overstated.	The audit team will need to agree the purchase price to supporting documentation and to confirm that the useful life is five years. The amortisation charge should be recalculated in order to ensure the accuracy of the charge and that the intangible is correctly valued at the year end.
The company has borrowed $1.2 million from the bank via a 5-year loan. This loan needs to be correctly split between current and non-current liabilities in order to ensure correct disclosure.	During the audit, the team would need to confirm that the $1.2 million loan finance was received. In addition, the split between current and non-current liabilities and the disclosures for this loan should be reviewed in detail to ensure compliance with relevant accounting standards. Details of security should be agreed to the bank confirmation letter.
Also, as the level of debt has increased, there should be additional finance costs. There is a risk that this has been omitted from the statement of profit or loss leading to understated finance costs and overstated profit.	The finance costs should be recalculated and any increase agreed to the loan documentation for confirmation of interest rates. Interest payments should be agreed to the cash book and bank statements to confirm the amount was paid and is not therefore a year-end payable.
During the year Aquamarine outsourced its payroll processing to an external service organisation. A detection risk arises as to whether sufficient and appropriate evidence is available at Aquamarine to confirm the completeness and accuracy of controls over payroll. If not, another auditor may be required to undertake testing at the service organisation.	Discuss with management the extent of records maintained at Aquamarine and any monitoring of controls undertaken by management over the payroll charge. Consideration should be given to contacting the service organisation's auditor to confirm the level of controls in place.
The payroll processing transferred to Coral Payrolls Co from 1 January. If any errors occurred during the transfer process, these could result in the payroll charge and related employment tax liabilities being under/overstated.	Discuss with management the transfer process undertaken and any controls put in place to ensure the completeness and accuracy of the data. Where possible, undertake tests of controls to confirm the effectiveness of the transfer controls. In addition, perform substantive testing on the transfer of information from the old to the new system.
The land and buildings are to be revalued at the year end; it is likely that the revaluation surplus/deficit will be material. The revaluation needs to be carried out and recorded in accordance with IAS 16 *Property, Plant and Equipment*, otherwise non-current assets may be incorrectly valued.	Discuss with management the process adopted for undertaking the valuation, including whether the whole class of assets was revalued and if the valuation was undertaken by an expert. This process should be reviewed for compliance with IAS 16.

Audit risks	Auditors' response
Receivables for the year to date are considerably higher than the prior year. If this continues to the year end, there is a risk that some receivables may be overvalued as they are not recoverable.	Discuss with management the reasons for the increase in receivables and management's process for identifying potential irrecoverable debt. Test controls surrounding management's credit control processes. Extended post year end cash receipts testing and a review of the aged receivables ledger are to be performed to assess valuation. Also consider the adequacy of any allowance for receivables.
Aquamarine is planning to make approximately 65 employees redundant after the year end. The timing of this announcement has not been confirmed; if it is announced to the staff before the year end, then under IAS 37 *Provisions, Contingent Liabilities and Contingent Assets* a redundancy provision will be required at the year end. Failure to provide will result in an understatement of provisions and expenses.	Discuss with management the status of the redundancy announcement; if before the year end, review supporting documentation to confirm the timing. In addition, review the basis of and recalculate the redundancy provision.

(c)   Payroll service organisations

Additional factors Amethyst & Co should consider in relation to Aquamarine's use of the service organisation, Coral Payrolls Co (Coral), include:

- The audit team should gain an understanding of the services being provided by Coral, including the materiality of payroll and the basis of the outsourcing contract.

- They will need to assess the design and implementation of internal controls over Aquamarine's payroll at Coral.

- The team may wish to visit Coral and undertake tests of controls to confirm the operating effectiveness of the controls.

- If this is not possible, Amethyst & Co should contact Coral's auditors to request either a type 1 report (on description and design of controls) or type 2 report (on description, design and operating effectiveness of controls).

- Amethyst & Co is responsible for obtaining sufficient and appropriate evidence, therefore no reference may be made in the auditor's report regarding the use of information from Coral's auditors.

77 Kangaroo Construction Co

Workbook reference. Chapter 6.

Top tips. This is a typical scenario-based exam question on audit risk, with a knowledge element. It is important to go through the scenario carefully, line by line, so that you can identify the risk factors as you will need to explain how they may impact on the financial statements in part (b)(ii). This part also requires you to describe the auditor's responses to the identified audit risks – vague answers here will not score well. For example, it is not sufficient to say 'Discuss with management'. Your answer needs to be more detailed and explain how you, as auditor, are going to undertake audit work to address the risk. This part of the question is best answered in a columnar format so that you can link the audit risks with the appropriate responses and give your answer more structure. Make sure you make reference to the ratios you calculated in part (b)(i) of the question.

Marking scheme

Marks

(a)   Up to 1 mark per well-explained point.

- Materiality for financial statements as a whole and also performance materiality levels
- Definition of materiality
- Amount or nature of misstatements, or both
- 5% profit before tax or 1% revenue or total expenses
- Judgement, needs of users and level of risk
- Small errors aggregated
- Performance materiality

5

(b)   (i)   ½ mark per ratio calculation per year.

- Gross margin
- Operating margin
- Inventory holding period
- Inventory turnover
- Receivables collection period
- Payables payment period
- Current ratio
- Quick ratio

5

(ii)   Up to 1 mark per well-described audit risk and up to 1 mark per well-explained audit response.
- Receivables valuation
- Inventory valuation
- Depreciation of plant and machinery
- Management manipulation of profit to reach bonus targets
- Completeness of warranty provision
- Disclosure of bank loan of £1 million
- Going concern risk

10
___
20
___

(a)   **Materiality and performance materiality**

Materiality is not specifically defined in ISA 320 *Materiality in Planning and Performing an Audit* but it does state that misstatements are material if they could reasonably be expected to influence the economic decisions of users (either individually or in aggregate) (ISA 320). ISA 320 also states that judgements about materiality are affected by the size and/or nature of a misstatement (ISA 320). Auditors set their own materiality levels, based on their judgement of risk. During audit planning, the auditor will set materiality for the financial statements as a whole and this involves the exercise of professional judgement. Benchmarks and percentages are often used to calculate a materiality level for the financial statements as a whole, eg 5% of profit before tax or 1–2% of total assets, but ultimately, the level of materiality set is down to the auditor's professional judgement, and may be revised during the course of the audit.

BPP
LEARNING
MEDIA

The auditor also has to set performance materiality, which is lower than materiality for the financial statements as a whole. Performance materiality is defined in ISA 320 as the amount or amounts set by the auditor at less than materiality for the financial statements as a whole to reduce to an appropriately low level the probability that the aggregate of uncorrected and undetected misstatements exceeds materiality for the financial statements as a whole (ISA 320).

(b)   (i)   **Ratios**

Ratio	20X3	20X2
Gross profit margin (gross profit/sales × 100)	5.5/12.5 × 100 = 44%	7.0/15.0 × 100 = 47%
Operating margin (profit before interest and taxation/sales × 100)	0.5/12.5 × 100 = 4%	1.9/15 × 100 = 13%
Inventory turnover (cost of sales/inventory)	7/1.9 = 3.7	8/1.4 = 5.7
Inventory holding period (inventory/cost of sales × 365)	1.9/7 × 365 = 99 days	1.4/8 × 365 = 64 days
Receivables collection period (receivables/sales × 365)	3.1/12.5 × 365 = 91 days	2/15 × 365 = 49 days
Payables payment period (payables/cost of sales × 365)	1.6/7 × 365 = 83 days	1.2/8 × 365 = 55 days
Current ratio (current assets/current liabilities)	(1.9 + 3.1 + 0.8)/(1.6 + 1.0) = 2.2	(1.4 + 2.0 + 1.9)/1.2 = 4.4
Quick ratio (current assets except inventory/current liabilities)	(3.1 + 0.8)/(1.6 + 1.0) = 1.5	(2.0 + 1.9)/1.2 = 3.3

Note. Only five ratios were required.it risk and responses

Audit risk	Auditor's response
The company offers a five-year building warranty on its houses. During the year, as a result of switching to a cheaper supplier, some customers have claimed on their guarantees. There is a risk that the warranty provision is understated in the financial statements.	As this is a judgemental area, the auditors need to discuss the basis of calculating the provision with the directors and assess the reasonableness of any assumptions made. They should also review a sample of guarantees claimed during the year and vouch amounts to repairs invoices. They should review the level of claims made in the year and assess whether the provision needs revising in light of this.
The company has had a difficult year due to a fall in house prices. Gross profit margin has fallen by 3% and operating margin has fallen significantly from 13% to 4%. In addition, the company has had to take out a loan of $1m during the year to help with operating cash flow. The payables collection period has also increased from 55 days to 83 days, indicating that the company is having	The auditors must discuss with directors whether they believe that the company is still a going concern in light of the results of the ratio analysis, and review cash flow forecasts and budgets for the forthcoming year.

Audit risk	Auditor's response
problems paying suppliers. The current and quick ratios have also fallen significantly from the prior year. There is therefore a risk that the company may not be a going concern.	
The receivables collection period has increased from 49 days to 91 days as a result of the directors increasing the credit terms offered to customers. There is a risk that the receivables balance at year end is materially misstated as customers may not be able to pay.	The auditors should carry out post year end testing and cut-off testing on receivables balances to verify the accuracy of the year-end balance. The auditors should also review the aged receivables listing to identify any balances that need writing off.
There is a risk that inventory is overstated in the financial statements as there may be some houses whose selling price is less than cost. The inventory holding period has also increased from 64 days to 99 days, and inventory turnover has fallen from 5.7 to 3.7. Inventory should be valued at the lower of cost and net realisable value.	Detailed audit work on inventory should be carried out as this is likely to be a material balance. An auditor's expert may need to be used to independently verify the value of inventory at the year end.
There is a risk that revenue and costs have been deliberately misstated in the financial statements in order for the directors to meet the target profit before interest and taxation figure of $0.5m so as to get their bonuses (window dressing). This is also indicated by the fact that the directors have changed the useful economic life of plant and machinery from three to five years to reduce the depreciation charge for the year and hence inflate the profit figure to attain the minimum target figure.	The auditors need to maintain professional scepticism throughout the audit and carry out detailed cut-off testing on revenue and expenses to confirm that the figures are correctly stated.
There is a risk that the depreciation charge for the year is understated and non-current assets on the statement of financial position are overstated as the directors have amended the useful economic life of plant and machinery from three to five years.	The auditors should discuss the change and the reasons for it with the directors and assess whether it is reasonable or not. They should also examine a sample of plant and machinery assets to assess whether the change is appropriate.
The company has taken out a loan of $1m from the bank which is repayable within a year. There is a risk that this loan has been incorrectly disclosed in the financial statements. It should be disclosed as a current liability as it is repayable within a year.	The auditors should review the terms of the loan agreement to verify the repayment date and the amount borrowed. They should review the draft financial statements to confirm the correct disclosure of the loan.

Note. Only **five** audit risks were required.

78 Hurling Co

Top tips. This question is a typical scenario based question testing the area of audit risk. To score well in part (b) it is essential that your audit risk is properly explained (in terms of what could be over/under stated in the financial statements) and also that you come up with practical actions that the auditor would take to gain evidence. Part (c) on ethical threats and safeguards is another area where it is very important to fully explain both the threat and the safeguard.

Easy marks. You should have found parts (a) and (c) reasonably straightforward.

Examining team's comments.

Regarding part (a): Questions on assessing audit risks tend to be scenario based; the candidates having to identify and explain the risks from a scenario and give an auditor's response to address the risks. Other questions in this area of the syllabus tend to be more factual, knowledge based questions and hence depends on the ability of students to recall their knowledge in the exam.

As noted in previous Examining Team's Reports a fundamental factor in planning and assessing the risks of an audit of an entity is an assessment of audit risk, and this remains a highly examinable area. Audit risk questions typically require a number of audit risks to be identified (½ marks each), explained (½ marks each) and an auditor's response to each risk (1 mark each).

The scenarios usually contain more issues than are required to be discussed. It is pleasing that candidates planned their time carefully and generally only attempted to list the required number of issues. However, a large number of candidates often did not explain how each issue could impact on the audit risk and therefore were not awarded the second ½ mark. To explain audit risk candidates need to state the area of the accounts impacted with an assertion (eg cut off, valuation etc), or, a reference to under/over/misstated, or, a reference to inherent, control or detection risk. Misstated was only awarded if it was clear that the balance could be either over or understated.

Auditor's responses continue to be weak and while an auditor's response does not have to be a detailed audit procedure, rather an approach the audit team will take to address the identified risk, the responses given were sometimes too weak eg 'discuss with management'.

A minority of candidates discussed business risks and therefore concentrated their responses on what management should do rather than the auditor.

Regarding part (b): Questions in this area may present candidates with a scenario-based ethics question and performance in this area remains satisfactory, Candidates are generally asked to identify and explain a set number of issues from a given scenario and give relevant recommendations to counter the risks identified.

It is pleasing to note evidence of candidates planning their time carefully and generally only listing the required number of issues.

One mark was available for each well explained issue. As in previous sittings, while it was pleasing that candidates were able to identify relevant issues from the scenario, candidates often did not explain the issues correctly, or in sufficient detail, therefore many candidates scored ½ marks rather than one mark for each issue.

Therefore, a candidate who identified an issue and stated the type of threat scored ½ marks, to be awarded the second ½ mark the candidate had to explain why this caused an ethical problem. The explanation was often weak, for example explaining the threat of 'self-interest` resulting from contingent audit fees, as 'the auditor will not be independent' is not sufficient. The candidates needed to comment on the possibility of the auditor 'ignoring audit adjustments that reduce profits' to obtain the second ½ mark.

		Marks
(a)	**Define audit risk and its components**	
	– Audit risk	2
	– Inherent risk	1
	– Control risk	1
	– Detection risk	1
	Maximum	4
(b)	**Audit risks and responses**	
	– Capitalisation of website costs	2
	– Warehouse acquisition	2
	– Classification of preference shares	2
	– Appropriateness of asset useful lives	2
	– Irrecoverable receivable	2
	– Sales staff bonus scheme	2
	– Product recall	2
	– Legal action	2
	– Audit timetable, increased detection risk	2
	– Accounting for proposed dividend	2
	Maximum	16
(c)	**Ethical threats and safeguards**	
	– Intimidation threat – audit timetable	2
	– Self-interest threat – recruitment	2
	– Familiarity threat – ECQR review	2
	– Self-interest/intimidation threat – fees	2
	– Self-interest threat – contingent fee	2
	– Self-interest threat – outstanding fees	2
	Maximum	10
	Total	30

(a) Audit risk and the components of audit risk

Audit risk is the risk that the auditor expresses an inappropriate audit opinion when the financial statements are materially misstated. Audit risk is a function of two main components, being the risk of material misstatement and detection risk. Risk of material misstatement is made up of a further two components, inherent risk and control risk.

BPP
LEARNING
MEDIA

Inherent risk is the susceptibility of an assertion about a class of transaction, account balance or disclosure to a misstatement which could be material, either individually or when aggregated with other misstatements, before consideration of any related controls.

Control risk is the risk that a misstatement which could occur in an assertion about a class of transaction, account balance or disclosure and which could be material, either individually or when aggregated with other misstatements, will not be prevented, or detected and corrected, on a timely basis by the entity's internal control.

Detection risk is the risk that the procedures performed by the auditor to reduce audit risk to an acceptably low level will not detect a misstatement which exists and which could be material, either individually or when aggregated with other misstatements. Detection risk is affected by sampling and non-sampling risk.

(b)   Audit risks and auditor's responses

Audit risk	Auditor's response
Hurling Co upgraded their website during the year at a cost of $1.1m. The costs incurred should be correctly allocated between revenue and capital expenditure. As the website has been upgraded, there is a possibility that the new processes and systems may not record data reliably and accurately. This may lead to a risk over completeness and accuracy of data in the underlying accounting records.	Review a breakdown of the costs and agree to invoices to assess the nature of the expenditure and if capital, agree to inclusion within the asset register or agree to the statement of profit or loss. The audit team should document the revised system and undertake tests over the completeness and accuracy of data recorded from the website to the accounting records.
Hurling Co has entered into a transaction to purchase a new warehouse for $3.2m and it is anticipated that the legal process will be completed by the year end. Only assets which physically exist at the year end should be included in property, plant and equipment. If the transaction has not been completed by the year end, there is a risk that assets are overstated if the company incorrectly includes the warehouse at the year end.	Discuss with management as to whether the warehouse purchase was completed by the year end. If so, inspect legal documents of ownership, such as title deeds ensuring these are dated prior to 1 April 20X7 and are in the company name.
Significant finance has been obtained in the year, as the company has issued $5m of irredeemable preference shares. This finance needs to be accounted for correctly, with adequate disclosure made. As the preference shares are irredeemable, they should be classified as equity rather than non-current liabilities. Failing to correctly classify the shares could result in understated equity and overstated non-current liabilities.	Review share issue documentation to confirm that the preference shares are irredeemable. Confirm that they have been correctly classified as equity within the accounting records and that total financing proceeds of $5m were received. In addition, the disclosures for this share issue should be reviewed in detail to ensure compliance with relevant accounting standards.

Audit risk	Auditor's response
The finance director has extended the useful lives of fixtures and fittings from three to four years, resulting in the depreciation charge reducing. Under IAS 16 *Property, Plant and Equipment*, useful lives are to be reviewed annually, and if asset lives have genuinely increased, then this change is reasonable. However, there is a risk that this reduction has occurred in order to boost profits. If this is the case, then fixtures and fittings are overvalued and profit overstated.	Discuss with the directors the rationale for any extensions of asset lives and reduction of depreciation rates. Also, the four-year life should be compared to how often these assets are replaced, to assess the useful life of assets.
A customer of Hurling Co has been encountering difficulties paying their outstanding balance of $1.2m and Hurling Co has agreed to a revised credit period. If the customer is experiencing difficulties, there is an increased risk that the receivable is not recoverable and hence is overvalued.	Review the revised credit terms and identify if any after date cash receipts for this customer have been made. Discuss with the finance director whether he intends to make an allowance for this receivable. If not, review whether any existing allowance for uncollectable accounts is sufficient to cover the amount of this receivable.
A sales-related bonus scheme has been introduced in the year for sales staff, with a significant number of new customer accounts on favourable credit terms being opened pre year end. This has resulted in a 5% increase in revenue. Sales staff seeking to maximise their current year bonus may result in new accounts being opened from poor credit risks leading to irrecoverable receivables. In addition, there is a risk of sales cut-off errors as new customers could place orders within the two-month introductory period and subsequently return these goods post year end.	Increased sales cut-off testing will be performed along with a review of any post year-end returns as they may indicate cut-off errors. In addition, increased after date cash receipts testing to be undertaken for new customer account receivables.
Hurling Co has halted further sales of its new product Luge and a product recall has been initiated for any goods sold in the last four months. If there are issues with the quality of the Luge product, inventory may be overvalued as its NRV may be below its cost. Additionally, products of Luge sold within the last four months are being recalled, this will result in Hurling Co paying customer refunds. The sale will need to be removed; a refund liability should be recognised along with the reinstatement of inventory, although the NRV of this inventory could be of a minimal value. Failing to account for this correctly could result in overstated revenue and understated liabilities and inventory.	Discuss with the finance director whether any write downs will be made to this product, and what, if any, modifications may be required with regards the quality. Testing should be undertaken to confirm cost and NRV of the Luge products in inventory and that on a line-by-line basis the goods are valued correctly. Review the list of sales made of product Luge prior to the recall, agree that the sale has been removed from revenue and the inventory included. If the refund has not been paid pre year end, agree it is included within current liabilities.

Audit risk	Auditor's response
Petanque Co, a customer of Hurling Co, has announced that they intend to commence legal action for a loss of information and profits as a result of the Luge product sold to them. If it is probable that the company will make payment to the customer, a legal provision is required. If the payment is possible rather than probable, a contingent liability disclosure would be necessary. If Hurling Co has not done this, there is a risk over the completeness of any provisions or the necessary disclosure of contingent liabilities.	Caving & Co should write to the company's lawyers to enquire of the existence and likelihood of success of any claim from Petanque Co. The results of this should be used to assess the level of provision or disclosure included in the financial statements.
The finance director has requested that the audit completes one week earlier than normal as he wishes to report results earlier. A reduction in the audit timetable will increase detection risk and place additional pressure on the team in obtaining sufficient and appropriate evidence. In addition, the finance team of Hurling Co will have less time to prepare the financial information leading to an increased risk of errors arising in the financial statements.	The timetable should be confirmed with the finance director. If it is to be reduced, then consideration should be given to performing an interim audit in late March or early April; this would then reduce the pressure on the final audit. The team needs to maintain professional scepticism and be alert to the increased risk of errors occurring.
The company is intending to propose a final dividend once the financial statements are finalised. This amount should not be provided for in the 20X7 financial statements, as the obligation only arises once the dividend is announced, which is post year end. In line with IAS 10 *Events after the Reporting Period* the dividend should only be disclosed. If the dividend is included, this will result in an overstatement of liabilities and understatement of equity.	Discuss the issue with management and confirm that the dividend will not be included within liabilities in the 20X7 financial statements. The financial statements need to be reviewed to ensure that adequate disclosure of the proposed dividend is included.

Note. Only eight risks and eight related responses were required.

(c) Ethical threats and safeguards

(I) Ethical threat	(II) Possible safeguard
The finance director is keen to report Hurling Co's financial results earlier than normal and has asked if the audit can be completed in a shorter time frame. This may create an intimidation threat on the team as they may feel under pressure to cut corners and not raise issues in order to satisfy the deadlines and this could compromise the objectivity of the audit team and quality of audit performed.	The engagement partner should discuss the timing of the audit with the finance director to understand if the audit can commence earlier, so as to ensure adequate time for the team to gather evidence. If this is not possible, the partner should politely inform the finance director that the team will undertake the audit in accordance with all relevant ISAs and quality control procedures. Therefore the audit is unlikely to be completed earlier. If any residual concerns remain or the intimidation threat continues, then Caving & Co may need to consider resigning from the engagement.

(I) Ethical threat	(II) Possible safeguard
A non-executive director (NED) of Hurling Co has just resigned and the directors have asked whether the partners of Caving & Co can assist them in recruiting to fill this vacancy. This represents a self-interest threat as the audit firm cannot undertake the recruitment of members of the board of Hurling Co, especially a NED who will have a key role in overseeing the audit process and audit firm.	Caving & Co is able to assist Hurling Co in that they can undertake roles such as reviewing a shortlist of candidates and reviewing qualifications and suitability. However, the firm must ensure that they are not seen to undertake management decisions and so must not seek out candidates for the position or make the final decision on who is appointed.
The engagement quality control reviewer (ECQR) assigned to Hurling Co was until last year the audit engagement partner. This represents a familiarity threat as the partner will have been associated with Hurling Co for a long period of time and so may not retain professional scepticism and objectivity.	As Hurling Co is a listed company, then the previous audit engagement partner should not be involved in the audit for at least a period of five years. An alternative ECQR should be appointed instead.
Caving & Co provides taxation services, the audit engagement and possibly services related to the recruitment of the NED. There is a potential self-interest or intimidation threat as the total fees could represent a significant proportion of Caving & Co's income and the firm could become overly reliant on Hurling Co, resulting in the firm being less challenging or objective due to fear of losing such a significant client.	Caving & Co should assess whether audit, recruitment and taxation fees would represent more than 15% of gross practice income for two consecutive years. If the recurring fees are likely to exceed 15% of annual practice income this year, additional consideration should be given as to whether the recruitment and taxation services should be undertaken by the firm. In addition, if the fees do exceed 15%, then this should be disclosed to those charged with governance at Hurling Co. If the firm retains all work, it should arrange for a pre-issuance (before the audit opinion is issued) or post-issuance (after the opinion has been issued) review to be undertaken by an external accountant or by a regulatory body.
The finance director has suggested that the audit fee is based on the profit before tax of Hurling Co which constitutes a contingent fee. Contingent fees give rise to a self-interest threat and are prohibited under ACCA's *Code of Ethics and Conduct*. If the audit fee is based on profit, the team may be inclined to ignore audit adjustments which could lead to a reduction in profit.	Caving & Co will not be able to accept contingent fees and should communicate to those charged with governance at Hurling Co that the external audit fee needs to be based on the time spent and levels of skill and experience of the required audit team members.
At today's date, 20% of last year's audit fee is still outstanding and was due for payment three months ago. A self-interest threat can arise if the fees remain outstanding, as Caving & Co may feel pressure to agree to certain accounting adjustments in order to have the previous year and this year's audit fee paid. In addition, outstanding fees could be perceived as a loan to a client which is strictly prohibited.	Caving & Co should discuss with those charged with governance the reasons why the final 20% of last year's fee has not been paid. They should agree a revised payment schedule which will result in the fees being settled before much more work is performed for the current year audit.

79 Prancer Construction Co

Workbook references. Chapters 4 and 6.

Top tips. This question is a typical scenario based question testing the area of audit risk. Part (a), on the preconditions of an audit, is an area that can easily be tested for a few marks and so you need to be familiar with them.

Both parts (a) and (b) were for 3 marks each, so you need to be looking for at least 2 marks on each question part to pass this part of the question.

Part (c) accounted for the majority of marks in this question, and required you to read the scenario closely in order to identify audit risks. The requirement asks you to 'describe' the audit risks, so it is important that you do not just state what the risk is, but also say why it is a risk, thinking in particular about how it might affect the financial statements and specifically which balances might be over or understated.

Easy marks. You should have found parts (a) and (b) reasonably straightforward.

Examining team's comments. This area of the syllabus requires an understanding of how the auditor obtains and accepts audit engagements, obtains an understanding of the entity and its environment, assesses the risk of material misstatement and plans an audit of the financial statements.

Questions on assessing audit risks tend to be scenario based with candidates having to identify and explain the risks from a scenario and give an auditor's response to address the risks. Other questions in this area of the syllabus tend to be more factual knowledge based questions and hence depend on the ability of students to recall their knowledge in the exam.

In this session it was disappointing to see a significant number of candidates were unable to answer the knowledge marks in this syllabus area. Some answers scored zero marks as points made were completely unrelated to the question asked. It is important in factual questions that candidates answer the question set rather than the one they would like to see. This unsatisfactory performance also indicates a lack of preparation and awareness of the knowledge areas relating to planning and risk.

As noted in previous Examining team's Reports a fundamental factor in planning and assessing the risks of an audit of an entity is an assessment of audit risk, and this remains a highly examinable area. Audit risk questions require a number of audit risks to be identified (½ marks each), explained (½ marks each) and an auditor's response to each risk (1 mark each). Typically candidates can be required to identify and explain in the region of six to eight risks and responses.

The scenarios usually contain more issues than are required to be discussed. It is pleasing that candidates planned their time carefully and generally only attempted to list the required number of issues. However, in common with other sessions, a significant number of candidates often did not explain how each issue could impact on the audit risk and therefore were not awarded the second ½ mark. To explain audit risk candidates need to state the area of the accounts impacted with an assertion (eg cut off, valuation, etc), or, a reference to under/over/misstated, or, a reference to inherent, control or detection risk. Misstated was only awarded if it was clear that the balance could be either over or understated.

Auditor's responses still continue to be weak and while an auditor's response does not have to be a detailed audit procedure, rather an approach the audit team will take to address the identified risk. The responses given were sometimes too vague, eg "discuss with the finance director" or they were impractical such as "recruit more audit staff" for the risk of the auditor not attending all the company's inventory counts. Additionally, candidates continue to concentrate their responses on what management should do rather than the auditor.

Marks

(a)   **Preconditions for the audit**

Determination of acceptable framework   1

Agreement of management responsibilities   1

Preparation of financial statements   1

Internal control   1

Access to information   1

Restricted to   3

(b)   **Audit strategy document**

Main characteristics of the audit   1

Reporting objectives   1

Significant factors affecting the audit   1

Preliminary engagement activities   1

Nature, timing and extent of resources   1

Restricted to   3

(c)   **Audit risks and responses** (only 7 risks required)

New client   2

Work in progress   2

Increased inventory   2

Warranty provision   2

Attendance at inventory counts   2

Deferred income not correctly recognised   2

Receivables allowance and valuation   2

Overdraft covenants   2

Trade payables   2

Max 7 issues, 2 marks each   14

Total marks   20

(a)   **Preconditions for the audit**

ISA 210 *Agreeing the Terms of Audit Engagements* states that auditors should only accept a new audit engagement when it has been confirmed that the preconditions for an audit are present.

To assess whether the preconditions for an audit are present, Cupid & Co should have determined whether the financial reporting framework to be applied in the preparation of Prancer Construction Co's financial statements is acceptable. In considering this, the auditor should have assessed the nature of the entity, the nature and purpose of the financial statements and whether law or regulation prescribes the applicable reporting framework

In addition, the firm should have obtained the agreement of Prancer Construction Co's management that it acknowledges and understands its responsibility for the following:

- Preparation of the financial statements in accordance with the applicable financial reporting framework, including where relevant their fair presentation;

- For such internal control as management determines is necessary to enable the preparation of financial statements which are free from material misstatement, whether due to fraud or error; and

- To provide Cupid & Co with access to all relevant information for the preparation of the financial statements, any additional information which the auditor may request from management and unrestricted access to personnel within Prancer Construction Co from whom the auditor determines it necessary to obtain audit evidence.

(b) **Areas to be included in the audit strategy document**

The audit strategy sets out the scope, timing and direction of the audit and helps the development of the audit plan. ISA 300 *Planning an Audit of Financial Statements* sets out areas which should be considered and documented as part of the audit strategy document and are as follows:

Main characteristics of the engagement

The audit strategy should consider the main characteristics of the engagement, which define its scope. For Prancer Construction

Co, the following are examples of things which should be included:

- Whether the financial information to be audited has been prepared in accordance with the relevant financial reporting framework.

- Whether computer-assisted audit techniques will be used and the effect of IT on audit procedures.

- The availability of key personnel at Prancer Construction Co.

Reporting objectives, timing and nature of communication

It should ascertain the reporting objectives of the engagement to plan the timing of the audit and the nature of the communications required, such as:

- The audit timetable for reporting including the timing of interim and final stages.

- Organisation of meetings with Prancer Construction Co's management to discuss any audit issues arising.

- Any discussions with management regarding the reports to be issued.

- The timings of the audit team meetings and review of work performed.

Significant factors affecting the audit

The strategy should consider the factors which, in the auditor's professional judgement, are significant in directing Prancer Construction Co's audit team's efforts, such as:

- The determination of materiality for the audit.

- The need to maintain a questioning mind and to exercise professional scepticism in gathering and evaluating audit evidence.

Preliminary engagement activities and knowledge from previous engagements

It should consider the results of preliminary audit planning activities and, where applicable, whether knowledge gained on other engagements for Prancer Construction Co is relevant, such as:

- Results of any tests over the effectiveness of internal controls.

- Evidence of management's commitment to the design, implementation and maintenance of sound internal controls.

- Volume of transactions, which may determine whether it is more efficient for the audit team to rely on internal controls.

- Significant business developments affecting Prancer Construction Co, such as the improvement in building practices and construction quality.

Nature, timing and extent of resources

The audit strategy should ascertain the nature, timing and extent of resources necessary to perform the audit, such as:

- The selection of the audit team with experience of this type of industry.

- Assignment of audit work to the team members.

- Setting the audit budget.

(c)   **Audit risks and auditor's responses**

Audit risk	Auditor's response
Prancer Construction Co is a new client for Cupid & Co. As the team is not familiar with the accounting policies, transactions and balances of the company, there will be an increased detection risk on the audit.	Cupid & Co should ensure they have a suitably experienced team. In addition, adequate time should be allocated for team members to obtain an understanding of the company and the risks of material misstatement including a detailed team briefing to cover the key areas of risk.
Prancer Construction Co is likely to have a material level of work in progress at the year end, being construction work in progress as well as ongoing maintenance services, as Prancer Construction Co has annual contracts for many of the buildings constructed. The level of work in progress will need to be assessed at the year end. Assessing percentage completion for partially constructed buildings is likely to be quite subjective, and the team should consider if they have the required expertise to undertake this. If the percentage completion is not correctly calculated, the inventory valuation may be under or overstated.	The auditor should discuss with management the process they will undertake to assess the percentage completion for work in progress at the year end. This process should be reviewed by the auditor while attending the year-end inventory counts. In addition, consideration should be given as to whether an independent expert is required to value the work in progress or if a management expert has been used. If the work of an expert is to be used, then the audit team will need to assess the competence, capabilities and objectivity of the expert.

Audit risk	Auditor's response
The August 20X7 management accounts contain $2.1 million of completed properties; this balance was $1.4 million in September 20X6. The increase in inventory may be due to an increased level of pre year-end orders. Alternatively, it may be that Prancer Construction Co is struggling to sell completed properties, which may indicate that they are overvalued. IAS 2 *Inventories* requires that inventory should be stated at the lower of cost and NRV.	Detailed cost and net realisable value (NRV) testing to be performed at the year end and the aged inventory report to be reviewed to assess whether inventory requires to be written down.
At the year end there will be inventory counts undertaken at all 11 of the building sites in progress. It is unlikely that the auditor will be able to attend all of these inventory counts, increasing detection risk, and therefore they need to ensure that they obtain sufficient evidence over the inventory counting controls, and completeness and existence of inventory for any sites not visited.	The auditor should assess for which of the building sites they will attend the counts. This will be those with the most material inventory or which according to management have the most significant risk of misstatement. For those not visited, the auditor will need to review the level of exceptions noted during the count and discuss with management any issues, which arose during the count.
Prancer Construction Co offers its customers a building warranty of five years, which covers any construction defects. A warranty provision will be required under IAS 37 *Provisions, Contingent Liabilities and Contingent Assets*. Calculating warranty provisions requires judgement as it is an uncertain amount. The finance director anticipates this provision will be lower than last year as the company has improved its building practices and the quality of its finished properties. However, there is a risk that this provision could be understated, especially in light of the overdraft covenant relating to a minimum level of net assets and is being used as a mechanism to manipulate profit and asset levels.	Discuss with management the basis of the provision calculation, and compare this to the level of post year-end claims, if any, made by customers. In particular, discuss the rationale behind reducing the level of provision this year. Compare the prior year provision with the actual level of claims in the year, to assess the reasonableness of the judgements made by management.
Customers who wish to purchase a property are required to place an order and a 5% non-refundable deposit prior to the completion of the building. These deposits should not be recognised as revenue in the statement of profit or loss until the performance obligations as per the contracts have been satisfied, which is likely to be when the building is finished and the sale process is complete. Instead, they should be recognised as deferred income within current liabilities. Management may have incorrectly treated the deferred income as revenue, resulting in overstated revenue and understated liabilities.	Discuss with management the treatment of deposits received in advance, to ensure it is appropriate. During the final audit, undertake increased testing over the cut-off of revenue and completeness of deferred income.

Audit risk	Auditor's response
An allowance for receivables has historically been maintained, but it is anticipated that this will be reduced. There is a risk that receivables will be overvalued; some balances may not be recoverable and so will be overstated if not provided for. In addition, reducing the allowance for receivables will increase asset values and would improve the covenant compliance, which increases the manipulation risk further. Prancer Construction Co has a material overdraft which has minimum profit and net assets covenants attached to it. If these covenants were to be breached, the overdraft balance would become instantly repayable. If the company does not have sufficient cash to meet this repayment, then there could be going concern implications. In addition, there is a risk of manipulation of profit and net assets to ensure that covenants are met.	Review and test the controls surrounding how the finance director identifies old or potentially irrecoverable receivables balances and credit control to ensure that they are operating effectively. Discuss with the director the rationale for reducing the allowance for receivables. Extended post year-end cash receipts testing and a review of the aged receivables ledger to be performed to assess valuation and the need for an allowance for receivables. Review the covenant calculations prepared by the company at the year end and identify whether any defaults have occurred; if so, determine the effect on the company. The team should maintain their professional scepticism and be alert to the risk that profit and/or net assets have been overstated to ensure compliance with the covenants.
Preliminary analytical review of the August management accounts shows a payables payment period of 56 days for August 20X7, compared to 87 days for September 20X6. It is anticipated that the year-end payables payment period will be even lower. The forecast profit is higher than last year, indicating an increase in trade, also the company's cash position has continued to deteriorate and therefore, it is unusual for the payables payment period to have decreased. There is an increased risk of errors within trade payables and the year-end payables may be understated.	The audit team should increase their testing on trade payables at the year end, with a particular focus on completeness of payables. A payables circularisation or review of supplier statement reconciliations should be undertaken.

80 Blackberry Co

Examining team's comments. This area of the syllabus requires an understanding of how the auditor obtains and accepts audit engagements, obtains an understanding of the entity and its environment, assesses the risk of material misstatement and plans an audit of the financial statements.

As noted in previous Examining team's Reports a fundamental factor in planning and assessing the risks of an audit of an entity is an assessment of audit risk, and this remains a highly examinable area. Audit risk questions typically require a number of audit risks to be identified (½ marks each), explained (½ marks each) and an auditor's response to each risk (1 mark each). Typically candidates can be required to identify and explain in the region of six to eight risks and responses.

The scenarios usually contain more issues than are required to be discussed. It is pleasing that candidates planned their time carefully and generally only attempted to list the required number of issues. However, in common with other sessions, a significant number of candidates often did not explain how each issue could impact on the audit risk and therefore were not awarded the second ½ mark. To explain audit risk candidates need to state the area of the financial statements impacted with an assertion (e.g. cut off, valuation etc.), a reference to under/over/misstated, or, a reference to inherent, control or detection risk. Misstated was only awarded if it was clear that the balance could be either over or understated.

Candidates should note that an auditor's response does not have to be a detailed audit procedure, rather an approach the audit team will take to address the identified risk. However, the responses given were sometimes too weak e.g. "discuss with management". Responses also sometimes focussed on what management should do rather than the auditor, and/or, were inappropriate to the scenario.

Marking scheme

		Marks
(a)	**Fraud and error**	
	ISA 240 responsibilities	2
	Respond appropriately	2
		4
(b)	**Audit risks and responses (only 8 risks required)**	
	Inventory valuation	2
	Inventory count after year-end date	2
	Accounting treatment of patent	2
	Share issue	2
	Sales ledger fraud	2
	Use of service organisation	2
	Transfer of data to service organisation	2
	Claim for unfair dismissal	2
	Key controls not performed	2
	Contingent asset	2
	Max 8 issues, 2 marks each	16
	Total marks	20

(a)   **Fraud responsibility**

Loganberry & Co must conduct an audit in accordance with ISA 240 *The Auditor's Responsibilities Relating to Fraud in an Audit of Financial Statements* and is responsible for obtaining reasonable assurance that the financial statements taken as a whole are free from material misstatement, whether caused by fraud or error.

In order to fulfil this responsibility, Loganberry & Co is required to identify and assess the risks of material misstatement of the financial statements due to fraud.

They need to obtain sufficient appropriate audit evidence regarding the assessed risks of material misstatement due to fraud through designing and implementing appropriate responses. In addition, Loganberry & Co must respond appropriately to fraud or suspected fraud identified during the audit.

When obtaining reasonable assurance, Loganberry & Co is responsible for maintaining professional scepticism throughout the audit, considering the potential for management override of controls and recognising the fact that audit procedures which are effective in detecting error may not be effective in detecting fraud.

To ensure that the whole engagement team is aware of the risks and responsibilities for fraud and error, ISA 240 requires that a discussion is held within the team. For members not present at the meeting, Blackberry Co's audit engagement partner should determine which matters should be communicated to them.

(b)   **Audit risks and auditor's response**

Audit risk	Auditor's response
Blackberry Co values its inventory at the lower of cost and net realisable value. Cost includes both production and general overheads. IAS 2 *Inventories* requires that costs included in valuing goods and services should only be those incurred in bringing inventory to its present location and condition. Although production overheads meet these criteria, general overheads do not. If these are included in inventory cost, then this will result in over-valued inventory.	Discuss with management the nature of the overheads included in inventory valuation. If general overheads are included, request management remove them from the valuation to be included in the draft financial statements. Review supporting documentation to verify those overheads deemed to be of a production nature are valid.
The company is planning to undertake the full year-end inventory counts after the year end and then adjust for movements from the year end. If the adjustments are not completed accurately, then the year-end inventory could be under or overstated.	The auditor should attend the inventory count held after the year end and note details of goods received and despatched post year end, in order to agree to the reconciliation. During the final audit, the year-end inventory adjustments schedule should be reviewed in detail and agreed to supporting documentation obtained during the inventory count for all adjusting items. The audit team should increase the extent of inventory cut-off testing at the year end and at the date of the count.

Audit risk	Auditor's response
A patent has been purchased for $1.1m and this grants Blackberry Co the exclusive right for three years to customise their portable music players to gain a competitive advantage in their industry. Management has expensed the full amount paid to the current year statement of profit or loss. In accordance with IAS 38 *Intangible Assets*, this should have been included as an intangible asset and amortised over its three-year life. As the sum has been fully expensed and not treated in accordance with IAS 38, intangible assets and profits are understated. During the year Blackberry Co has raised new finance through issuing $1.2m of shares at a premium. This needs to be accounted for correctly, with adequate disclosure made and the equity finance needs to be allocated correctly between share capital and share premium. If this is not done, then the accounts may be misstated due to a lack of disclosure or share capital and share premium may be misstated.	The audit team will need to agree the purchase price to supporting documentation and confirm the useful life is three years as per the contract. Discuss with management the reason for fully expensing the $1.1m paid, and request they correct the treatment. The correcting journal should be reviewed and the amortisation charge should be recalculated in order to ensure the accuracy of the charge and that the intangible is correctly valued at the year end. The audit team should confirm that proceeds of $1.2m were received and that the split of share capital and share premium is correct and appropriately recorded. In addition, the disclosures for this finance should be reviewed in detail to ensure compliance with relevant accounting standards and local legislation.
In November 20X7, it was discovered that a significant teeming and lading fraud had been carried out by four members of the sales ledger department. There is a risk that the full impact of the fraud has not been quantified and any additional fraudulent transactions would need to be written off in the statement of profit or loss. If these have not been uncovered, the financial statements could be misstated.	Discuss with the finance director what procedures they have adopted to fully identify and quantify the impact of the teeming and lading fraud. In addition, discuss with the finance director, what controls have been put in place to identify any similar frauds. Review the receivables listing to identify any unusual postings to individual receivable balances as this could be further evidence of fraudulent transactions.
In addition, individual receivable balances may be under/overstated as customer receipts have been misallocated to other receivable balances. During the year Blackberry Co outsourced its sales ledger processing to an external service organisation. A detection risk arises as to whether sufficient and appropriate evidence is available at Blackberry Co to confirm the completeness and accuracy of controls over the sales and receivables cycle and balances at the year end.	In addition, the team should maintain their professional scepticism and be alert to the risk of further fraud and errors. Discuss with management the extent of records maintained at Blackberry Co for the period since February 20X8 and any monitoring of controls undertaken by management over sales and receivables. Consideration should be given to contacting the service organisation's auditor to confirm the level of controls in place.
The sales ledger processing transferred to the service organisation from 1 February 20X8. If any errors occurred during the transfer process, these could result in sales and receivables being under/overstated.	Discuss with management the transfer process undertaken and any controls put in place to ensure the completeness and accuracy of the data. Where possible, undertake tests of controls to confirm the effectiveness of the transfer controls. In addition, perform substantive testing on the transfer of information from the old to the new system.

Audit risk	Auditor's response
In December 20X7, the financial accountant of Blackberry Co was dismissed and is threatening to sue the company for unfair dismissal. If it is probable that Blackberry Co will make a payment to the financial accountant, a provision for unfair dismissal is required. If the payment is possible rather than probable, a contingent liability disclosure would be necessary. If Blackberry Co has not done this, there is a risk over the completeness of any provisions or contingent liabilities.	The audit team should request confirmation from the company's lawyers of the existence and likelihood of success of any claim from the former financial accountant.
No supplier statement or purchase ledger control account reconciliations have been performed in the period from December 20X7 to the year end. This a key control which is being overridden and as such there is an increased risk of errors within trade payables and the year-end payables balance may be under or overstated.	The audit team should increase their testing on trade payables at the year end, including performing supplier statement reconciliations, with a particular focus on completeness of trade payables. Request management prepare a year-end purchase ledger control account reconciliation. The audit team should undertake a detailed review of this reconciliation with a focus on any unusual reconciling items.
A current asset of $360,000 has been included within the statement of profit or loss and assets. It represents an anticipated pay out from liquidators handling the bankruptcy of a customer who owed Blackberry Co $0.9m. The sum of $0.9m was written off in the prior year accounts. However, the company has not received a formal notification from the liquidators confirming the payment and this would therefore represent a possible contingent asset. To comply with IAS 37 *Provisions, Contingent Liabilities and Contingent Assets*, this should not be recognised until the receipt is virtually certain. With no firm response to date, the inclusion of this sum overstates profit and current assets.	Discuss with management whether any notification of payment has been received from the liquidators and review the related correspondence. If virtually certain, the treatment adopted is correct. If payment has been received, agree to post-year end cash book. If receipt is not virtually certain, management should be requested to remove it from profit and receivables. If the receipt is probable, the auditor should request management include a contingent asset disclosure note.

81 Darjeeling Co

Workbook references. Chapter 6, 13 and 14.

Top tips. Part (a) was a simple knowledge requirement on which you should have a chance of scoring at least two marks. If you were not sure of your knowledge here, then you could think about what the stages of an audit would be, and then consider why analytical procedures might be used at each stage.

Part (b) simply asked for three ratios for both years – so six calculations in total. These did not need to be complex, but it is important that you worked carefully and picked up the right figures from the question. Be careful not to waste time by calculating more ratios than are needed, or writing out the formula for each ratio.

Part (c) was an application-based requirement. It is essential that you only include eight audit risks in your solution; the 16 marks available divide themselves into one each for describing the audit risk and then for the auditor's response to it. Your description of the audit risk should say what is happening and then, crucially, why this poses an audit risk. This statement of why could address a problem that could be encountered during the audit (eg due to lack of available information), or simply which balances could be over or understated. The auditor's response is then focused on reducing the audit risks.

Part (d) asked for substantive procedures on the faulty paint inventory. When writing your procedures you need to be as specific as possible, and should say **why** the procedure should be performed. Do not overlook procedures that begin with 'Discuss with management' – you could have scored two out of three marks here merely for 'discuss' procedures.

Part (e) was similar to (d) but focused on revenue. Many of these are generic points that would apply to many different situations, but there are easy marks available for thinking of procedures that are specific to Darjeeling Co and its sales price promise.

Easy marks. There are marks in (c) for giving a simple description of each audit risk from the scenario (the marks for identification), and these are easy to get.

Examining team's comments. As noted in previous examiner's reports a fundamental factor in planning and assessing the risks of an audit of an entity is an assessment of audit risk, and this remains a highly examinable area. Audit risk questions typically require a number of audit risks to be identified (½ marks each), explained (½ marks each) and an auditor's response to each risk (1 mark each). Typically candidates can be required to identify and explain in the region of six to eight risks and responses.

The scenarios usually contain more issues than are required to be discussed. It is pleasing that candidates planned their time carefully and generally only attempted to list the required number of issues. However, in common with other sessions, a significant number of candidates often did not explain how each issue could impact on the audit risk and therefore were not awarded the second ½ mark. To explain audit risk candidates need to state the area of the financial statements impacted with an assertion (eg cut off, valuation etc), a reference to under/over/misstated or, a reference to inherent, control or detection risk. Misstated was only awarded if it was clear that the balance could be either over or understated.

Candidates should note that an auditor's response does not have to be a detailed audit procedure, rather an approach the audit team will take to address the identified risk. However, the responses given were sometimes too weak eg 'discuss with management'. Responses also sometimes focussed on what management should do rather than the auditor, and/or, were inappropriate to the scenario.

As in previous sessions, in this session a number of audit risk questions were combined with a requirement to calculate ratios, these ratios then link into the risk and responses requirement. 'Darjeeling Co' from the 'Sample September/December 2018 Questions' is a good question to practice the skill of calculating ratios and applying these to a risk and response question. Candidates tend to score well in calculating ratios, however a few points to note are as follows:

- Do not calculate more than the required number of ratios as this wastes time
- Do not provide the formula for ratios, as no credit is available

		Marks
(a)	Analytical procedures	
	Must be used at planning as risk assessment tool	1
	Can be used to gather evidence during fieldwork	1
	Must be used at completion to confirm overall conclusion	1
		3

		Marks
(b)	Ratios	
	Gross profit margin	1
	Inventory holding period	1
	Receivables collection period	1
	Payables payment period	1
	Current ratio	1
	Quick ratio	1
	Max 3 ratios, ½ for each calc	3
(c)	Audit risks and responses (only 8 risks required)	2
	Treatment of research and development costs	2
	Incorrect capitalisation of PPE costs	2
	New significant loan finance	2
	Finance costs	2
	Risk of manipulation due to potential listing	2
	Recoverability of receivables	2
	Accounting for 'price promise'	2
	Product recall	2
	Inventory valuation	2
	Significant increase in revenue and gross margin	2
	Cash flow difficulties	2
	Max 8 issues, 2 marks each	16
(d)	Substantive procedures – faulty inventory	
	Obtain schedule of faulty inventory, cast and agree to inventory listing	1
	Agree quantities affected to manufacturing and sales records	1
	Agree a sample of returns to relevant documentation	1
	Discuss issue with management and likelihood of subsequent sale	1
	Agree any post year-end sales to invoice and assess NRV	1
	Agree costs of faulty goods to supporting documentation	1
	Discuss any write down with management	1
	Inspect board minutes for evidence of resale or additional costs	1
	Restricted to	3
	Total marks	30

(a) **Analytical procedures**

Analytical procedures can be used at all stages of an audit, however, ISA 315 Identifying and Assessing the Risks of Material Misstatement through Understanding the Entity and Its Environment and ISA 520 Analytical Procedures identify three particular stages.

During the planning stage, analytical procedures must be used as risk assessment procedures in order to help the auditor to obtain an understanding of the entity and assess the risk of material misstatement.

During the final audit, analytical procedures can be used to obtain sufficient appropriate evidence. Substantive procedures can either be tests of detail or substantive analytical procedures.

At the final review stage, the auditor must design and perform analytical procedures which assist them when forming an overall conclusion as to whether the financial statements are consistent with the auditor's understanding of the entity.

(b) **Ratios**

Ratios to assist the audit supervisor in planning the audit:

	20X8	*20X7*
Gross margin	7,410/19,850 = 37.3%	6,190/16,990 = 36.4%
Inventory holding period	1,850/12,440 * 365 = 54 days	1,330/10,800 * 365 = 45 days
OR		
Inventory turnover	12,440/1,850 = 6.7	10,800/1,330 = 8.1
Receivables collection period	2,750/19,850 * 365 = 51 days	1,780/16,990 * 365 = 38 days
Payables payment period	1,970/12,440 * 365 = 58 days	1,190/10,800 * 365 = 40 days
Current ratio	4,600/(1,970 + 810) = 1.65	3,670/1,190 = 3.08
Quick ratio	2,750/(1,970 + 810) = 0.99	(3,670 – 1,330)/1,190 = 1.97

(c)

Audit risk	Auditor's response
During the year, Darjeeling Co has spent $0.9m on developing new product lines, some of which are in the early stages of their development cycle. This expenditure is classed as research and development under IAS 38 *Intangible Assets*. The standard requires research costs to be expensed to profit or loss and only development costs to be capitalised as an intangible asset. The company has included all of this expenditure as an intangible asset. If research costs have been incorrectly classified as development expenditure, there is a risk that intangible assets could be overstated and expenses understated.	Obtain a breakdown of the expenditure and verify that it relates to the development of the new products. Review expenditure documentation to determine whether the costs relate to the research or development stage. Discuss the accounting treatment with the finance director and ensure it is in accordance with IAS 38.

Audit risk	Auditor's response
Darjeeling Co purchased and installed a new manufacturing line. The costs include purchase price ($2.2m), installation costs ($0.4m) and a five-year servicing and maintenance plan ($0.5m). As per IAS 16 *Property, Plant and Equipment*, the cost of an asset includes its purchase price and directly attributable costs only. IAS 16 does not allow servicing and maintenance costs to be capitalised as part of the cost of a non-current asset, as they are not directly related to the cost of bringing the asset to its working condition. The servicing costs relate to a five-year period and so should be charged to profit or loss over this time. The upfront payment represents a prepayment for five years; as the services are received, the relevant proportion of the cost should be charged to profit or loss. If the service for 20X8 has been carried out, then $0.1m ($0.5m/5) should be charged to profit or loss. Therefore property, plant and equipment (PPE) and profits are overstated and prepayments are understated.	Review the purchase documentation for the new manufacturing line to confirm the exact cost of the servicing and that it does relate to a five-year period. Discuss the accounting treatment with the finance director and the level of any necessary adjustment to ensure treatment is in accordance with IAS 16.
The company has borrowed $4m from the bank via an eight-year loan. This loan needs to be correctly split between current and non-current liabilities in order to ensure correct disclosure.	During the audit, the team would need to confirm that the $4 million loan finance was received. In addition, the split between current and non-current liabilities and the disclosures for this loan should be reviewed in detail to ensure compliance with relevant accounting standards and local legislation. Details of security should be agreed to the bank confirmation letter.
As the level of debt has increased, there should be additional finance costs as the loan has an interest rate of 5%. There is a risk that this has been omitted from the statement of profit or loss leading to understated finance costs and overstated profit.	The finance costs should be recalculated and any increase agreed to the loan documentation for confirmation of the 5% interest rate. Interest payments should be agreed to the cash book and bank statements to confirm the amount was paid and is not therefore a year-end payable.
Darjeeling Co intends to undertake a stock exchange listing in the next 12 months. In order to maximise the success of the potential listing, Darjeeling Co will need to present financial statements which show the best possible position and performance. The directors therefore have an incentive to manipulate the financial statements, by overstating revenue, profits and assets.	Earl & Co should ensure that there is a suitably experienced audit team. Also, adequate time should be allocated for team members to obtain an understanding of the company and the significant risks of overstatement of revenue, profits and assets, including attendance at an audit team briefing. The team needs to maintain professional scepticism and be alert to the increased risk of manipulation. Significant estimates and judgements should be carefully reviewed in light of the misstatement risk.

ANSWERS

Audit risk	Auditor's response
The receivables collection period has increased from 38 to 51 days and management has extended the credit terms given to customers on the condition that sales order quantities were increased. The increase in receivable days could be solely due to these increased credit terms. However, it could also be due to an increased risk over recoverability of receivables as they may be overvalued and expenses understated.	Review and test the controls surrounding how Darjeeling Co identifies receivables balances which may not be recoverable and procedures around credit control to ensure that they are operating effectively. Extended post year-end cash receipts testing and a review of the aged receivables ledger to be performed to assess valuation. Also consider the adequacy of any allowance for receivables
This year the company made a 'price promise' to match the price of its competitors for similar products. Customers are able to claim the difference from the company for one month after the date of purchase of goods. The company should account for the price promise in accordance with IFRS 15 *Revenue from Contracts with Customers*. As the company may be required to provide a refund, the anticipated refund amount should not be initially recognised as revenue but instead as a refund liability until the one-month price promise period has ended. This is a highly subjective area, with many judgements required with regards to the level of likely refund due. As this is a new liability, the directors may not have correctly accounted for this sum resulting in overstated revenue, under/overstated profits and liabilities.	Discuss with management the basis of the refund liability of $0.25m and obtain supporting documentation to confirm the reasonableness of the assumptions and calculations.
Darjeeling Co has stopped further sales of one of its paint products and a product recall has been initiated for any goods sold since June. This product recall will result in Darjeeling Co paying refunds to customers. The sales will need to be removed from the 20X8 financial statements and a refund liability recognised. Also inventory will need to be reinstated, albeit at a possibly written down value. Failing to account for this correctly could result in overstated revenue, understated liabilities and misstated inventory.	Review the list of sales of the paint product made between June and the date of the recall, agree that the sales have been removed from revenue and the inventory included. If the refunds have not been paid before the year end, review the draft financial statements to confirm that it is included within current liabilities.
The company is holding a number of damaged paint products in inventory and overall the inventory holding period has increased from 45 days to 54 days. Due to the issue with the paint consistency, the quality of these products is questionable and management is investigating whether these products can be rectified. There is a risk that this inventory may be overvalued as its net realisable value may be below cost.	Discuss with the finance director whether any write downs will be made to this product, and what, if any, modifications will be required to rectify the quality of the product. Testing should be undertaken to confirm cost and NRV of the affected paint products held in inventory and that on a line by line basis the goods are valued correctly.

Audit risk	Auditor's response
Revenue has increased by 16.8% in the year; and the gross margin has increased slightly from 36.4% to 37.3%. This is a significant increase in revenue and, along with the increase in gross margin, may be related to the increased credit period and price promise promotion or could be due to an overstatement of revenue.	During the audit a detailed breakdown of sales will be obtained, discussed with management and tested in order to understand the sales increase. Also increased cut-off testing should be undertaken to verify that revenue is recorded in the right period and is not overstated.
The payables payment period has increased from 40 to 58 days. The current ratio has decreased from 3.08 to 1.65. The quick ratio has also decreased from 1.97 to 0.99. In addition, the bank balance has moved from $0.56m to an overdraft of $0.81m. These are all indicators that the company could be experiencing a reduction in its cash flow which could result in going concern difficulties or uncertainties. These uncertainties may not be adequately disclosed in the financial statements.	Detailed going concern testing to be performed during the audit, including the review of cash flow forecasts and the underlying assumptions. These should be discussed with management to ensure that the going concern basis is reasonable.

(d)   **Faulty inventory**

- Obtain a breakdown of the damaged goods held in inventory and returned from customers and cast to confirm its accuracy.

- From the breakdown, agree the damaged goods quantities manufactured since June to production records; and agree to sales records the quantities sold.

- Agree on a sample basis the returns from customers as per the breakdown back to sales returns documentation to confirm the existence of the returns quantities.

- Discuss with management the current status of their plans for this product line and whether they are able to rectify the damage and then sell the goods on. If so, agree the costs of rectification to supporting documentation.

- If the damaged inventory has been rectified and sold post year end, agree to the sales invoice to assess NRV in line with the new cost of the product.

- Agree the cost of damaged goods to supporting documentation to confirm the raw material cost, labour cost and any overheads attributed to the cost.

- Discuss with management if the goods have been written down; if so, follow through the write down to the inventory valuation to confirm.

- Inspect monthly board meeting minutes from June 20X8 onwards to obtain further information regarding the faulty paint and its possible resale value.

(e)   **Revenue**

- Compare the overall level of revenue against prior years and budget for the year and investigate any significant fluctuations.

- Perform a proof in total calculation for revenue, creating an expectation of the average price for the main paint products multiplied by the increased sales volumes for this year. This expectation should be compared to actual revenue and any significant fluctuations should be investigated.

- Obtain a schedule of sales for the year broken down into the main product categories and compare this to the prior year breakdown and for any unusual movements, discuss with management.

BPP
LEARNING
MEDIA

- Calculate the final gross profit margin for Darjeeling Co and compare this to the prior year and investigate any significant fluctuations.

- Select a sample of sales invoices for customers and agree the sales prices back to the price list or customer master data information to ensure the accuracy of invoices.

- For a sample of invoices, recalculate invoice totals including discounts and sales tax.

- Select a sample of credit notes raised, trace through to the original invoice and ensure the invoice has been correctly removed from sales.

- Select a sample of customer orders and agree these to the despatch notes and sales invoices through to inclusion in the sales ledger and revenue general ledger accounts to ensure completeness of revenue.

- Select a sample of despatch notes both pre and post year end and follow these through to sales invoices in the correct accounting period to ensure that cut-off has been correctly applied.

- For sales made under the price promise, compare the level of claims made to date with the refund liability recognised and assess whether it is reasonable.

- For a sample of sales invoices issued between June and the product recall, trace to subsequent credit notes to confirm that the sale has been removed from revenue.

Flowers Anytime

82   The correct answer is:

(1)   Complete flowcharts and internal control evaluation questionnaires
(2)   Perform walkthrough tests
(3)   Perform tests of control
(4)   Revise the audit strategy and audit plan

The first step should be to document the system of internal control – this is done using the flowchart and internal control evaluation questionnaire. The second step should be to confirm the auditor's understanding of the system – this is done with a walkthrough test. Tests of control are then performed to obtain audit evidence about the effectiveness of the design and operation of internal controls. Finally, if controls testing reveals any deficiencies in internal controls that have not been previously identified, the audit strategy and the audit plan should be revised as required.

83   The correct answer is:

ICEQs are generally easier to apply to a variety of different systems than ICQs.

In the first option, the descriptions of ICQs and ICEQs are reversed. Neither ICQs nor ICEQs are likely to capture how internal controls deal with unusual transactions: narrative notes are needed to do this. Both ICQs and ICEQs give the impression that all controls are of equal importance. The significance of each control would only be highlighted in narrative notes.

84   The correct answer is:

Audit junior's notes	Yes	No
All orders are recorded on pre-printed, three-part sequentially numbered order forms. One copy is kept by the sales clerk, one copy is forwarded to the warehouse for the dispatch of inventory, and one copy is sent to the customer as evidence of the order.		X
The sales clerk regularly performs reviews of the standing data on the system, matching the price of flowers against an up to date price list.		X

Audit junior's notes	Yes	No
To ensure completeness of orders, a sequence check is performed on the sales invoices manually by the sales clerk and any missing documents are investigated.	X	
Sales invoices are posted on a weekly basis to the sales day book and accounts receivable ledger.		X

A sequence check of the invoices is an effective control, be it carried out manually or electronically. Order forms should have four, not three, parts. No copy of the order is sent to the accounts receivables clerk – as a result, the recording of receivables may be incomplete or delayed, and outstanding balances may remain uncollected. The sales clerk should not be reviewing the standing data themselves – this review should be performed by an independent, senior member of staff. Sales invoices should be posted automatically to the sales day book and the accounts receivables ledger immediately after the order is taken.

85 The correct answer is:

1 only

This simply reduces the risk that cash will be misappropriated. It does not provide any assurance that subsequent recording will be complete or accurate.

86 The correct answer is:

The deficiencies identified in the sales system only

ISA 265 *Communicating Deficiencies in Internal Control to those Charged with Governance and Management* requires the auditor to communicate significant deficiencies in internal control (ISA 265). The fact that the amounts exposed to the deficiencies in the sales system were high and that it is likely that the deficiencies would result in material misstatements in the financial statements are indicators that the deficiencies are significant (ISA 265).

KLE Co

87 The correct answer is: Purchases may be made unnecessarily at unauthorised prices.

The fact that the ordering clerk transfers information from the order requisition to the order form without any subsequent approval increases the risk that errors on the order form go unnoticed. The fact that the order requisition is thrown away means that any subsequent queries cannot be traced back to the original order. The facts that the ordering department does not retain copies of the order forms means that orders may be duplicated, either in error or deliberately. The chief buyer authorises the order requisitions and determines the appropriate supplier, so the risk of purchases being made at unauthorised prices is reduced.

88 The correct answer is: 1, 3 and 4

It is important that the ordering department receives a copy of the GRN, so that they can monitor which orders are closed and which remain outstanding. To ensure efficiency and to avoid delays, a three-part GRN could be used – one for the ordering department, one for the goods inwards department and one for the accounts department.

89 The correct answer is: For a sample of GRNs check that there is an authorised purchase order

The direction of the test is important here. The sample is taken from goods received notes as these represent deliveries. The auditor can then check that each delivery is supported by a valid order. If the sample is chosen from purchase orders (as in the first option) the test would confirm whether orders have been fulfilled. The remaining options are tests of controls regarding completeness of accounting information.

90   The correct answer is: Undertake 'mystery shopper' reviews, where they enter the store as a customer, purchase goods and rate the overall shopping experience

Bank confirmations should always be carried out by the auditor. Providing advice on the implementation of a new payroll system would impair the internal auditors' independence. Reviewing the financial statements on behalf of the board is the responsibility of the audit committee, not internal audit.

91   The correct answer is: The relationship between goods and services produced and the resources used to produce them

A value for money audit focuses on three Es: Economy, Efficiency and Effectiveness. The first option describes economy. The third option describes effectiveness. The second option only describes one aspect of efficiency.

SouthLea

92   The correct answers are:

Cut-off of starters' and leavers' wages

Potential fraud risk factors

The facts that the foreman is authorised to issue new employee numbers, and that the two wages clerks are responsible for setting up employee records, make it more likely for bogus employees to be set up on the system than for bona fide employees to be omitted. This is likely to give rise to questions around the occurrence of wages, not their completeness. The fact that a wages clerk reviews the calculations for the deductions from gross pay should reduce the risk of computerised errors.

93   The correct answer is:

Review the log of amendments to standing data for evidence of review

Reviewing overtime lists for evidence of authorisation is a test of control over the authorisation of wages. The other two procedures can identify unauthorised amendments to standing data, but they are substantive procedures.

94   The correct answer is:

The internal auditor must always consider the potential of management overriding controls and modify their audit procedures accordingly when performing internal audit engagements.

The need to consider the potential of management override applies mainly to the external auditors. The external auditor's objective is to conclude whether the financial statements are free from material misstatement, whether from error or fraud. Audit procedures that are effective in detecting error may not be appropriate in detecting fraud due to the nature of fraud.

95   The correct answer is:

(1) and (2) only

In the absence of the audit committee the work of the internal audit department should be directed by the board. The scope being set by the finance director reduces independence.

96   The correct answers are:

Full testing procedures using test data when developing computer applications

Disaster recovery procedures

One for one checking and hash totals are application controls.

Cherry

97   The correct answer is: The selection and application of accounting policies

The selection and application of accounting policies is one of the areas in which the auditor is required to gain an understanding, as part of the auditor's risk assessment procedures. It is not a component of internal control. The other components of internal control are the risk assessment process and monitoring of controls.

98   The correct answer is: 2 and 3

The fact that raw materials are being ordered without reviewing inventory levels means that both stock-outs and excess obsolescent inventory are likely. The lack of authorisation means that fraudulent purchases could be made, but there is an approved supplier list and money-laundering risks seem far-fetched. Likewise, poorer quality goods may be ordered but the approved supplier list does act as a control here – and going concern risks are irrelevant.

99   The correct answer is: Completeness of payables

The fact that goods received notes (GRNs) are not sequentially numbered means that GRNs may be omitted from accounting records and it would be difficult to trace the unrecorded GRNs. As a result, the risk is that payables (and inventory) is understated.

100   The correct answer is: Because there are likely to be fewer capital purchases than standard purchases in the year, it may not be cost efficient to undertake tests of controls.

It is likely that the number of capital purchases in the year will be less than the number of standard purchases in the year. If the invoices are not segregated, it may not be cost efficient to test the controls over this area, in which case substantive testing would have to be undertaken. Although controls around the non-current assets cycle will probably resemble those around the purchases cycle, the auditor should still understand how the company's system records capital invoices. The risk of material misstatement in relation to the non-current assets cycle is high, because orders are likely to be of a less routine nature, larger amounts may be involved, and there may be an incentive to account creatively for tax or other purposes.

101   The correct answer is: 1 and 3

The direction of the test is important here. If the sample of serial numbers were taken from the non-current assets register, the physical assets which were not assigned serial numbers and/or were not recorded would not be identified. Reviewing the non-current register to identify duplicate serial numbers will identify instances when the serial numbers assigned were not unique, making it difficult to trace the related assets. Observation is a valid audit procedure, but it provides a weak form of audit evidence, since it does not assure the auditor that the control would be operated when the auditor is not there to observe it.

Swan

102   The correct answer is:

The company is able to fulfil the orders.

It is a deficiency in the system that the other three objectives do not appear to be met.

103   The correct answers are:

Goods are sent out but not invoiced.

Wrong goods are sent to customers.

This is because there is a risk that the printed orders will not be invoiced properly as they may be lost or overlooked (being outside the electronic system), hence the second risk. In addition, if the reason the GRN details do not match is that they have been fulfilled incorrectly (rather than due to simple typographical errors), the staff member may assume it is a typing issue and simply print the order, but not double check the goods properly against it, hence the fourth risk. In this situation, a customer might be sent 50 goods rather than the ordered 5, but only be invoiced for 5, as the invoice is generated from the order.

This issue should not cause goods to be invoiced without being sent out, as invoices are generated from goods out notes or orders being used as goods out notes.

It should also not cause orders not to be fulfilled, as the issue arises when the order has been processed, so the order has not been overlooked.

104   The correct answers are:

Review a sample of invoices to ensure their numerical sequence.

Review a sample of goods out notes to ensure they have been matched to sales invoices.

The other two procedures relate to accuracy.

105   The correct answers are:

The likelihood of material misstatement resulting

The number of deficiencies identified

The likelihood of material misstatement occurring is a key factor in determining whether the deficiency is significant. The number of deficiencies is a factor, as deficiencies may become significant if there is a significant combination of deficiencies.

A control deficiency does not increase in significance simply due to the area of business it relates to, but may become significant if there is a risk of fraud. There is no more significant risk of fraud in the sales system than in other systems, for example, the purchases system or payroll system, so the business area is not a critical factor.

Similarly, a deficiency is a deficiency regardless of whether the related control is new or not. In fact, an old deficiency might be more significant than a new one if, say, it had been previously reported and not acted on.

106   The correct answer is:

A computerised ICEQ

This is the only option that has the element of evaluation that the partner requires. The fact that it is computerised should also influence how easy it is to update, therefore addressing her second issue.

107 Chuck

Workbook references. Chapters 6, 10, 11, 17 and 20.

Top tips. As always in the long 30-mark questions you should make sure you keep to time for each individual part and the question as a whole.

In part (a) you should identify and explain the deficiencies of the payroll system from the scenario and recommend a control to address each one. Make sure you use a two-column tabular approach as noted in the requirement, one column for control deficiency and one for control recommendations.

In (b) keep your answers focused on substantive procedures, not tests of control. Also your procedures should remain relevant to the assertions stated in the question – completeness and accuracy of the payroll charge. Don't forget simple procedures such as casting the payroll records since this will also help to confirm accuracy and completeness.

Part (c) was on the auditor's responsibility in relation to laws and regulations. Remember the auditor's opinion will be on the financial statements, so the auditor's responsibility will be focused on those laws and regulations that could have a material effect on the financial statements, whether direct or indirect. There are a number of substantive procedures you could have suggested in (d) in respect of the redundancy provision, but the most you could gain is four marks so it is important you did not carry on stating more than four procedures and risk exceeding your time allocation of eight minutes. Part (e) was relatively straightforward in relation to reliance on internal audit as long as you knew the four key factors of objectivity, technical competence, due professional care and communication.

Easy marks. These were available in parts (d) and (e), but all in all it was possible to score well in every part of this question.

Examining team's comments. In part (a) the scenario contained an abundance of deficiencies and so on the whole candidates were able to easily identify enough points. A small minority of candidates provided implications and recommendations for general deficiencies which were not specified within the scenario; these points would not have gained credit as the question requirement clearly stated that points needed to be raised for the deficiencies identified in the scenario. A significant proportion of candidates wasted time by writing out the deficiencies from the scenario; there were no marks available for deficiencies, only for the implications and recommendations.

Performance was mixed in part (b). As noted in previous examining team's reports, candidates are often confused with the differences between tests of controls and substantive tests. The requirement verb was to 'describe' therefore sufficient detail was required to score the one mark available per test.

Part (c) was answered unsatisfactorily by most candidates. Most candidates focused on management's responsibility for preparing financial statements and implementing controls and auditors' responsibility to provide a true and fair opinion. These points are not related to laws and regulations. Part (d) was answered unsatisfactorily by many candidates. Candidates must tailor their knowledge to the scenario in order to pick up application marks and those candidates who performed well were able to produce detailed procedures which related to the scenario. In relation to the popular answer of obtaining written representations this procedure needs to be phrased with sufficient detail to obtain credit. 'Obtain a written representation from management' would not have scored any marks as it does not specify what the representation is for. Candidates performed well on part (e), with many attaining full marks.

Marking scheme

Marks

(a) Up to 1 mark per well-explained control deficiency and up to 1 mark for each well-explained recommendation.

No monitoring/supervision of clocking in and out

Payroll calculations not checked

Verbal notification of payroll changes by HR

Night shift wages susceptible to risk of theft

Absent night shift employees' pay not secure over weekend

Joiners not notified on timely basis   12

(b) Up to 1 mark per substantive procedure.

Agree wages and salaries per payroll to trial balance

Cast payroll records

Recalculate gross and net pay

BPP
LEARNING
MEDIA

Recalculate statutory deductions, agree relevant to current year rates

Compare total payroll to prior year

Review monthly payroll to prior year and budget

Proof in total of payroll

Verify joiners/leavers and recalculate first/last pay

Agree salaries paid per payroll to bank transfer list and cash book

Agree total cash withdrawn from bank equates to wages paid and surplus cash banked

Agree tax liabilities to payroll and post year end cash book

Agree the individual wages and salaries as per the payroll to the personnel records and records of hours worked per clocking in cards 6

(c)   Up to 1 mark per valid point.

Management responsibility to comply with law and regulations

Auditors not responsible for preventing non-compliance

Auditors – reasonable assurance financial statements free from material error

Law and regulations – direct effect responsibility

Law and regulations – indirect effect responsibility

Remain alert/Professional scepticism 4

(d)   Up to 1 mark per substantive procedure.

Discuss with directors whether formal announcement made of redundancies

Review supporting documentation to confirm present obligation

Review board minutes to confirm payment probable

Cast breakdown of redundancy provision

Recalculate provision and agree components of calculation to supporting documentation

Review post year end period to compare actual payments to amounts provided

Written representations to confirm completeness

Review disclosures for compliance with IAS 37 *Provisions, Contingent Liabilities and Contingent Assets* 5

(e)   Up to 1 mark per well-explained point.

Objectivity – independence, status and to whom report

Technical competence – qualifications and experience

Due professional care – properly planned and performed

Communication – between internal and external auditors <u>3</u>

<u><u>30</u></u>

(a)   Chuck Industries – payroll system

Control deficiency	Control recommendation
There are no monitoring/supervision procedures relating to the clocking in and clocking out of employees. This means that staff may ask colleagues to clock them in when they are not actually present resulting in a payroll cost in excess of that expected for the actual hours worked.	Clocking in and out should be monitored by a supervisor of an appropriate level, or by CCTV cameras installed to deter employees from clocking in for one another. Furthermore, employees should be automatically clocked out at the end of their shift, and should be required to clock back in if they are completing pre-agreed overtime.
Payroll calculations are not reviewed and 100% reliance is placed on the accuracy of the payroll system. This means that any errors made, for example as a result of standing or underlying data being incorrect or errors occurring during payroll processing, then they would not be discovered. This may lead to overpayments or underpayments (and incorrect payroll costs) and may result and lead to losses or disgruntled employees.	A payroll supervisor should periodically recalculate the net pay based on the gross pay and expected deductions, then compare the result with the computer generated figures for a sample of employees. The review should be evidenced by a signature and wages should not be paid until this signed review is completed.
The HR department has used verbal authorisation to inform the payroll department of pay increases. This indicates a lack of authorisation at board level and could lead to invalid increases in employee wages (eg for HR personnel's friends or relatives).	HR should be required to gain written board authorisation for any proposed wage increase before passing this to payroll. Similarly, payroll should be informed only to action a wage increase or other change on receipt of written authorisation approved by the board.
The factory supervisor is trusted with substantial cash sums in advance of the distribution of wages to the night shift. This cash is susceptible to theft and loss while not with employees or securely stored.	Payroll officials should be available for certain hours during the night shift to distribute wages. The night shift workers should also be required to produce identification before they are given their pay packets. Alternatively Chuck may decide to pay the night shift via bank transfer.
The factory supervisor keeps absent employees' wages over the weekend before handing back to payroll and this further increases the risk of loss or theft of cash wages.	Any amounts not paid out on Fridays should be kept by payroll in a safe or other secure means until Monday when the employee can collect from payroll.
Staff holidays in the HR department have meant that payroll information relating to new joiners was not communicated on a timely basis, which in turn meant that joiners were not paid on time leading to disgruntled employees and inaccurate payroll records.	HR staff duties and responsibilities should be reallocated when staff are ill or on holiday, including the responsibility of immediate communication of new joiners (and leavers) to payroll. In addition, new joiner forms showing start date should be completed and authorised, and then passed to payroll so that they are aware of the need to update the payroll records.

(b)   **Substantive procedures – Payroll cost**

(i)   Compare the total payroll expense to the previous year and investigate any significant variances.

(ii)   Review monthly payroll charges and compare this to the prior year monthly charges and to budgets. Discuss significant variances with management.

(iii)   Reconcile the total wages and salaries expense per the payroll records to the cost in the financial statements and investigate any differences.

(iv)   Agree amounts owed to the tax authorities to the payroll records and with the amount subsequently paid and clearing the bank statement post year end to ensure completeness.

(v)   Cast a sample of payroll records to confirm completeness and accuracy of the payroll expense.

(vi)   Recalculate the gross and net pay for a sample of employees and agree to the payroll to confirm accuracy.

(vii)   Recalculate statutory deductions to confirm whether the correct deductions are included within the payroll expense.

(viii) Perform a proof in total of total factory workforce wages by taking last year's expense, dividing by last year's average employee numbers to arrive at an average wage and multiplying by current year average employee numbers (the calculation should also incorporate the pay increase). Compare this estimate of the current year charge with the actual wages cost in the financial statements and investigate significant differences.

(ix)   Agree the start or leaving date to supporting documentation for a sample of joiners and leavers, and recalculate their first or last pay packet to ensure it was accurately calculated and properly recorded.

(x)   Agree the total net salaries paid on the payroll records to the bank transfer listing of payments for sales and administrative staff, and to the cash book for weekly paid employees.

(xi)   Agree the total cash withdrawn for wage payments equates to the weekly wages paid plus any leftover cash subsequently banked to confirm completeness and accuracy.

(xii)   Agree individual wages and salaries per the payroll to the personnel records and records of hours worked per the swipe card system.

Note. Only six procedures were needed to gain full marks.

(c)   **Responsibilities – Laws and regulations**

It is Chuck Industries Co's management that have a responsibility to ensure that the entity complies with the relevant laws and regulations (ISA 250). It is not the auditor's responsibility to prevent or detect non-compliance with laws and regulations.

The auditor's responsibility is to obtain reasonable assurance that the financial statements are free from material misstatement and, in this respect, the auditor must take into account the legal and regulatory framework within which the entity operates (ISA 250).

ISA 250 (Revised) *Consideration of Laws and Regulations in an Audit of Financial Statements* distinguishes the auditor's responsibilities in relation to compliance with two different categories of laws and regulations:

- Those that have a direct effect on the determination of material amounts and disclosures in the financial statements

- Those that do not have a direct effect on the determination of material amounts and disclosures in the financial statements but where compliance may be fundamental to the operating aspects, ability to continue in business, or to avoid material penalties (ISA 250).

For the first category, the auditor's responsibility is to obtain sufficient appropriate audit evidence about compliance with those laws and regulations (ISA 250). For the second category, the auditor's responsibility is to undertake specified audit procedures to help identify non-compliance with laws and regulations that may have a material effect on the financial statements (ISA 250).

Blair & Co must also maintain professional scepticism and be alert to the possibility that other audit procedures may bring instances of identified or suspected non-compliance with laws and regulations. (ISA 250)

(d)   **Substantive procedures – Redundancy provision**

- Obtain an analysis of the redundancy calculations (cost by employee) and cast it to ensure completeness.

- Obtain written representation from management confirming the completeness of the provision.

- In order to establish that a present obligation exists at the year end, ask the directors whether they formally announced their intention to make the sales ledger department redundant during the year.

- If the redundancies have been announced pre year end, review any documentation corroborating that the decision has in fact been formally announced.

- Review the board minutes to assess the probability the redundancy payments will be paid.

- Recalculate the redundancy provision to confirm completeness and agree components of the calculation to supporting documents.

- Confirm whether any redundancy payments have been made post year end and compare any amounts paid to amounts provided to assess the adequacy of the provision.

- Review the disclosure of the redundancy provision to ensure it complies with IAS 37 *Provisions, Contingent Liabilities and Contingent Assets*.

Note. Only five procedures were needed to gain full marks.

(e)   **Factors to consider – Reliance on work performed by internal audit**

The following important criteria will be considered by the external auditors when determining if the work of internal auditors is likely to be adequate.

Extent to which its objectivity is supported

The auditor must consider the extent to which the internal audit function's objectivity is supported by its organisational status, relevant policies and procedures. Considerations include to whom the internal auditors report, any conflicting responsibilities, any constraints or restrictions, whether those charged with governance oversee employment decisions regarding internal auditors and whether management acts on recommendations made.

Level of technical competence

The auditor must consider whether internal auditors are members of relevant professional bodies, whether they have adequate technical training and proficiency and whether there are established policies for hiring and training.

Whether a systematic and disciplined approach is taken

The auditor must also consider whether internal audit activities are systematically and properly planned, supervised, reviewed and documented; and whether suitable audit manuals, work programmes and internal audit documentation exist. The auditor must also consider whether the function has appropriate quality control procedures in place.

108 Greystone

Workbook reference. Chapters 5, 9, 10, 16 and 19.

Top tips. Part (a) is a standalone requirement which asks for an explanation of matters to be considered when determining whether a deficiency is significant. So, assuming a deficiency has been identified, what would make it a significant one? Remember that a significant deficiency is one that the auditor judges to be of sufficient importance to merit the attention of those charged with governance (TCWG) – so even if you couldn't remember the factors listed in the ISA, you could have tried to think of what sort of factors will influence the need to report to TCWG and which might not.

In part (b), you don't want miss out on the two marks for the presentation of your answer, so make sure you include a suitable covering letter with your report to management. As you look through a scenario such as this, you should look out for any clue you are given that there is a deficiency in a particular area. For example, here there is a lot of potential for running out of inventory where you have a four-week wait for orders to arrive. In the absence of a robust control, you should be able to pick up that the current ordering system is not up to the job and suggest viable improvements, such as setting minimum reorder levels.

Part (c) is a relatively straightforward requirement if you know your trade payables substantive procedures. Remember to focus on year-end trade payable procedures and only include substantive procedures, not tests of controls.

For part (d) you may well be familiar with the sorts of assignments internal audit carry out. You should always bear the scenario in mind though and prioritise your suggestions according to how well they fit the scenario.

Easy marks. You should be very comfortable with substantive procedures over trade payables, making (c) relatively straightforward.

Examining team's comments. Part (a) was unrelated to the Greystone Co scenario and hence tested candidates' knowledge as opposed to application skills. This question related to ISA 265 *Communicating Deficiencies in Internal Control to those Charged with Governance and Management*, and candidates performed inadequately on this part of the question. The main reason for this is that candidates failed to read the question properly or did not understand what the requirement entailed. The question asked for matters which would mean internal control deficiencies were significant enough to warrant reporting to those charged with governance. The question was not asking for examples of significant internal control deficiencies; however, this is what the majority of candidates gave.

Part (b) was answered well by the vast majority of candidates with some scoring full marks. The scenario was quite detailed and hence there were many possible deficiencies which could gain credit. Where candidates did not score well this was mainly due to a failure to explain the deficiency and/or the implication in sufficient detail.

Many candidates failed to score the full two marks available for presentation as they did not produce a covering letter. A significant minority just gave the deficiencies, implications and recommendations without any letter at all; this may be due to a failure to read the question properly. Also even when a letter was produced this was often not completed.

The question asked for four deficiencies, implications and recommendations; however, many candidates provided much more than the required four points. It was not uncommon to see answers which had six or seven points. Whilst it is understandable that candidates wish to ensure that they gain credit for four relevant points, this approach can lead to time pressure and subsequent questions can suffer.

Part (c) was answered satisfactorily for many candidates. The most common mistake made by some candidates was to confuse payables and purchases and hence provide substantive tests for purchases such as 'agree purchase invoices to goods received notes'. The requirement verb was to 'describe' therefore sufficient detail was required to score the one mark available per test. Candidates are reminded that substantive procedures is a core topic area and they must be able to produce relevant detailed procedures. Answers such as 'discuss with management to confirm ownership of payables' is far too vague to gain credit as there is no explanation of what would be discussed and also how such a discussion could even confirm ownership.

Part (d) required candidates to use their knowledge of internal audit assignments and apply it to a retailer scenario. On the whole candidates performed satisfactorily on this question. However, some candidates restricted their answers to assignments the auditors would perform in light of the control deficiencies identified in part (b) of their answer. This meant that their answers lacked the sufficient breadth of points required to score well.

Marking scheme

	Marks

(a) Up to 1 mark per valid point.

Likelihood of deficiencies leading to errors

Risk of fraud

Subjectivity and complexity

Financial statement amounts

Volume of activity

Importance of the controls

Cause and frequency of exceptions

Interaction with other deficiencies 5

(b) Up to 1 mark per well explained deficiency, up to 1 mark per recommendation and up to 1 mark per test of control. If not well explained 0.5 marks for each.

2 marks for presentation, 1 for address and intro, 1 for conclusion

Purchasing manager orders goods without consulting store

Purchase order reviewed in aggregate by purchasing director

Store managers reorder goods

No inter-branch transfer system

Deliveries accepted without proper checks

Sales assistants produce the goods received note

Goods received but not checked to purchase orders

Manual matching of goods received notes to invoice

Purchase invoice logged late 14

(c) Up to 1 mark per well-explained substantive procedure.

Agree purchase ledger to general and financial statements

Review payable to prior year

Calculate trade payables

After-date payments review

After-date invoices/credit notes review

Supplier statement reviews

Payables circularisation

Goods received not invoiced

Cut-off testing

Debit balances review

Disclosure within current liabilities   5

(d)   Up to 1 mark per well-explained point.

Cash controls testing

Mystery shopper

Financial/operational controls

Fraud investigations

IT systems review

Value for money review

Regulatory compliance   <u>6</u>

                                                                        <u><u>30</u></u>

(a)   ISA 265 includes examples of matters to consider when determining whether a deficiency in internal control is a significant deficiency. These include (ISA 265):

- The likelihood of the deficiencies resulting in material misstatements in the financial statements in the future

- The importance of the controls to the financial reporting process

- The susceptibility to loss or fraud of the related asset or liability

- The interaction of the deficiency with other deficiencies in internal control

- The amounts exposed to the deficiencies

> **Top tips.** In (a) you could have included the following factors:
> - The cause and frequency of the exceptions identified as a result of the deficiencies
> - The volume of activity that has occurred or could occur
> - The subjectivity and complexity of determining estimated amounts
>
> However, only five were needed to pick up all of the available marks.

(b)

ABC & Co

Certified Accountants

29 High Street

The Board of Directors

Greystone Co

15 Low Street

8 December 20X0

Members of the board,

Financial statements for the year ended 30 September 20X0

We set out, in an appendix to this letter, deficiencies in the purchases system which arose as a result of our review of the accounting systems and procedures operated by your company during our recent audit. The matters dealt with in this letter came to our notice during the conduct of our normal audit procedures which are designed primarily for the purpose of expressing our opinion on the financial statements.

This letter has been produced for the sole use of your company. It must not be disclosed to a third party, or quoted or referred to, without our written consent. No responsibility is assumed by us to any other person.

We should like to take this opportunity of thanking your staff for their co-operation and assistance during the course of our audit.

Yours faithfully

ABC & Co

Appendix

Control deficiency	Control recommendation	Test of control
The purchasing manager determines store inventory levels without consulting those who are best placed to judge the local market; the store or sales managers. Certain clothes and accessories may be initially over-ordered and may need to be sold at reduced prices. This may also result in overvalued inventory (if held at cost) in the management accounts and ultimately the financial statements. Also some inventory may not be ordered in enough volume to meet demand and the reputation of Greystone may suffer.	The purchasing manager should consult (in a meeting or by conference call) the store managers and a joint decision should be made on the initial inventory levels to be ordered for clothes/accessories.	Select a sample of the minutes of meetings held by the purchasing manager and store managers for evidence that the store managers have been consulted on inventory order levels. Discuss with/email a sample of store managers to request confirmation that they have been consulted on inventory order levels.
Store managers are responsible for reordering through the purchases manager and it can take four weeks for goods to be received. The reliance is on store managers to be proactive and order four weeks before a potential stock-out. Without prompting they may order too late and inventory may run out for a period of up to four weeks, resulting in lost revenue.	Realistic reorder levels should be established in the inventory system. When inventory is down to the predetermined level, the purchasing manager should be prompted to raise a purchase order (for example the system may generate an automatic reorder request which is emailed to the purchasing manager).	Use test data to process sufficient sales so that the inventory levels of a sample of items fall below the reorder level. Determine whether an automatic reorder request is emailed to the purchasing manager.

Control deficiency	Control recommendation	Test of control
Stores cannot transfer goods between each other to meet demand. Customers are directed to try other stores/the website when an item of clothing is sold out. Revenue may be lost because the system is inconvenient for the customer, who may not follow up at other stores, but may have purchased if the goods were transferred to their local store. Additionally the perceived lack of customer service may damage the store's reputation.	An internal ordering system should be set up which allows for the transfer of goods between stores. In particular, stores with very low inventory levels should be able to obtain excess inventories from those with high levels to meet demand while goods are reordered.	Process a sample of orders between different stores in order to determine whether the internal ordering system operates as documented.
Goods received are not checked against purchase orders. Goods which were not ordered in the first place could be received. Once received, it may be difficult to return these goods and they may need to be paid for. In any case there is a potential unnecessary administrative cost. Additionally, some goods ordered may not be received leading to insufficient inventory levels and potential lost revenue.	A copy of authorised orders should be kept at the relevant store and checked against goods received notes (GRNs). If all details are correct, the order should be marked completed and sent to head office. The purchasing clerk should review the purchase orders at regular intervals for incomplete items and investigate why these are not completed.	Inspect a sample of goods received notes (GRN) to confirm that they have been checked back to the original order, and that the GRN has been initialled to show that the check has been performed.

> **Top tips.** The answer to (b) includes four well-explained deficiencies, recommendations and tests of control as 4 were needed to gain 12 marks. Together with the 2 marks available for presentation, this would be enough for the full 14 marks.
>
> Please note, however, there were a number of alternative deficiencies, recommendations and controls you may have identified, including those shown in the table below:

Control deficiency	Control recommendation	Test of control
The purchase orders reviewed and authorised by the purchasing director are aggregated by region. The lack of detail does not allow the purchasing director to make an informed assessment of the buying policies and they may be unsuitable for specific markets within regions.	A country by country review of orders should be carried out by the purchasing director. Where appropriate, discussions should take place between the purchasing director and local purchasing managers before authorisation of orders.	Inspect the documentation relating to the review of orders to determine whether they have been reviewed in sufficient detail.

Control deficiency	Control recommendation	Test of control
Quality of goods is not checked by sales assistants, only quantity. Poor quality clothes may be accepted and may not be saleable (also inventory may be temporarily overvalued).	Goods should be checked on arrival for quantity and quality prior to acceptance.	Observe a sample of goods being received in order to determine whether goods are checked for both quality and quantity. Inspect GRN for evidence of a signature to show that the check has been performed.
Purchase invoices and GRNs are manually matched, which is time consuming. The manual processing of high a high volume of documents is prone to human error. Invalid invoices may be processed as a result.	A purchasing system should be adopted which allows for logging of GRNs against original invoices, and then electronic/automatic matching of invoices against GRNs. A regular review by the purchasing clerk should then be focused on unmatched items.	Process a sample of orders using test data. Trace the orders through the purchasing system to verify that all appropriate checks and authorisations are requested by the system.
A purchase invoice is not put on the system until it is ready for authorisation by the purchasing director. The purchase ledger will not have all invoices posted, understating liabilities. Also payables may be paid late.	A list of invoices not posted should be prepared on a monthly basis and passed to the purchasing director for authorisation and an accrual made to ensure completeness of payables.	Review the list of invoices not posted to ensure they are being prepared on a monthly basis, and that they are authorised by the purchasing director.

(c) Substantive procedures for year-end trade payables

(i) Obtain a trade payables purchase ledger listing and agree the total to the general ledger and the figure for trade payables included in the financial statements

(ii) Compare the list of trade payables with the previous years to identify any potentially significant omissions

(iii) Compare the payables turnover and payables payment period with the previous year and industry data

(iv) Reconcile a sample of payables balances with supplier statements and investigate differences which could indicate a significant misstatement

(v) Review the cash book entries or the bank statements after the end of the year for payments which could indicate the existence of unrecorded trade payables

> **Top tips.** Only five were needed for full marks, but other procedures include:
> * Reconcile the total of the purchase ledger accounts with the purchase ledger control account and cast the list of balances and the control account
> * Review after-date invoices and credit notes for evidence of unrecorded liabilities
> * For a sample of pre year end goods received notes, ensure the related payables have recorded pre year-end (ie that cut-off is appropriate)
> * Perform a trade payables circularisation for a sample of trade payable balances, following up non replies and reconciling the balance on the trade payables listing with that shown on the supplier response

> - Review the purchase ledger for debit balances that require reclassification as assets
> - Make sure that trade payables are classified as current liabilities in the financial statements

(d) **Additional assignments for internal audit**

Testing of controls over cash

Retail stores have a significant amount of cash at each shop and need robust controls over the cash receipts process. Internal audit could test the design and operation of these controls at each store on a periodic basis. They could also conduct cash counts at the same time they carry out inventory counts.

Fraud investigations

A retailer such as Greystone with large sums of cash and desirable, easily moveable, inventory is more susceptible to fraud than many other businesses. Internal audit assignments may therefore include reviewing the fraud risk areas and suggesting controls to mitigate these risks. Where fraud is uncovered, internal audit could also investigate these instances of fraud.

Value for money review

Internal audit could undertake value for money audits to examine the economy, efficiency and effectiveness of activities and systems, such as the just-in-time ordering system recently introduced.

Overall review of financial/operational controls

Internal audit could undertake reviews of central controls at head office, making recommendations to management over, for example, the sales, purchases and payroll systems.

Review of information technology (IT) systems

Greystone may have complex computer systems linking tills in the stores to head office. If internal audit has an IT specialist, they could be asked to perform a review over the computer controls for this system or other computer systems.

Compliance with laws and regulations

Like all businesses, Greystone will be subject to law and regulation, which will vary depending on the part of the world a store is operating in. The internal audit department could review compliance with these laws and regulations.

> **Top tips.** Six other assignments were needed for full marks. An alternative you may have come up with is the assignment of an internal auditor to test the customer experience in stores by posing as a customer. The level of perceived customer satisfaction is then fed back to each shop to improve customer service and form the basis for any further training that is required.

109 Tinkerbell

> **Workbook reference.** Chapters 9, 10 and 14.
>
> **Top tips.** Read the examining team's comments below carefully in relation to part (a). You must be able to differentiate between a test of control and a substantive procedure or you risk losing a high proportion of marks on some questions. A test of control must provide evidence that a control is operating effectively (or otherwise).
>
> Parts (b) and (d) were relatively straightforward and you should have been able to come up with enough procedures to gain the majority of marks. You should use the scenario to help you to generate tests, for example identifying procedures in relation to the discounts offered to large customers.

Part (c) could be answered in a tabular format to help address both mini-requirements – (1) identify and explain controls and (2) describe how the risk of fraud is mitigated. The description of the 'teeming and lading' fraud uncovered in the year pointed out the current lack of controls, so this could form the basis of your controls which should fill the gap. For example, customer statements were not sent out and this is one of the reasons the fraud was not uncovered before, so making sure that they are sent out in the future is a valid control.

Easy marks. These are available in parts (b) and (d) where you are asked for substantive procedures in relation to receivables and revenue.

Examining team's comments. In part (a) most candidates performed inadequately. The main problems encountered were that candidates struggled to differentiate between tests of control and substantive tests and hence often provided long lists of substantive procedures, which scored no marks. In addition, a significant minority of candidates did not read the question carefully and, instead of providing tests of controls, gave control procedures management should adopt. The approach candidates should have taken was to firstly identify from the scenario the controls present for Tinkerbell; they then should have considered how these controls could be confirmed by the auditor. In addition, candidates' explanations of tests were vague, such as 'check that credit limits are set for all new customers'. This procedure does not explain how the auditor would actually confirm that the control for new customer credit limits operates effectively. Tests that start with 'check' are unlikely to score many marks as they do not explain how the auditor would actually check the control. Future candidates should practise generating tests, both substantive and tests of controls, which do not start with the word 'check'.

The second part of this requirement was to explain the objective of the test of control provided. Again, this was not answered well. A common answer was to state that the objective was 'to ensure that the control is operating effectively'. This was far too vague. Instead, candidates should have considered the aim of the specific control being tested. Therefore the objective of a test over credit limits is 'to ensure that orders are not accepted for poor credit risks'.

As noted in previous examining team's reports candidates are often confused with the differences between tests of controls and substantive tests. Candidates must ensure that they understand when tests of controls are required and when substantive procedures are needed. They need to learn the difference between them and should practice questions requiring the generation of both types of procedures. A significant number of candidates presented their answers in a columnar format and this seemed to help them to produce concise and relevant answers.

Part (b) for eight marks required substantive procedures the auditor should perform on year-end receivables. This was answered well by many candidates. Candidates were able to provide variety in their procedures including both tests of detail and analytical review tests.

The most common mistakes made by some candidates were providing tests of control rather than substantive procedures, providing substantive procedures for revenue rather than receivables, not generating enough tests for eight marks and describing the process for a receivables circularisation at length (this was not part of the question requirement).

Part (c) for six marks required identification and explanation of controls that Tinkerbell should adopt to reduce the risk of fraud occurring again, as well as an explanation of how this control would mitigate the fraud risk. This question was answered well by most candidates, with some scoring full marks.

The scenario provided details of a 'teeming and lading fraud' which had occurred during the year and candidates needed to think practically about how Tinkerbell could reduce the risk of this occurring again. However, candidates' performance on the second requirement to describe how the control would mitigate the risk of fraud occurring again was mixed.

The main problem was that answers were not specific enough; frequently vague answers such as 'this will reduce the risk of fraud and error occurring' were given.

Part (d) for four marks required substantive procedures the auditor should perform on Tinkerbell's revenue. This requirement was not answered well. Some candidates confused this requirement with that of 1b, which required receivables tests, and so provided the same tests from 1b again. In addition, a significant number of candidates provided procedures to confirm bank and cash rather than revenue.

Those candidates who performed well were able to provide a good mixture of analytical procedures such as 'compare revenue to prior year or to budget' and 'review monthly sales against prior year' and also detailed tests such as confirming cut-off of sales.

Marking scheme

Marks

(a) Up to 1 mark per well-explained point and up to 1 mark for each objective.

Process order for fictitious order

Sales order over credit limit

Inspect credit applications

Agree prices used to relevant price list

Confirm discounts used on invoices agree to customer master file

Attempt to process a discount for a small customer

Inspect orders to confirm order acceptance generated

Observe sales order clerk processing orders to see if acceptance generated

Observe goods dispatch process

Agree goods dispatch notes (GDN) to invoices

Sequence checks over invoices   12

(b) Up to 1 mark per well-explained procedure.

Trade receivables circularisation, follow up any non-replies

Review the after-date cash receipts

Calculate average receivables collection period

Reconciliation of sales ledger control account

Cut-off testing of GDN

Aged receivables report to identify any slow-moving balances

Review customer correspondence to assess whether there are any invoices in dispute

Review board minutes

Review post year end credit notes

Review for any credit balances

Agree to GDN and sales order to ensure existence   8

(c)   Up to 1 mark per well-explained control and up to 1 mark for how it
        mitigates risk.

        Relatives not permitted to work in the same department

        Cash receipts processed by two members of staff

        Monthly customer statements sent

        Bank reconciliations reviewed by responsible official

        Rotation of duties within finance department

        Sales ledger control account reconciliation regularly performed

        Consider establishing an internal audit department   6

(d)   Up to 1 mark per well-explained procedure.

        Analytical review over revenue compared to budget and prior year

        Analytical review of major categories of toy sales compared to prior year

        Gross margin review

        Recalculate discounts allowed for larger customers

        Recalculate sales tax

        Follow order to goods dispatched note to sales invoice to sales ledger

        Sales cut-off

        Review post year end credit notes   4
                                                                              ――
                                                                              30
                                                                              ══

(a)   **Tinkerbell – Tests of control and test objectives for the sales cycle**

Test of control	Test objective
Enter an order for a fictitious customer account number and ensure the system does not accept it.	To ensure that orders are only accepted and processed for valid customers.
Inspect a sample of processed credit applications from the credit agency and ensure the same credit limit appears in the sales system.	To ensure that goods are only supplied to customers with acceptable credit ratings.
For a sample of invoices, agree that current prices have been used by comparing them with prices shown on the current price list.	To ensure that goods are only sold at authorised prices.
For a sample of invoices showing discounts, agree the discount terms back to the customer master file information.	To ensure that sales discounts are only provided to those customers the sales director has authorised.
For a sample of orders ensure that an order acceptance email or letter was generated.	To ensure that all orders are recorded completely and accurately.
Visit a warehouse and observe whether all goods are double checked against the GDN and dispatch list before sending out.	To ensure that goods are dispatched correctly to customers and are of an adequate quality.

Test of control	Test objective
With the client's permission, attempt to enter a sales order which will take a customer over the agreed credit limit and ensure the order is rejected as expected.	To ensure that goods are not supplied to poor credit risks.
Attempt to process an order with a sales discount for a customer not normally entitled to discounts to assess the application controls.	To ensure that sales discounts are only provided to valid customers.
Observe the sales order clerk processing orders and look for proof that the order acceptance is automatically generated (eg email in sent folder).	To ensure that all orders are recorded completely and accurately.
Inspect a sample of GDNs and agree that a valid sales invoice has been correctly raised.	To ensure that all goods dispatched are correctly invoiced.
Review the latest report from the computer sequence check of sales invoices for omissions and establish the action taken in respect of any omissions found.	To ensure completeness of income for goods dispatched.

(b) **Substantive procedures to confirm Tinkerbell's year-end receivables balance**

(i) Circularise trade receivables for a representative sample of the year-end balances. If authorised by Tinkerbell's management, send an email or reminder letter to follow up non-responses.

(ii) Review cash receipts after the year end in respect of pre year end receivable balances to establish if anything is still outstanding. Where amounts are unpaid investigate whether an allowance is needed.

(iii) Review the reconciliation of the receivables ledger control account (sales ledger control account) to the list of receivables (sales ledger) balances and investigate unusual reconciling items.

(iv) Review the aged receivables report to identify any old balances and discuss the probability of recovery with the credit controller to assess the need for an allowance.

(v) Calculate average receivables collection period and compare this to prior year and expectations, investigating any significant differences.

(vi) Select a sample of goods dispatched notes just before and just after the year end to ensure the related invoices are recorded in the correct accounting period.

(vii) Review a sample of credit notes raised after the year end to identify any that relate to pre year end transactions and confirm that they have not been included in receivables.

(viii) Review the aged receivables ledger for any credit balances and inquire of management whether these should be reclassified as payables.

(ix) For slow-moving/aged balances, review customer correspondence files to assess whether there are any invoices in dispute which require an allowance.

(x) Review board minutes to assess whether there are any material disputed receivables.

(xi) Select a sample of year-end receivable balances and agree back to a valid GDN and sales order to ensure existence.

(c) Controls to reduce the risk of fraud reoccurring and explanation of how the risk is mitigated

Control	Explanation of how risk is mitigated by control
Related members of staff should not be allowed to work in the same department where they can seek to override segregation of duty controls.	The risk of related staff colluding and being able to commit a fraud without easily being discovered will be reduced.
Customer statements should be sent out each month to all customers. The receivables ledger supervisor should check that all customers have been sent statements.	Customers receiving statements may notice anomalies in the allocation of payments (either timing or amount) and may alert the company of these anomalies. This may draw attention to the sort of fraud that occurred at Tinkerbell (known as 'teeming and lading').
Bank reconciliations should be reviewed regularly by someone of an appropriate level of management who is not involved in its preparation. Unreconciled amounts should be investigated and resolved at the time of review.	Any compensating material balances netted off to a small difference on the bank reconciliation will be discovered quickly, increasing the probability of uncovering fraud on a timely basis.

Top tips. Three controls such as those shown above along with three explanations were enough to gain the six marks available. However, other valid controls and explanations are given below.

Control	Explanation of how risk is mitigated by control
Two members of staff should process cash receipts.	This would mean another collusion would be necessary (on top of the one that has already occurred) to steal cash receipts. This therefore reduces the risk of reoccurrence.
Staff within the finance department should rotate duties on a regular basis.	Rotation will act as a deterrent to fraud. This is because staff will be less likely to commit fraudulent activities due to an increased risk of the next person to be rotated to their position uncovering any wrongdoing.

Control Study	Explanation of how risk is mitigated by control
The receivables ledger should be reconciled to the receivables ledger control account on at least a monthly basis. The reconciliation should be reviewed by a responsible official and anomalies investigated.	This will increase the chance of discovering errors in the receivable balances and help to create a strong control environment likely to deter fraud.

BPP
LEARNING
MEDIA

Control Study	Explanation of how risk is mitigated by control
Management should consider establishing an internal audit department to assess and monitor the effectiveness of controls, identify any deficiencies, and carry out specific fraud investigations.	The presence of an internal audit department would help to deter employees committing fraud and identification of fraud would be more likely due to ongoing monitoring of internal controls.

(d)   **Substantive procedures to confirm Tinkerbell's revenue**

(i)   Compare the total revenue with that reported in previous years and the revenue budgeted, and investigate any significant fluctuations.

(ii)   For a sample of customer orders, trace the details to the related dispatch notes and sales invoices and ensure there is a sale recorded in respect of each (to test the completeness of revenue).

(iii)   For a sample of sales invoices for larger customers, recalculate the discounts allowed to ensure that these are accurate.

(iv)   Select a sample of dispatch notes in the month immediately before and month immediately after the year end. Trace these through to the related sales invoices and resultant accounting entries to ensure each sale was recorded in the appropriate period.

> **Top tips.** Four procedures such as those shown above would have been sufficient to gain full marks on this part of the question. However, other procedures are given below.

(v)   Obtain an analysis of sales by major categories of toys manufactured and compare this to the prior year breakdown and discuss any unusual movements with management.

(vi)   Calculate the gross profit margin for Tinkerbell for the year and compare this to the previous year and expectations. Investigate any significant fluctuations.

(vii)   Recalculate the sales tax for a sample of invoices and ensure that the sales tax has been correctly applied to the sales invoice.

(viii) Select a sample of credit notes issued after the year end and trace these through to the related sales invoices to ensure sales returns were recorded in the proper period.

110 Trombone

> **Workbook references.** Chapters 7, 9 and 10.
>
> **Top tips.** Part (a) asks you to identify deficiencies in the control system for payroll, to recommend improvements and to describe a relevant test of control. Make sure that your answer addresses all three requirements. A tabular format is a particularly useful way of presenting your answer.
>
> Part (c) tests your knowledge of the difference between an interim audit and a final audit. You should find this relatively straightforward.
>
> **Easy marks.** Easy marks can be found in part (b).
>
> **Examining team's comments.** The first two parts of part (a) were answered satisfactorily by candidates; however, the tests of controls proved challenging for many.
>
> The requirement for tests of controls was answered unsatisfactorily. Many candidates are still confusing substantive procedures and test of controls. A significant number of candidates suggested substantive procedures such as 'recalculating gross and net pay calculations', rather than a test of control which might be to 'review evidence of the recalculation of payroll'. Candidates need to review their understanding of these different types of audit procedures and ensure that they appreciate that substantive tests focus on the number within the financial statements whereas tests of controls are verifying if client procedures are operating.

x

x

x

In many instances candidates focused on reperforming the control rather than testing that it had operated. Observation of a control was commonly suggested by candidates; however, in many cases this is not an effective way of testing that a control has operated throughout the year. Part (c) was answered very poorly by a significant number of candidates, demonstrating a worrying lack of knowledge about substantive procedures and tests of controls. This is an important area which needs to be addressed.

Part (b) was generally answered well by candidates. A minority of candidates incorrectly suggested that planning procedures would be undertaken at the interim audit and that they were undertaken by internal auditors. Also a significant minority confused this requirement with a comparison of internal and external audit roles. Candidates must remember to read the question carefully and think and plan before writing to ensure that they answer the question asked.

Marking scheme

Marks

(a) **Internal control deficiencies, recommendations and tests of control**
Up to 1 mark per well-explained deficiency, up to 1 mark for each well-explained recommendation and up to 1 mark for each well-described test of control. Overall maximum of 5 marks each for deficiencies, controls and tests of control.
Payroll calculations not checked
Payroll clerks update standing data for wages increases
Authorisation of overtime sheets only undertaken if overtime exceeds 30% of standard hours
Time off as payment for overtime not checked to overtime worked report
Review of overtime worked reports by department heads
Authorisation of overtime sheets when department heads on annual leave
Finance director only reviews totals of payroll records and payments list

Maximum marks   15

(b) **Final audit and interim audit**
Up to 1 mark per well-explained point, maximum of 3 marks each for interim and final audit, overall maximum of 5 marks.
Interim audit
Final audit   5

(c) Up to 1 mark per well-described substantive procedure.
Agree wages and salaries per payroll to trial balance
Cast payroll records
Recalculate gross and net pay
Recalculate statutory deductions
Compare total payroll to prior year
Review monthly payroll to prior year and budget
Proof in total of payroll and agree to the financial statements
Verify joiners/leavers and recalculate first/last pay
Agree wages and salaries paid per payroll to bank transfer list and cash book
Agree the individual wages and salaries as per the payroll to the personnel records
Agree sample of weekly overtime sheets to overtime payment in payroll   6
records

Marks

(d) Up to 1 mark per well-described procedure.
Agree to the payroll records to confirm the accuracy of the accrual
Reperform the calculation of the accrual
Agree the subsequent payment to the post year end cash book and
bank statements
Review any correspondence with tax authorities to assess whether there
are any additional outstanding payments due, if so, agree they are
included in the year- end accrual
Review disclosures and assess whether these are adequate and in
compliance

4

Maximum marks

30

(a)

Deficiencies	Recommended controls	Test of control
The gross and net pay automatically calculated by the payroll package are not checked at all. The lack of checking increases the risk that errors are being accumulated without being detected. This could lead to wages being over- or understated. Additional wages may be paid as a result. Statutory deductions may be over- or underpaid, giving rise to compliance issues. There is also likely to be a loss of employee goodwill.	A senior member of the payroll department should reperform a sample of the gross and net pay calculations. Any discrepancies should be investigated. The automatic gross and net pay calculations must be reviewed and approved before payments are made.	Obtain the recalculations performed by the senior payroll reviewer for evidence that the automatic calculations have been reviewed. Review a sample of the gross and net pay calculations generated by the payroll system for evidence that they have been approved and signed off.
The clerks update the standing data to reflect the increase of wages each year. The apparent lack of authorisation to changes in standing data increases the risk of errors, leading to the over- or understatement of wages, and the incorrect payment of wages. This also increases the risk of fraud, as the clerks have the ability to make unauthorised changes to standing data.	Payroll clerks should not be allowed to make standing data changes. Changes to the standing data to reflect the annual wage increase should be made by a senior member of the payroll department. These changes should be checked by another responsible official to identify any errors or inconsistencies.	Observe a payroll clerk attempting to make changes to payroll standing data, to determine whether the system rejects the changes. Review the log of changes made to the standing data for evidence that they were made by a senior member of the payroll department. Review the log of changes made to the standing data for evidence that they have been reviewed by another responsible official.

214   Audit and Assurance (AA)

Deficiencies	Recommended controls	Test of control
Only payment for overtime in excess of 30% of the standard hours are authorised by department heads. This increases the risk of employees claiming for overtime not worked, leading to additional payroll costs.	All overtime hours worked, whether in lieu of pay or holidays, must be authorised by the relevant department head. The authorisation should be evidenced by signatures.	Review a sample of the weekly overtime sheets for evidence of signature by the head of the department concerned.
The payroll clerks do not always check the overtime worked report before employees take time off in lieu of overtime worked. This increases the risk of employees taking unauthorised leave, leading, again, to wages being paid for days which have not been worked.	Payroll clerks must agree holidays taken in lieu to the overtime report, and record that this has been done. Where inconsistencies are identified, the payroll clerks should notify the relevant department head.	Review a sample of holidays taken in lieu of overtime to verify whether the payroll clerk has agreed the time taken in lieu to the overtime report.
The overtime worked report is emailed by the payroll department to department heads, who report only by exception if errors are identified. The authorisation of overtime sheets by an alternative responsible official while the department heads are on leave does not always occur. The fact that the department heads only report by exception can cause the payroll department to mistakenly assume that the overtime report is correct when it is not – leading to the payment of incorrect overtime. The lack of holiday cover for the authorisation of overtime can lead to overtime pay being delayed, resulting in the loss of employee goodwill.	Departments should be required to respond to the payroll department regarding each overtime worked report, regardless of whether it is correct. The department heads should be reminded of the procedures with regards to holiday cover. No payment should be made until the report has been authorised by the relevant official. The payroll department should monitor the authorisation of the overtime worked report and follow up with each relevant head where no response has been received.	For a sample of overtime worked reports, inspect the responses received from each department head. For a sample of overtime payments, compare the dates on which authorisation has been received with the dates on which overtime payment is made, to confirm that payment is only made after authorisation has been obtained. Make enquiries of payroll clerks regarding the process of obtaining authorisation for overtime sheets while the department heads are on leave.

Deficiencies	Recommended controls	Test of control
The finance director reviews the total list of bank transfers and compares this to the total payable per the payroll records. This process does not prevent employees to be omitted from the payroll. There is equally a risk of fictitious employees, or employees who have left the company, appearing on payroll. As a result, fraudulent payments could be made.	The finance director should agree a sample of the employees on the payroll records to the payment list, and vice versa, to ensure that payments are complete, and made only to bona fide employees. These checks should be evidenced by the finance director's signature.	Inspect payment lists for evidence that the finance director has agreed a sample of payees to the payroll records, and vice versa.

(b)   The differences between an interim and a final audit can be summarised as follows:

Type of audit	When it occurs	Purpose	Procedures performed
Interim audit	During the period of review	To carry out procedures that would be difficult to perform at the year end because of time constraints. No statutory requirement to perform interim audit.	<ul><li>Inherent risk assessment and gaining an understanding of the entity</li><li>Documenting and evaluating the entity's system of internal control</li><li>Carrying out tests of control on the company's internal controls to ensure they are operating as expected</li><li>Performing substantive testing of profit or loss transactions/balances to gain evidence that the books and records are a reliable basis for the preparation of financial statements</li><li>Identification of issues that may have an impact on work to take place at the final audit</li></ul>

Final audit	After the year end	To express an audit opinion on the financial statements covering the entire period being audited. The performance of the final audit is a statutory requirement.	Substantive procedures involving verification of statement of financial position balances and amounts in the statement of profit or loss • Obtaining third-party confirmations • Analytical procedures relating to figures in the financial statements • Subsequent events review • Agreeing the financial statements to the accounting records • Examining adjustments made during the process of preparing the financial statements • Consideration of the going concern status of the entity • Performing tests to ensure that the conclusions formed at the interim audit are still valid • Obtaining written representations

(c) **Payroll substantive procedures**

(i) Agree the total wages and salaries expense per the payroll system to the trial balance, investigate any differences.

(ii) Cast a sample of payroll records to confirm completeness and accuracy of the payroll expense.

(iii) For a sample of employees, recalculate the gross and net pay and agree to the payroll records to confirm accuracy.

(iv) Reperform the calculation of statutory deductions to confirm whether correct deductions for this year have been made in the payroll.

(v) Compare the total payroll expense to the prior year and investigate any significant differences.

(vi) Review monthly payroll charges, compare this to the prior year and budgets and discuss with management for any significant variances.

(vii) Perform a proof in total of total wages and salaries, incorporating joiners and leavers and the annual pay increase. Compare this to the actual wages and salaries in the financial statements and investigate any significant differences.

(viii) Select a sample of joiners and leavers, agree their start/leaving date to supporting documentation, recalculate that their first/last pay packet was accurately calculated and recorded.

(ix) Agree the total net pay per the payroll records to the bank transfer listing of payments and to the cash book.

(x) Agree the individual wages and salaries per the payroll to the personnel records for a sample.

(xi) Select a sample of weekly overtime sheets and trace to overtime payment in payroll records to confirm completeness of overtime paid.

(d)   **Accrual for income tax payable on employment income**

Procedures the auditor should adopt in respect of auditing this accrual include:

(i)   Agree the year-end income tax payable accrual to the payroll records to confirm accuracy.

(ii)   Reperform the calculation of the accrual to confirm accuracy.

(iii) Agree the subsequent payment to the post year end cash book and bank statements to confirm completeness.

(iv)   Review any correspondence with tax authorities to assess whether there are any additional outstanding payments due; if so, agree they are included in the year-end accrual.

(v)   Review any disclosures made of the income tax accrual and assess whether these are in compliance with accounting standards and legislation.

111 Fox Industries Co

Workbook references. Chapters 3, 9, 10 and 15.

Top tips. The requirements for this question are typical of the Audit and Assurance exam, with the scenario being about control deficiencies within a particular system. There is a lot to do in this question, so there is a risk of overrunning on the time. Make sure you stick to time for each part of the question and move on to the next requirement once the time is up.

Part (b) should be presented in a tabular format for the deficiencies, impacts and recommendations but do note the requirement for a covering letter – this is relatively unusual for this type of question. Note also that there are two marks available for this letter, so make sure your covering letter is addressed and dated appropriately and that you use a ruler for the table and headings. These two marks could be the difference between passing and failing. You must ensure that you identify deficiencies from both the purchases system and the payments system – go through the scenario line by line and make notes on areas where there are weaknesses. Your recommendations need to be sufficiently detailed and useful to the organisation. Imagine that you are drafting a real report to management to a real client. Saying things like 'Discuss with management' or 'Reconciliations' will not score many marks.

Part (c) is on application controls. This is a notorious area of weakness for Audit and Assurance students. Make sure you know the difference between application and general IT controls and that the controls you describe are relevant to the scenario in the question.

Easy marks. Part (a) on ISA 260 is knowledge based for five marks and relatively straightforward. Part (d) asks for substantive procedures for bank and cash. This is worth six marks and, provided your procedures are adequately detailed, you should be able to score well here.

			Marks

(a)   (i)   Up to 1 mark per well-explained point.

- Assists the auditor and those charged with governance in understanding matters related to the audit

- Obtains information relevant to the audit

- Helps those charged with governance in fulfilling their responsibility to oversee the financial reporting process   **2**

(ii)   Up to 1 mark for each example matter to be communicated to those charged with governance   **3**

(b) Requirement – Control weaknesses and recommendations (only 6 issues required)

- No approved suppliers list   2
- Purchase orders not sequentially numbered   2
- Orders below $5,000 are not authorised by a responsible official   2
- No application controls over input of purchase invoices   2
- Purchase ledger manually posted to general ledger   2
- Saving (deposit) bank accounts only reconciled every two months   2
- Payments to suppliers delayed   2
- Finance director only reviews the total of the payment list prior to payment authorising   2
- Covering letter presentation   2

Maximum   14

(c) Up to 1 mark per well-explained application control.

- Document counts
- Control totals
- One for one checking
- Review of output to expected value
- Check digits
- Range checks
- Existence checks   5

(d) Up to 1 mark per substantive procedure.

- Check additions of bank reconciliation
- Obtain bank confirmation letter
- Bank balance to statement/bank confirmation
- Cash book balance to cash book
- Outstanding lodgements
- Unpresented cheques review

- Old cheques write back
- Agree all balances on bank confirmation
- Unusual items/window dressing
- Security/legal right set-off
- Review reconciliations for saving (deposit) accounts
- Cash counts for significant cash balances
- Review disclosure of bank and cash in financial statements   <u>6</u>

<u><u>30</u></u>

(a)   **ISA 260 requirements**

(i)   It is important that auditors communicate throughout the audit with those charged with governance for the following reasons (ISA 260):

- It assists the auditor and those charged with governance to understand audit-related matters in context and allows them to develop a constructive working relationship.

- It allows the auditor to obtain information relevant to the audit.

- It assists those charged with governance to fulfil their responsibility to oversee the financial reporting process, thus reducing the risks of material misstatement in the financial statements.

(ii)   Examples of matters to be communicated to those charged with governance (ISA 260):

- The auditor's responsibilities in relation to the audit of the financial statements, including that the auditor is responsible for forming and expressing an opinion on the financial statements and that the audit does not relieve management or those charged with governance of their responsibilities

- The planned approach to, and timing of, the audit

- Significant deficiencies in internal control

- The auditor's views about significant qualitative aspects of the entity's accounting practices, including accounting policies, accounting estimates and financial statement disclosures

- Significant difficulties encountered during the audit

- Significant matters arising from the audit that were discussed or subject to correspondence with management

- Written representations requested by the auditor

- Other matters that, in the auditor's professional judgement, are significant to the oversight of the financial reporting process

- For listed entities, a statement that the engagement team and others in the firm, the firm, and network firms have complied with relevant ethical requirements regarding independence, any relationships between the firm and entity that might affect independence, and safeguards applied to eliminate identified threats to independence or reduce them to an acceptable level

Note. Only three matters were required.

(b)   Purchasing and payments system

Board of Directors

Fox Industries Co

Trading Estate

Any Town

AB1 3DE

Dear Sirs,

Audit of Fox Industries Co for the year ended 31 March 20X6

Please find enclosed the report to management on deficiencies in internal controls identified during the audit for the year ended 31 March 20X6. The appendix to this report considers deficiencies in the purchasing and payments system, the implications of those deficiencies and recommendations to address those deficiencies.

Please note that this report only addresses the deficiencies identified during the audit and if further testing had been performed, then more deficiencies may have been reported. This report is solely for the use of management and if you have any further questions, then please do not hesitate to contact us.

Yours faithfully,

An audit firm

Appendix

Control deficiency	Control recommendation
When raising purchase orders, the clerks choose whichever supplier can despatch the goods the fastest. This could result in Fox Industries Co ordering goods at a much higher price or a lower quality than they would like, as the only factor considered was speed of delivery.	It is important that goods are despatched promptly, but this is just one of many criteria that should be used in deciding which supplier to use. An approved supplier list should be compiled; this should take into account the price of goods, their quality and also the speed of delivery. Once the list has been produced, all orders should only be placed with suppliers on the approved list
Purchase orders are not sequentially numbered. Failing to sequentially number the orders means that Fox Industries Co's ordering team are unable to monitor if all orders are being fulfilled in a timely manner; this could result in stock outs. If the orders are numbered, then a sequence check can be performed for any unfulfilled orders	All purchase orders should be sequentially numbered and on a regular basis a sequence check of unfulfilled orders should be performed

BPP
LEARNING
MEDIA

Control deficiency	Control recommendation
Purchase orders below $5,000 are not authorised and are processed solely by an order clerk. This can result in goods being purchased which are not required by Fox Industries Co. In addition, there is an increased fraud risk as an order clerk could place orders for personal goods up to the value of $5,000, which is significant.	All purchase orders should be authorised by a responsible official. Authorised signatories should be established with varying levels of purchase order authorisation.
Purchase invoices are input daily by the purchase ledger clerk and due to his experience, he does not utilise any application controls. Without application controls there is a risk that invoices could be input into the system with inaccuracies or they may be missed out entirely. This could result in suppliers being paid incorrectly or not all, leading to a loss of supplier goodwill.	The purchase ledger clerk should input the invoices in batches and apply application controls, such as control totals, to ensure completeness and accuracy over the input of purchase invoices.
The purchase day book automatically updates with the purchase ledger but this ledger is manually posted to the general ledger. Manually posting the amounts to the general ledger increases the risk of errors occurring. This could result in the payables balance in the financial statements being under or overstated.	The process should be updated so that on a regular basis the purchase ledger automatically updates the general ledger. A responsible official should then confirm through purchase ledger control account reconciliations that the update has occurred correctly
Fox Industries Co's saving (deposit) bank accounts are only reconciled every two months. If these accounts are only reconciled periodically, there is the risk that errors will not be spotted promptly. Also, this increases the risk of employees committing fraud. If they are aware that these accounts are not regularly reviewed, then they could use these cash sums fraudulently.	All bank accounts should be reconciled on a regular basis, and at least monthly, to identify any unusual or missing items. The reconciliations should be reviewed by a responsible official and they should evidence their review.
Fox Industries Co has a policy of delaying payments to their suppliers for as long as possible. While this maximises Fox Industries Co's bank balance, there is the risk that the company is missing out on early settlement discounts. Also, this can lead to a loss of supplier goodwill as well as the risk that suppliers may refuse to supply goods to Fox Industries Co.	Fox Industries Co should undertake cash flow forecasting/budgeting to maximise bank balances. The policy of delaying payment should be reviewed, and suppliers should be paid in a systematic way, such that supplier goodwill is not lost

Control deficiency	Control recommendation
The finance director authorises the bank transfer payment list for suppliers; however, he only views the total amount of payments to be made. Without looking at the detail of the payments list, as well as supporting documentation, there is a risk that suppliers could be being paid an incorrect amount, or that sums are being paid to fictitious suppliers.	The finance director should review the whole payments list prior to authorising. As part of this, he should agree the amounts to be paid to supporting documentation, as well as reviewing the supplier names to identify any duplicates or any unfamiliar names. He should evidence his review by signing the bank transfer list.

Note. Only six deficiencies were required.

(c) **Application controls**

Document counts – the number of invoices to be input are counted, the invoices are then entered one by one, at the end the number of invoices input is checked against the document count. This helps to ensure completeness of input.

Control totals – here the total of all the invoices, such as the gross value, is manually calculated. The invoices are input, the system aggregates the total of the input invoices' gross value and this is compared to the control total. This helps to ensure completeness and accuracy of input.

One for one checking – the invoices entered into the system are manually agreed back one by one to the original purchase invoices. This helps to ensure completeness and accuracy of input.

Review of output to expected value – an independent assessment is made of the value of purchase invoices to be input, this is the expected value. The invoices are input and the total value of invoices is compared to the expected value. This helps to ensure completeness of input.

Check digits – this control helps to reduce the risk of transposition errors. Mathematical calculations are performed by the system on a particular data field, such as supplier number, a mathematical formula is run by the system, this checks that the data entered into the system is accurate. This helps to ensure accuracy of input.

Range checks – a pre-determined maximum is input into the system for gross invoice value, for example, $10,000; when invoices are input if the amount keyed in is incorrectly entered as being above $10,000, the system will reject the invoice. This helps to ensure accuracy of input.

Existence checks – the system is set up so that certain key data must be entered, such as supplier name, otherwise the invoice is rejected. This helps to ensure accuracy of input.

Tutorial note: Marks will be awarded for any other relevant application controls.

(d) **Substantive procedures on bank and cash balances**

(i) Send out a standard bank confirmation letter to each bank where the company holds bank accounts to confirm the year-end balance.

(ii) Review the year-end reconciliation of the bank balance per the general ledger against the bank balance per the bank letter.

(iii) Reperform the arithmetic of the bank reconciliation for each bank account held.

(iv) Trace cheques shown as outstanding from the bank reconciliation to the cash book prior to the year end and to the after-date bank statements and obtain explanations for any large or unusual items not cleared at the time of the audit.

(v) Compare cash book(s) and bank statements in detail for the last month of the year, and match items outstanding at the reconciliation date to bank statements.

(vi) Review the bank reconciliation previous to the year-end bank reconciliation and test whether all items are cleared in the last period or taken forward to the year-end bank reconciliation.

BPP
LEARNING
MEDIA

(vii) Obtain satisfactory explanations for all items in the cash book for which there are no corresponding entries in the bank statement and vice versa by discussion with finance staff.

(viii) Verify contra items appearing in the cash books or bank statements with original entry.

(ix) Verify by inspecting paying-in slips that uncleared bankings are paid in prior to the year end.

(x) Examine all lodgements in respect of which payment has been refused by the bank; ensure that they are cleared on representation or that other appropriate steps have been taken to effect recovery of the amount due.

(xi) Verify balances per the cash book according to the bank reconciliation by inspecting cash book, bank statements and general ledger.

(xii) Verify the bank balances with the reply to standard bank letter and with the bank statements.

(xiii) Inspect the cash book and bank statements before and after the year end for exceptional entries or transfers which have a material effect on the balance shown to be in hand.

(xiv) Identify whether any accounts are secured on the assets of the company by discussion with management.

(xv) Consider whether there is a legal right of set-off of overdrafts against positive bank balances.

(xvi) Determine whether the bank accounts are subject to any restrictions by inquiries with management.

(xvii) Count year-end cash balances and match to cash records such as the petty cash book.

(xviii) Obtain certificates of cash in hand from responsible officers.

(xix) Review draft financial statements to confirm that all amounts and relevant disclosures relating to cash and bank have been correctly stated.

112 Bluesberry

Workbook reference. Chapters 5 and 12.

Top tips. You should have been familiar with the purpose of a value for money audit in part (a) – just remember to focus on the **purpose** and not just provide a definition of a value for money audit.

The most important thing for (b)(i) is to understand the requirement. Don't be fazed by the fact you are asked for strengths instead of weaknesses or deficiencies. The scenario actually gives examples of problems that have been solved by certain procedures, so you should have recognised that these were strengths (for example the overtime scheme has seen reliance on expensive temporary staff reduced). As you were pulling out the strengths in the operating environment you could also have been considering the areas for improvement to help in answering part (b)(ii). In fact a good approach would have been to lay out your answer so that you could answer (b)(i) and (b)(ii) together.

Part (c) depends on you knowing your assertions so you can stay focused on the relevant substantive procedures. For each assertion ask yourself, what am I trying to prove with this procedure? For example, with completeness you are trying to prove no material items are missing from non-current assets. You therefore need to suggest procedures that might highlight missing assets.

Easy marks. Parts (a) and (c) were more straightforward than (b).

Examining team's comments. Candidates performed satisfactorily on part (a) of the question.

Part (b) required identification and explanation of four strengths within the hospital's operating environment and a description of an improvement to provide best value for money for the hospital. Candidates performed well in the explanations of the strengths within Bluesberry, with many scoring full marks. Where candidates failed to score well this was due to a failure to explain their strengths. The requirement was to 'identify and explain'; where a strength was identified then ½ mark was available, and another 1 mark was available for a clear explanation of each strength. In addition, a significant minority misread the question requirement and identified weaknesses rather than strengths.

The second part of this question required improvements to the strengths identified. Performance on this question was adequate. The majority of candidates attempted this part of the question, and were able to identify a few relevant points. However, answers were often too vague or unrealistic.

Candidates' performance was mixed for part (c), with many confusing their assertions. It was common to have existence tests provided for completeness. In addition, too many answers were vague; candidates are still giving substantive procedures such as 'check the invoices'.

Marking scheme

		Marks
(a)	Up to 1 mark per valid point.	
	Explanation of value for money audit	
	Economy – description	
	Efficiency – description	
	Effectiveness – description	4
(b)	0.5 marks for identification and up to 1 mark for explanation of each well-explained strength and up to 1 mark per improvement. If not well explained 0.5 marks for each, but overall maximum of 4 points.	
	Internal audit department	
	Centralised buying department buys from lowest cost supplier	
	Authorisation of all purchase orders by purchasing director	
	Reduction in use of temporary staff	
	Employee clocking in cards to monitor hours worked	
	New surgical equipment leading to better recovery rates	
	Capital expenditure committee	10
(c)	Up to 1 mark per substantive procedure.	
	Valuation (i)	
	Review depreciation policies for reasonableness	
	Recalculate the depreciation charge	
	Proof in total calculation of depreciation	

For revalued assets, consider reasonableness of valuer

For revalued assets, agree the revalued amounts to valuation report

Surgical equipment additions – vouch the cost to invoice   2

Completeness (ii)

Reconcile PPE schedule to general ledger

Physical inspection of assets

Reconciliation of non-current asset register to the general ledger

Review the repairs and maintenance expense account   2

Rights and obligations (iii)

Verify ownership of property via inspection of title deeds

Additions agree to purchase invoices to verify invoice relates to entity

Review any new lease agreements

Inspect vehicle registration documents   2

Total for (c)   <u>6</u>

<u>20</u>

(a) **Purpose of a value for money (VFM) audit**

VFM focuses on the best combination of services for the lowest level of resources. The purpose of a VFM audit is to examine the **economy, efficiency** and **effectiveness** of the activity or process in question.

- **Economy**: attaining the appropriate quantity and quality of physical, human and financial resources (inputs) at lowest cost

- **Efficiency**: the relationship between goods or services produced (outputs) and the resources used to produce them

- **Effectiveness**: concerned with how well an activity is achieving its policy objectives or other intended effects

(b)

Strength (i)	Improvement (ii)
The buying department researches the lowest price from suppliers before raising a purchase order. This helps with economy of the process, attaining resources at the lowest cost.	In order to also ensure the goods are of the required quality, an approved list of suppliers could be built up, with purchases only being permitted from those suppliers on the list.

Strength (i)	Improvement (ii)
Overtime rates have been increased and this has incentivised staff to fill staffing gaps. As a result the hospital has saved money by decreasing the level of expensive temporary staff. Additionally, the permanent staff may be more effective as they are familiar with the hospital's systems and the level of patient care expected at Bluesberry.	The increased hours will affect overall efficiency given that the same staff are now carrying out extended shifts, as overtime rates are higher than basic rates, even though overtime cost appears to be lower than temporary staff. There is also an increased risk of mistakes due to tiredness which could have adverse effects on the reputation of the hospital. Ideally the hospital should recruit enough permanent staff of the required level to fill shifts without then working overtime.
The hospital has implemented time card clocking in to ensure employees are only paid for those hours worked. It also provides a means for recording hours worked which is valuable management information. Before this there would have been no definitive record of actual hours worked.	The system appears to allow payable overtime to accumulate simply because an employee clocks out late, even if there is no staff gap to fill. The system should be set to automatically clock out after the normal number of shift hours. Staff will then need to clock back in for their overtime if they have an authorised shift. Overtime hours each month should be reviewed by the department head for consistency with agreed extra shifts.
A capital expenditure committee of senior managers has been set up to authorise significant capital expenditure items. This will help prevent cash outflows for unnecessary assets, or assets not budgeted for.	In a hospital there will be very expensive equipment purchases, such as the recently acquired new surgical equipment. It is better that these are authorised at board level rather than by senior managers. An authorisation policy should be drawn up setting out the different levels of authorisation needed (the highest being at board level) depending on the amount of expenditure for capital items.

Top tips. You were only asked for four strengths and related improvements. Others you may have come up with in place of those given in the answer above are as follows.

Strength (i)	Improvement (ii)
The hospital has an internal audit department monitoring the internal control environment and advising on value for money.	The remit of internal audit could be extended to advising on implementation.
Orders are authorised by a purchasing director to help ensure expenditure incurred is necessary expenditure.	The volume of forms (200 per day) will no doubt take valuable time away from the director which could be used on more pressing matters. Orders below a certain monetary level should be authorised by the next level (down) of management. Orders over the specified monetary value should still be reserved for purchase director authorisation.
New surgical equipment purchased has improved the rate of operations and patient recovery rates. This is an improvement in the effectiveness of the hospital.	The equipment is not used as efficiently as it could be due to lack of trained medical staff. The hospital should look at providing targeted training for existing medical staff and look to recruit staff that have the appropriate skills.

(c)   **Substantive procedures – property, plant and equipment (non-current assets)**

(i)   *Valuation*

- Review depreciation rates applied in relation to asset lives, past experience of profits and losses on disposals, and consistency with prior years and disclosed accounting policies.

- If assets have been revalued, consider:
    - Experience and independence of valuer
    - Scope of the valuer's work
    - Methods and assumptions used
    - Whether valuation bases are in line with IFRSs

(ii)   *Completeness*

- Compare non-current assets in the general ledger with the non-current assets register and obtain explanations for differences.

- For a sample of assets which physically exist agree that they are recorded in the non-current asset register.

(iii)   *Rights and obligations*

- Verify title to land and buildings by inspection of:
    - Title deeds
    - Land registry certificates
    - Leases

- Examine documents of title for other assets (including purchase invoices, contracts, hire purchase or lease agreements).

Top tips. Only two substantive procedures were needed for each assertion. You may have come up with alternative procedures including:

Valuation

- Recalculate the depreciation charge for a sample of assets and agree the charges to the asset register

- Perform a depreciation proof in total taking into account timing of additions/disposals and investigate any differences

- Agree the cost of a sample of additions of surgical equipment to purchase invoices

Completeness

- Reconcile the schedule of non-current assets with the general ledger

- Review the repairs and maintenance expense account in the SOCI for capital items

Rights and obligations

- Review new lease agreements to ensure properly classified as a finance lease or an operating lease in accordance with IFRSs

- Inspect vehicle registration documents (eg ambulances) to confirm ownership of motor vehicles

---

113 Bronze Industries Co

Marking scheme

Marks

(a) Up to 1 mark each per well-explained key control. If not well explained, then just give ½ mark for each, overall maximum of 5 marks for 5 points.

- Sequentially numbered clock cards
- Automatic calculations of gross, net pay and deductions
- Sample of calculations double checked
- Separate human resources and payroll department
- Bonus communicated in writing to payroll
- List of bank payments agreed in detail to payroll records

5

(b) Up to 1 mark each per well-explained deficiency and recommendation.

If not well explained, then just give ½ mark for each. Overall maximum of 6 marks each for deficiencies and recommendations.

- Clock in/out process unsupervised

- Employee breaks not monitored

- Temporary staff are not appointed by human resources department

- Overtime report reviewed after payment

- Authorisation of discretionary bonus

- No input checks over entry of bonus into payroll

- Payroll manager reviews the bank transfer listing prior to payment

  and can change payroll records

- No identity checks prior to cash wages pay out

12

(c) Up to 1 mark per well-described procedure, overall maximum of 3 marks.

- Compare total payroll expense to the prior year and investigate

  any significant differences

- Review monthly payroll charges, compare to the prior year,

  budgets, discuss with management

- Compare overtime pay as a percentage of factory normal hours against prior year, investigate any significant differences

- Perform a proof in total of total wages and salaries, compare

  to actual, and investigate any significant differences

3
___
20
___

(a) **Bronze Industries Co (Bronze) payroll system key controls**

Key controls in Bronze's payroll system are as follows:

(i) Factory staff are each issued a sequentially numbered clock card which details their employee number and name. This should ensure that employees are only paid for hours they have worked and-that the payroll records record completely all employees, as any gaps in the sequence would be identified.

(ii) The payroll system automatically calculates gross and net pay along with any statutory deductions. This should reduce the risk of employees' wages and statutory deductions being incorrect as there is a reduced risk of errors occurring.

(iii) A sample of the calculations made by the automated system is checked by the payroll supervisor to ensure the system is operating effectively; this tests the automated controls within the system.

(iv)	Bronze has a human resources department which is responsible for setting up new permanent employees and leavers. Having a segregation of roles between human resources and payroll departments reduces the risk of fictitious employees being set up and also being paid.

(v)	The discretionary bonus is communicated in writing to the payroll department. As this is in writing rather than verbal, this reduces the risk of the bonus being recorded at an incorrect amount in the payroll records.

(vi)	For employees paid by bank transfer, the list of the payments is reviewed in detail and agreed to the payroll records prior to authorising the bank payment. This reduces the risk of fraudulent payments being made through the creation of fictitious employees and other employees being omitted from the payment run.

(b)	**Bronze payroll system deficiencies and controls**

Deficiencies	Controls
Employees swipe their cards at the beginning and end of the eight-hour shift; this process is not supervised. This could result in a number of employees being swiped in as present when they are not. This will result in a substantially increased payroll cost for Bronze.	The clocking in and out process should be supervised by a responsible official to prevent one individual clocking in multiple employees. A supervisor should undertake a random check of employees by reviewing who has logged in with a swipe card and confirming visually that the employee is present.
Employees are entitled to a 30-minute paid break and do not need to clock out to access the dining area. Employees could be taking excessive breaks resulting in a decrease in productivity and increased payroll costs.	Employees should be allocated set break times and there should be a supervisor present to ensure that employees only take the breaks they are entitled to.
Although there is a human resources department, appointments of temporary staff are made by factory production supervisors. The supervisor could appoint unsuitable employees and may not carry out all the required procedures for new joiners. This could result in these temporary employees not receiving the correct pay and relevant statutory deductions.	All appointment of staff, whether temporary or permanent, should only be made by the human resources department.
Overtime reports which detail the amount of overtime worked are sent out quarterly by the payroll department to production supervisors for review. These reports are reviewed after the payments have been made which could result in unauthorised overtime or amounts being paid incorrectly and Bronze's payroll cost increasing.	All overtime should be authorised by a responsible official prior to the payment being processed by the payroll department. This authorisation should be evidenced in writing.
Production supervisors determine the amount of the discretionary bonus to be paid to employees. Production supervisors are not senior enough to determine this as they could pay extra bonuses to friends or family members.	The bonus should be determined by a more senior individual, such as the production director, and this should be communicated in writing to the payroll department.

Deficiencies	Controls
The bonus is input by a clerk into the payroll system. There is no indication that this input process is reviewed. This could result in input errors or the clerk could fraudulently change the amounts leading to incorrect bonus payments.	Once the clerk has input the bonus amounts, all entries should be double checked against the written confirmation from the production director by another member of the team to identify any amounts entered incorrectly.
The payroll manager reviews the bank transfer listing prior to authorising the payments and also amends the payroll records for any changes required. There is a lack of segregation of duties as it is the payroll team which processes the amounts and the payroll manager who authorises payments. The manager could fraudulently increase the amounts to be paid to certain employees and process this payment as well as amend the records.	The payroll manager should not be able to process changes to the payroll system as well as authorise payments. The authorisation of the bank transfer listing should be undertaken by an individual outside the payroll department, such as the finance director.
A payroll clerk distributes cash pay packets to employees without requesting proof of identity. Even if most employees are known to the clerk, there is a risk that without identity checks wages could be paid to incorrect employees.	The payroll clerks should be informed that all cash wages can only be paid upon sight of the employee's clock card and photographic identification as this confirms proof of identity.

(c)   Substantive analytical procedures to confirm payroll expense

(i)   Compare the total payroll expense to the prior year and investigate any significant differences.

(ii)   Review monthly payroll charges, compare this to the prior year and budgets and discuss with management any significant variances.

(iii)   Compare overtime pay as a percentage of factory normal hours pay to investigate whether it is at a similar level to the prior year and within an acceptable range. Investigate any significant differences.

(iv)   Perform a proof in total of total wages and salaries, incorporating joiners and leavers and any pay increase. Compare this to the actual wages and salaries in the financial statements and investigate any significant differences.

114 Lemon Quartz Co

Workbook references. Chapter 10.

Top tips. The key to a good answer to part (a) is to adopt a sensible structure. In this instance the question lends itself to a three-column approach. This will ensure that each aspect of the requirement is dealt with. Notice that the question specifies the number of deficiencies you should identify (five) so make sure that you do not waste time by addressing more points than necessary. Notice that you are asked to identify and explain deficiencies. You must include the explanation to score well. Make sure that you are clear on the difference between a test of control and a substantive procedure. Requirement (a)(iii) asks for tests of control. Remember that these are audit procedures designed to evaluate the operating effectiveness of controls as opposed to substantive procedures whose purpose is to identify material misstatements.

Easy marks. Part (b) should have represented easy marks as there was no application of knowledge required.

Examining team's comments. Internal control questions remain a highly examinable area and, in common with prior sittings, performance in the internal control question in June 2016 was mixed.

Candidates were able to identify the control deficiency from the scenario; however, some candidates did not clearly explain the implication of the deficiency. Additionally some candidates did not understand or incorrectly identified deficiencies eg renting space in warehouses to third parties or completing inventory count sheets in ink.

The scenario in the exam contained more issues than was required to be discussed and it was therefore pleasing that candidates generally only identified the required number of issues noted in the question.

Most candidates were able to provide good recommendations to address the deficiencies. However, some of the recommendations were poorly described, did not clearly address the specific control weakness identified or were impractical suggestions.

The tests of controls that the auditor could perform were often not well explained by candidates (eg 'ensure the bays are flagged' without saying how the auditor would ensure this, or just using the word 'check' or 'observe', did not address the controls identified or were substantive audit procedures rather than tests of control).

It was pleasing to note that many candidates presented their answers well using a three-column approach with internal control deficiencies in one column, the related recommendation in the other and the related test of control in the third column.

Marking scheme

Marks

(a)   Up to 1 mark per well-explained deficiency, up to 1 mark for each well- explained recommendation and up to 1 mark for each well-described test of control.
Overall maximum of 5 marks each for deficiencies, controls and tests of control.

- Warehouse employees undertaking the count
- Inventory counting sheets contain quantities per records
- No clear division of roles within counting teams
- Third-party inventory included in the count
- Access to high value finished goods
- Each location counted once only
- No flagging of bays once counted
- No sequence checks of inventory sheets   15

(b)   Up to 1 mark per well-explained element.

- Intended user, responsible party, practitioner
- Subject matter
- Suitable criteria
- Appropriate evidence
- Assurance report $\underline{5}$
                                                                              $\underline{\underline{20}}$

(a)   Deficiencies, controls and test of controls

Deficiencies (i)	Controls (ii)	Test of controls (iii)
The count will be undertaken by teams of warehouse staff. There should be a segregation of roles between those who have day to day responsibility for inventory and those who are checking it. If the same team are responsible for maintaining and checking inventory, then errors and fraud could be hidden.	The counting teams should be independent of the warehouse; hence members of alternative departments should undertake the counting rather than the warehouse staff.	Attend the year-end count and enquire of the counting teams which department they normally work in. Inspect the updated inventory count instructions to verify that they have been communicated to members of staff outside the warehouse department.
The inventory sheets contain quantities as per the inventory records. There is a risk that the counting teams may simply agree with the pre-printed quantities rather than counting the balances correctly, resulting in significant errors in inventory.	The count sheets should be sequentially numbered and contain product codes and descriptions but no quantities.	Inspect a sample of the counting sheets being used by the counting teams to verify that only the inventory product codes and description are pre-printed on them.
There are 15 teams of counters, each team having 2 members of staff. However, there is no clear division of responsibilities within the team. Therefore, both members of staff could count together rather than checking each other's count; and errors in their count may not be identified.	Each team should be informed that both members are required to count their assigned inventory separately. Therefore, one member counts and the second member also undertakes a count and then records the inventory on the count sheets correctly. In addition, the financial controller supervising the count should undertake some sample checks of inventory counted by each team.	Observe the counting teams to assess if they are counting together or if one counts and the other then double checks the quantities counted. Review the records of the sample checks undertaken by the supervisor of the inventory count.
Inventory owned by third parties is also being counted by the teams, with adjustments being made by the finance team to split these goods out later. There does not appear to be a method for counters to identify which items are third-party inventory. There is a risk that these goods may not be correctly removed from the inventory count sheets, resulting in inventory being overstated.	All inventories belonging to third parties should be moved to one location. This area should be clearly marked and excluded from the counting process.	Enquire of the count supervisor where the third-party inventory is to be stored, confirm through inspection of the counting sheets that these bays are not included on any pre-printed forms.

Deficiencies (i)	Controls (ii)	Test of controls (iii)
High value inventory which is normally stored in a secure location will be accessible by all team members as they will be given the access code. This significantly increases the risk of theft as any member of the counting team could subsequently access these goods.	The high value inventory should be kept in the locked area of the warehouse. Senior members of the team should be allocated to count these goods, and they should be given the access code to enter the area. Upon completion of the count the access code should be changed.	Attempt to access the area where the high value inventory is stored; this should not be possible without the access code. At the year-end visit attempt to access with the code which was supplied during the inventory count.
Each bay of the warehouse is counted once only. If inventory is only checked once, then counting errors may arise resulting in under- or overstated inventory.	Once all inventories have been counted once, each area should be recounted by a different team. Any differences on the first count should be promptly notified to the count supervisor and a third count undertaken if necessary. If a full second count would be too time consuming for the company, then sample checks on the inventory counted should be undertaken by a different counting team.	Observe the counting team undertake second counts of all areas; confirm that different teams undertake this process.
Once areas are counted, the teams are not marking the bays as completed. Therefore there is the risk that some areas of the warehouse could be double counted or missed out.	All bays should be flagged as completed, once the inventory has been counted. In addition, the count supervisor should check at the end of the count that all of the bays with Quartz's inventory have been flagged as completed.	Physically confirm that the completed bays of the warehouse have been flagged to indicate that the goods have been counted. At the end of the count, review any bays containing Quartz's goods which have not been flagged.
The inventory sheets are sequentially numbered and at the end of the count they are given to the count supervisor who confirms with each team that they have returned all sheets. However, no sequence check of the sheets is performed. If sheets are missing, then the inventory records could be understated.	After the counting has finished, each team should return all of their sequentially numbered sheets and the supervisor should check the sequence of all sheets at the end of the count.	Review the sequence of the inventory sheets for any gaps in the sequence and obtain an explanation from the count supervisor.

BPP
LEARNING
MEDIA

(b) **Elements of an assurance engagement**

In accordance with ISAE 3000 *Assurance Engagements Other than Audits or Reviews of Historical Financial Information*, an assurance engagement will require a three-party relationship comprising of:

- The intended user who is the person who requires the assurance report

- The responsible party, which is the organisation responsible for preparing the subject matter to be reviewed

- The practitioner (ie an accountant) who is the professional who will review the subject matter and provide the assurance

A second element which is required for an assurance engagement is suitable subject matter. The subject matter is the data which the responsible party has prepared and which requires verification. Thirdly this subject matter is then evaluated or assessed against suitable criteria in order for it to be assessed and an opinion provided.

Fourth, the practitioner must ensure that they have gathered sufficient appropriate evidence in order to give the required level of assurance. Last, an assurance report provides the opinion which is given by the practitioner to the intended user.

115 Equestrian Co

Marking scheme

		Marks
(a)	**Control activities**	
	– Segregation of duties	1
	– Information processing	1
	– Authorisation	1
	– Physical controls	1
	– Performance reviews	1
	Maximum	4

(b)   **Control deficiencies and recommendations**

- Assets not physically verified   2

- Internal audit staff shortages   2

- Payroll setting up new staff   2

- Lack of approval for wage increase   2

- Credit limits not reviewed regularly   2

- Inappropriate access to high value inventory   2

- Perpetual inventory counts not complete   2

- Bank reconciliations not always reviewed   2

- Invoices not paid in line with suppliers' terms   2

Maximum   <u>16</u>

Total   <u>20</u>

(a)   Control activities

- Segregation of duties – assignment of roles or responsibilities to ensure the tasks of authorising and recording transactions and maintaining custody of assets are carried out by different people, thereby reducing the risk of fraud and error occurring. For example, the purchase ledger clerk recording invoices onto the purchase ledger, and the finance director authorising the payment of those purchase invoices.

- Information processing – controls including application and general IT controls, which ensure the completeness, accuracy and authorisation of information being processed. For example, use of batch control totals when entering transactions into the system.

- Authorisation – approval of transactions by a suitably responsible official to ensure transactions are genuine. For example, authorisation by a responsible official of all purchase orders.

- Physical controls – restricting access to physical assets as well as computer programs and data files, thereby reducing the risk of theft. For example, cash being stored in a safe which only a limited number of employees are able to access.

- Performance reviews – comparison or review of the performance of the business by looking at areas such as budget versus actual results. For example, the review by department heads of monthly results of actual trading to budget and prior year, with analysis of variances.

(b)   Equestrian Co deficiencies and controls

Control deficiency	Control recommendation
Physical verification of assets within the non-current asset register has not been undertaken for some time. A current programme has started but is only 15% complete, due to staff shortages. If non-current assets are not physically verified on a regular basis, there is an increased risk of assets being misappropriated or misplaced as there is no check that the assets still exist in their correct location.	Additional resources should be devoted to completing the physical verification of all assets within the register. If any assets cannot be located, they should be written off. Following this full review, on a monthly basis a sample of assets at the sites should be agreed back to the register to confirm existence.
Equestrian Co has experienced significant staff shortages within their internal audit (IA) department. In addition, several members of the current IA team are new to the company. Maintaining an IA department is an important control as it enables senior management to test whether controls are operating effectively within the company. If the team has staff shortages or lack of experience, this reduces the effectiveness of this monitoring control.	Senior management should consider recruiting additional employees to join the IA department. In the interim, employees from other departments, such as finance, could be seconded to IA to assist them with the internal audits, provided these reviews do not cover controls operating in the department where the employees normally work.
During the year, the human resources (HR) department has been busy; therefore the payroll department has set up new joiners to the company. This is a lack of segregation of duties, as employees are able to set up new joiners in the payroll system and process their pay, this leads to an increased risk of fictitious/duplicate employees being set up.	The HR director should as a matter of urgency review the workloads of the department to assess whether other tasks can be reprioritised as payroll should cease to set up new joiners. This role must immediately revert back to HR to undertake. Additionally, a review should be undertaken of all new joiners set up by payroll with agreement to employee files to confirm that all new employees are *bona fide*.
The wage rate has been increased by the HR director and notified to the payroll supervisor by email. As payroll can be a significant expense for a business, any decision to increase this should be made by the board as a whole and not just by the HR director. In addition, the notification of the payroll increase was via email and the payroll supervisor was able to make changes to the payroll standing data without further authorisation. This increases the risk of fraud or errors arising within payroll.	All increases of pay should be proposed by the HR department and then formally agreed by the board of directors. Upon agreement of the pay rise, a written notification of the board decision should be sent to the payroll supervisor who enters the revised pay rate into the system. This change should trigger an exception report for the payroll director, and the new rate should not go live until the director has signed off the changes.
New customers undergo a credit check, after which a credit limit is proposed by the sales staff and approved by the sales director, these credit limits are not reviewed after this. Over a period of time it may be that the customers' credit limits have been set too high, leading to irrecoverable debts, or too low, leading to a loss of sales.	Credit limits should continue to be approved by the sales director; however, on a regular basis the sales director should review these limits based on order history and payment record.

Control deficiency	Control recommendation
High value inventory is stored in a secure location across all nine warehouses and access is via a four digit code, which is common to all sites. As the code is the same across all sites, this significantly increases the risk of fraud. A considerable number of people will be aware of the codes and could access inventory at any of the nine sites.	The access codes for all of the sites should be changed. Each site should have a unique code, known to a small number of senior warehouse employees. These codes should be changed on a regular basis.
Monthly perpetual inventory counts are supposed to be undertaken at each of the nine warehouses, but some of these are outstanding. In order to rely on inventory records for decision making and the year-end financial statements, all lines of inventory must be counted at least once a year, with high value or high turnover items counted more regularly. If the counts are outstanding, some goods may not be counted, and the inventory records may be incorrect.	The programme of perpetual inventory counts should be reviewed for omissions. Any lines which have been missed out should be included in the remaining counts. At the year end, if any lines are identified as having not been counted, the company should organise an additional count to ensure that all items are confirmed to inventory records.
The bank reconciliations are only reviewed by the financial controller if the sum of reconciling items is significant; therefore some reconciliations are not being reviewed. The financial controller relies solely on the accounts clerk's notification that the bank reconciliations require review. The bank reconciliations could contain significant errors, but a low overall amount of reconciling items, as there could be compensating errors which cancel each other out. Bank reconciliations are a key control which reduces the risk of fraud. If they are not reviewed, then this reduces its effectiveness and also results in a lack of assurance that bank reconciliations are being carried out at all or on a timely basis.	The bank reconciliations should be reviewed by the financial controller on a monthly basis, even if the reconciling items are not significant, and he should evidence his review by way of signature on the bank reconciliation.
Invoices are authorised by the finance director, but payment is only made 75 days after receipt of the invoice. There is the risk that Equestrian Co is missing out on early settlement discounts. Also, failing to pay in accordance with the supplier's payment terms can lead to a loss of supplier goodwill as well as the risk that suppliers may refuse to supply goods to the company.	The policy of making payment after 75 days should be reviewed. Consideration should be given to earlier payment if the settlement discounts are sufficient. If not, invoices should be paid in accordance with the supplier's payment terms.

116 Comet Publishing Co

Marking scheme

		Marks
(a)	Safeguards to deal with conflict of interest	
	Notify both parties and obtain consent	1
	Advise clients to seek independent advice	1
	Separate engagement teams	1
	Prevent access to information	1
	Clear guidelines on security and confidentiality provided to client	1
	Confidentiality agreements	1
	Monitor safeguards	1
	Restricted to	5

(b) Steps to confirm prior year flowcharts and system notes

Review PY notes and confirm all stages covered	1
Review PY file for weaknesses not actioned	1
Review PY report to management	1
Review client system documentation for changes	1
Interview client staff to confirm client processes	1
Walk-through tests to confirm notes	1
Walk-through tests to confirm procedures	1
Restricted to	5

(c) Control deficiencies, recommendations and tests of control (only 5 issues required)

No inter-branch transfers	3
Not all purchase orders are authorised	3
GRNs not processed regularly	3
GRNs not sent to purchasing department	3
Segregation of duties in relation to purchases	3
Authorisation of bank payments	3
Supplier statement reconciliations not performed	3
Max 5 issues, 3 marks each	15

(d) Substantive tests for purchases and other expenses

Calculate operating and gross margin and compare to PY	1
Review monthly purchases and investigate unexpected difference	1
Discuss changes in key suppliers and compare to PL	1
Recalculate a sample of invoices	1
Recalculate prepayments and accruals	1
Review post year-end invoices for pre year-end liabilities	1
Sample of cash book payments to appropriate expense account	1
GRNs to purchase invoice to purchase day book	1
Cut-off testing using GRNs	1
Restricted to	5
Total marks	30

(a) **Safeguards to deal with conflict of interest**

- Both Comet Publishing Co and its rival competitor, Edmond Co, should be notified that Halley & Co would be acting as auditors for each company and, if necessary, consent should be obtained from each.

- Advising one or both clients to seek additional independent advice.

- The use of separate engagement teams, with different engagement partners and team members; once an employee has worked on one audit, such as Comet Publishing Co, then they would be prevented from being on the audit of the competitor for a period of time.

- Procedures to prevent access to information, for example, strict physical separation of both teams, confidential and secure data filing.

- Clear guidelines for members of each engagement team on issues of security and confidentiality. These guidelines could be included within the audit engagement letters.

- Potentially the use of confidentiality agreements signed by employees and partners of the firm.

- Regular monitoring of the application of the above safeguards by a senior individual in Halley & Co not involved in either audit.

(b) **Steps to confirm prior year flowcharts and system notes**

- Obtain the system notes from last year's audit and ensure that the documentation on the purchases and payables system covers all expected stages and is complete.

- Review the audit file for indications of weaknesses in the system and note these for investigation this year.

- Review the prior year report to management to identify any recommendations which were made over controls in this area as this may highlight potential changes which have been made in the current year.

- Obtain system documentation from the client, potentially in the form of a procedure manual. Review this to identify any changes made in the last 12 months.

- Interview client staff to ascertain whether systems and controls have changed including the stores and warehouse to ensure that the flowcharts and notes produced last year is correct.

- Perform walk-through tests by tracing a sample of transactions through the purchases and payables system to ensure that the flowcharts and systems notes contained on the audit file are accurate.

- During the walk-through tests, confirm the systems notes and flowcharts accurately reflect the control procedures which are in place and can be used to identify controls for testing.

(c) **Control deficiencies, control recommendations and tests of control**

Control deficiency	Control recommendation	Test of control
It is not possible for a store to order goods from other local stores for customers who request them. Instead, customers are told to contact the other stores or use the company website. Customers are less likely to contact individual stores themselves and this could result in the company losing valuable sales. In addition, some goods which are slow moving in one	An inter-branch transfer system should be established between stores, with inter-branch inventory forms being completed for store transfers. This should help stores whose inventory levels are low but are awaiting their deliveries from the suppliers.	During the interim audit, arrange to visit a number of the stores, discuss with the store manager the process for ordering of inventory items, in particular whether it is possible to order from other branches. At each store, inspect a sample of completed inter-branch inventory forms for confirmation the control is operating.

Control deficiency	Control recommendation	Test of control
store may be out of stock at another; if goods could be transferred between stores, then overall sales may be maximised.		
Purchase orders below $1,000 are not authorised and are processed solely by the purchase order clerk who is also responsible for processing invoices. This could result in non-business related purchases and there is an increased fraud risk as the clerk could place orders for personal goods up to the value of $1,000, which is significant.	All purchase orders should be authorised by a responsible official. Authorised signatories should be established with varying levels of purchase order authorisation.	Select a sample of purchase orders and review for evidence of authorisation, agree this to the appropriate signature on the approved signatories list.
Goods received notes (GRNs) are sent to the accounts department every two weeks. This could result in delays in suppliers being paid as the purchase invoices could not be agreed to a GRN and also recorded liabilities being understated. Additionally, any prompt payment discounts offered by suppliers may be missed due to delayed payments.	A copy of the GRNs should be sent to the accounts department on a more regular basis, such as daily. The accounts department should undertake a sequence check of the GRNs to ensure none are missing for processing.	Enquire of the accounts clerk as to the frequency of when GRNs are received to assess if they are being sent promptly. Undertake a sequence check of GRNs held by the accounts department, discuss any missing items with the accounts clerk.
GRNs are only sent to the accounts department. Failing to send a copy to the ordering department could result in a significant level of unfulfilled orders leading to a loss of sales and stock-outs.	The GRN should be created in three parts and a copy of the GRN should be sent to the purchase order clerk, Oliver Dancer, who should agree this to the order and change the order status to complete. On a regular basis he should then review for all unfulfilled orders and chase these with the relevant supplier	Review the file of copy GRNs held by the purchase ordering clerk, Oliver Dancer, and review for evidence that these are matched to orders and flagged as complete. Review the file of unfulfilled purchase orders for any overdue items and discuss their status with Oliver Dancer.
The purchase ordering clerk, Oliver Dancer, has responsibility for ordering goods below $1,000 and for processing all purchase invoices for payment. There is a lack of segregation of duties and this increases the risk of fraud and non-business related purchases being made.	The roles of purchase ordering and processing of the related supplier invoices should be allocated to separate members of staff.	Observe which member of staff undertakes the processing of purchase invoices and confirm this is not the purchase ordering clerk, Oliver Dancer. Inspect a copy of the company's organisation chart to identify if these tasks have now been allocated to different roles.

Control deficiency	Control recommendation	Test of control
The finance director authorises the bank transfer payment list for suppliers; however, she only views the total amount of payments to be made. Without looking at the detail of the payments list, as well as supporting documentation, there is a risk that suppliers could be being paid an incorrect amount, or that sums are being paid to fictitious suppliers.	The finance director should review the whole payments list prior to authorising. As part of this, she should agree the amounts to be paid to supporting documentation, as well as reviewing the supplier names to identify any duplicates or any unfamiliar names. She should evidence her review by signing the bank transfer list.	Review the payments list for evidence of review by the finance director. Enquire of accounts staff what supporting documentation the finance director requests when undertaking this review.
Supplier statement reconciliations are no longer performed. This may result in errors in the recording of purchases and payables not being identified in a timely manner.	Supplier statement reconciliations should be performed on a monthly basis for all suppliers and these should be reviewed by a responsible official.	Review the file of reconciliations to ensure that they are being performed on a regular basis and that they have been reviewed by a responsible official. Re-perform a sample of the reconciliations to ensure that they have been carried out appropriately.

(d)   Substantive procedures for purchases and other expenses

- Calculate the operating profit and gross profit margins and compare them to last year and budget and investigate any significant differences.

- Review monthly purchases and other expenses to identify any significant fluctuations and discuss with management.

- Discuss with management whether there have been any changes in the key suppliers used and compare this to the purchase ledger to assess completeness and accuracy of purchases.

- Recalculate the accuracy of a sample of purchase invoice totals and related taxes and ensure expense has been included in the correct nominal code.

- Recalculate the prepayments and accruals charged at the year end to ensure the accuracy of the expense charge included in the statement of profit or loss.

- Select a sample of post year-end expense invoices and ensure that any expenses relating to the current year have been included.

- Select a sample of payments from the cash book and trace to expense account to ensure the expense has been included and classified correctly.

- Select a sample of goods received notes (GRNs) from throughout the year; agree them to purchase invoices and the purchase day book to ensure the completeness of purchases.

- Select a sample of GRNs just before and after the year end; agree to the purchase day book to ensure the expense is recorded in the correct accounting period.

BPP
LEARNING
MEDIA

117 Raspberry Co

Workbook references. Chapters 5, 10 and 16.

Top tips. In part (a), it was important that you stuck to the number of controls required (five). The ten available marks divide themselves into five for part (i) and five for part (ii). Notice that (a)(i) asks you to identify and explain the controls – there is half a mark available for each of these things (ie half for identifying and half for explaining). Your answer must therefore contain the right level of detail to get both of them and so you should extract the information from the scenario to identify the control and then explain the benefit of the control to Raspberry Co.

As with (a), so with (b) – the requirement is to 'identify and explain' each deficiency, which suggests that your answer could be structured as two sentences / paragraphs within the left column, the first of which says what is happening (identifying the problem), and the second of which says why this is a problem (or why it is wrong). You must also make a practical recommendation to address the deficiency, this should be clearly explained with sufficient detail to know what specific action to take to solve the problem.

Part (c) was fairly knowledge-based, and was a matter of recalling the possible assignments for internal audit, and then thinking about how they might apply to Raspberry Co.

Part (d) required you to suggest substantive procedures. It was therefore critical that you did not suggest tests of control here, which would not garner any marks.

Easy marks. Part (c) was knowledge-based and should have been within your reach.

Examination team comments. This 30-mark question was based on Raspberry Co, a company which operates an electric power station. This question tested candidates' knowledge of key controls and control deficiencies, recommendations and tests of control, internal audit departments, and, substantive procedures for accruals.

Part (a) for 10 marks required candidates to identify and explain from the scenario five key controls in respect of the payroll system described which the auditor may seek to place reliance on, and, describe a test of control the auditor should perform to assess if each of the key controls is operating effectively. Candidates' performance on this requirement was disappointing.

In common with previous exams, candidates continue to find tests of control challenging. Many candidates confused substantive procedures for tests of control and tests were often vague or incomplete.

Part (b) for 10 marks, required candidates to identify and explain from the scenario five deficiencies in respect of the payroll system and provide a recommendation to address each of these deficiencies. Many candidates performed well in this requirement.

The scenario in the exam contained more issues than were required to be discussed and it was pleasing that many candidates identified the required number of issues noted in the question.

Many candidates were able to provide good recommendations to address the deficiencies identified. However, some of the recommendations were not described in enough detail.

Internal controls questions remain a highly examinable area and future candidates need to ensure that they have undertaken adequate question practice.

Part (c) for five marks required candidates to describe assignments the internal audit department of Raspberry Co would carry out. Up to 1 mark was awarded for each well described point. Performance was mixed.

Common misunderstandings by a number of candidates were 'the internal auditor prepares the financial statements' and 'internal auditors implement the controls'.

Some candidates described the differences between internal and external audit, which was not the purpose of the requirement.

In addition some candidates described assignments, which would not be relevant to an electric power station client, for example 'internal auditors undertaking mystery shopping'. This is principally a knowledge area, which has been tested in previous exams.

Part (d) for five marks required candidates to describe substantive procedures the auditor should perform to confirm the year-end accrual for tax payable on employment income.

The substantive procedures were often vague, for example 'agree payment' rather than 'agree to the post year-end cashbook'. Candidates are once again reminded that a well described substantive procedure will clearly detail the source of the evidence.

In addition, many candidates did not focus on the year-end accrual and noted general substantive procedures for tax, which did not gain credit.

Candidates are reminded to read the question requirement carefully and to ensure that they are not only answering the question set but also fully describing each substantive procedure.

Marking scheme

		Marks
(a)	**Key controls and tests of control (only 5 controls required)**	
	Separate HR department set up employees	2
	Pre-printed joiners forms	2
	Data processing checks on bonus information	2
	Use of clock cards and process supervised	2
	Direct transfer between clock card and payroll systems	2
	Exception reports for changes to payroll data	2
	Security process over cash	2
	SOD over pay packets	2
	Restricted to	**10**
(b)	**Control deficiencies, and control recommendations (only 5 issues required)**	
	Production bonus set by supervisor	2
	No independent checks on wage calculations	2
	No monitoring of student loan payments	2
	Holiday requests not always authorised	2
	Lack of SOD in payroll department	2
	Pay packets not delivered by independent staff/no evidence of distribution	2
	Monthly management accounts not analysed	2
	Max 5 issues, 2 marks each	**10**
(c)	**Internal audit assignments**	
	Value for money	1
	Financial/operational review	1
	Monitoring assets	1
	Regulatory compliance	1
	IT systems	1
	Cash controls	1
	Fraud investigation	1

BPP
LEARNING
MEDIA

ANSWERS

		Marks
	Restricted to	<u>5</u>
(d)	Substantive procedures – tax payable accrual	
	Compare to prior year and investigate differences	1
	Agree to TB and payroll records	1
	Reperform accrual calculation and discuss with management	1
	Agree subsequent payment to cash book and bank statement	1
	Review correspondence with tax authorities	1
	Review disclosures	<u>1</u>
	Restricted to	<u>5</u>
Total marks		<u>30</u>

(a) Key controls and tests of control

Key control	Test of control
Raspberry Co has a separate human resources (HR) department which is responsible for setting up all new employees.	Review the job descriptions of payroll and HR to confirm the split of responsibilities with regards to setting up new joiners.
Having a segregation of roles between human resources and payroll departments reduces the risk of fictitious employees being set up and also being paid.	Discuss with members of the payroll department the process for setting up new joiners and for confirmation that the process is initiated by HR.
Pre-printed forms are completed by HR for all new employees, and includes assignment of a unique employee number, and once verified, a copy is sent to the payroll department. Payroll is unable to set up new joiners without information from these forms.	Select a sample of new employees added to the payroll during the year, review the joiner forms for evidence of completion of all parts and that the information was verified as accurate and was received by payroll prior to being added to the system.
The use of pre-printed forms ensures that all relevant information, such as tax IDs, is obtained about employees prior to set up. This minimises the risk of incorrect wage and tax payments. In addition, as payroll is unable to set up new joiners without the forms and employee number, it reduces the risk of fictitious employees being set up by payroll.	Select a sample of edit reports for changes to payroll during the year; agree a sample of new employees added to payroll to the joiners forms.

Key control	Test of control
The quarterly production bonus is input by a clerk into the payroll system, each entry is checked by a senior clerk for input errors prior to processing, and they evidence their review via signature. This reduces the risk of input errors resulting in over/underpayment of the bonus to employees.	If attending Raspberry Co at the time of bonus processing, observe the clerk inputting and senior clerk checking the bonus payments into the payroll system. In addition, obtain listings of quarterly bonus payments and review for evidence of signature by the senior clerk who checks for input errors.
Production employees are issued with clock cards and are required to swipe their cards at the beginning and end of their shift, this process is supervised by security staff 24 hours a day. This ensures that genuine employees are only paid for the work actually done, and reduces the risk of employees being paid but not completing their eight-hour shift. In addition, due to the supervision it is unlikely that one employee could swipe in others.	Observe the use of clock cards by employees when entering the power station. Confirm the security team is supervising the process and following up on discrepancies through discussions with the security staff.
The clock card information identifies the employee number and links into the hours worked report produced by the payroll system. As the hours worked are automatically transferred into the payroll system, this reduces the risk of input errors in entering hours to be paid in calculating payroll, ensuring that employees are paid the correct amount.	Utilise test data procedures to input dummy clock card information, verify this has been updated into the payroll system.
On a quarterly basis, exception reports of changes to payroll standing data are produced and reviewed by the payroll director. This ensures that any unauthorised amendments to standing data are identified and resolved on a timely basis.	Select a sample of quarterly exception reports and review for evidence of review and follow up of any unexpected changes by the payroll director.
For production employees paid in cash, cash is received weekly from the bank by a security company.	Enquire of payroll clerks how cash is delivered to Raspberry Co for weekly pay packets.
It is likely the sum of money required to pay over 175 employees would be considerable. It is important that cash is adequately safeguarded to reduce the risk of misappropriation.	Review a sample of invoices from the security company to Raspberry Co for delivery of cash.

Key control	Test of control
The pay packets are prepared by two members of staff with one preparing and one checking the pay packets and this is evidenced by each staff member signing the weekly listing.	Observe the preparation of the pay packets ensuring that two members of staff are involved and that pay packets are checked for accuracy.
This ensures there is segregation of duties which prevents fraud and errors not being identified.	For a sample of weeks throughout the year, inspect the weekly payroll listing for evidence of signature by the two members of staff involved in the preparation of the pay packets.

(b)   Deficiencies and recommendations

Control deficiency	Control recommendation
Production supervisors determine the amount of the discretionary bonus to be paid to employees.	The bonus should be determined by a responsible official, such as the production director and should be formulated based on a written policy. If significant in value, the bonus should be formally agreed by the board of directors.
Production supervisors should not determine this as they could pay extra bonuses to friends or family members, resulting in additional payroll costs.	The bonus should be communicated in writing to the payroll department.
The wages calculations are generated by the payroll system and there are no checks performed.	A senior member of the payroll team should recalculate the gross to net pay workings for a sample of employees and compare their results to the output from the payroll system. These calculations should be signed as approved before payments are made.
Therefore, if system errors occur during the payroll processing, this would not be identified. This could result in wages being over or under calculated, leading to an additional payroll cost or loss of employee goodwill.	The payroll department should maintain a schedule, by employee, of payments made to third parties, such as the central government as well as the cumulative balance owing. On a regular basis, at least annually, this statement should be reconciled to the loan statement received from the government and sent to the employee for agreement.
Student loan deduction forms are completed by relevant employees and payments are made directly to the third party until the employee notifies HR that the loan has been repaid in full.	In accordance with the schedule, payments which are due to cease shortly should be confirmed in writing with the third party, prior to stopping.
As the payments continue until the employee notifies HR, and employees are unlikely to be closely monitoring payments, there is the risk that overpayments may be made, which then need to be reclaimed, leading to employee dissatisfaction.	
In the case of underpayments, Raspberry Co has an obligation to remit funds on time and to reconcile to annual loan statements. If the company does not make payments in full and on time, this could result in non-compliance by both the company and employee, which could result in fines or penalties.	

Control deficiency	Control recommendation
Holiday request forms are required to be completed and authorised by relevant line managers, however, this does not always occur. This could result in employees taking unauthorised leave, resulting in production difficulties if an insufficient number of employees are present to operate the power plant. In addition, employees taking unauthorised leave could result in an overpayment of wages.	Employees should be informed that they will not be able to take holiday without completion of a holiday request form, with authorisation from the line manager. Payroll clerks should not process holiday payments without agreement to the authorised holiday form.
The senior payroll manager reviews the bank transfer listing prior to authorising the payments and also amends the payroll records for any changes required.	The senior payroll manager should not be able to process changes to the payroll system as well as authorise payments.
There is a lack of segregation of duties as it is the payroll team which processes the amounts and the senior payroll manager who authorises payments. The senior manager could fraudulently increase the amounts to be paid to certain employees, process this payment as well as amend the records.	The authorisation of the bank transfer listing should be undertaken by an individual outside the payroll department, such as the finance director.
The pay packets are delivered to the production supervisors, who distribute them to employees at the end of their shift. The supervisor is not sufficiently independent to pay wages out. They could adjust pay packets to increase those of close friends whilst reducing others. In addition, although the production supervisors know their team members, payment of wages without proof of identity increases the risk that wages could be paid to incorrect employees.	All pay packets should be distributed by the payroll department, directly to employees, upon sight of the employee's clock card and photographic identification as this confirms proof of identity. Payroll should undertake a reconciliation of pay packets issued to production supervisors, wages distributed with employee signatures to confirm receipt and pay packets returned to payroll due to staff absences. Any differences should be investigated immediately. As employees work eight-hour shifts over 24 hours,
Monthly management accounts do not analyse the variances between actual and budgeted wages and salaries; this is because there are no overtime costs. However, wages and salaries are a significant expense and management needs to understand why variances may have arisen. These could occur due to extra employees being recruited which were not budgeted for, or an increase in wage pay out rates. The board would need to monitor the wages and salaries costs as if they are too high, then this would impact the profitability of the company.	consideration should be given to operating a shift system for the payroll department on wages pay out day. This will ensure that there are sufficient payroll employees to perform the wages pay out for each shift of employees, with the same level of controls in place. The monthly management accounts should be amended to include an analysis of wages and salaries compared to the budgeted costs. These should be broken down to each relevant department and could also include an analysis of headcount numbers compared to budget.

(c)   **Assignments for internal audit department (IAD)**

Value for money review – The IAD could be asked to assess whether Raspberry Co is obtaining value for money in areas such as capital expenditure.

Review of financial/operational controls – The IAD could undertake reviews of controls at head office and the power station and make recommendations to management over such areas as the purchasing process as well as the payroll cycle.

Monitoring asset levels – The IAD could undertake physical verification of property, plant and equipment (PPE) at the production site and head office and compare the assets seen to the PPE register. There is likely to be a significant level of PPE and the asset register must be kept up to date to ensure continuous production. If significant negative differences occur, this may be due to theft or fraud.

Regulatory compliance – Raspberry Co produces electricity and operates a power station, hence it will be subject to a large number of laws and regulations such as health and safety and environmental legislation. The IAD could help to monitor compliance with these regulations.

IT system reviews – Raspberry Co is likely to have a relatively complex computer system linking production data to head office. The IAD could be asked to perform a review over the computer environment and controls.

Cash controls – Raspberry Co's internal auditors could undertake controls testing over cash payments. 70% of employees are paid in cash rather than bank transfer, therefore on a weekly basis cash held is likely to be significant, therefore the cash controls in payroll should be tested to reduce the level of errors.

Fraud investigations – The IAD can be asked to investigate any specific cases of suspected fraud as well as review the controls in place to prevent/detect fraud.

(d)   **Accrual for income tax payable on employment income**

Procedures the auditor should adopt in respect of auditing this accrual include:

*   Compare the accrual for income tax payable to the prior year, investigate any significant differences.

*   Agree the year-end income tax payable accrual to the general ledger and payroll records to confirm accuracy.

*   Re-perform the calculation of the accrual to confirm accuracy and discuss any unexpected variances with management.

*   Agree the subsequent payment to the post year-end cash book and bank statements to confirm completeness.

*   Review any correspondence with tax authorities to assess whether there are any additional outstanding payments due; if so, agree they are included in the year-end accrual.

*   Review any disclosures made of the income tax accrual and assess whether these are in compliance with accounting standards and legislation.

118 Camomile Co

Marks

(a) (i) **Importance of communicating with TCWG**

Assists understanding of matters related to the audit   1

Obtains information relevant to the audit   1

Assists TCWG discharge their responsibilities   1

Promotes effective two-way communication   1

Restricted to   2

(ii) Matters to communicate to TCWG

1 mark for any relevant and well described example   2

(b) **Control deficiencies and recommendations (only 8 issues required)**

Petty cash differences   2

Access to tills   2

Tills reconciled in total   2

Lack of SOD – reconciling cash   2

Risk of incomplete daily sales sheets   2

Security of cash – access to safes   2

Lack of SOD – cashier   2

Credit card statements are not reconciled   2

Frequency of bank reconciliations   2

Payment list not adequately reviewed   2

Max 8 issues, 2 marks each   16

Total marks   20

(a) (i) Importance of communicating with those charged with governance

In accordance with ISA 260 *Communication with Those Charged with Governance*, it is important for the auditors to report to those charged with governance as it helps in the following ways:

- It assists the auditor and those charged with governance in understanding matters related to the audit, and in developing a constructive working relationship. This relationship is developed while maintaining the auditor's independence and objectivity.

- It helps the auditor in obtaining, from those charged with governance, information relevant to the audit. For example, those charged with governance may assist the auditor in understanding the entity and its environment, in identifying appropriate sources of audit evidence and in providing information about specific transactions or events.

- It helps those charged with governance in fulfilling their responsibility to oversee the financial reporting process, thereby reducing the risks of material misstatement of the financial statements.

- It promotes effective two-way communication between the auditor and those charged with governance.

(ii)   Matters to be communicated to those charged with governance

- The auditor's responsibilities with regards to providing an opinion on the financial statements and that they have carried out their work in accordance with International Standards on Auditing.

- The auditor should explain the planned approach to the audit as well as the audit timetable.

- Any key audit risks identified during the planning stage should be communicated.

- In addition, any significant difficulties encountered during the audit should be communicated.

- Also significant matters arising during the audit, as well as significant accounting adjustments.

- During the audit, any significant deficiencies in the internal control system identified should be communicated in writing or verbally.

- How the external auditor and internal auditor may work together and any planned use of the work of the internal audit function.

- Those charged with governance should be notified of any written representations required by the auditor.

- Other matters arising from the audit which are significant to the oversight of the financial reporting process.

- If any suspected frauds are identified during the audit, these must be communicated.

- If the auditors are intending to make any modifications to the audit opinion, these should be communicated to those charged with governance.

- For listed entities, a confirmation that the auditors have complied with ethical standards and appropriate safeguards have been put in place for any ethical threats identified.

(b)   **Control deficiencies and recommendations**

Control deficiency	Control recommendation
Each restaurant maintains a petty cash float of $400, and at any point in time the receipts and funds present should equal the float. It has been noted by the internal audit (IA) department that on occasions there are differences due to the fact that no log is maintained of petty cash requests. This could be as a result of sundry items being purchased without the relevant receipt or voucher being returned. There is also a possibility that the cash is being misappropriated by staff members, or being spent on non-business related items.	A petty cash log should be maintained so the purchase of sundry items is recorded in the log along with the sum borrowed, date and employee. On purchase of the items, the relevant employee should return the relevant receipt or voucher and any funds not spent. The log should be updated to confirm return of funds and receipts. On a weekly basis, the restaurant manager should reconcile the petty cash and if any receipts are missing, these should be followed up with the relevant employee. If it is cash which is missing, then this should be

Control deficiency	Control recommendation
	investigated further with the employees who made petty cash purchases during that period.
To speed up the cash payment by customers, for each venue the tills have the same log on code and these codes are changed fortnightly. In the event of cash discrepancies arising in the tills, it would be difficult to ascertain which employees may be responsible as there is no way of tracking who used which till. This could lead to cash being easily misappropriated.	Each employee should be provided with a unique log on code and this is required to be entered when using the tills. In order to facilitate the investigation of till differences, employees should be allocated to a specific till point for their shift. Any discrepancies which arise should initially be double checked to ensure they are not arithmetical errors. If still present, the relevant employees who had access to the till can be identified and further investigations can be undertaken.
The reconciliations of the tills to the daily sales readings are performed in total for all five tills at each venue rather than for each till. This means that when exceptions arise, it will be difficult to identify which till caused the difference and therefore which employees may require further till training or may have undertaken fraudulent transactions.	The reconciliations should be undertaken on an individual till by till basis rather than in aggregate and any discrepancies noted should be investigated immediately.
The cashing up of tills along with the recording of any cash discrepancies is undertaken by just one individual, the restaurant manager. There is a fraud risk as the manager could remove some of the cash and then simply record that there was an exception on the daily sales list. In addition, as there is no segregation of duties, the restaurant manager could, fraudulently or by error, record the total sales as per each till incorrectly leading to incorrect identification of discrepancies.	The cashing up process should be undertaken by two individuals together, ideally an assistant manager and the restaurant manager. One should count the cash and the other record it. Any exceptions to the till reading should be double checked to confirm that they are not simply arithmetical errors. If still present, the relevant employees who had access to the till can be identified and further investigations can be undertaken.
Daily sales sheets are scanned and emailed to head office on a weekly basis. There is a possibility that some sales sheets could be misplaced by the restaurant manager resulting in incomplete sales and cash receipts data being recorded into the accounting system	Daily sales sheets for each venue should be sequentially numbered and remitted to head office on a daily basis. At head office, a sequence check should be undertaken on a regular basis to identify any missing sheets and any gaps should be investigated further. Once received, the cashier should post the sales and cash data for all six venues on a daily basis. Once processed, they should then be signed as posted by the cashier and filed away securely.

Control deficiency	Control recommendation
Cash is stored in a safe at each venue and the restaurant manager stores the safe key in a drawer of their desk when not in use. Although cash is banked on a daily basis, there could still be a significant sum of cash onsite each day. There is a risk of significant cash losses due to theft if access to the safe key is not carefully controlled.	The current key lock safe should be replaced with a safe with a digital code. Only authorised personnel should have the code which should be updated on a regular basis.
The cashier is responsible for several elements of the cash receipts system. She receives the daily sales sheets from restaurants, agrees that cash has cleared into the bank statements, updates the cash book and undertakes the bank reconciliations.

There is a lack of segregation of duties and errors will not be identified on a timely basis. | These key roles should be split between different members of the finance team, with ideally the bank reconciliations being undertaken by another member of the team. |
| The cashier is not checking that payments made by credit card have resulted in cash being received by Camomile Co. The credit card statements are not reviewed or reconciled, they are just filed away.

There is a risk that receipts of cash by credit card may have been omitted and this would not be identified on a timely basis as the bank is only reconciled every two months and may result in difficulties in resolving any discrepancies with the credit card company | The cashier should reconcile the credit card vouchers per restaurant to the monthly statement received from the card company. The daily amounts per the statement should be agreed to the bank statement to ensure that all funds have been received.

This reconciliation should be reviewed by a responsible official, such as the financial controller, who should evidence by signature that the review has been undertaken |
| The bank reconciliations are only carried out every two months.

For a cash-based business, the bank reconciliation is a key control which reduces the risk of fraud. If it is not reconciled regularly enough, then this reduces its effectiveness as fraud and errors may not be identified on a timely basis. | The bank reconciliations should be performed on a monthly basis rather than every two months. The financial controller should continue to review each reconciliation and evidence her review by way of signature on the bank reconciliation. |
| The finance director only views the total amount of payments to be made rather than the amounts to be paid to each supplier.

Without looking at the detail of the payments list, as well as supporting documentation, there is a risk that suppliers could be being paid an incorrect amount, or that sums are being paid to fictitious suppliers. | The finance director should review the whole payments list prior to authorising.

As part of this, he should agree the amounts to be paid to supporting documentation, as well as reviewing the supplier names to identify any duplicates or any unfamiliar names.

He should evidence his review by signing the bank transfer list. |

ANSWERS

Expert

119   The correct answers are:

The revaluation constitutes a change in accounting policy, so we will need to consider the adequacy of the disclosures made in respect of this.

The flagship store should be depreciated on its revalued amount.

IAS 16 *Property, Plant and Equipment* permits non-current assets to be revalued (16). However, if an item of property, plant and equipment is revalued, the entire class of property, plant and equipment to which that asset belongs must be revalued (IAS 16). Truse Co is therefore entitled to revalue the shop, but it will also need to revalue all of the other shops if it is to comply with IAS 16.

The revaluation does constitute a change of accounting policy, so disclosures do need to be reviewed.

Under IAS 16, all non-current assets used by the entity should be depreciated, even if the fair value is in excess of the carrying amount. Repair and maintenance does not negate the need to depreciate the shop over its useful life (IAS 16).

Repairs and maintenance costs should be expensed as incurred, not capitalised.

120   The correct answer is:

Assertion	Yes	No
Existence	X	
Occurrence		X
Classification	X	
Presentation	X	

Existence, classification and presentation are all assertions related to tangible non-current assets. Completeness and accuracy, valuation and allocation are also relevant assertions (ISA 315). Occurrence and classification relate to classes of transactions and events recorded in profit or loss (ISA 315).

121   The correct answer is:

For a sample of assets selected by physical inspection, agree that they are listed on the non-current assets register

Physically inspecting assets listed in the non-current assets register tests for existence. Recalculating the carrying amount tests for accuracy, valuation and allocation. Inspecting relevant purchase invoices or deeds tests for rights and obligations.

122   The correct answer is:

The existence of any interests in or relationships with Truse Co that might pose a threat to the expert's objectivity

The existence of threats to the expert's objectivity should be considered as part of determining the competence, capability and objectivity of the auditor's expert (ISA 620). However, it is not a matter to be considered when the auditor determines the overall nature, timing and extent of the audit procedures required to evaluate the auditor's expert and the auditor's expert's work.

Besides the other three matters listed, the auditor should also consider the nature of the matter to which the auditor's expert's work relates (ie the nature of Truse Co's properties)

and the significance of the auditor's expert's work in the context of the audit (this depends, in part, on the materiality of the property account).

123 The correct answer is:

(1) Bank confirmation report from Truse Co's bank

(2) Cash count carried out by the audit junior himself

(3) Bank reconciliation carried out by the cashier

(4) Verbal confirmation from the directors that the overdraft limit is to be increased

Third-party evidence is the most reliable, followed by auditor-generated evidence. Client-generated evidence is deemed to be less reliable – more so when the evidence is verbal.

Newthorpe

124 The correct answers are:

The auditor observes client staff to determine whether inventory count procedures are being followed.

The auditor reviews procedures for identifying damaged, obsolete and slow-moving inventory.

Management is responsible for organising the inventory count, not the auditor. If the results of the auditor's test counts are not satisfactory, the auditor can request that inventory is recounted, but the auditor cannot insist on a recount. However, if management refuses the auditor's request then the auditor will need to consider the implications of this on the auditor's report.

125 The correct answer is:

For a sample of inventory sold just before and just after the year end, match dates of sales invoices/date posted to ledgers with date on related goods dispatched notes.

All of the suggested audit procedures test the valuation assumption, except for matching the dates of sales invoices with the dates on the related goods dispatched notes, which is an audit procedure around cut-off.

126 The correct answer is:

The legal claim should **not be recorded as a provision but disclosed as a contingent liability** because **a present obligation exists, but the outflow of economic resources is not probable.**

Management believe that there is a 35% chance of the claim succeeding. For an event to be 'probable', it should be more likely than not to occur (ie a 50% probability) (IAS 37). In this case, the outflow of economic resources is therefore not probable, so a provision should not be recognised. A present obligation (not a possible obligation) exists, since the former managing director has sued Newthorpe for unfair dismissal. It is because the likelihood of him succeeding in his claim is not probable that the claim should be treated as a contingent liability instead of a provision.

127 The correct answer is:

Send an enquiry letter to Newthorpe's lawyers to obtain their view as to the probability of the claim being successful

Independent third-party audit evidence is generally considered to be more reliable than client generated or auditor-generated audit evidence. Although all the procedures are valid, only the written confirmation from Newthorpe's lawyers provides an expert, third-party confirmation on the likelihood of the claim being successful. It is also sent directly to the auditor rather than to the client.

128   To perform specific procedures to identify possible non-compliance

ISA 250 (Revised) distinguishes between those laws and regulations which have a direct effect on the financial statements, and those which have an indirect effect (ISA 250). For those which have a direct effect on the financial statements the auditor must undertake specified audit procedures to help identify non-compliance with laws and regulations that may have a material effect on the financial statements (ISA 250).

Tirrol

129   The correct answers are:

We should budget for the extra time required to document an understanding of the entity, its environment and its systems, and to verify material opening balances.

We must agree a clear timetable with the client for the testing of the computerised inventory systems, setting out availability of access to the system, files and personnel required to complete testing.

As this is Cal & Co's first year of auditing Tirrol Co, additional time should be budgeted for documenting an understanding of the entity and for verifying the opening balances. Because Cal & Co's audit software has to be rewritten and the testing is taking place on a live basis, it is particularly important to plan our CAATs procedures carefully.

The ACCA's *Code of Ethics and Conduct* does not prohibit lowballing as such stating that 'a professional accountant in public practice may quote whatever fee is deemed appropriate' (ACCA *Code of Ethics and Conduct*: para. 330.3 A2), so withdrawing from the audit engagement on this basis is disproportionate. However, the firm should be able to demonstrate that appropriate time and qualified staff are assigned to the audit, and that all applicable standards are being adhered to (ACCA *Code of Ethics and Conduct*: para. 330.3 A3-7). It may not be appropriate to adopt a combined approach if the control risk is deemed to be high. The appropriate audit approach should be determined by the risk assessment, not by time or fee constraints.

130   The correct answers are:

The ability to test all 25 of Tirrol Co's locations using the same audit software, resulting in time and cost savings

The ability to select and extract a sample of inventory data for testing, thus reducing sampling risk

Audit software is used to perform substantive procedures rather than tests of controls and therefore this would not include testing internal controls relating to the input of data. Similarly, the error rate in a sample refers to the number of times a control deficiency is projected to occur in a population and therefore is not relevant to audit software.

131   The correct answer is:

A sampling method which involves having a constant sampling interval, the starting point for testing is determined randomly

The first option describes monetary unit sampling. The third option is an example of block selection. The fourth option describes haphazard sampling.

132   The correct answer is:

Whether there are any significant threats to the objectivity of the internal auditor

The objectivity of the internal auditor should be considered in determining whether or not the work of the internal auditors can be used in the first place. It is not part of evaluating the work itself.

133 The correct answer is:

Inventory should be $43,500, inventory is overstated.

Inventory should be measured at the lower of cost and net realisable value (IAS 2). Net realisable value is defined by IAS 2 as estimated selling price less estimated costs necessary to make the sale (IAS 2). In this case, inventory should be written down by $6,000 and shown at a value of $43,500 in the financial statements.

Wright

134 The correct answer is: 1 and 3

Material items will require more evidence to support them than immaterial items, which might be tested by comparative analytical review only. If the evidence is of high quality, then less may be required than if it were of poorer quality. Time and budget constraints should never influence the auditor's judgement regarding the sufficiency of audit evidence. The size of the account is considered in determining materiality (ie materiality may be determined as 5% of profit before tax), but the auditor's judgement regarding the sufficiency of audit evidence depends on the level of audit risks associated with each account. The operating effectiveness of the company's internal control systems will also influence this judgement.

135 The correct answer is: 2 only

The goods were received before the year end and have been recognised in inventory. A liability should therefore be recognised in the current accounting period. Although the cheque cleared the bank account after the year end it was issued before the year end and there is nothing to suggest that it has been deliberately held back. The cash in transit is therefore a legitimate reconciling item.

136 The correct answer is: No further evidence is required

As the supplier statement balance agrees with that on the purchase ledger, no further work is required in respect of this account.

Purchase orders made after the year end would not have any effect on current year liabilities.

As a supplier statement is available there would be no need to ask for a direct confirmation of the balance from supplier XX3.

Credit notes issued by Wilbur Co would potentially affect receivables, not payables, balances.

137 The correct answer is: Written on the audit firm's headed paper; information requested to be sent directly to the auditor

The bank confirmation letter must be sent identifiably by the auditor, and responses should be provided directly to the auditor. This is to prevent the information being distorted by any lack of objectivity, or tampering by client management.

138 The correct answer is: The bank's date stamp on the paying-in slip

The bank's stamp on the paying-in slip is the most reliable as it is third-party evidence and shows the date the lodgements were actually paid into the bank.

The bank statement would be a useful source of evidence but there may be a delay between the paying-in date and the date that the balance is cleared by the banking system. Therefore the bank statement date is not necessarily an accurate reflection of when the lodgement was made. There may also be a delay between the date on the cheques/remittance advice and the date it is actually received by Wilbur Co.

Lodestar

139   The correct answer is: The sample selection does not address the risk of understatement as it has focused on the ten largest balances.

Option A is incorrect as the sample is not appropriate. In order to test **completeness**, the sample selection for a receivables circularisation should consider incorporating nil balances and balances written off in the year to ensure that the balance is not understated. (Hence Option C is correct.)

Option B is incorrect as the nature of sampling means that a percentage of the balance will not be sampled, but conclusions can still be drawn.

Option D is incorrect as stratification is not required (although it may be helpful) and would not necessarily give a 'representative' sample, due to the risks discussed above in relation to Option A.

140   The correct answer is: 1, 2 and 4

Appropriateness refers to relevance and reliability. All the procedures are relevant to the assertion, but only some of them are reliable. Simply asking the credit controller if the client exists is not reliable, as it gives oral evidence generated by management and does not add value to the sales ledger.

Sending out a follow-up request gives the auditor a chance of obtaining evidence direct from a third party, which would be considered very reliable.

Reviewing cash receipts after date gives indirect evidence from a third party as, if someone is paying the debt, it implies it existed in the first place.

Reviewing the sales invoices is auditor-generated evidence that the sale was generated in the first place. It is based on relatively weak internally generated evidence (the invoices) but as it involves auditor analysis (for example, whether the relevant invoices appear in numerical sequence with other genuine invoices and have associated goods outwards notes) it adds a degree of reliability. This evidence would not be sufficient on its own but it might corroborate other evidence.

141   The correct answer is: Trade receivables should be £6,000 lower, current assets are overstated.

The difference caused by the payment by the customer does not require adjustment. The auditor has verified that the payment was received by Lodestar on 2 October, which is consistent with the
third-party evidence that it was sent out on 30 September. As far as Lodestar is concerned, the debt was genuine at 30 September and there is good evidence about its existence and valuation provided by the subsequent payment.

The customer is disputing an invoice and declaring its intention not to accept the debt. Regardless of management's intention to dispute this credit request, that suggests that the **valuation** of the debt is inappropriate (as the customer is only prepared to pay £0 in effect for that invoice), even if the **existence** of the debt can be proved. The invoice should be written off, hence receivables and current assets are overstated by £6,000.

142   The correct answer is: Auditors should use their own estimate in the financial statements, as auditor-generated evidence is more conclusive than management-generated evidence.

Auditors do not prepare the financial statements, management do. It is inappropriate to suggest that the auditors should prepare a figure for the financial statements (and this might cause an ethical threat of self-review). Auditor-generated evidence is considered reliable, so if the auditors did make an estimate which was significantly different from management's, this would be evidence that the allowance was misstated. The auditor will have to bear in mind the risk of management bias in making an estimate, and it is true that it can be difficult to obtain evidence relating to management judgement (particularly in this case if no events occur to 'prove' the debt is doubtful, such as the customer going into liquidation, or management writing the debt off – which they are likely to want to defer in case the debt is eventually paid).

143 The correct answer is: 1, 2, 3, 4

The assertion being tested is **valuation**.

(1) Gives indirect third-party evidence that the valuation of the debt is appropriate (ie in proving that some debts have not been paid)

(2) Gives auditor-generated evidence of the age of some debt and therefore the fact that its valuation is likely to be in doubt (otherwise it would have been paid before)

(3) Gives management evidence relating to the valuation of the debt, which might give the auditor insight into issues they might otherwise be unaware of, such as conversations with customers about when debts are to be paid

(4) Gives very little evidence about current valuation, as it only shows what the value was at the time the invoice was sent, and is of low reliability anyway, as it is internally generated

Porthos

144 The correct answer is: 2, 4, 1, 3

The steps should be undertaken in this order. The objective of the CAAT procedures should be determined first and foremost. The accessibility of the data files must be considered before the scope and nature of the procedures are determined.

145 The correct answer is: (i), (ii), (iii) and (iv)

Testing orders for unusually large quantities identifies whether any reject controls requiring special authorisation for large orders are effective. Testing orders with fields left blank determines whether controls are in place to prevent orders being placed that can't be fulfilled due to missing information (ie incomplete delivery address). Testing orders with invalid inventory codes identifies whether controls are in place to ensure that the correct goods are dispatched. Finally, orders with correct and complete details should be accepted by the system. This will allow the auditor to inspect the order confirmation to determine whether the order details are transferred accurately into the dispatch system.

146 The correct answer is: For sales invoices issued before 31 December 20X7 use audit software to determine whether there is a matching GDN dated before 31 December 20X7

Sales cut-off will have been correctly applied where goods are dispatched and recognised as sales in the same accounting period. Therefore all GDNs relating to goods dispatched before 31 December 20X7 should be matched by a sales invoice also dated before 31 December 20X7.

The fact that goods are picked and dispatched in the same accounting period does not provide evidence that sales have been recognised in the correct accounting period. Therefore the third and fourth options are not relevant.

147 The correct answer is: To provide audit evidence over the completeness of the recording of sales

Sequence checks on sales invoices provide evidence on the completeness of sales.

148 The correct answer is: (21,600 × 2/12) + (24,000 × 10/12)

The rent recognised in the year should reflect that earned in the period. For January and February this will be based on an annual rental income of $21,600. For the remaining 10 months this would be based on the increased rental. The proof in total should be calculated on the same basis.

149 Lily

Marking scheme

Marks

(a)   Up to 1 mark per well-explained deficiency and up to 1 mark per recommendation. If not well explained then just give ½ mark for each.

Warehouse manager supervising the count

No division of responsibilities within each counting team

Internal audit teams should be checking controls and performing sample counts

No flagging of aisles once counting complete

Additional inventory listed on sheets which are not sequentially numbered

Inventory sheets not signed by counters

Damaged goods not moved to central location

Movements of inventory during the count

Warehouse manager not qualified to assess the level of work in progress

Warehouse manager not experienced enough to assess the quantities of raw materials

12

(b) Up to 1 mark per well-described procedure.

Observe the counters to confirm if inventory count instructions are being followed

Perform test counts inventory to sheets and sheets to inventory

Confirm procedures for damaged goods are operating correctly

Inspect damaged goods to confirm whether the level of damage is correctly noted

Observe procedures for movements of inventory during the count

Obtain a photocopy of the completed inventory sheets

Identify and make a note of the last goods received notes and goods dispatched notes

Observe the procedures carried out by warehouse manager in assessing the level of work in progress

Discuss with the warehouse manager how he has estimated the raw materials quantities

Identify inventory held for third parties and ensure excluded from count

6

(c) (i) Up to 1 mark per well-described procedure, max of 4 procedures.

Calculate inventory holding period

Produce an aged inventory analysis to identify any slow-moving goods

Cast the inventory listing

Select a sample of items for testing to confirm net realisable value (NRV) and/or cost

Recalculate cost and NRV for sample of inventory

Computer-assisted audit techniques (CAATs) can be used to confirm cut-off

CAATs can be used to confirm whether inventory adjustments noted during the count have been updated to inventory records

4

(ii) Up to 1 mark per well-explained advantage.

Test a large volume of inventory data accurately and quickly

Cost effective after set-up

CAATs can test program controls as well as general IT controls

Test the actual inventory system and records rather than printouts from the system

CAATs reduce the level of human error in testing

CAAT results can be compared with traditional audit testing

Free up audit team members to focus on judgemental and high risk areas

4

(iii) Up to 1 mark per well-explained disadvantage.

Costs of using CAATs in this first year will be high

Team may require training on the specific CAATs to be utilised

Changes in the inventory system may require costly revisions to the CAATs

The inventory system may not be compatible with the audit firm's CAATs

If testing the live system, there is a risk the data could be corrupted or lost

If using copy files rather than live data, there is the risk that these files are not genuine copies

Adequate systems documentation must be available

$$\frac{4}{30}$$

(a)

Deficiency (i)	Recommendation (ii)
The warehouse manager will supervise the inventory count and is not independent as he has overall responsibility for the inventory. He therefore has an incentive to conceal or fail to report any issues that could reflect badly upon him.	An independent supervisor should be assigned, such as a manager from the internal audit department.
Aisles or areas counted will not be flagged. This could result in items being double counted or not counted at all.	Once areas have been counted they should be flagged. At the end of the count the supervisor should check all areas have been flagged and therefore counted.
There is no one independent reviewing controls over the count or test counting to assess the accuracy of the counts.	Instead of the internal auditors being involved in the count itself, they should perform secondary test counts and review controls over the count.
Damaged goods are being left in their location rather than being stored separately. This makes it more difficult for finance to assess the level of damage to the goods and establish the level of write down needed. Also, if not moved, damaged goods could be sold by mistake.	Damaged goods should be clearly marked as such during the count and at the end of the count they should be moved to a central location. A manager from the finance team should then inspect these damaged goods to assess the level of allowance or write down needed.

Deficiency (i)	Recommendation (ii)
Due to the continuous production process, there will be movement of goods in and out of the warehouse during the count, increasing the risk of double counting or failing to count inventory. This could mean inventory in the financial statements is under- or overstated.	Although it is not practicable to disrupt the continuous production process, raw materials (RM) required for 31 December should be estimated and separated from the remainder of inventory. These materials should be included as part of work in progress (WIP). Goods manufactured on 31 December should be stored separately, and at the end of the count should be counted once and included as finished goods. Goods received from suppliers should also be stored separately, counted once at the end and included in RM. Goods dispatched to customers should be kept to a minimum during the count.
The warehouse manager is going to estimate WIP levels. The warehouse manager is unlikely to have the necessary experience to estimate the WIP levels which is something the factory manager would be more familiar with. Alternatively a specialist may be needed to make the estimate. This could ultimately result in an inaccurate WIP balance in the financial statements.	A specialist should be used to assess the work in progress.
The warehouse manager is going to approximate RM quantities. Although he is familiar with the RM, and on the basis that a specialist has been required in the past, the warehouse manager may not have the necessary skill and experience to carry out these measurements. This could result in an inaccurate RM balance in the financial statements.	As in previous years, a specialist should assess the quantities of raw materials, or at least check the warehouse manager's estimate to give comfort that the manager's estimates will be reasonable going forward.
There is no indication that inventory sheets are signed or initialled by the counting team, nor a record kept of which team counted which area. This means it will be difficult to follow up on any anomalies noted, as the identity of the counters may not be known.	Inventory sheets should be signed by both team members once an aisle is completed. The supervisor should check the sheets are signed when handed in.
Inventory not listed on the sheets is to be entered onto separate sheets. These sheets are not sequentially numbered and the supervisor will be unable to ensure the completeness of all inventory sheets.	Every team should be given a blank sheet on which they can enter any inventory counted which is not on their sheets. The blank sheets should be sequentially numbered, with any unused sheets returned at the end of the count. The supervisor should then check the sequence of all sheets.
The responsibilities of each of the two staff members within a counting team is unclear. It does not appear that one has been told to count and the other to check. Therefore errors in counting may not be picked up.	For each area one team member should be asked to count and the second member asked to check that the inventory has been counted correctly. The roles of each can then be reversed for the next area.

Note. Only six deficiencies and six related recommendations were needed to gain 12 marks.

(b) **Procedures undertaken during the inventory count**

- For a sample of inventory items, carry out test counts from aisle to inventory sheet to test completeness and from inventory sheets to aisle to test existence.

- Obtain and record details of the last goods received notes (GRNs) and goods dispatched notes (GDNs) for 31 December to form the basis for cut-off procedures at the audit.

- Observe whether teams carrying out the count are adequately following the inventory count instructions.

- For a sample of items marked as damaged on the inventory sheets, inspect the windows to verify that the level of damage has been correctly recorded.

- Observe the procedures for movements of inventory during the count and assess the risk that raw materials or finished goods have been missed or double counted.

- Photocopy the inventory sheets for follow-up and use when performing procedures at the final audit.

- Ascertain how the warehouse manager is assessing the level of work in progress by observing the assessment and by reviewing his assumptions, and consider how consistent his estimate is with observed levels.

- Ask the warehouse manager how he has estimated the raw materials quantities and review his calculations and any assumptions for reasonableness. Reperform a sample of the measurements of height and width forming the basis of any calculation to see if they are accurate.

- Confirm any third-party inventory observed has been excluded from the count.

- Confirm that the procedures for identifying and separately storing damaged goods are operating effectively.

Note. Only six procedures were needed to gain full marks.

(c) **Computer-assisted audit techniques (CAATs)**

(i) Audit procedures

Software can be used to cast the inventory listing to confirm the total is complete and accurate.

Audit software could be used to extract a statistical sample of inventory items in order to verify their cost or net realisable value (NRV).

Calculations of the inventory holding period or inventory turnover could be carried out by audit software, before being used to compare against the same ratios for the prior year or of competitors. This will help to assess the risk of inventory being overstated.

Audit software could be used to help extract an aged inventory analysis. This could in turn be used to identify any obsolete or slow-moving items, which may require a write-down or an allowance.

Audit software can be used to perform calculations during testing of inventory, such as recorded cost (eg weight or quantity multiplied by cost per kg or unit).

CAATs can be used to confirm whether inventory adjustments recorded during attendance at the count have been correctly recorded in the final inventory records forming the basis of inventory in the financial statements.

CAATs can be used to verify cut-off by testing whether the dates of the last GRNs and GDNs recorded relate to pre year end, and that any with a date after the year end have been excluded from the inventory records.

Note. Only four procedures were required.

(ii)   **CAATs – advantages**

- CAATs allow the audit team to test a large volume of inventory data more accurately and more quickly than if tested manually.

- CAATs decrease the scope for human error during testing and can provide evidence of a higher quality.

- By using CAATs, auditors can test actual inventory transactions within the system rather than working on printouts from spool or previewed files which are dependent on other software (and therefore could contain errors or could have been tampered with following export).

- Assuming the inventory system remains unchanged, CAATs used in the audit of Lily year on year should bring time (and therefore cost) savings in the long term, which should more than compensate for any set-up costs.

- Auditors can utilise CAATs to test program controls as well as general internal controls associated with computers.

- Results from CAATs can be compared with results from traditional testing. If the results correlate, overall confidence is increased.

- The use of CAATs allows audit team members more time to focus on risk areas and issues requiring judgement, rather than performing routine calculations that can be carried out by audit software.

Note. Only four advantages were needed to gain full marks.

(iii)   **CAATs – disadvantages**

- Setting up the software needed for CAATs in the first year is likely to be time consuming and expensive.

- Audit staff working on Lily's audit will need to be trained so they have a sufficient level of IT knowledge to apply CAATs when auditing the inventory system.

- If testing is performed on data in the live inventory system, there is a risk that live client data may be corrupted and lost.

- If the inventory system at Lily changed then it may be expensive and time consuming to redesign the CAATs.

- If the inventory system at Lily is not compatible with Daffodil & Co's CAATs then they will need to be tailored to Lily's system, which may be costly.

- If testing is performed on data from copies of the live files rather than the live data itself, there is the risk that these files have been affected by the copying process or have been tampered with.

- If there is not adequate systems documentation available, it will be difficult to design appropriate CAATs due to a lack of understanding of the inventory system at Lily.

Note. Only four advantages were needed to gain full marks.

150 Westra Co

Marking scheme

Marks

(a) **Audit procedures – purchases**, 12 marks. 1 for procedure and 1 for the reason. Limit to 5 marks in each category where stated briefly without full detail.

Audit procedure	Reason for procedure
Parts to GRN	Check completeness
Parts no GRN number	System error or cut-off error
GRN to computer	Parts received were ordered – occurrence
GRN agree to invoice	Completeness of recording
Review unmatched GRN file	Completeness of recording of liabilities
Paid invoice – GRN attached	Confirms invoice in PDB
Invoice details to payables ledger	Completeness and accuracy of recording
Review unmatched invoices file	Indicate understatement of liability (lack of completeness)
Payables ledger to purchase invoice	Liability belongs to Westra
Payables ledger to payments list	Liability properly discharged – payments complete
Payment list entries to invoice	Payment made for bona fide liability
Payments list to bank statement	Confirms payment to supplier
Bank statement entry to payments list	Confirms payment relates to Westra
GRN cut-off testing	Accuracy of cut-off

Maximum marks

(b) **Audit procedures – payables**, 8 marks. 1 for procedure and 1 for reason. Limit to ½ mark in each category where stated briefly without full detail.

Audit procedure	Reason for procedure
Obtain and cast list of payables	Ensure that the list is accurate
Total of payables to the general ledger and financial statements	Confirm that the total has been accurately recorded
Analytical procedures	Indicates problems with the accuracy and completeness of payables
Agree payables to supplier statements	Confirm balance due from Westra
Supplier statement reconciliation	Liabilities exist and belong to Westra
Reconcile invoices	Confirms completeness and cut-off assertions
Reconcile payments	Payment to correct supplier
Review ledger old unpaid invoices	Credits O/S or going concern indicator
After-date credit notes	Payables not overstated
FS categorisation payables	Classification objective

Maximum marks 8

(c) **Controls over standing data**, 5 marks. 1 mark for explaining each control. ½ for poor/limited explanation.

Amendments authorised

How authorised (form or access control)

Reject deletion where outstanding balance

Keep record of amendments

Review list of suppliers – unauthorised amendments

Update supplier list on computer regularly

Review computer control log

Review list of suppliers – unauthorised additions

Other relevant points (each)

Maximum marks 5

(d) **Use of data analytics**

Link together with other cycles

Analysis of ageing, problem entries

Use of data analytics may be limited by lack of computer system integration

Cost effective – may improve audit effectiveness

Analysis of journal entries

Ratio analysis

Other relevant points (each)

Maximum marks $\underline{5}$

                                                         $\underline{\underline{30}}$

(a) **Substantive procedures**

Completeness

Audit procedure	Purpose
Perform analytical procedures on purchases, eg comparison to the prior year on a month by month basis, ratio of purchases to payables, gross profit percentage etc and investigate any significant fluctuations	To provide assurance on the completeness of amounts recorded in the accounts and to highlight any areas of concern for further investigation
For a sample of supplier invoices, trace amounts to the GRN, order and payables ledger	To confirm completeness of recording of purchases
Inspect the unmatched GRN file and seek explanations for any old unmatched items and trace these to the year-end accruals listing	To provide assurance on completeness as these should be included in the year-end accrual
For a sample of amounts on the ledger, agree to the computerised payments list to verify the amount and supplier	To provide assurance that the payment list is complete and accurate

Occurrence

Audit procedure	Purpose
For a sample of amounts in the payables ledger, trace these to the invoice and other supporting documentation such as GRNs	To provide assurance on the occurrence assertion
For a sample of GRNs, agree back to the original order details	To provide assurance on occurrence
For a sample of payees on the computerised payments list, agree amounts back to the supporting documentation such as invoices and GRNs	To provide assurance that payment has been made for a bona fide liability of the company

Audit procedure	Purpose
For a sample of payments made after the year end, trace back to the computerised payments list	To provide assurance that payment relates to the company
For a sample of payees on the computerised payments list, trace payment to post year end bank statements	To confirm that payment was made to authorised suppliers of the company

Cut-off

Audit procedure	Purpose
For a sample of GRNs dated shortly before and after the year end, agree that the amounts on invoices are posted to the correct financial year	To ensure that amounts are included in the correct financial period
Review the schedule of accruals and agree to GRNs, inspecting the date of receipt of goods to ensure that goods received after the year end are not included	To ensure that amounts are included in the correct financial period
Inspect outstanding orders on the 'orders placed' file for any orders completed but not yet invoiced	To ensure that amounts are included in the correct financial period

(b) **Audit procedures on trade payables**

Audit procedure	Purpose
Cast the list of payables balances from the ledger at the year end	To provide assurance that the list is complete and accurate
Reconcile the payables list from the payables ledger to the general ledger and accounts	To provide assurance that the figures are complete and accurate and correctly reflected in the financial statements
Perform analytical procedures on trade payables, comparing balance to prior year and investigating any significant fluctuations	To provide assurance on completeness and accuracy and to highlight areas of concern
For a sample of balances, trace amount to supporting supplier statements	To confirm the existence and accuracy of the amount outstanding at the year end
Test cut-off by taking a sample of GRNs either side of the year end and verifying that amounts are included on the payables ledger for goods received before the year end	To ensure that amounts are included in the correct financial period
Review disclosure of payables in the draft financial statements	To ensure that payables have been disclosed appropriately in the statement of financial position and notes as either current or long-term liabilities

ANSWERS

(c)   Control procedures over standing data on trade payables master file

- Access to the trade payables master file is limited only to authorised staff

- Amendments to standing data can only be made by authorised staff and all amendments must be authorised prior to input

- Access to the file is controlled by logins and passwords and passwords must be prompted to be changed regularly (say, every 90 days)

- Computer log is reviewed regularly by IT department to detect any unauthorised access or attempts to access the trade payables master file

- The list of suppliers should be reviewed regularly by a senior manager and those no longer used should be removed from the system

(d)   Use of data analytics techniques in audit of Westra

Data analytics could be used in the audit of purchases and payables at Westra in a number of ways.

Data analytics routines can be used to link together purchase expenses with payables, which could be helpful in testing a variety of areas. This would include the application of the cut-off at the beginning and end of the reporting period, as well as the completeness of payables, all of which should be matched to expenses.

These routines may be able to go further still, and link together several cycles for a sample of transactions, for example; the purchase order could be linked to the expense, which could in turn be linked to the liability (payable). This is then connected to the cash movement for the payment, and to the accounting for the item in inventory (depending on the item being purchased). Finally it may then be possible to trace the inventory item being sold, with entries to revenue, receivables and, ultimately, the cash receipt. In this way, the audit of payables changes from being an isolated area of the financial statements to one that is connected to the wider accounting context.

Within payables, data analytics software could be used to generate detailed payables ageing reports, allowing the auditor to identify potential problem balances. The software can perform a check that all payables calculations are arithmetically accurate, and can highlight gaps in the expected sequence of entries, as well as zero or duplicated entries.

An analysis of journal entries to payables can be made, helping to identify eg unexpected journals, journals posted to unusual combinations of accounts or by unauthorised users, or to identify trends such as high numbers of postings just below authorisation limits.

Data analytics software could also be used to **reperform** the cost of the total on the file to ensure the file is a complete record of transactions. The software can also be used to perform **ratio calculations** for analytical procedures on the purchases and payables data, and to compare the results of this analysis with expectations.

For this audit, the use of data analytics may be **limited** by the fact that the company uses a mixture of manual and computerised systems. However, it may still be possible for the auditor to improve both audit efficiency and audit quality by making using of data analytics routines where it is appropriate to do so.

151 Dashing Co

Marking scheme

		Marks
(a)	**Steps for a receivables circularisation**	
	Obtain consent from client	1
	Agree receivables listing to SL	1
	Select sample including nil, credit, old and large balances	1
	Prepare letters on company letterhead	1
	Sent by auditor	1
	Where no response, perform alternative procedures	1
	For replies received reconcile and investigate differences	1
	Restricted to	4
(b)	**Receivables substantive procedures**	
	Accuracy, valuation and allocation tests	2
	Completeness tests	2
	Rights and obligation tests	2
		6
(c)	**Substantive procedures for redundancy provision**	
	Discuss with directors when announcement was made	1
	If before year end, agree to supporting documentation	1
	Review board minutes for details of redundancy payments	1
	Obtain a breakdown of redundancy calculations	1
	Recalculate the redundancy provision	1
	Review post y/e cash book for evidence of payments	1

	Marks
Obtain written representation	1
Review disclosure in FS	1
Restricted to	$\overline{5}$
(d) **Impact on auditor's report**	
Discussion of issue	1
Calculation of materiality	1
Type of auditor's report modification required	2
Impact on auditor's report	$\underline{1}$
	$\overline{5}$
Total marks	$\overline{\underline{20}}$

(a) **Steps in undertaking a positive receivables circularisation for Dashing Co**

The following steps should be undertaken in carrying out a positive receivables circularisation:

- Obtain consent from the finance director of Dashing Co in advance of undertaking the circularisation.

- Obtain a list of trade receivables at the year end, cast this and agree it to the sales ledger control account total.

- Select a sample from the receivables list ensuring that a number of nil, old, credit and large balances are selected.

- Circularisation letters should be prepared on Dashing Co's letterhead paper, requesting a confirmation of the year-end receivables balance, and for replies to be sent directly to the audit team using a pre-paid envelope.

- The finance director of Dashing Co should be requested to sign all the letters prior to them being sent out by a member of the audit team.

- Where no response is received, follow this up with another letter or a phone call and where necessary alternative procedures should be performed

- When replies are received, they should be reconciled to Dashing Co's receivables records, any differences such as cash or goods in transit should be investigated further.

(b) **Receivables substantive procedures**

Accuracy, valuation and allocation

- Review the after date cash receipts and follow through to pre year-end receivable balances.

- Inspect the aged receivables report to identify any slow moving balances, discuss these with the credit control manager to assess whether an allowance or write down is necessary.

- For any slow moving/aged balances review customer correspondence to assess whether there are any invoices in dispute.

- Review board minutes of Dashing Co to assess whether there are any material disputed receivables.

Completeness

- Select a sample of goods despatched notes from before the year end, agree to sales invoices and to inclusion in the sales ledger and year-end receivables ledger.

- Agree the total of individual sales ledger accounts to the aged receivables listing and to the trial balance.

- Obtain the prior year aged receivables listing and for significant balances compare to the current year receivables listing for inclusion and amount due. Discuss with management any missing receivables or significantly lower balances.

- Review the sales ledger for any credit balances and discuss with management whether these should be reclassified as payables.

Rights and obligations

- Review bank confirmations and loan agreements for any evidence that receivables have been assigned as security for amounts owed by Dashing Co.

- Review board minutes for evidence that legal title to receivables has been sold onto a third party such as a factor.

- For a sample of receivables, agree the balance recorded on the sales ledger to the original name of the customer on a sales order or a contract.

Tutorial note: Marks will be awarded for any other relevant receivables tests.

(c) **Substantive procedures to confirm the redundancy provision**

- Discuss with the directors of Dashing Co as to whether they have formally announced their intention to close the production site and make their employees redundant, to confirm that a present obligation exists at the year end.

- If announced before the year end, review supporting documentation to verify that the decision has been formally announced.

- Review the board minutes to ascertain whether it is probable that the redundancy payments will be paid.

- Obtain a breakdown of the redundancy calculations by employee and cast it to ensure completeness and agree to trial balance.

- Recalculate the redundancy provision to confirm completeness and agree components of the calculation to supporting documentation such as employee contracts.

- Review the post year-end cash book to identify whether any redundancy payments have been made, compare actual payments to the amounts provided to assess whether the provision is reasonable.

- Obtain a written representation from management to confirm the completeness of the provision.

- Review the disclosure of the redundancy provision to ensure compliance with IAS 37 *Provisions, Contingent Liabilities and Contingent Assets.*

(d) **Impact on auditor's report**

The company has included a redundancy provision of $110,000 in the draft financial statements, however, audit fieldwork testing has confirmed that the provision should actually be $305,000. The provision is understated and profit before tax overstated if the finance director does not amend the financial statements.

The provision included is $110,000, it should be $305,000 hence an adjustment of $195,000 is required which represents 7.5% of profit before tax (195/2,600) or 1.1% of total assets (195/18,000) and hence is a material matter.

If management does not adjust the redundancy provision, the auditor's report will need to be modified. As provisions are understated and profit overstated, there is a material misstatement, which is not pervasive. Therefore, a qualified opinion would be necessary, stating that the opinion is qualified 'except for'. A basis for qualified opinion paragraph would also need to be included subsequent to the opinion paragraph. This would explain the material misstatement in relation to the redundancy provision and the effect on the financial statements.

152 Rose

Marking scheme

Marks

(a) **Trade payables and accruals**

Calculate trade payables payment period

Compare total trade payables and list of accruals against prior year

Discuss with management process to quantify understatement of payables

Discuss with management whether any correcting journal adjustment posted

Sample invoices received between 25 March and year end and follow to inclusion in year-end accruals or trade payables   correcting journal

Review after-date payments

Review supplier statements reconciliations

Perform a trade payables circularisation

Cut-off testing pre- and post-year end GRN

Maximum   6

(b) **Receivables**

For non-responses arrange to send a follow-up circularisation

With the client's permission, telephone the customer and ask for a response

For remaining non-responses, undertake alternative procedures to confirm receivables

For responses with differences, identify any disputed amounts, identify whether these relate to timing differences or whether there are possible errors in the records

Cash in transit should be vouched to post year end cash receipts in the cashbook

Review receivables ledger to identify any possible mispostings

Disputed balances, discuss with management whether a write down is necessary

Maximum   5

(c) **Reorganisation**

Review the board minutes where decision taken

Review the announcement to shareholders in late October

Obtain a breakdown and confirm that only direct expenditure from restructuring is included

Review expenditure to ensure retraining costs excluded

Cast the breakdown of the reorganisation provision

    Agree costs included to supporting documentation
    Obtain a written representation
    Review the adequacy of the disclosures

Maximum   4

(d)   **Written representations**

    Written representations are necessary evidence
    Required to confirm directors' responsibilities
    Required to support other evidence or required by ISAs
    Required to confirm management have communicated all deficiencies in
    internal controls
    Letter addressed to the auditor
    Throughout fieldwork identify that require written representations

Maximum

Total

(a)   **Trade payables and accruals**

    (1)   Ask management about the action they have taken to establish the value of the misstatement of trade payables. If they have ascertained the value of the error assess the materiality of it and the impact of it remaining uncorrected.

    (2)   Enquire whether any correcting journal entry has been calculated and whether it has been processed in relation to the misstatement.

    (3)   For a sample of purchase invoices received between 25 March and the end of 31 March 20X6, verify that they are included within accruals or as part of trade payables via a journal adjustment.

    (4)   Reconcile supplier statements to purchase ledger balances, and investigate any reconciling items.

    (5)   Calculate and compare the trade payables payment period with prior years. Significant differences should be investigated.

    (6)   Compare trade payables and accruals against the previous year and expectations. Investigate any significant differences and corroborate any explanations for differences to supporting evidence.

    (7)   Review the cash book payments and bank statements in the period immediately after the year end for evidence of payments relating to current year liabilities. Ensure any found are included in accruals, trade payables or the trade payables journal.

    (8)   For a sample of payable balances, perform a trade payables circularisation. Any non-replies should be followed up and reconciling items between the balance confirmed and the trade payables balance should be investigated.

    (9)   For a sample of goods received notes before the year end and after the year end, ensure the related invoices have been recorded in the period to which they relate.

    Note. Only six valid procedures were needed.

(b)   **Receivables**

    (1)   For those receivables who don't respond, the team should arrange to send a follow-up circularisation if agreed by the client.

    (2)   For non-responses to the follow-up, and after obtaining client consent, the audit senior should telephone the customer and request the customer responds in writing to the circularisation request.

    (3)   Where all follow-ups are unsuccessful, alternative procedures must be carried out to confirm receivables, such as reviewing after-date cash receipts for year-end receivables.

(4) Where responses highlight differences, these should be investigated to establish if any amounts are disputed or require adjustment.

(5) Where it is found that differences are in relation to disputed invoices, they should be discussed with management and the need for an allowance or write-off assessed.

(6) For timing differences identified on responses or otherwise (eg cash in transit), these should be agreed to post year end cash receipts in the cash book and bank statement.

(7) For those responses highlighting an unresolved difference, the receivables ledger should be reviewed for unusual entries that could suggest errors made when posting transactions.

Note. Only five valid procedures were needed.

(c) **Reorganisation**

(1) Verify the announcement to shareholders was actually made in late March by inspecting documentary evidence of the announcement.

(2) Board minutes should also be reviewed to confirm that the decision to reorganise the business was taken pre year end.

(3) Obtain an analysis of the reorganisation provision and confirm that only expenditure attributable to the restructuring is included.

(4) Cast the breakdown of the reorganisation provision to ensure it has been correctly calculated.

(5) Review the expenditure and confirm retraining costs are not included.

(6) Agree costs included within the provision to supporting documentation to confirm the appropriateness and accuracy of items included.

(7) Review the related disclosures in the financial statements to assess whether they comply with the requirements of IAS 37 Provisions, Contingent Liabilities and Contingent Assets.

(8) Obtain a written representation confirming management discussions in relation to the announcement of the reorganisation.

Note. Only four valid procedures were needed.

(d) **Written representations**

Written representations are necessary information that the auditor requires in connection with the audit of the entity's financial statements. Accordingly, similar to responses to inquiries, written representations are audit evidence.

The auditor needs to obtain written representations from management and, where appropriate, those charged with governance that they believe they have fulfilled their responsibility for the preparation of the financial statements and for the completeness of the information provided to the auditor.

Written representations are needed to support other audit evidence relevant to the financial statements or specific assertions in the financial statements, if determined necessary by the auditor or required by other ISAs. This may be necessary for judgemental areas where the auditor has to rely on management explanations.

Written representations can be used to confirm that management have communicated to the auditor all deficiencies in internal controls of which management are aware.

Written representations are normally in the form of a letter, written by the company's management and addressed to the auditor. The letter is usually requested from management but can also be requested from the chief operating officer or chief financial officer. Throughout the fieldwork, the audit team will note any areas where representations may be required.

During the final review stage, the auditors will produce the written representations which the directors will review and then produce it on their letterhead. It will be signed by the directors and dated as at the date the auditor's report is signed, but not after.

153 Andromeda Industries Co

Workbook references. Chapters 8, 12, 13 and 20.

Top tips. Note that in part (b) you are asked to consider the procedures you would carry out **before** and **during** the inventory count. One of the key procedures which the auditor must perform before the count is a review of the count instructions to determine whether the count is to be conducted in such a way that it will provide reliable evidence. Remember however it is not the auditor's responsibility to organise the count itself. That is the responsibility of management so make sure that you answer the question from the auditor's perspective. Other planning issues will be relevant; for example in this case there are a number of warehouses so the auditor will need to consider which counts to attend.

During the count, remember that the auditor carries out tests of controls and substantive procedures. The tests of controls provide evidence that the count is being conducted properly eg observing the count teams. Substantive procedures include the carrying out of test counts.

For the research and development expenditure, one approach would be to think about what the balance is made up of ie opening balance, plus additional expenses capitalised, less amortisation. Then think about how you would obtain evidence relating to each of these elements. For example, the opening balances would be agreed to prior year financial statements and so on. You must also try to make your answer specific to the scenario. For example, when you talk about the amortisation charge you should refer to the policy stated. This demonstrates that you are applying your knowledge and not just repeating a list of pre-learned procedures.

Part (c) asks you to consider the impact on the auditor's report. With this type of requirement, if you are given the information, calculate materiality and consider the implications of this in your response. If you decide that a modified opinion is required explain the grounds on which you think a modification is required (ie material misstatement or inability to obtain sufficient appropriate evidence) and the degree of seriousness (ie material or pervasive).

Easy marks. Part (a) should represent four easy marks. You should be comfortable explaining factors which influence the reliability of audit evidence.

Examining team's comments. Candidates were firstly asked to explain four factors, which influence the reliability of audit evidence. One mark was available for each factor; candidates were required to either fully explain the factor or compare that factor to another source. This question was generally well answered. A minority of candidates did not fully describe each factor eg they noted written evidence was reliable but did not explain why it was reliable or, alternatively, did not make a comparison such as written evidence is stronger than oral evidence. It was pleasing that candidates planned their time carefully and generally only described the required number of factors.

Candidates were further provided with a short scenario-based question and were required to describe audit procedures that would be performed before and during an inventory count (eight marks) and audit procedures in relation to the research and development costs (four marks). As in previous sittings and as noted in previous examining team's reports, the provision of audit procedures relevant to particular circumstances was not well attempted by the majority of candidates.

Most candidates were able to identify that the count procedures should be obtained before the inventory count; however, a significant number did not expand to explain the purpose of obtaining this information or the importance of the auditor reviewing the adequacy of these instructions. Candidates often then listed further details to be obtained eg location of count, assembling the audit team and whether to use an expert. A number of candidates referred to third-party inventory; however, this was not mentioned in the scenario and therefore any related procedures were not valid. Only the better candidates suggested looking at prior year audit files or considered the materiality of the sites and control issues.

Most candidates did note that during the count the auditor should observe the counters to ensure the instructions were being followed. However, a significant number of candidates then proceeded to list the count procedures that the company's counting team should follow thereby straying into management responsibilities rather than the procedures relevant to the auditor. Some candidates correctly suggested undertaking test counts, while only a minority suggested obtaining copies of the completed count sheets. Overall it was disappointing that candidates did not seem familiar with the auditor's role at an inventory count.

In relation to research and development costs, some candidates correctly suggested that the auditor needed to ensure compliance with the capitalisation criteria in IAS 38 and also suggested recalculating the amortisation charge, but few candidates identified any other relevant procedures. Many candidates did not score any marks for this requirement. Although many candidates suggested a review of invoices, the procedure described was most often testing valuation or rights and obligations rather than to ensure correct classification.

Marking scheme

Marks

(a) Up to 1 mark per well-explained point, maximum of 4 points.

- Reliability increased when it is obtained from independent sources

- Internally generated evidence more reliable when the controls are effective

- Evidence obtained directly by the auditor is more reliable than evidence obtained indirectly or by inference

- Evidence in documentary form is more reliable than evidence obtained orally

4

- Evidence provided by original documents is more reliable than evidence provided by copies

(b) (i) Up to 1 mark per well-described procedure, overall maximum of 8 marks.

Before the count

- Review the prior year audit files to identify significant inventory issues from last year

- Discuss with management if any new warehouses or any sites have significant control issues

- Decide which of the 12 warehouses the audit team members will attend

- Review a copy of the proposed inventory count instructions

During the count

- Observe the counters to confirm if inventory count instructions are being followed
- Perform test counts inventory to sheets and sheets to inventory
- Confirm procedures for damaged goods are operating correctly
- Observe procedures for movements of inventory during the count
- Obtain a photocopy of the completed inventory sheets
- Identify and make a note of the last goods received notes and goods dispatched notes
- Discuss with the internal audit supervisor how they have estimated the raw materials quantities

8

(ii) Up to 1 mark per well-described procedure, overall maximum of 4 marks.

- Cast the schedule of intangible assets
- Agree the opening balances to the prior year financial statements
- Agree the closing balances to the general ledger, trial balance and draft financial statements
- Recalculate amortisation charged in the year and confirm in line with the policy of straight line over five years
- For new projects, discuss with management the stage of development and if capitalised or expensed
- For those expensed as research, agree costs to invoices, supporting documentation and to inclusion in profit or loss
- For those capitalised as development, agree costs to invoice and confirm technically feasible by discussion with development managers or review of feasibility reports
- Review market research reports to confirm Andromeda has the ability to sell the product
- Review the disclosures in the financial statements in accordance with IAS 38 *Intangible Assets*

4

(c) Up to 1 mark per valid point, overall maximum of 4 marks.

- Discussion of issue
- Calculation of materiality
- Type of auditor's report modification required
- Impact on auditor's report

4

20

(a)   **Reliability of audit evidence**

The following factors or generalisations can be made when assessing the reliability of audit evidence:

(i)   The reliability of audit evidence is increased when it is obtained from independent sources outside the entity.

(ii) The reliability of audit evidence which is generated internally is increased when the related controls imposed by the entity, including those over its preparation and maintenance, are effective.

(iii) Audit evidence obtained directly by the auditor is more reliable than audit evidence obtained indirectly or by inference.

(iv) Audit evidence in documentary form, whether paper, electronic or other medium, is more reliable than evidence obtained orally.

(v)   Audit evidence provided by original documents is more reliable than audit evidence provided by photocopies or facsimiles, the reliability of which may depend on the controls over their preparation and maintenance.

(b)   (i)   **Inventory count procedures**

Before the count

(1)   Review the prior year audit files to identify whether there were any particular warehouses where significant inventory issues arose last year.

(2)   Discuss with management whether any of the warehouses this year are new, or have experienced significant control issues.

(3)   Decide which of the 12 warehouses the audit team members will attend, basing this on materiality and risk of each site.

(4)   Obtain a copy of the proposed inventory count instructions, review them to identify any control deficiencies and, if any are noted, discuss them with management prior to the counts.

During the count

(1)   Observe the counting teams of Andromeda to confirm whether the inventory count instructions are being followed correctly.

(2)   Select a sample of inventory and perform test counts from inventory sheets to warehouse aisle and from warehouse aisle to inventory sheets.

(3)   Confirm that the procedures for identifying and segregating damaged goods are operating correctly, and assess inventory for evidence of any damaged or slow-moving items.

(4)   Observe the procedures for movements of inventory during the count, to confirm that all movements have ceased.

(5)   Obtain a photocopy of the completed sequentially numbered inventory sheets for follow-up testing on the final audit.

(6)   Identify and make a note of the last goods received notes and goods dispatched notes for 31 December in order to perform cut-off procedures.

(7)   Discuss with the internal audit supervisor how any raw materials quantities have been estimated. Where possible, reperform the procedures adopted by the supervisor.

(ii) Research and development

Obtain and cast a schedule of intangible assets, detailing opening balances, amount capitalised in the current year, amortisation and closing balances.

(1) Agree the opening balances to the prior year financial statements.

(2) Agree the closing balances to the general ledger, trial balance and draft financial statements.

(3) Recalculate the amortisation charge for a sample of intangible assets which have commenced production and confirm it is in line with the amortisation policy of straight line over five years.

(4) For the five new projects, discuss with management the details of each project along with the stage of development and whether it has been capitalised or expensed.

(5) For those expensed as research, agree the costs incurred to invoices and supporting documentation and to inclusion in profit or loss.

(6) For those capitalised as development, agree costs incurred to invoices and confirm technically feasible by discussion with development managers or review of feasibility reports.

(7) Review market research reports to confirm Andromeda has the ability to sell the product once complete and probable future economic benefits will arise.

(8) Review the disclosures for intangible assets in the draft financial statements to ensure that they are in accordance with IAS 38 *Intangible Assets*.

(c) Auditor's reports

One of the projects Andromeda has developed in the year does not meet the recognition criteria under IAS 38 for capitalisation but has been included within intangible assets. This is contrary to IAS 38 as, if the criteria are not met, then this project is research expenditure and should be expensed to profit or loss rather than capitalised.

The error is material as it represents 11.8% of profit before tax (0.98m/8.3m) and hence management should adjust the financial statements by removing this project from intangible assets and charging it to profit or loss instead. The finance director's argument that the balance is immaterial is not correct.

If management refuses to amend this error, then the auditor's report will need to be modified. As management has not complied with IAS 38 and the error is material but not pervasive, then a qualified opinion would be necessary.

A basis for qualified opinion paragraph would be needed and would explain the material misstatement in relation to the incorrect treatment of research and development and the effect on the financial statements. The opinion paragraph would be qualified 'except for'.

154 Traffic Lights

In part (b), think about all the elements that go into the **valuation** assertion. Usually you need to verify **cost** and **depreciation**. Here, where items are held at **fair value**, you need to consider **fair value** and **depreciation**. You might also direct procedures to whether valuations are updated sufficiently regularly, given the potential weakness in controls. Remember that a procedure should include what will be done and why in order to be well explained.

In part (c), think about each type of income being verified and the documentation available in respect of them. Remember that donations fall into two categories that will need to be tackled differently. Think also about the **assertions** relevant to income as this will help you generate tests. You must not include tests of controls in your answer, as you are specifically asked for substantive tests.

Easy marks. The easiest marks available in this question are those relating to evidence over depreciation (in parts (a) and (b)).

Marks

(a)   1 mark per well-explained point.

- Expectation of comparability
- Controls
- Suitability of analytical procedures for particular assertions
- Nature of income and assets (donations, grants)
- Proof in total for depreciation   3

(b)   1 mark per well-explained procedure.

(i)   Properties

- Review donated assets register for additions

- Compare value of properties with local valuation data, eg estate agents

- Consider time since previous revaluation of assets

- Calculate expectation of proof in total for depreciation on properties

- Compare calculation to trustee's calculation

- Enquire of trustees concerning any disposals

- Visit play premises/review any advertising to confirm disposals or not of premises   4

(ii) Play equipment

- Review purchased asset ledger for any donations in year

- Trace purchased assets to invoice/receipts (cost is likely to represent fair value in this case)

- Review donated asset ledger for any donations/write-offs in year

- Attend play sessions to assess whether any written off assets appear to be in use

- Compare fair value of donated assets to suitable evidence, eg:
  - Toy retailers' websites
  - eBay for quality used items
  - Local 'secondhand' shops

- Recalculate depreciation (as for properties)

- Review useful life   5

(c) (i) Legacies

- Review correspondence to assess existence of legacies in year

- Enquire of legal advisers about any legacies in year

- Review cash books for legacies (or any unspecified items), trace to bank statements

- Discuss whether any legacies have occurred with trustees   2

(ii) Donations

- Observe cash counting

- Trace a sample of weekly bankings from cash books to bank statements

- Review cash books for unusual items, eg gaps

- Review correspondence to assess existence of donations from businesses/individuals

- Review cash books for donations, trace to bank statements

- Review local press for mention of donations to the charity, trace to bank statements

- Ask trustees about any specific fundraising activity during the year relating to assets

- Cross-check between new purchased assets and related donated funds

- Attend play sessions to gain an impression of any new equipment which might not be included in register   6
                                                   ——
                                                   20

(a) **Use of substantive analytical procedures at TL**

When judging whether to use substantive analytical procedures, auditors must consider factors such as (ISA 520):

- Internal controls in the related area
- The suitability of analytical procedures for particular assertions
- The auditor's expectation of comparability, given their understanding of the entity

Substantive procedures tend to be appropriate for large volumes of transactions which tend to be predictable over time.

In TL's case, given that income is donated and relatively low volume, there is likely to be a high degree of unpredictability. Donations related to play are voluntary and therefore are likely to be unpredictable, as are other income and legacies. In addition, asset donations are likely to be unpredictable.

It might be possible to establish a degree of correlations between particular appeals and subsequent donations but, given the assumption that controls are weak, it is unlikely that the auditor will judge that analytical procedures could give strong evidence over the completeness of income.

The local authority grants are applied for annually. This also implies a degree of unpredictability. However, actual practice over past years could be appraised, as it is possible that this is in fact predictable, if TL has been granted the same amount for a number of years and has a reasonable expectation of this continuing.

One area where Amber might be able to make use of analytical procedures is in relation to depreciation, where it will be possible to calculate an expectation of the depreciation charge for the year and compare it to TL's (a proof in total).

(b) **Procedures over valuation of assets**

    (i) Donated property

        The following procedures could be carried out in relation to the valuation of donated property:

- Review donated assets register to identify if there have been any additions in the year

- Compare the valuation of properties to third-party evidence, for example, comparable properties in local estate agents, to assess reasonableness of valuation

- Consider length of time since previous revaluations and discuss with trustees whether any class of asset requires revaluation to conform with accounting requirements

- Enquire of the trustees of any disposals of properties

- Visit play premises to confirm they are still in use in the charity and hence fair value is reasonable (if properties are not in use their fair value may be affected)

- Review charity advertising to ensure all properties are in use (ie they have not been disposed of)

- Calculate an expectation of the depreciation charge on properties for the year and compare to the trustees' calculation to assess whether the charge is reasonable

- Alternatively, recalculate depreciation

(ii)   Play equipment

The following procedures could be carried out in relation to the valuation of play equipment:

- Review purchased asset register for any bought assets in the year

- Trace purchased assets to invoice as cost price should be a good indicator of fair value

- Consider assumptions relating to any difference in valuation between cost and fair value of purchased assets

- Review purchased asset register for any written off assets and attend play sessions to identify if written off assets are still in use in the centres

- Review donated asset register for any additions/disposals in the year

- Compare fair value of donated assets to suitable third-party sources, such as toy retailers' websites, eBay for quality secondhand toys, local secondhand shops

- As above, consider if revaluations have been considered on a timely basis (although secondhand toys in frequent use are unlikely to increase in value, the trustees should be considering revaluations on a regular basis to comply with IAS 16)

- As above, perform a proof in total of depreciation and compare to trustees'

- Alternatively, recalculate depreciation

- Review asset write-offs to analyse whether a useful life of ten years is appropriate (it seems potentially long for secondhand toys in frequent use)

- Consider whether the sub-category 'play equipment' is sufficient, or whether there are different classes of play equipment which may have different useful lives

(c)   **Substantive procedures over income**

(i)   Legacies

- Discuss whether any legacies have occurred with trustees

- Review correspondence to assess occurrence of legacies in year

- Enquire of legal advisers about any legacies in year, to confirm occurrence and completeness

- Review cash books for legacies and trace to bank statements

- Review cash books and bank statements for unspecified items which might be legacies

(ii)   Donations

Cash donations

- Observe a series of cash counts during the year under review and perform some cash counts to ensure accuracy

- Trace a number of entries in the branch cash book for donations to the bank statements

- Review the branch cash books for any weeks with lack of entries

- Discuss weeks with no entries with volunteers and assess reasonableness of answers (eg volunteer absence, centre closure)

- Corroborate answers where possible (for example, staff may have a rota which can be used to corroborate absence)

Note. It is important to remember here that you have been asked for substantive procedures – answers including tests of controls, for example, observing whether two staff carry out the cash count, will not receive credit.

Other donations

- Review correspondence to assess existence of donations from businesses/individuals

- Review cash books for donations, trace to bank statements

- Review bank statements for direct donations and trace to donation records

- Review local press for mention of donations to the charity, trace to bank statements

- Ask trustees about any specific fundraising activity during the year relating to assets

- Cross-check between new purchased assets and related donated funds having been recorded

- Attend play sessions to gain an impression of any new equipment which might not be included in register (as this could suggest that income re associated equipment has not been recorded)

155 Hawthorn Enterprises Co

Workbook references. Chapters 8, 14, 15 and 16.

Top tips. The key issue for both part (a)(ii) and part (b) is the description of substantive procedures. There are two important points that you must bear in mind here. Firstly, make sure that you do not include any tests of controls. Confusing these two types of test is a common mistake identified by the examining team. A substantive procedure provides evidence regarding an assertion, whilst a test of control provides evidence regarding the effectiveness of controls operated by the entity. The second point is to note the use of the word 'describe'. Vague responses such as 'Check the year-end statements' will score no marks. You need to make it clear how you obtain the evidence and what the evidence actually is eg 'Select a representative sample of year-end supplier statements and agree the balance to the purchase ledger. If the balance agrees, then no further work is required'.

Easy marks. Part (a)(i) is straightforward but you must ensure that you explain the assertion as well as identifying it.

Marking scheme

Marks

(a) Up to 1 mark per assertion, ½ mark for stating assertion and ½ mark for explanation, max of 4 marks; up to 1 mark per relevant revenue substantive procedure, max of 4 marks.

- Occurrence – explanation and relevant substantive procedure
- Completeness – explanation and relevant substantive procedure
- Accuracy – explanation and relevant substantive procedure
- Cut-off – explanation and relevant substantive procedure
- Classification – explanation and relevant substantive procedure

8

(b)   Up to 1 mark per well-described procedure, overall maximum of 3
        marks for supplier statement reconciliations, maximum of 4
        marks for bank and maximum of 5 marks for receivables.

    (i)   **Supplier statement reconciliation**

- Select a sample of supplier statements and agree the balance to the purchase ledger

- Invoices in transit, confirm via GRN if receipt of goods was pre year end, if so confirm included in year-end accruals

- Cash in transit, confirm from cash book and bank statements the cash was sent pre year end

- Discuss any further adjusting items with the purchase ledger supervisor to understand the nature of the reconciling item, and whether it has been correctly accounted for   **3**

    (ii)   **Bank reconciliation**

- Bank balance to statement/bank confirmation

- Cash book balance to cash book

- Outstanding lodgements

- Unpresented cheques review

- Old cheques write back   **4**

    (iii)   **Receivables**

- Aged receivables report to identify any slow-moving balances

- Review the after-date cash receipts

- Review customer correspondence to assess whether there are any invoices in dispute

- Review board minutes

- Calculate average receivables collection period

- Post year end sales returns/credit notes

- Cut-off testing of GDN

- Agree to GDN and sales order to ensure existence $\underline{\text{5}}$
        $\underline{\underline{\text{20}}}$

(a)   **Assertions for classes of transactions and events** (ISA 315)

Occurrence

Transactions and events that have been recorded or disclosed have occurred, and such transactions and events pertain to the entity.

BPP
LEARNING
MEDIA

Substantive procedures

Select a sample of sales transactions recorded in the sales day book; agree the details back to a goods dispatched note (GDN) and customer order.

Review the monthly breakdown of sales per key product, compare to the prior year and budget and investigate any significant differences.

Completeness

All transactions and events that should have been recorded have been recorded, and all related disclosures that should have been included in the financial statements have been included.

Substantive procedures

Select a sample of GDNs raised during the year; agree to the sales invoice and that they are recorded in the sales day book.

Review the total amount of sales, compare to the prior year and budget and investigate any significant differences.

Accuracy

The amounts and other data relating to recorded transactions and events have been recorded appropriately, and related disclosures have been appropriately measured and described.

Substantive procedures

Select a sample of sales invoices and recalculate that the totals and calculation of sales tax are correct.

For a sample of sales invoices, confirm the sales price stated agrees to the authorised price list.

Cut-off

Transactions and events have been recorded in the correct accounting period.

Substantive procedures

Select a sample of pre and post year end GDNs and agree that the sale is recorded in the correct period's sales day books.

Review the post year end sales returns and agree if they relate to pre year end sales that the revenue has been correctly removed from the sales day book.

Classification

Transactions and events have been recorded in the proper accounts.

Substantive procedures

Agree for a sample of sales invoices that they have been correctly recorded within revenue nominal account codes and included within revenue in the financial statements.

Presentation

Transactions and events are appropriately aggregated or disaggregated and clearly described, and related disclosures are relevant and understandable in the context of the requirements of the applicable financial reporting framework.

Substantive procedures

For an entity applying IFRS 15 *Revenue from Contracts with Customers*, obtaining a breakdown of trade receivables and for a sample of receivables, reviewing the related sales contract to ensure that the entity's right to consideration is not conditional. (Conditional consideration should be recorded as contract assets.)

Note. Only four assertions and substantive procedures are required.

(b)   (i)   **Substantive procedures for supplier statement reconciliations**

       (1)   Select a representative sample of year-end supplier statements and agree the balance to the purchase ledger of Hawthorn. If the balance agrees, then no further work is required.

       (2)   Where differences occur due to invoices in transit, confirm from goods received notes (GRN) whether the receipt of goods was pre year end; if so, confirm that this receipt is included in year-end accruals.

       (3)   Where differences occur due to cash in transit from Hawthorn to the supplier, confirm from the cash book and bank statements that the cash was sent pre year end.

       (4)   Discuss any further adjusting items with the purchase ledger supervisor to understand the nature of the reconciling item, and whether it has been correctly accounted for.

   (ii)   **Substantive procedures for bank reconciliation**

       (1)   Obtain Hawthorn's bank account reconciliation and cast to check the additions to ensure arithmetical accuracy.

       (2)   Agree the balance per the bank reconciliation to an original year-end bank statement and to the bank confirmation letter.

       (3)   Agree the reconciliation's balance per the cash book to the year-end cash book.

       (4)   Trace all the outstanding lodgements to the pre year end cash book and post year end bank statement and also to paying-in book pre year end.

       (5)   Trace all unpresented cheques through to a pre year end cash book and post year end statement. For any unusual amounts or significant delays, obtain explanations from management.

       (6)   Examine any old unpresented cheques to assess if they need to be written back into the purchase ledger as they are no longer valid to be presented.

  (iii)   **Substantive procedures for receivables**

       (1)   Review the aged receivable ledger to identify any slow-moving or old receivable balances, discuss the status of these balances with the credit controller to assess whether they are likely to pay.

       (2)   Select a significant sample of receivables and review whether there are any after-date cash receipts; ensure that a sample of slow-moving/old receivable balances is also selected.

       (3)   Review customer correspondence to identify any balances which are in dispute or unlikely to be paid.

       (4)   Review board minutes to identify whether there are any significant concerns in relation to payments by customers.

       (5)   Calculate average receivables collection period and compare this with prior year; investigate any significant differences.

       (6)   Inspect post year end sales returns/credit notes and consider whether an additional allowance against receivables is required.

       (7)   Select a sample of GDNs before and just after the year end and follow through to the sales ledger to ensure they are recorded in the correct accounting period.

       (8)   Select a sample of year-end receivable balances and agree back to valid supporting documentation of GDN and sales order to ensure existence.

ANSWERS

156 Airsoft Co

Workbook references. Chapters 11, 15, 16, 17 and 20.

Top tips. This question tests audit evidence (including audit software) and has several requirements which are presented alongside some scenario information. When generating your audit procedures it is essential that you give audit procedures that address the specific issues relating, for example, to the closing of the purchase ledger, rather than simply preparing generic procedures on payables.

Easy marks. The audit of bank balances has been tested reasonably regularly and so you should have found part (c) straightforward.

Examining team's comments. This area of the syllabus requires a description of the work and evidence obtained by the auditor required to meet the objectives of audit engagements and the application of International Standards on Auditing.

A key requirement of this part of the syllabus is an ability to describe relevant audit procedures for a particular class of transactions or event. Overall performance in this key syllabus area in this exam session was very disappointing. The March 2017 exam contained a number of questions in this syllabus area covering a variety of areas including trade payables and accruals, bank balances, directors' remuneration, property plant and equipment, inventory and receivables, illustrating that candidates must be prepared to tailor their knowledge of substantive testing to any area of the financial statements. In most cases candidates remain unable to tailor their knowledge of general substantive procedures to the specific issues in the question requirements, with many providing tests of controls rather than substantive procedures, or, provided vague tests. As addressed in previous reports by the examining team candidates must strive to understand substantive procedures. Learning a generic list of tests will not translate to exam success – procedures must be tailored to the specific requirements of the question.

Marking scheme

		Marks
(a)	**Substantive procedures for completeness of Airsoft Co's payables and accruals**	
	– Compare to prior year and investigate differences	1
	– Post y/e cash book payments to ledger	1
	– Supplier statement reconciliations	1
	– Trade payables circularisation	1
	– Review after date invoices and credit notes	1
	– Enquiry of management process for identifying accruals	1
	Maximum	4
(b)	**Audit software procedures over trade payables and accruals**	
	– Calculate trade payables payment period	1
	– Cast the payables and accruals schedule	1
	– Select sample for circularisation	1
	– Recalculate accruals	1
	– Cut-off testing on GRNs	1
	Maximum	3
(c)	**Substantive procedures in relation to year-end bank balances**	
	– Bank confirmation letter	1
	– Agree to bank reconciliation and TB	1
	– Cast bank reconciliations	1
	– Testing on bank reconciliations (1 mark per relevant procedure)	4
	– Review cash book and bank statements for window dressing	1

	Marks

– Examine bank letter for evidence of security granted	1
– Review financial statement disclosure	1
Maximum	5

(d) **Substantive procedures in relation to directors' remuneration**

– Cast schedule of remuneration	1
– Agree payments to payroll records	1
– Confirm bonus payments to cash book	1
– Review board minutes for additional remuneration	1
– Review board minutes for approval	1
– Obtain written representation confirming completeness	1
– Review financial statement disclosure	1
Maximum	3

(e) **Key audit matters (KAM)**

– Definition of KAM	1
– Purpose of KAM	1
– Significant matters and areas of judgement	1
– Examples of KAM	2
– KAM disclosure	1
Maximum	5
Total	20

(a) Trade payables and accruals

- Compare the total trade payables and list of accruals against prior year and investigate any significant differences.

- Select a sample of post year-end payments from the cash book; if they relate to the current year, follow through to the purchase ledger or accruals listing to ensure they are recorded in the correct period.

- Obtain supplier statements and reconcile these to the purchase ledger balances, and investigate any reconciling items.

- Select a sample of payable balances and perform a trade payables' circularisation, follow up any
non-replies and any reconciling items between the balance confirmed and the trade payables' balance.

- Review after date invoices and credit notes to ensure no further items need to be accrued.

- Enquire of management their process for identifying goods received but not invoiced or logged in the purchase ledger and ensure that it is reasonable to ensure completeness of payables.

(b) Audit software procedures using computer assisted audit techniques (CAATs)

- The audit team can use audit software to calculate payables payment period for the year-to-date to compare against the prior year to identify whether the payables payment period has changed in line with trading levels and expectations. If the payables payment period has decreased, this may be an indication that payables are understated.

- Audit software can be used to cast the payables and accruals listings to confirm the completeness and accuracy of trade payables and accruals.

- Audit software can be used to select a representative sample of items for further testing of payables balances.

- Audit software can be utilised to recalculate the accruals for goods received not invoiced at the year end.

- CAATs can be used to undertake cut-off testing by assessing whether the dates of the last GRNs recorded relate to pre year end; and that any with a date of 1 January 20X6 onwards were excluded from trade payables.

(c)   Substantive procedures for bank balances

- Obtain a bank confirmation letter from Airsoft Co's bankers for all of its bank accounts.

- Agree all accounts listed on the bank confirmation letter to Airsoft Co's bank reconciliations and the trial balance to ensure completeness of bank balances.

- For all bank accounts, obtain Airsoft Co's bank account reconciliation and cast to ensure arithmetical accuracy.

- Agree the balance per the bank reconciliation to an original year-end bank statement and to the bank confirmation letter.

- Agree the reconciliations balance per the cash book to the year-end cash book.

- Trace all the outstanding lodgements to the pre year-end cash book, post year-end bank statement and also to the paying-in-book pre year end.

- Trace all unpresented cheques through to a pre year-end cash book and post year-end statement. For any unusual amounts or significant delays, obtain explanations from management.

- Examine any old unpresented cheques to assess if they need to be written back into the purchase ledger as they are no longer valid to be presented.

- Review the cash book and bank statements for any unusual items or large transfers around the year end, as this could be evidence of window dressing.

- Examine the bank confirmation letter for details of any security provided by Airsoft Co or any legal right of set-off as this may require disclosure.

- Review the financial statements to ensure that the disclosure of bank balances is complete and accurate.

(d)   Substantive procedures for directors' remuneration

- Obtain a schedule of the directors' remuneration, split by salary and bonus paid in December and cast the schedule to ensure accuracy.

- Agree a sample of the individual monthly salary payments and the bonus payment in December to the payroll records.

- Confirm the amount of each bonus paid by agreeing to the cash book and bank statements.

- Review the board minutes to identify whether any additional payments relating to this year have been agreed for any directors.

- Agree the amounts paid per director to board minutes to ensure the sums included are genuine.

- Obtain a written representation from management confirming the completeness of directors' remuneration including the bonus.

- Review the disclosures made regarding the directors' remuneration and assess whether these are in compliance with local legislation.

(e)   Key audit matters

Key audit matters (KAM) are those matters which, in the auditor's professional judgement, were of most significance in the audit of the financial statements of the current period. Key audit matters are selected from matters communicated with those charged with governance.

The purpose of including key audit matters in the auditor's report is to help users in understanding the entity, and to provide a basis for the users to discuss with management and those charged with governance about matters relating to the entity and the financial statements. A key part of the definition is that these are the most significant matters. Identifying the most significant matters involves using the auditor's professional judgement.

ISA 701 *Communicating Key Audit Matters in the Independent Auditor's Report* suggests that in determining key audit matters the auditor should take the following into account:

- Areas of higher assessed risk of material misstatement, or significant risks.

- Significant auditor judgements relating to areas in the financial statements which involved significant management judgement.

- The effect on the audit of significant events or transactions which occurred during the period.

The description of each KAM in the Key Audit Matters section of the auditor's report should include a reference to the related disclosures in the financial statements and covers why the matter was considered to be one of most significance in the audit and therefore determined to be a KAM; and how the matter was addressed in the audit.

157 Gooseberry Co

Workbook references. Chapters 12, 17 and 20.

Top tips. This question tests audit evidence in relation to different types of non-current assets, and then links in with auditor reporting.

Part (a) is on development costs and IAS 38 *Intangible assets*. This is a standard that you will need to be familiar with, but this is a difficult requirement at AA level. Most of the audit procedures come from the financial reporting, so you can use this to help generate your answers.

For part (b), you can use the scenario as a starting point for your description of the procedures to perform to determine whether the depreciation charge is fairly stated.

Part (c) was another detailed requirement on audit evidence, and should be approached by thinking practically about how these bonuses should have been processed, and then considering how you would test them. The bonuses have been awarded to the directors and so these amounts would be material by their nature. Furthermore the scenario tells you that disclosure is required by local legislation and so it is important that your substantive procedures include reviewing whether the required disclosures have been made.

Part (d) probably came as a relief. This is a familiar requirement on the auditor's report and should have been within your reach.

Easy marks. Part (d) was likely to have been the easiest part of the question; the marks for materiality were among the simplest to obtain.

Examining team's comments. This 20-mark question was based on Gooseberry Co, a company which develops and manufactures health and beauty products and distributes these to wholesale customers. This question tested candidates' knowledge of substantive procedures for research and development, depreciation and directors' bonuses, and, auditor's reports.

Part (a) for five marks required candidates to describe substantive procedures the auditor should perform to obtain sufficient and appropriate audit evidence in relation to Gooseberry's research and development expenditure. Performance on this requirement was mixed.

One mark was awarded for each well described substantive procedure. Hence for a five mark requirement, candidates should have provided at least five substantive procedures. Disappointingly this was not the case, as some answers only contained one or two procedures for each area and these were often not well described, resulting in a maximum of ½ mark each. Candidates are severely limiting the opportunity to score marks and are reminded to ensure that they employ effective exam technique.

Many procedures were vague, often not giving the source for the test, or, stating 'ensure' without explaining how the test would achieve this.

Part (b) for five marks required the candidates to describe substantive procedures the auditor should perform to obtain sufficient and appropriate audit evidence in relation to depreciation. Performance on this requirement was disappointing.

As in part (a), one mark was awarded for each well described substantive procedure. Disappointingly often the substantive procedures were either not well described, or, were not related to depreciation. A significant number of candidates did not clearly answer the specific requirement of the question to describe depreciation substantive procedures.

In general there was clear evidence of a lack of tailoring of knowledge to the specific scenario provided. Candidates have clearly learned that the depreciation charge should be compared to the prior year. However, this substantive procedure is not relevant if there is a change in the useful life of the assets in the year as was detailed in this scenario. As addressed in previous examining team's reports candidates must strive to understand substantive procedures. Learning a generic list of tests will not translate to exam success, as they must be applied to the question requirement.

Part (c) for five marks required the candidates to describe substantive procedures the auditor should perform to obtain sufficient and appropriate audit evidence in relation to the directors' bonuses. Performance on this requirement for many candidates was pleasing.

Part (d) for five marks required a discussion of an issue and the impact on the auditor's report if the issue remained unresolved. The issue presented related to $440,000 of development costs which had been incorrectly capitalised by the client.

Auditor's report questions have shown a gradual improvement in recent exams so it is disappointing that performance for this question was mixed.

A number of candidates described the impact on the auditor's report if the issue was resolved and also if the issue remained unresolved. The question clearly asked for the impact if the issue remained unresolved. Once again, candidates are advised to read the question requirements carefully.

Marking scheme

		Marks
(a)	**Substantive procedures – Research & development**	
	Cast and agree closing balance to TB and draft FS	1
	Discuss amortisation policy with management and assess reasonableness	1
	Recalculate amortisation charge/commenced in line with production	1
	Discuss new projects and stage of development	1
	For research costs agree invoices and to profit or loss	1
	For development costs agree to invoices and confirm meets criteria	1
	Review market research to confirm ability to sell	1
	Review disclosures in line with IAS 38	1
	Restricted to	5
(b)	**Substantive procedures – depreciation**	
	Discuss reasons for change with management	1
	Compare to industry averages and knowledge of business	1
	Review capex budgets to assess revised lives appropriate	1

		Marks
	Agree new rates to non-current asset register	1
	Recalculate profit/loss on disposal and consider new rates	1
	Recalculate depreciation charge for a sample of assets	1
	Perform a proof-in-total on depreciation charge	1
	Review disclosure is in line with IAS 16	1
	Restricted to	5
(c)	**Substantive procedures – directors' bonuses**	
	Cast schedule of bonuses and agree to TB	1
	Confirm bonus accrual as current liability	1
	Agree bonus payments to payroll records	1
	Recalculate bonus payments in line with contracts	1
	Confirm post year-end payment to bank statement	1
	Review board minutes for additional sums	1
	Obtain written representation confirming completeness	1
	Review disclosures in line with local legislation	1
	Restricted to	5
(d)	**Impact on auditor's report**	
	Discussion of issue	1
	Materiality calculation and conclusion	1
	Type of modification required	2
	Impact on auditor's report	1
		5
Total marks		20

(a)   **Substantive procedures for research and development**

- Obtain and cast a schedule of intangible assets, detailing opening balances, amounts capitalised in the current year, amortisation and closing balances.

- Agree the closing balances to the general ledger, trial balance and draft financial statements.

- Discuss with the finance director the rationale for the three-year useful life and consider its reasonableness.

- Recalculate the amortisation charge for a sample of intangible assets which have commenced production and confirm it is in line with the amortisation policy of straight line over three years and that amortisation only commenced from the point of production.

- For the nine new projects, discuss with management the details of each project along with the stage of development and whether it has been capitalised or expensed.

- For those expensed as research, agree the costs incurred to invoices and supporting documentation and to inclusion in profit or loss.

- For those capitalised as development, agree costs incurred to invoices and confirm technically feasible by discussion with development managers or review of feasibility reports.

- Review market research reports to confirm Gooseberry Co has the ability to sell the product once complete and probable future economic benefits will arise.

- Review the disclosures for intangible assets in the draft financial statements to verify that they are in accordance with IAS 38 *Intangible Assets*.

BPP
LEARNING
MEDIA

(b)   **Substantive procedures for depreciation**

- Discuss with management the rationale for the changes to property, plant and equipment (PPE) depreciation rates, useful lives, residual values and depreciation methods and ascertain how these changes were arrived at.

- Confirm the reasonableness of these changes, by comparing the revised depreciation rates, useful lives and methods applied to PPE to industry averages and knowledge of the business.

- Review the capital expenditure budgets for the next few years to assess whether the revised asset lives correspond with the planned period until replacement of the relevant asset categories.

- Review the non-current asset register to assess if the revised depreciation rates have been applied.

- Review and recalculate profits and losses on disposal of assets sold/scrapped in the year, to assess the reasonableness of the revised depreciation rates.

- Select a sample of PPE and recalculate the depreciation charge to ensure that the non-current assets register is correct and ensure that new depreciation rates have been appropriately applied.

- Obtain a breakdown of depreciation by asset categories, compare to prior year; where significant changes have occurred, discuss with management and assess whether this change is reasonable.

- For asset categories where there have been a minimal number of additions and disposals, perform a proof in total calculation for the depreciation charged on PPE, discuss with management if significant fluctuations arise.

- Review the disclosure of the depreciation charges and policies in the draft financial statements and ensure it is in line with IAS 16 *Property, Plant and Equipment*.

(c)   **Substantive procedures for directors' bonuses**

- Obtain a schedule of the directors' bonus paid in February 20X8 and cast the schedule to ensure accuracy and agree amount disclosed in the financial statements.

- Review the schedule of current liabilities and confirm the bonus accrual is included as a year-end liability.

- Agree the individual bonus payments to the payroll records.

- Recalculate the bonus payments and agree the criteria, including the exclusion of intangible assets, to supporting documentation and the percentage rates to be paid to the directors' service contracts.

- Confirm the amount of each bonus paid post year end by agreeing to the cash book and bank statements.

- Agree the amounts paid per director to board minutes to ensure the sums included in the current year financial statements are fully accrued and disclosed.

- Review the board minutes to identify whether any additional payments relating to this year have been agreed for any directors.

- Obtain a written representation from management confirming the completeness of directors' remuneration including the bonus.

- Review the disclosures made regarding the bonus paid to directors and assess whether these are in compliance with local legislation.

(d)   **Impact on auditor's report**

One of the new health and beauty products Gooseberry Co has developed in the year does not meet the recognition criteria under IAS 38 *Intangible Assets* for capitalisation but has been included within intangible assets. This is contrary to IAS 38, as if the criteria are not met, then this project is research expenditure and should be expensed to the statement of profit or loss rather than capitalised.

The error is material as it represents 6.9% of profit before tax (0.44m/6.4m) and 1.2% of net assets (0.44m/37.2m) and hence management should adjust the financial statements by removing this amount from intangible assets and charging it to the statement of profit or loss instead. IAS 38 requires costs to date to be expensed; if the project meets the recognition criteria in 20X9, then only from that point can any new costs incurred be capitalised. Any costs already expensed cannot be written back to assets.

If management refuses to amend this error, then the auditor's opinion will need to be modified. As management has not complied with IAS 38 and the error is material but not pervasive, then a qualified opinion would be necessary.

A basis for qualified opinion paragraph would be needed after the opinion paragraph and would explain the material misstatement in relation to the incorrect treatment of research and development and the effect on the financial statements. The opinion paragraph would be qualified 'except for'.

158 Jasmine Co

Workbook references. Chapters 14, 15, 19 and 20.

Top tips. Parts (a) and (b) of this question deal with substantive procedures in relation to trade receivables and bank balances respectively. As ever, your answer here will likely be made up of general procedures that you have tailored to the specific circumstances of the scenario. The difference between passing and failing questions of this nature is often the way that you write your answer – you need to be as clear as possible about exactly what procedure should be performed, and why it should be performed. Saying 'why' is a theme in the AA exam.

Part (c) asks for going concern procedures, which will involve pre-learned areas of focus but again, these should be applied to the question. This need not be a source of difficulty – the scenario here contains a few hints at going concern difficulties, which in turn suggest areas of testing. For instance, the statement that the overdraft is to be renewed and that the directors are confident that this is will be done: this 'confidence' needs to be tested, so the auditor should look to obtain evidence about whether what the directors are saying is true. This suggests a procedure such as reviewing written correspondence to assess whether this is likely.

Part (d) moves us on in time from the evidence gathering stage to the completion stage; the theme of going concern continues, this time in the context of auditor reporting. The question itself should not be too difficult, provided that you had not exceeded your timings on the previous parts of the question and thus had enough time to get some of the marks on offer here. Going concern is a topical area and is therefore likely to be examined again in future exams.

Easy marks. Part (d) was likely to have been the easiest part of the question.

Examining team's comments. A key requirement of this part of the syllabus is an ability to describe relevant audit procedures for a particular class of transactions or event. Overall performance in this key syllabus area in this exam session was once again disappointing.

The December 2018 exam session contained a number of questions in this syllabus area covering a variety of areas across both the statement of profit or loss and statement of financial position, illustrating that candidates must be prepared to tailor their knowledge of substantive testing to any area of the financial statements.

As addressed in previous Examiner's Reports candidates must strive to understand substantive procedures. Learning a generic list of tests will not translate to exam success – procedures must be tailored to the specific requirements of the question. Additionally tests must be sufficiently detailed noting clearly which source document should be used. A significant number of candidates suggest tests such as 'review disclosures' however this would only have scored ½ marks as they did not go on to say 'in accordance with accounting standards'. Also recommending 'obtain a management representation' without explaining what for, e.g. to ensure completeness/reasonableness of a provision, will not generate any marks.

Marking scheme

		Marks
(a)	**Substantive procedures – trade receivables**	
	Obtain aged receivables listing, cast and agree to TB	1
	Review listing for old balances and discuss with management	1
	Perform cash after-date testing	1
	Inspect customer correspondence for evidence of disputed items and discuss with mgt	1
	Calculate receivables collection period, compare to PY and investigate differences	1
	Inspect post year-end returns and consider need for additional allowance	1
	Obtain a breakdown of the allowance, recalculate and consider adequacy	1
	Select sample of GDNs from before and after year end and confirm recorded in correct period	1
	Select a sample of balances and agree to order, GDN and invoice	1
	Restricted to	5
(b)	**Substantive procedures – bank balances**	
	Bank confirmation letter	1
	Agree to bank reconciliation and TB	1
	Cast bank reconciliations	1
	Testing on bank reconciliations (1 mark per relevant procedure)	4
	Review cash book and bank statements for window dressing	1
	Examine bank letter for evidence of security granted	1
	Review financial statement disclosure	1
	Restricted to	5
(c)	**Going concern procedures**	
	Obtain cash flow forecast and assess assumptions	1
	Perform sensitivity analysis on cash flow forecast	1
	Evaluate management's plans for future actions	1
	Review post year-end order book to assess levels of trade	1
	Review agreements with the bank to determine whether any covenants breached	1
	Review bank correspondence for evidence of renewal	1
	Review correspondence with suppliers for dispute/legal action	1
	Obtain confirmation from company lawyers about any legal action	1
	Review post year-end board minutes for any indications of financial difficulties	1
	Review management accounts to assess if in line with cash flow	1
	Review financial statement disclosure	1
	Consider if going concern basis is appropriate	1
	Obtain a written representation	1
	Restricted to	5
(d)	**Impact on auditor's report**	
	Discussion of issue	1
	Disclosure adequate	2
	Disclosure inadequate	2
		5
Total marks		20

(a) **Substantive procedures for trade receivables**

- Obtain the aged receivables listing and agree to the balance on the sales ledger control account and trial balance.

- Review the aged trade receivables ledger to identify any slow moving or old balances, discuss the status of these balances with the credit controller to assess whether they are likely to pay.

- Select a representative sample of trade receivables and review for any after-date cash receipts. Ensure that a sample of slow moving/old receivable balances is also selected.

- Review customer correspondence to identify any balances which are in dispute or unlikely to be paid and discuss with management.

- Review board minutes to identify whether there are any significant concerns in relation to payments by customers.

- Calculate the average receivables collection period and compare this to the prior year and investigate any significant differences.

- Inspect post year-end sales returns/credit notes and consider whether an additional allowance against receivables is required.

- Obtain a breakdown of the allowance for trade receivables, recalculate and compare to any potentially irrecoverable balances to assess if the allowance is adequate.

- Select a sample of goods despatched notes (GDN) immediately before and after the year end and follow through to the receivables ledger to ensure they are recorded in the correct accounting period.

- Select a sample of year-end receivables balances and agree back to valid supporting documentation of sales invoices, GDNs and sales orders to ensure existence.

(b) **Substantive procedures for bank balances**

- Obtain a bank confirmation letter from Jasmine Co's bankers for all of its accounts.

- Agree all accounts listed on the bank confirmation letter to the company's bank reconciliations or the trial balance/general ledger to ensure completeness of bank balances.

- For the current account, obtain Jasmine Co's bank reconciliation and cast to check the additions to ensure arithmetical accuracy.

- Agree the balance per the bank reconciliation to an original year-end bank statement and to the bank confirmation letter.

- Agree the reconciliation's balance per the cash book to the year-end cash book.

- Trace all the outstanding lodgements to the pre year-end cash book, post year-end bank statement and also to the paying-in book pre year end.

- Trace all unpresented cheques through to a pre year-end cash book and post year-end bank statement. For any unusual amounts or significant delays, obtain explanations from management.

- Examine any old unpresented cheques to assess whether they need to be written back.

- Review the cash book and bank statements for any unusual items or large transfers around the year end, as this could be evidence of window dressing.

- Examine the bank confirmation letter for details of any security provided by Jasmine Co, with regards to the bank overdraft or any legal right of set-off as this may require disclosure.

- For the savings bank accounts, review any reconciling items on the year-end bank reconciliations and agree to supporting documentation.

- Review the financial statements to ensure that the disclosure of bank balances is complete and accurate and classified appropriately between current assets and current liabilities.

(c) **Going concern procedures**

- Obtain the company's cash flow forecast and review the cash inflows and outflows. Assess the assumptions for reasonableness and discuss the findings with management to understand if the company will have sufficient cash.

- Perform a sensitivity analysis on the cash flows to understand the margin of safety the company has in terms of its net cash in/outflow.

- Evaluate management's plans for future actions, including their contingency plans in relation to ongoing financing and plans for generating revenue, and consider the feasibility of these plans.

- Review the company's post year-end sales and order book to assess if the levels of trade are likely to increase and if the revenue figures in the cash flow forecast are reasonable.

- Review any agreements with the bank to determine whether any covenants have been breached, especially in relation to the overdraft.

- Review any bank correspondence to assess the likelihood of the bank renewing the overdraft facility.

- Review post year-end correspondence with suppliers to identify if any have threatened legal action or any others have refused to supply goods.

- With the client's permission, enquire of the lawyers of Jasmine Co as to the existence of any litigation and if so, the likely outcome of any litigation.

- Perform audit tests in relation to subsequent events to identify any items which might indicate or mitigate the risk of going concern not being appropriate.

- Review the post year-end board minutes to identify any other issues which might indicate further financial difficulties for the company.

- Review post year-end management accounts to assess if in line with cash flow forecast.

- Consider whether any additional disclosures as required by IAS 1 *Presentation of Financial Statements* in relation to material uncertainties over going concern should be made in the financial statements.

- Consider whether the going concern basis is appropriate for the preparation of the financial statements.

- Obtain a written representation confirming the directors' view that Jasmine Co is a going concern.

(d) **Auditor's report**

As the outcome regarding the negotiations for the overdraft facility renewal will not be known at the time of signing the auditor's report, there is a material uncertainty which may cast significant doubt on the company's ability to continue as a going concern.

The impact on the auditor's report depends on whether this uncertainty is deemed to be adequately disclosed in the financial statements.

Disclosure adequate

If the disclosures are adequate, then the auditor's report will need to include a material uncertainty related to going concern section. The section will state that the audit opinion is not modified, indicate that there is a material uncertainty and will cross reference to the disclosure note made by management. It would be included after the opinion and basis for opinion paragraph.

Disclosure inadequate

If the disclosures made by management are not adequate, the audit opinion will need to be modified as there is a material misstatement relating to inadequate disclosure. The failure to adequately disclose is likely to be material but not pervasive due to the ongoing nature of the negotiations and so a qualified opinion will be issued.

The opinion paragraph will state that 'except for' the failure to adequately disclose the uncertainty, the financial statements give a true and fair view. The report will contain a basis for opinion paragraph, subsequent to the opinion paragraph, explaining that a material uncertainty exists and that the financial statements do not adequately disclose this matter.

Chestnut

159 The correct answers are:

Review whether any payments have subsequently been made by this customer since the audit fieldwork was completed	**PERFORM**	DO NOT PERFORM
Match the total of the aged receivables listing to the sales ledger control account	PERFORM	**DO NOT PERFORM**
Vouch the balance owed by the customer at the year end to sales invoices	PERFORM	**DO NOT PERFORM**
Review the latest customer correspondence with regards to an assessment of the likelihood of the customer making payment	**PERFORM**	DO NOT PERFORM

The audit concern here is that receivables are overstated as the balance from this customer does not appear to be recoverable. Audit procedures should therefore focus on the valuation of receivables. Vouching the balance owed by the customer at the year end to sales invoices will provide audit evidence in relation to the existence, rights and obligations of receivables, but not their valuation. Matching the total of the aged receivables listing to the sales ledger control account will provide evidence of completeness.

160 The correct answer is:

Material	Financial statement impact
Yes	Gross profit may be overstated

Chestnut & Co was only appointed as auditors subsequent to Ash's year end and hence did not attend the year-end inventory count. Therefore, it has not been able to gather sufficient and appropriate audit evidence with regards to the completeness and existence of inventory. This may mean that closing inventory is over- or understated and this will have a resultant impact on gross profit and current assets.

Inventory is a material amount as it represents 21.3% (0.51/2.4m) of profit before tax and 5% (0.51/10.1m) of revenue.

161 The correct answers are:

Review the internal auditor's reports of the inventory count to identify the level of adjustments made to the records, in order to assess the reasonableness of relying on the inventory records for the purpose of the year-end audit.

Perform test counts of inventory in the warehouse and compare these first to the inventory records, and then from inventory records to the warehouse, in order to assess the reasonableness of the inventory records maintained by Ash.

Audit procedures should focus on testing the accuracy of the work performed by the internal audit department at the year end in order to determine whether the year-end inventory quantity exists and is complete.

Testing the accuracy of the aged inventory report will provide evidence over the valuation of inventory.

Reviewing the sales order book for February, March and April 20X5 could provide audit evidence as to the quantity of inventory at the year end but only if it is assessed to determine whether there would have been sufficient inventory at the year end to fulfil customer demand.

162 The correct answer is:

Evaluation of all significant audit judgments	INCLUDE	EXCLUDE
Evaluation of the performance of specific audit procedures performed	INCLUDE	EXCLUDE
Evaluation of the cost-effectiveness of the audit process	INCLUDE	EXCLUDE
Evaluation of conclusions reached in formulating auditor's report	INCLUDE	EXCLUDE

The evaluation of specific audit procedures would not be part of an engagement quality control review – this would be part of the audit team's internal processes of monitoring and review, but is too detailed to be included within this review.

The cost-effectiveness of the audit is not relevant to the engagement quality control review, since it does not have a bearing on whether the auditor expresses an appropriate audit opinion.

163 The correct answer is:

Audit opinion	Disclosure in the auditor's report
Qualified	Basis for qualified opinion

The auditor will need to express a modified opinion as they are unable to obtain sufficient appropriate evidence in relation to inventory. The effect of this is material but not pervasive. Therefore a qualified 'except for' opinion will be required.

The opinion paragraph will explain that the audit opinion is qualified 'except for'. A basis for qualified opinion paragraph will be required to explain the limitation in relation to the lack of evidence over inventory.

Humphries

164 The correct answer is:

1, 2, 3 and 4

All the procedures are valid in identifying subsequent events occurring up to the date of the auditor's report.

165 The correct answers are:

Inventory should not be written down, because the damage is not an adjusting event.

If a material amount of inventory is uninsured, it may be necessary to disclose the event and an estimate of the financial losses.

The flood damage does not provide evidence of conditions that existed at the year end, and therefore is not an adjusting event as defined by IAS 10 *Events After The Reporting Period*. On this basis, the inventory should not be written down, but the nature and amount of expected uninsured losses may need to be disclosed. It is incorrect to recognise a contingent asset in the 20X1 financial statements: contingent assets should be disclosed, not recognised, and it should only be disclosed when an inflow of economic benefits is probable (IAS 37).

166 The correct answers are:

Reviewing the post year end period for payments received from the customer in respect of the year-end debt

Reviewing correspondence with the customer to assess the likelihood of Humphries Co recovering the $0.3 million

Writing to the customer is likely to be unproductive. In addition, it would only provide persuasive evidence that the receivable existed at the year end, not that it was recoverable. Requesting a cash flow forecast is irrelevant, as it does not give evidence as to the recoverability of the receivable itself and there is no evidence that the going concern assumption needs to be revised.

167 The correct answer is:

The lawsuit relating to the breach of contract is considered to be **material** and therefore if the financial statements are not revised in the light of the new information then the auditor's opinion will be **qualified 'except for' due to material misstatement.**

The probable payment and anticipated adjustment needed is $0.6m representing 8% of profit ($0.6m/$7.5m × 100%). This is material and if management refuse to adjust for the provision, the audit opinion will need to be modified on the basis management has not complied with IAS 37 *Provisions, Contingent Liabilities and Contingent Assets*. The misstatement is material but not pervasive, so a qualified opinion would be expressed. The opinion paragraph would state that 'except for' this issue the financial statements are presented fairly (or show a true and fair view). A 'basis for qualified opinion' section would explain the material misstatement in relation to the $0.6m not provided, and describe the effect on the financial statements.

168 The correct answer is:

If the auditor becomes aware of a fact that, had it been known to the auditor at the date of the auditor's report, may have caused the auditor to amend the auditor's report, the auditor shall discuss the need for any adjustments with management.

The first two options describe the auditor's responsibility with regards to subsequent events occurring before the date of the auditor's report. It is true that the auditor does not have any obligation to perform procedures or make enquiries but, should an adjusting event come to light, adjustments to the financial statements about to be issued must be considered and further audit procedures must be performed as necessary at the time, rather than deferring to next year, hence the third option is incorrect.

Greenfields

169 The correct answer is: Warranty provision only

The audit team has already carried out some procedures in testing the calculations and assumptions relating to the warranty provision, and has found them to be in line with prior years (and presumably in accordance with expectations). All of the evidence to date is from internal sources, but there is unlikely to be readily available reliable external sources.

It will be difficult for anyone to predict how many warranty claims there will be in the future and the value of any future claims, and written representation on this matter will be one of the few sources of evidence available.

Management have offered a written representation over the recoverability of the receivables balance but have not allowed circularisation of the receivable. The written representation cannot be used as a substitute for evidence which should otherwise be available. The written representation proposed by management is focused on the recoverability and gives only weak evidence over the relevant assertions. Despite being in writing and more reliable than a verbal representation, the internally generated representation is not as good as evidence from an external source (such as any potential response from Yellowmix to the circularisation).

With the other evidence available being limited due to the lack of payment activity over the last six months, without further, more compelling evidence, the representation alone would appear insufficient to conclude that receivables are free from material misstatement.

170 The correct answers are:

Review correspondence with Yellowmix Co regarding the late payment

Perform a review of post year-end cash receipts

Reviewing correspondence with Yellowmix may provide details confirming the likelihood of the debt being repaid. If cash is received in after the period end from Yellowmix this provides evidence that the debt was recoverable at the period end.

Tracing a sample of goods dispatched notes (Option 2) provides evidence of completeness.

Tracing of entries in Yellowmix's account in the receivables ledger provides evidence of existence and accuracy.

171 The correct answers are:

Discuss with management why they have refused to provide the representations requested	PERFORM	DO NOT PERFORM
Reassess the integrity of management and consider the implications for any other representations	PERFORM	DO NOT PERFORM
Seek legal advice	PERFORM	DO NOT PERFORM
Resign as auditor	PERFORM	DO NOT PERFORM

Management has not provided a requested written representation, therefore ISA 580 *Written Representations* requires the auditor to discuss the matter with management and ask why they will not provide the representation relating to the warranty provision.

ISA 580 also requires the auditor to re-evaluate the integrity of management and evaluate the effect this may have on the reliability of any other representations (such as on the Yellowmix balance) and audit evidence in general (ISA 580).

The auditor must then take appropriate actions, including determining the impact on the auditor's opinion in the auditor's report.

172   The correct answer is:

Audit opinion	Reason
Qualified	Inability to obtain sufficient appropriate evidence

Given the limited evidence available other than the representation, the auditor will be unable to obtain sufficient appropriate evidence over the material warranty provision. Therefore a modification of the auditor's opinion is required. A qualified opinion will be issued because the misstatement, although material, will not be pervasive. A qualified or adverse opinion on the grounds of material misstatement would not be appropriate as the auditor has not been able to obtain sufficient evidence to determine whether a material misstatement has occurred or not.

173   The correct answer is:

Audit opinion	Disclosure
Unmodified	Other Information section including a description of the uncorrected misstatement

The audit opinion would not be modified as the audit opinion relates to the financial statements and not the 'Other information'. In accordance with ISA 700 *Forming an Opinion and Reporting on Financial Statements* (ISA 700) and ISA 720 *The Auditor's Responsibilities Relating to Other Information* (ISA 720) the auditor's report would be required to include an Other Information section as other information is issued with the financial statements and is available to the auditors. As there is a material misstatement this would be disclosed in the Other Information section. An Other Matter paragraph is not used for these purposes.

Strawberry

174   The correct answer is: 1, 2 and 4

The fall in inventory holding period means that Strawberry is turning over its inventory more quickly, which if anything would improve its cash cycle and have a positive rather than negative impact on the ability of the company to continue. In this case the change is relatively small so is unlikely to be a significant factor either way.

175   The correct answer is: At least 12 months from the date of the financial statements

In accordance with ISA 570 the assessment must cover a period of at least 12 months from the date of the financial statements. If the period covered is less than this the auditor must request that the assessment period is extended.

176   The correct answer is: Identification during your subsequent events review of a cash receipt for the full amount

The receipt of the balance after the year end confirms that the debt is recoverable at the year end.

The written representation is written evidence but is internally generated.

The response to the circularisation provides evidence of existence but does not provide evidence of recoverability.

The correspondence between the lawyers is externally generated and from trusted parties but is less reliable than the receipt of the payment as it would still be possible for Grape Co to default.

177   The correct answer is: Agreement by an alternative financial institution to lend Strawberry $4.8m in September 20X2

As part of the going concern review the auditor must consider mitigating circumstances. In this case, the agreement with the alternative finance provider gives the most assurance as there is a greater degree of certainty that Strawberry will receive the cash. The first three options may provide the cash required but this cannot be guaranteed. There is also a timing issue as the property may not sell for some time and cost savings will not have an immediate effect.

178   The correct answer is:

Auditor's opinion	Explanation of circumstances
Adverse opinion	Basis for adverse opinion

An adverse opinion would be issued as the matter is material and pervasive ie the auditors disagree with the whole basis on which the financial statements have been prepared. A description of the circumstances would be included in the Basis for adverse opinion paragraph in accordance with ISA 705 (ISA 705).

A qualified opinion would apply if the issue were material, but not pervasive. Disclosure in the Material uncertainty related to going concern section is made when the auditor agrees that the company is a going concern but believes that there is a material uncertainty which needs to be brought to the attention of the shareholders (ISA 570). This does not apply in this case.

Clarinet

179   The correct answer is:

Material	Adjust in 20X4 financial statements
Yes	Yes

The uncorrected misstatement amounts to 15% of profit after tax (PAT) and on this basis would be material (ie it is over 10% of PAT). It is an adjusting event as the discovery provides evidence as to the value of the inventory at the year end. The 20X4 financial statements should therefore be adjusted.

Adjustment in the 20X4 financial statements would not be required for non-adjusting events ie those which do not provide evidence of conditions which existed at the period end.

180   The correct answer is: 1, 2 and 4

The entry of the competitor has resulted in a loss of market share and the loss of a major customer. There is a risk that this sizeable loss of market share will result in a significant loss of future revenues, as well as reducing future cash flows.

The overdraft has increased significantly and is due for renewal. This suggests liquidity problems. If the bank does not renew the overdraft, and the company fails to obtain alternative finance it may not be able to continue trading.

The failure of Clarinet's shareholders to invest indicate doubts in relation to the company's ability to generate healthy profits in future, or possible liquidity problems. It may also make it less likely for others to invest.

The existence of a bank loan in itself does not give rise to going concern issues. The bank loan is long term so there is no imminent requirement to repay the balance. To date all payments have been made therefore there is no breach of any loan terms which could trigger early repayment.

181   The correct answer is: A review of post year end sales and the order book

All of the procedures provide evidence regarding the assumption used in the cash flow forecast. However, the review of post year end sales and the order book is the most reliable as this shows sales which have actually taken place or sales to which the customer has shown a commitment. Procedures described in A, B and D are based on possible events.

182   The correct answer is: 1, 2 and 3

The disclosures are set out in ISA 570 paragraph 25.

(4) is incorrect. The management assessment should be at least 12 months from the date of the financial statements. If not the auditors will ask that the assessment period is extended.

183   The correct answer is:

Opinion	Disclosure
Unmodified	Material uncertainty related to going concern

As the auditors agree with the basis of preparation of the financial statements and have concluded that the disclosures are adequate, an unmodified opinion is issued. As a material uncertainty regarding going concern exists, this must be highlighted for the benefit of the shareholders. In accordance with ISA 570 (ISA 570) and ISA 701 (ISA 701) this must be disclosed in a 'Material uncertainty related to going concern' section, and not as a Key audit matter.

Czech & Dawson

184   The correct answer is: A written representation should be requested from management to confirm whether they believe that the effects of the unadjusted misstatements are immaterial, both individually and in aggregate, to the financial statements as a whole

ISA 450 *Evaluation of Misstatements Identified During the Audit* states that the auditor has a responsibility to accumulate misstatements identified during the audit, other than those that are clearly trivial (ISA 450).

All the accumulated misstatements should be communicated to the appropriate level of management on a timely basis (ISA 450). The auditor must request that management correct the misstatements.

If management refuses to correct some or all of the misstatements, the auditor must obtain an understanding of the reasons for not making the corrections, and take these into account when determining whether the financial statements are free from material misstatement (ISA 450). This may affect the auditor's opinion if this results in the financial statements being materially misstated, but the refusal to correct the misstatements does not affect the opinion.

The auditor should determine whether uncorrected misstatements are material, both individually and in aggregate (ISA 450).

185   The correct answers are:

Discuss the requirements of IAS 38 *Intangible Assets* with the directors in order to determine whether they understand the required accounting treatment of research and development expenditure

Obtain a breakdown of the $5.3m capitalised as an intangible asset and agree to supporting documentation to determine the nature of the projects to which the expenditure relates

Audit procedures should focus on determining the extent of research expenditure which has been incorrectly capitalised.

Whilst it is generally important to authorise expenditure, the issue is not authorisation or occurrence but its classification.

186   The correct answer is: Qualified opinion

Research expenditure of $2.1m has been capitalised within intangible assets. This accounting treatment is incorrect, as IAS 38 *Intangible Assets* requires research expenditure to be expensed to profit or loss (IAS 38).

The error is material as it represents 8% of profit before tax ($2.1m/$26.3m).

Management should adjust the financial statements by removing the $2.1m research expenditure from intangibles and debiting the amount to profit or loss.

If management refuse to make the adjustment, the auditor's opinion will need to be modified. As the error is material but not pervasive, a qualified opinion would seem appropriate.

The basis of opinion section would need to include a paragraph explaining the misstatement and its effect on the financial statements. The opinion paragraph would be qualified 'except for'.

187   The correct answer is:

Material	Financial statement impact
Yes	Wages may be materially misstated

Two months' worth of wages records have been lost and so audit evidence has not been gained in relation to this expense. Wages and salaries for the 2-month period represent 11% of profit before tax ($1.1m/$10m) and so wages and salaries may be materially misstated.

188   The correct answer is:

Audit opinion	Disclosure in the auditor's report
Qualified	Basis for qualified opinion

The auditors should seek alternative audit procedures to audit the wages and salaries account. If no alternative audit procedures are possible, the loss of data would constitute a lack of sufficient appropriate audit evidence.

The auditors will need to modify the auditor's opinion on the basis that they are unable to obtain sufficient appropriate evidence in relation to a material amount in the financial statements. As the two months' salary and wages are not pervasive, a qualified opinion would seem appropriate.

The basis of opinion section would require an explanation of the insufficient audit evidence in relation to wages and salaries. The opinion paragraph would be qualified on the grounds of an inability to obtain sufficient appropriate audit evidence.

Medimade

189   The correct answers are:

The going concern basis of accounting is used when the entity will be able to continue in business for the foreseeable future.

The going concern basis of accounting assumes that the entity will be able to realise its assets and discharge its liabilities in the normal course of business.

The term 'foreseeable future' is not defined within ISA 570 *Going Concern*, but IAS 1 *Presentation of Financial Statements* deems the foreseeable future to be a period of 12 months from the end of the entity's reporting period (IAS 1). When financial statements are prepared using the going concern basis of accounting, the assertion is that there is neither the intention nor the need to liquidate the company's operations.

190   The correct answers are:

Medimade now has to pay cash on delivery and this adds further cash flow strain imposed by the overdraft

Some suppliers may end their relationship with Medimade, preventing the company from producing its products, thus further reducing sales

Although all of the stated options are possible consequences, only these two options describe the most direct effect on going concern: cash flow difficulties and reducing sales. The main concern with bank covenants (which should already be in place) is that the bank can withdraw finance if and when the covenants are breached – bank covenants do not usually restrict the way in which a company conducts its business.

191   The correct answer is:

Review board minutes for meetings held after the year end for evidence which indicates further financial difficulties or evidence of alternative sources of finance

The bank letter will provide evidence of the current level of overdraft but not about the likelihood of the overdraft being renewed in future.

The scenario clearly states that the bank will not make a decision on the extension of the overdraft facility until after the auditor's report is signed, and banks will not agree to disclose such information to the auditor. While written representations are a valid form of audit evidence, they do not provide sufficient appropriate audit evidence on their own about any of the matters with which they deal.

192   The correct answer is:

Audit opinion	Disclosure in the auditor's report
Unmodified opinion	Describe the nature of the going concern uncertainty in the Material uncertainty related to going concern section

An unmodified opinion is issued as the auditor agrees with the use of the going concern basis of accounting and the level of disclosure provided. The existence of a material uncertainty in relation to going concern would be disclosed in the 'Material uncertainty related to going concern' section (ISA 570). A qualified opinion would be issued if the going concern basis of accounting is appropriate, but a material uncertainty exists which is not adequately disclosed (ISA 570). An adverse opinion would be issued where the going concern basis of accounting is inappropriate (ISA 570). A disclaimer of opinion would be issued if the auditor is unable to form an opinion.

193   The correct answer is:

Discuss with management about their plans for the company and determine whether the 20X7 financial statements should now be prepared on a break-up basis. If yes, request management to adjust the financial statements, audit the adjustments and provide a new auditor's report.

If Medimade is no longer able to continue its operations, this constitutes an adjusting event and the financial statements must be revised accordingly. IAS 10 *Events After the Reporting Period* states that an entity must not prepare its financial statements on a going concern basis if management determine after the year end that it has no other alternative but to liquidate the company (IAS 10). Now that the bank has withdrawn its overdraft facility, closure has become a very real possibility. In this case, disclosure in the financial statements is no longer appropriate – the financial statements must be prepared on a break-up basis.

Before the financial statements are issued, the auditors have a passive duty to consider the impact of matters which, had they been known at the date of the auditor's report, would have caused the auditor to amend the auditor's report.

194 Panda

Marking scheme

Marks

(a)   Up to 1 mark per well-explained element.

- Intended user, responsible party, practitioner
- Subject matter
- Suitable criteria
- Appropriate evidence
- Assurance report   5

(b)   Up to 1 mark per valid point, overall maximum of 6 marks per event.

Event 1 – Defective chemicals
- Provides evidence of conditions at the year end
- Inventory to be adjusted to lower of cost and net realisable value
- Calculation of materiality
- Review board minutes/quality control reports
- Discuss with the directors, adequate inventory to continue to trade
- Obtain written representation re going concern
- Obtain schedule of defective inventory, agree to supporting documentation
- Discuss with directors basis of the scrap value   6

Event 2 – Explosion
- Provides evidence of conditions that arose subsequent to the year end
- Non-adjusting event, requires disclosure if material
- Calculation of materiality
- Obtain schedule of damaged property, plant and equipment and agree values to asset register
- Obtain latest inventory records to confirm damaged inventory levels
- Discuss with the directors if they will make disclosures
- Discuss with directors why no insurance claim will be made   6

(c) Up to 1 mark per well-explained valid point.

- Disclosure required in 20X3 financial statements and adjustment to the assets in 20X4 financial statements
- Material but not pervasive misstatement, modified auditor's report, qualified opinion
- Basis for qualified opinion paragraph required
- Opinion paragraph – except for

$$\frac{3}{20}$$

(a) Elements of an assurance engagement

There are five elements of an assurance engagement and these are explained below (IFAC, 2016).

A three party relationship

The three parties are the intended user, the responsible party and the practitioner. Intended users are the person, persons or class of persons for whom the practitioner prepares the assurance report. The responsible party is the person (or persons) responsible for the subject matter (in a direct engagement) or subject matter information of the assurance engagement.

The practitioner is the individual providing professional services that will review the subject matter and provide the assurance.

A subject matter

This is the data to be evaluated that has been prepared by the responsible party. It can take many forms, including financial performance (eg historical financial information), non-financial performance (eg key performance indicators), processes (eg internal control) and behaviour (eg compliance with laws and regulations).

Suitable criteria

The subject matter is evaluated or measured against criteria in order to reach an opinion.

Evidence

Sufficient appropriate evidence needs to be gathered to support the required level of assurance.

Assurance report

A report containing the practitioner's opinion is issued to the intended user.

(b) Event 1: Defective chemicals

A batch of chemicals produced before the year end, costing $0.85m to produce, has been found to be defective after the year end. Its scrap value is $0.1m. Inventory should be valued at the lower of cost and net realisable value in accordance with IAS 2 *Inventories* (IAS 2). This is an adjusting event in accordance with IAS 10 *Events after the Reporting Period* (IAS 10). As it stands, the inventory is overstated by $0.75m. This represents 13.4% of profit before tax and 1.4% of revenue and is therefore material to the financial statements.

Audit procedures to be performed

- Obtain a schedule to confirm the cost value of the defective batch of $0.85m and documentary proof of the scrap value of $0.1m.

- Discuss with management whether this is the only defective batch or whether there are likely to be other batches affected.

- Review quality control reports to assess the likelihood of other batches being affected and discuss results of testing with technical team members at Panda.

Event 2: Explosion

An explosion shortly after the year end has resulted in damage to inventory and property, plant and equipment. The amount of inventory and property, plant and equipment damaged is estimated to be $0.9m. It has no scrap value. Inventory and property, plant and equipment are therefore overstated by $0.9m. This represents 16.1% of profit before tax and 1.6% of revenue, and is therefore material. The explosion represents a non-adjusting event in accordance with IAS 10 *Events after the reporting period*. It therefore does not require adjustment in the financial statements but should be disclosed as it is material (IAS 10).

Audit procedures to be performed

- Obtain a schedule of the inventory and property, plant and equipment damaged in the explosion to verify the value of $0.9m.

- Visit the site where the explosion took place to assess damage.

- Discuss with directors the need to make disclosure in the financial statements and review any disclosure note drafted.

- Inspect insurance agreement to assess whether any claim can be made on the insurance.

(c)   **Effect on auditor's report of the explosion**

The directors should make disclosures in the financial statements about the explosion and the effect on inventory and property, plant and equipment. This is because the amount involved is material and affects the value of opening inventory and property, plant and equipment in the following financial year.

If the directors refuse to make the disclosure, then the auditors would modify the opinion on the financial statements on the basis of a material misstatement. The opinion would be qualified 'except for' as the matter is material but unlikely to be pervasive.

A 'Basis for qualified opinion' paragraph would be included in the auditor's report, describing the auditor's reason for modifying the opinion and the effect of the explosion on the opening balances in the financial statements for the following financial year (ISA 705). The 'basis for qualified opinion' would be placed immediately after the Opinion paragraph.

Q195–196 March 2017

195   The correct answer is:

There has been an increase in the average time taken to manufacture each individual jewellery piece.

An increase in the average time to manufacture individual items is likely to increase the costs of production (labour and other direct production costs) meaning costs will rise relative to the net realisable value.

The other answers are incorrect for the following reasons:

- The general market price for individual stones remaining static will have no impact on net realisable value or cost.

- An increase in demand for completed items should increase the net realisable value in comparison to cost.

- An increase in trade discounts will reduce the cost of gems being bought for manufacture into jewellery items therefore should increase the difference between net realisable value and cost.

196   The correct answer is:

   (1)   Basis for opinion paragraph
   (2)   Other reporting responsibilities
   (3)   Key audit matters

   (1)   A 'basis for opinion' paragraph explains how the audit was conducted

   (2)   An 'other reporting responsibilities' paragraph is included if the auditor addresses
          other reporting responsibilities in the auditor's report on the financial statements that
          are in addition to the auditor's responsibilities under the ISAs. This paragraph must
          therefore be included in the auditor's report for a listed company

   (3)   Key audit matters are those matters, in the auditor's judgement, which are the most
          significant from the audit. A 'key audit matters' paragraph is required for all listed
          companies.

   (4)   Is incorrect as an 'other matters paragraph 'draws users' attention to issues outside
          the scope of the financial statements. This would result in a modified report with an
          unmodified opinion.

Q197–198 June 2017

197   The correct answers are:

The availability of alternative sources of audit evidence

The technical expertise required to perform the valuation

Candidates were told in the scenario that management had appointed an expert during
the year and therefore the requirements of ISA 500 *Audit Evidence* were applicable in
determining whether reliance can be placed on the expert. ISA 500 states that in order to
determine reliance, the auditor should consider whether there are other sources of evidence
available as if so the level of reliance will be reduced and to consider the technical expertise
that the expert should possess in order to carry out the work.

It is not appropriate for the auditor to consider at this stage whether staff can be allocated
to perform the work as the availability of staff and the ability to perform the work should
have been considered at the acceptance stage.

While the auditor in certain circumstances may need to refer to the fact that an expert has
been used the responsibility to gather sufficient and appropriate evidence on which to base
the audit opinion remains solely with the auditor. Therefore considering the extent to which
reference can be made to the expert is not an appropriate parameter on which to base
reliance.

198   The correct answer is:

   (1)   Recalculate the depreciation charge for the year using the updated valuation.

   (2)   Verify that all the assets in the same class have been revalued in line with IAS 16
          Property, Plant and Equipment.

   (3)   Agree the value to the expert's report and recalculate the revaluation adjustment
          recorded by Gates Co.

The procedures listed as (1), (2) and (3) would all be reliable and relevant tests for the
auditor to perform to verify a revaluation surplus. The test listed at (4) is not valid as the
surplus, in the circumstances described, should not be recorded in the statement of profit
or loss, but rather should be recorded in other comprehensive income. As such this is not a
suitable test to obtain sufficient and appropriate evidence. Many candidates incorrectly
selected all four options demonstrating that accounting knowledge in this area was lacking
and therefore they were not able to identify procedures to verify appropriate accounting
treatment by the client.

Q199–200 September 2017

199   The correct answer is: Attend the cash count at the year-end and re-perform the count.

Candidates are reminded that tests for existence need to focus on ascertaining whether the balance is genuine at the year end and is not overstated. A good way to approach this style of question is to think about the objective of a test in relation to the identified assertion before assessing each of the procedures in turn to consider whether it would satisfy that objective.

The first test is a test for Rights & Obligations as this test would only confirm that the account was held in the client's name and therefore that the client has the right to the account, but it would not confirm that the balance was not overstated at the year end.

The third test is a Completeness test as starting at the bank confirmation letter and agreeing to the trial balance allows the auditor to confirm that all accounts on the letter are recorded. It would not allow the auditor to confirm that all accounts on the trial balance are genuine.

The fourth test is a Presentation test as it is focused on the disclosure that is included in the financial statements at the year end.

The only test that would confirm that a recorded balance is both genuine and not overstated is to attend the cash count and to re-perform the count.

200   The correct answer is: Qualified opinion as the financial statements are materially misstated

The share issue represents a material non-adjusting subsequent event. So while the transaction will not be recorded until after the year end the event should be disclosed in the financial statements for the year ended 31 July 20X7. This lack of disclosure means that the financial statements are materially misstated and therefore if no changes are made the auditor should issue a qualified opinion.

The majority of candidates selected the fourth answer and candidates are once again reminded that an Emphasis of Matter paragraph can only be used to draw shareholder attention to an issue that is ALREADY disclosed within the financial statements.

Q201–202 December 2017

201   The correct answer is:

Select a sample of employees from the final week's payroll listing and recalculate deductions.

Candidates are reminded that testing for understatement is about ascertaining whether the balance is COMPLETE at the year end. In this question candidates were asked to identify which of the procedures would NOT cover this objective. Therefore candidates were being asked to identify which of the tests is NOT a test for completeness. A good way to approach this style of question is to think about the objective of a test in relation to the identified assertion before assessing each of the procedures in turn.

The first three tests would all test for understatement of the accrual through agreement to the subsequent payment, year-end client listing or prior year accrual.

The final option, however, would not test for understatement/completeness as the recalculation of deductions is a test for accuracy and will provide the auditor will no assurance that the correct amount has been accrued at the year end.

202   The correct answers are:

Was the audit plan suitably modified to allow for changing circumstances?

Has work been performed in accordance with relevant auditing, legal and professional standards?

While all of these questions will be considered in preparation for finalising the auditor's report only consideration of the suitability of the audit plan and whether the work has been performed in accordance with relevant standards will have an impact on the audit opinion.

Q203–204 March 2018

203 The correct answers are:

A code of professional ethics allows a professional accountant to apply fundamental ethical principles to a given situation

A code of professional ethics encourages professional accountants to think about more than just legal compliance

Codes of professional ethics, including ACCA's *Code of Ethics and Conduct* adopt a principles based approach rather than being a prescriptive set of rules. This approach identifies fundamental principles, threats to these principles and safeguards which can be put in place. This approach requires the professional accountant to use professional judgment when applying ethical principles to any given situation. Compliance with codes of professional ethics is a professional requirement.

On this basis, the first and fourth statements are incorrect.

204 The correct answer is:

Gross profit margin.

The key to this question is to consider the assertions which would be relevant to the testing of inventory. In this instance the gross profit margin is relevant to the valuation of inventory. As closing inventory is a component of cost of sales, changes in the gross profit margin could indicate that inventory is misstated.

Candidates should be reminded of the importance of understanding what the results of a ratio show, rather than just having knowledge of the balances which would be included in its calculation. For example, in this instance whilst the inventory balance is included in the current ratio, it is difficult to derive conclusions regarding inventory specifically from its calculation.

Q205–206 June 2018

205 The correct answer is: (1), (3) and (4) only.

Candidates are reminded to ensure that they understand the different between the auditor's and management responsibilities in relation to going concern and to ensure that they understand the requirements set out in ISA 570 *Going Concern*. Statement (2), which relates to determining the basis on which the financial statements should be prepared, is a management responsibility.

206 The correct answer is:

Limited assurance, negative conclusion.

Candidates should ensure that they understand the difference between reasonable and limited assurance and the circumstances in which each will be offered. Reasonable assurance is a high level of assurance and should only be provided when sufficient and appropriate evidence can be gathered. In the circumstances, which were described, the most appropriate level is assurance was limited assurance provided through a negative conclusion.

Q207–208 September 2018

207 The correct answers are:

To consider the adequacy of the accounting records which have been maintained

To obtain an understanding of the internal control system in place

The auditor does not guarantee the going concern status of the company. Accessing the books and records of the company represents one of the rights of the auditor which enables them to achieve their objectives.

This question is a straightforward knowledge-based question. Candidates should be reminded of the importance of having a good understanding of the basic principles of the role of the auditor.

This question was not well-answered in the exam, with many candidates misunderstanding the auditor's responsibility regarding going concern and confusing the auditor's rights and responsibilities.

208 The correct answer is: 2 and 3 only.

This question demonstrates two important points. Firstly, candidates should ensure that they understand the difference between a test of control and substantive procedures. The test described in (1) is a test of control (ie it provides evidence as to whether the control of board approval has operated effectively) and therefore does not provide substantive evidence.

The question also highlights the importance of reading all information provided carefully. The test described in (4) is a valid procedure but it provides evidence regarding other assets, not the headquarters as specified in the requirement.

Q209–210 December 2018

209 The correct answer is: 1, 3 and 4 only.

The effective date of the revaluation, the amount of the revaluation increase and the carrying amount of the head office under the cost model are disclosures required by IAS 16 Property, Plant and Equipment.

This question demonstrates two key points. Firstly it highlights the importance of disclosures to the audit. Obtaining sufficient appropriate evidence during the audit requires an assessment of the adequacy of disclosures included in the financial statements. Secondly candidates should also note the need for accounting knowledge to answer this question. An understanding of key accounting principles is critical to the audit process therefore candidates must ensure that they are familiar with these.

Guidance for candidates regarding the accounting knowledge assumed for this exam is included in the examinable documents list.

210 The correct answer is: Unmodified opinion with no further disclosure.

The amount of the disputed adjustment is not material, being 2.2% of profit before tax, therefore there is no material misstatement. An unmodified opinion would be issued meaning that options three and four are not correct.

The nature of the issue is such that it would not be disclosed in an emphasis of matter paragraph so option two is incorrect. A significant number of candidates chose this option.

Candidates should note the applied nature of this question and the importance of using the information provided in the scenario to come to a conclusion. Candidates must also ensure that they understand that an emphasis of matter paragraph is included in the auditor's report where a matter, appropriately presented or disclosed in the financial statements, is of such importance that it is fundamental to the users' understanding of the financial statements and the auditor wishes to draw attention to that disclosure.

Q211–212 March 2019

211   The correct answer is: 1, 2, 3 and 4.

An unmodified auditor's report includes a statement that the auditor believes the audit evidence obtained is sufficient and appropriate	TRUE	FALSE
Only an auditor's report with a modified opinion includes a statement indicating the report is that of the independent auditor	TRUE	FALSE
Only an auditor's report with a modified opinion includes a description of the meaning of materiality	TRUE	FALSE
An unmodified auditor's report includes a statement that the auditor is independent of the entity and has fulfilled their ethical responsibilities	TRUE	FALSE

Although straightforward many candidates found this question challenging. This question demonstrates the level of detailed knowledge of an ISA which may be tested, in this case ISA 700 *Forming an Opinion and Reporting on Financial Statements*.

The items described in the first and last rows would be included in the basis for opinion paragraph. The item in the second row would appear at the start of the auditor's report so that the auditor's report is clearly distinguished from reports issued by others.

The item described in the third row would be included as part of the auditor's responsibilities for the audit of the financial statements section.

212   The correct answer is:

If the directors refuse to amend the inconsistency, then the auditor's opinion will be **unmodified** and the inconsistency will be explained in an **other information section**.

As with the previous question this question requires a detailed knowledge and understanding of an ISA, in this case ISA 720 *The Auditor's Responsibilities Relating to Other Information*.

As the financial statements are not misstated the audit opinion will be unmodified. However, in accordance with ISA 720 as there is an uncorrected material misstatement in the other information, the auditor's report must include a statement describing the issue in the other information section.

Q213–214 June 2019

213   The correct answer is:

The audit committee's terms of reference should include reviewing and monitoring the external auditor's independence and objectivity	TRUE	
The audit committee's terms of reference should include appointing and removing the external auditors		FALSE
The audit committee's terms of reference should include evaluating and monitoring the effectiveness of the internal audit function	TRUE	

This question tests knowledge of corporate governance responsibilities and in particular those of the audit committee and demonstrates the level of detailed knowledge which is required. It also demonstrates the level of care which must be taken when reading the question and thinking through the options.

The audit committee makes recommendations in relation to the appointment and removal of the external auditors but it is the shareholders who are responsible for their appointment and removal. Candidates who rush through this type of question or who word spot without considering the whole of the context of the question are likely to answer incorrectly.

214   The correct answer is:

A & Co's evaluation of management's assessment of Z Co's ability to continue as a going concern must cover the period up to **31 December 20X9**

As with the previous question, this question requires detailed knowledge, in this case of ISA 570 *Going Concern*. However, it also demonstrates the need to be able to apply knowledge to a practical scenario. In accordance with ISA 570, the auditor is required to review the same period as that used by management to determine whether the going concern basis is appropriate. This must be at least 12 months from the end of the reporting period.

The management of Z Co has used a cash flow forecast for 12 months to December 20X9. As this is at least 12 months from the end of the reporting period, this is date to which A & Co's assessment must cover.

Q215–216 September 2019

215   The correct answer is: Attend the cash count at the year end and reperform the count

This question tests audit procedures relevant to bank and cash but also an ability to relate procedures to a specific assertion. It demonstrates the importance of understanding why a procedure is performed and the specific objective which it achieves.

By attending the cash count and reperforming the count the auditor is able to physically verify the existence of the cash. Agreeing a sample of accounts detailed on the bank confirmation letters to the trial balance provides evidence of completeness of bank and cash balances. Reviewing bank statements to verify that they are in the name of the company provides evidence of rights and obligations and the review of disclosures provides evidence relating to presentation.

216   The correct answer is: 1 and 4

This question demonstrates the need for candidates to have a thorough understanding of all aspects of the syllabus. While the topic of auditors' reports is an important one, candidates are reminded that section E of the syllabus also includes subsequent events, going concern, written representations and audit finalisation and the final review.

Revising the audit plan to allow for changing circumstances helps to ensure that sufficient and appropriate audit evidence is obtained. Performing audit work in accordance with relevant auditing, legal and professional standards enhances the quality of the audit work and therefore the evidence on which the audit opinion is based. The audit firm should ensure that it remains independent throughout the audit and the auditor is required to communicate deficiencies which are of sufficient importance to merit management's attention. However, neither of these issues has a direct effect on the evaluation of audit evidence at the review stage and its suitability for providing the basis for the audit opinion.

Q217–218 December 2019

217   The correct answer is: A

This question tests knowledge of corporate governance guidelines. It demonstrates not only the level of detailed knowledge which is required but also the importance of reading the question carefully rather than rushing to a conclusion. It is the chairman, not the chief executive officer who is responsible for the board. The audit committee will liaise with the external auditor, although this is not its key role, but is not responsible for their appointment. The audit committee may make recommendations regarding the appointment of the external auditor but appointment is normally by the shareholders at a general meeting.

218   The correct answer is: B

This question examines knowledge of ISA 570 *Going Concern*. However it also demonstrates the need to be able to apply the principles to a practical scenario. ISA 570 requires that in evaluating the entity's ability to continue as a going concern the auditor must cover the same period as that used by management to make its assessment. If management's assessment covers a period of less than twelve months from the date of the financial statements the auditor is required to request management to extend its assessment period. In this case the auditor must request that management extend the assessment period to 30 April 20X6. Performing additional audit procedures would not resolve the fact that the assessment period is not as required by ISA 570, therefore option C is not an appropriate response in this instance.

ANSWERS

BPP
LEARNING
MEDIA

Mock exams

ACCA

Applied Skills

Audit and Assurance

Mock Examination 1

September 2016 CBE

Time allowed: 3 hours

This mock exam is divided into two sections:

Section A – ALL 15 questions are compulsory and MUST be attempted

Section B – ALL 3 questions are compulsory and MUST be attempted

Section A – ALL 15 questions are compulsory and MUST be attempted

Each question is worth 2 marks.

The following scenario relates to questions 1–5.

Note. Assume it is 1 July 20X5

You are an audit senior of Viola & Co and are currently conducting the audit of Poppy Co for the year ended 31 March 20X5.

Materiality has been set at $50,000, and you are carrying out the detailed substantive testing on the year-end payables balance. The audit manager has emphasised that understatement of the trade payables balance is a significant audit risk.

Below is an extract from the list of supplier statements as at 31 March 20X5 held by the company and corresponding payables ledger balances at the same date along with some commentary on the noted differences:

Supplier	Statement balance $'000	Payables ledger balance $'000
Carnation Co	70	50
Lily Co	175	105

Carnation Co

The difference in the balance is due to an invoice which is under dispute due to faulty goods which were returned on 30 March 20X5.

Lily Co

The difference in the balance is due to the supplier statement showing an invoice dated 29 March 20X5 for $70,000 which was not recorded in the financial statements until after the year end. The payables clerk has advised the audit team that the invoice was not received until 2 April 20X5.

1   The audit manager has asked you to review the full list of trade payables and select balances on which supplier statement reconciliations will be performed.

   Indicate on the table below if the following items should be included in, or excluded from, your sample.

Suppliers with material balances at the year end	Include	Exclude
Suppliers which have a high volume of business with Poppy Co	Include	Exclude
Major suppliers with nil balances at the year end	Include	Exclude
Major suppliers where the statement agrees to the ledger	Include	Exclude

2   Which of the following audit procedures should be performed in relation to the balance with Lily Co to determine if the payables balance is understated?

   ☐   Inspect the goods received note to determine when the goods were received

   ☐   Inspect the purchase order to confirm it is dated before the year end

   ☐   Review the post year end cash book for evidence of payment of the invoice

   ☐   Send a confirmation request to Lily Co to confirm the outstanding balance

3   Which of the following audit procedures should be carried out to confirm the balance owing to Carnation Co?

(1)   Review post year end credit notes for evidence of acceptance of return

(2)   Inspect pre year end goods returned note in respect of the items sent back to the supplier

(3)   Inspect post year end cash book for evidence that the amount has been settled

☐ 1, 2 and 3

☐ 1 and 3 only

☐ 1 and 2 only

☐ 2 and 3 only

4   The audit manager has asked you to review the results of some statistical sampling testing, which resulted in 20% of the payables balance being tested.

The testing results indicate that there is a $45,000 error in the sample: $20,000 which is due to invoices not being recorded in the correct period as a result of weak controls and additionally there is a one-off error of $25,000 which was made by a temporary clerk.

What would be an appropriate course of action on the basis of these results?

☐ The error is immaterial and therefore no further work is required.

☐ The effect of the control error should be projected across the whole population.

☐ Poppy Co should be asked to adjust the payables figure by $45,000.

☐ A different sample should be selected as these results are not reflective of the population.

5   To help improve audit efficiency, Viola & Co is considering introducing the use of computer-assisted audit techniques (CAATs) for some audits. You have been asked to consider how CAATs could be used during the audit of Poppy Co.

Which of the following is an example of using test data for trade payables testing?

☐ Selecting a sample of supplier balances for testing using monetary unit sampling

☐ Recalculating the ageing of trade payables to identify balances which may be in dispute

☐ Calculation of trade payables payment period to use in analytical procedures

☐ Inputting dummy purchase invoices into the client system to see if processed correctly

The following scenario relates to questions 6–10.

Note. Assume it is 1 July 20X5

You are an audit manager at Blenkin & Co and are approaching the end of the audit of Sampson Co, which is a large listed retailer. The draft financial statements currently show a profit before tax of $6.5m and revenue of $66m for the financial year ended 31 March 20X5. You have been informed that the finance director left Sampson Co on 28 Feb 20X5.

As part of the subsequent events audit procedures, you reviewed post year end board meeting minutes and discovered that a legal case for unfair dismissal has been brought against Sampson Co by the finance director. During a discussion with the human resources (HR) director of Sampson Co, you established that the company received notice of the proposed legal claim on 10 April 20X5.

The HR director told you that Sampson Co's lawyers believe that the finance director's claim is likely to be successful, but estimate that $150,000 is the maximum amount of compensation which would be paid. However, management does not intend to make any adjustments or disclosures in the financial statements.

6   Blenkin & Co has a responsibility to perform procedures to obtain sufficient, appropriate evidence that subsequent events are appropriately reflected in the financial statements of Sampson Co.

      Indicate, by clicking on the timeline, up until which date the auditor should perform subsequent events procedures.

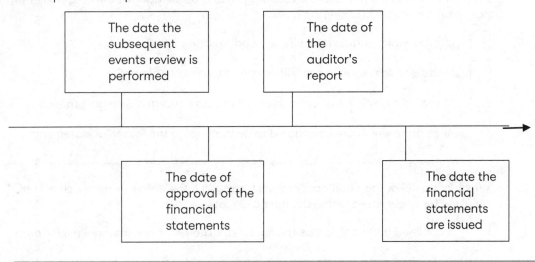

7   If, after the financial statements have been issued, Blenkin & Co becomes aware of a fact which may have caused its report to be amended, the firm should consider several possible actions.

      Which **TWO** of the following are appropriate actions for Blenkin & Co to take?

      ☐ Discuss the matter with management and, where appropriate, those charged with governance

      ☐ Obtain a written representation from management

      ☐ Consider whether the firm should resign from the engagement

      ☐ Enquire how management intends to address the matter in the financial statements where appropriate

8   Which of the following audit procedures should be performed to form a conclusion as to whether the financial statements require amendment in relation to the unfair dismissal claim?

(1)   Inspect relevant correspondence with Sampson Co's lawyers

(2)   Write to the finance director to confirm the claim and level of damages

(3)   Review the post year end cash book for evidence of payments to the finance director

(4)   Request that management confirm their views in a written representation

☐   1, 2 and 3

☐   1, 2 and 4

☐   1, 3 and 4

☐   2, 3 and 4

9   You are drafting the auditor's report for Sampson Co and the audit engagement partner has reminded you that the report will need to reflect the requirements of ISA 701 *Communicating Key Audit Matters in the Independent Auditor's Report*.

According to ISA 701, which of the following should be included in the 'Key audit matters' paragraph in the auditor's report?

☐   Matters which required significant auditor attention

☐   Matters which result in a modification to the audit opinion

☐   All matters which were communicated to those charged with governance

☐   All matters which are considered to be material to the financial statements

10   Which of the following audit opinions will be issued if the unfair dismissal case is **NOT** adjusted for or disclosed within the financial statements?

☐   A qualified audit opinion as the financial statements are materially misstated

☐   A qualified audit opinion as the auditor is unable to obtain sufficient appropriate evidence

☐   An unmodified opinion with an emphasis of matter paragraph

☐   An unmodified audit opinion

The following scenario relates to questions 11–15.

Note. Assume it is 1 July 20X5

Sycamore & Co is the auditor of Fir Co, a listed computer software company. The audit team comprises an engagement partner, a recently appointed audit manager, an audit senior and a number of audit assistants. The audit engagement partner has only been appointed this year due to the rotation of the previous partner who had been involved in the audit for seven years. Only the audit senior has experience of auditing a company in this specialised industry. The previous audit manager, who is a close friend of the new audit manager, left the firm before the completion of the prior year audit and is now the finance director of Fir Co.

The board of Fir Co has asked if Sycamore & Co can take on some additional work and have asked if the following additional non-audit services can be provided:

Payroll: Routine maintenance of payroll records

Recruitment: Assistance with the selection of a new financial controller including the checking of references

Tax: Tax services whereby Sycamore & Co would liaise with the tax authority on Fir Co's behalf

Sycamore & Co has identified that the current year fees to be received from Fir Co for audit and other services will represent 16% of the firm's total fee income and totalled 15.5% in the prior year. The audit engagement partner has asked you to consider what can be done in relation to this self-interest threat.

11   Complete the following sentences regarding the audit team by selecting from the options provided.

In relation to the composition of the current audit team, the fundamental principle of

[   ] is at risk.

An appropriate safeguard to deal with this risk would be to [   ]

Fundamental principle
confidentiality

professional competence

Safeguard
reinstate the previous partner

appoint a completely new audit team

resign from the engagement

provide industry training for team members

12   Which of the following identifies the threat which could arise as a result of the finance director's previous employment at Sycamore & Co and recommends an appropriate safeguard?

☐   A self-review threat; review the work performed by the previous audit manager

☐   A familiarity threat; a different audit manager should be appointed

☐   A self-review threat; change the existing audit plan

☐   A familiarity threat; the firm should resign from the engagement

13 Ignoring the potential effect on total fee levels, match the non-audit service to the threat to independence which would be created if Sycamore & Co were to provide the proposed services.

Non-audit service	Threat to independence
Recruitment	Self-review
Tax	Self-interest
Payroll	Advocacy

14 Which of the following safeguards would **NOT** be relevant in mitigating the threat identified in relation to fees?

☐ Disclosure to those charged with governance that fees from Fir Co represent more than 15% of Sycamore & Co's total fee income

☐ A pre-issuance review to be conducted by an external accountant

☐ The use of separate teams to provide the audit and non-audit services

☐ A post-issuance review to be conducted by an external accountant or regulatory body

15 During the course of the audit of Fir Co, a suspicious cash transfer has been identified. The audit team has reported this to the relevant firm representative as a potential money-laundering transaction.

Which of the following statements is true regarding the confidentiality of this information?

☐ Details of the transaction can only be disclosed with the permission of Fir Co.

☐ If there is a legal requirement to report money laundering, this overrides the principle of confidentiality.

☐ Sycamore & Co is not permitted to disclose details of the suspicious transaction as the information has been obtained during the course of the audit.

☐ In order to maintain confidentiality, Sycamore & Co should report its concerns anonymously.

(Total = 30 marks)

Section B – ALL THREE questions are compulsory and MUST be attempted

Question 16

Heraklion Co is a manufacturer of footballs and is a new audit client for your firm. You are an audit supervisor of Spinalonga & Co and are currently preparing for the forthcoming interim and final audit for the year ending 30 June 20X5. It is 1 July 20X5. You are required to document and assess the sales system, recommend control improvements to deal with a specific fraud issue and undertake substantive testing of revenue.

Sales ordering, goods dispatched and invoicing

Heraklion Co sells footballs to a range of large and small sports equipment retailers in several countries. Sales are made through a network of sales staff employed by Heraklion Co, but new customer leads are generated through a third-party company. Sales staff are responsible for assessing new customers' creditworthiness and proposing a credit limit which is then authorised by the sales director. The sales staff have monthly sales targets and are able to use their discretion in granting sales discounts up to a maximum of 10%. They then record any discount granted in the customer master data file.

The sales staff visit customer sites personally and orders are completed using a two-part pre-printed order form. One copy is left with the customer and the other copy is retained by the salesperson. The sales order number is based on the salesperson's own identification (ID) number.

The company markets itself on being able to dispatch all orders within three working days. Once the order is taken, the salesperson emails the finance department and warehouse dispatch team with the customer ID and the sales order details and from this a pick list is generated. Sequentially numbered goods dispatched notes are completed and filed in the warehouse.

Sequentially numbered invoices are generated using the pick lists for quantities and the customer master data file for prices. Standard credit terms for customers are 30 days and on a monthly basis sales invoices which are over 90 days outstanding are notified to the relevant salesperson to chase payment directly with the customer.

Payroll fraud

The finance director, Montse Mirabelle, has informed you that a significant fraud took place during the year in the payroll department. A number of fictitious employees were set up on the payroll and wages were paid into one bank account. This bank account belonged to two supervisors, who were married, and were employed by Heraklion Co. One had sole responsibility for setting up new joiners in the payroll system and the other processed and authorised bank transfer requests for wages and supplier payments. These employees no longer work for the company and Montse has asked the audit firm for recommendations on how to improve controls in this area to prevent this type of fraud occurring again. Heraklion Co operates a human resources department.

Required

(a) Describe **TWO** methods for documenting the sales system, and for each explain **ONE** advantage and **ONE** disadvantage of using this method. **(6 marks)**

(b) Identify and explain **SEVEN** deficiencies in the sales system of Heraklion Co and provide a recommendation to address each of these deficiencies.

Note. Prepare your answer using two columns headed Control deficiency and Control recommendation respectively. **(14 marks)**

(c)   In relation to the payroll fraud, identify and explain **THREE** controls Heraklion Co should implement to reduce the risk of this type of fraud occurring again and, for each control, describe how it would mitigate the risk.   (6 marks)

(d)   Describe substantive procedures the auditor should perform to obtain sufficient and appropriate audit evidence in relation to Heraklion Co's revenue.   (4 marks)

(Total = 30 marks)

Question 17

Elounda Co manufactures chemical compounds using a continuous production process. Its year end was 30 April 20X5 and the draft profit before tax is $13.6 million. You are the audit supervisor and the year-end audit is due to commence shortly. It is 1 July 20X5. The following matters have been brought to your attention:

(i)   **Revaluation of property, plant and equipment (PPE)**

At the beginning of the year, management undertook an extensive review of Elounda Co's non-current asset valuations and as a result decided to update the carrying value of all PPE. The finance director, Peter Dullman, contacted his brother, Martin, who is a valuer and requested that Martin's firm undertake the valuation, which took place in July 20X4.

(5 marks)

(ii)   **Inventory valuation**

Your firm attended the year-end inventory count for Elounda Co and ascertained that the process for recording work in progress (WIP) and finished goods was acceptable. Both WIP and finished goods are material to the financial statements and the quantity and stage of completion of all ongoing production was recorded accurately during the count.

During the inventory count, the count supervisor noted that a consignment of finished goods, compound E243, with a value of $720,000, was defective in that the chemical mix was incorrect. The finance director believes that compound E243 can still be sold at a discounted sum of $400,000.   (6 marks)

(iii)   **Bank loan**

Elounda Co secured a bank loan of $2.6 million on 1 July 20X3. Repayments of $200,000 are due quarterly, with a lump sum of $800,000 due for repayment in October 20X5. The company met all loan payments in 20X4 on time, but was late in paying the January and April 20X5 repayments.   (4 marks)

Required

(a)   Describe substantive procedures you should perform to obtain sufficient, appropriate audit evidence in relation to the above three matters.

Note. The mark allocation is shown against each of the three matters above.

(b)   Describe the procedures which the auditor of Elounda Co should perform in assessing whether or not the company is a going concern.   (5 marks)

(Total = 20 marks)

Question 18

You are an audit supervisor of Chania & Co and are planning the audit of your client, Sitia Sparkle Co, which manufactures cleaning products. Its year end was 30 April 20X5 and the draft profit before tax is $33.6 million. It is 1 July 20X5. You are supervising a large audit team for the first time and will have specific responsibility for supervising and reviewing the work of the audit assistants in your team.

Sitia Sparkle Co purchases most of its raw materials from suppliers in Africa and these goods are shipped directly to the company's warehouse and the goods are usually in transit for up to three weeks. The company has incurred $1.3 million of expenditure on developing a new range of cleaning products which are due to be launched into the marketplace in August 20X5. In June 20X4, Sitia Sparkle Co also invested $0.9 million in a complex piece of plant and machinery as part of the development process. The full amount has been capitalised and this cost includes the purchase price, installation costs and training costs.

This year, the bonus scheme for senior management and directors has been changed so that, rather than focusing on profits, it is instead based on the value of year-end total assets. In previous years an allowance for receivables, made up of specific balances, which equalled almost 1% of trade receivables, was maintained. However, the finance director feels that this is excessive and unnecessary and has therefore not included it for 20X5 and has credited the opening balance to the profit or loss account.

A new general ledger system was introduced in February 20X5; the finance director has stated that the data was transferred and the old and new systems were run in parallel until the end of May 20X5. As a result of the additional workload on the finance team, a number of control account reconciliations were not completed as at
30 April 20X5, including the bank reconciliation. The finance director is comfortable with this as these reconciliations were completed successfully for both March and May 20X5. In addition, the year-end close down of the purchase ledger was undertaken on 8 May 20X5.

Required

(a) ISA 300 *Planning an Audit of Financial Statements* provides guidance to assist auditors in planning an audit.

 Required

 Explain the benefits of audit planning. (4 marks)

(b) Describe **SIX** audit risks, and explain the auditor's response to each risk, in planning the audit of Sitia Sparkle Co.

 Note. Prepare your answer using two columns headed Audit risk and Auditor's response respectively. (12 marks)

(c) In line with ISA 220 *Quality Control for an Audit of Financial Statements*, describe the audit supervisor's responsibilities in relation to supervising and reviewing the audit assistants' work during the audit of Sitia Sparkle Co. (4 marks)

(Total = 20 marks)

Answers

DO NOT TURN THIS PAGE UNTIL YOU HAVE
COMPLETED THE MOCK EXAM

Plan of attack

If this were the real Audit and Assurance exam and you had been told to turn over and begin, what would be going through your mind?

An important thing to say (while there is still time) is that it is vital to have a good breadth of knowledge of the syllabus because all the questions are compulsory. However, don't panic. Below we provide guidance on how to approach the exam.

Looking through the exam

Section A has three objective test cases, each with five questions. This is the section of the exam where the examining team can test knowledge across the breadth of the syllabus. Make sure you read these cases and questions carefully. The distractors are designed to present plausible, but incorrect, answers. Don't let them mislead you. If you really have no idea – guess. You may even be right.

Section B has three longer questions:

- **Question 16** is a 30-mark internal controls question mainly focused on control deficiencies and recommendations in a payroll system. You are also asked to consider controls that would help to prevent fraud. Don't panic – take your time to read the scenario and what you are asked to do. Try to relate your answers to the specific scenario as much as you can.

- **Question 17** is a 20-mark question on audit procedures relating to PPE, inventory, a bank loan and for assessing going concern. You have a number of individual areas to cover here so take care with timing.

- **Question 18** is a 20-mark planning and audit risk question. Make sure you have noticed that part (b) requires you to identify risks **and** explain the auditor's response to these.

Allocating your time

BPP's advice is to always allocate your time **according to the marks for the question**. However, **use common sense**. If you're doing a question but haven't a clue how to do part (b), you might be better off reallocating your time and getting more marks on another question, where you can add something you didn't have time for earlier on. Make sure you leave time to recheck the OTs and make sure you have answered them all.

Forget about it!

And don't worry if you found the exam difficult. More than likely other candidates will too. If this were the real thing you would need to forget the exam the minute you left the exam hall and think about the next one. Or, if it is the last one, celebrate!

BPP
LEARNING
MEDIA

Section A

ALL 15 questions are compulsory and MUST be attempted

1   The correct answer is:

Suppliers with material balances at the year end	Include	
Suppliers which have a high volume of business with Poppy Co	Include	
Major suppliers with nil balances at the year end	Include	
Major suppliers where the statement agrees to the ledger		Exclude

Where completeness is the key assertion, the sample should be selected to verify where the balance may be understated and therefore should include suppliers with material balances, suppliers with a high volume of business with Poppy Co and major suppliers with no outstanding balance at the year end.

2   The correct answer is: Inspect the goods received note to determine when the goods were received.

In order to determine if the balance with Lily Co is understated, the auditor should determine if the goods should be included in payables at the year end by inspecting the goods received note.

3   The correct answer is: 1 and 2 only

To confirm the balance with Carnation Co, the auditor must determine if the liability exists for the disputed items at the year end by reviewing pre year end goods returned notes and post year end credit notes to verify that the goods have been returned and the order cancelled by the supplier.

4   The correct answer is: The effect of the control error should be projected across the whole population.

Although the error is immaterial, the auditor must reach a conclusion on the sample selected and in order to do so the effect of the error must be considered in relation to the whole population.

5   The correct answer is: Inputting dummy purchase invoices into the client system to see if processed correctly

Test data involves inputting fake transactions into the client's system to test how the transactions are processed. The other options are examples of audit software.

6

The date the subsequent events review is performed		The date of the auditor's report

───▶

| The date of approval of the financial statements | | The date the financial statements are issued |

As per ISA 560 *Subsequent Events*, the auditor has an active responsibility to carry out subsequent events procedures between the date of the financial statements and the date of the auditor's report.

7   The correct answers are:

Discuss the matter with management and, where appropriate, those charged with governance

Enquire how management intends to address the matter in the financial statements where appropriate

As per ISA 560 paragraph 15, in the circumstances described the auditor should initially discuss the matter with management and understand how management intends to address the matter in the financial statements.

8   The correct answer is: 1, 3 and 4

The auditor is unlikely to ask the finance director, who is no longer an officer of the company and the party involved in the claim, to confirm the level of damages payable. All other procedures would be appropriate.

9   The correct answer is: Matters which required significant auditor attention

As per paragraph 9 of ISA 701 *Communicating Key Audit matters in the Independent Auditor's Report*, in determining key audit matters, the auditor shall determine, from the matters communicated to those charged with governance, those which required significant auditor attention.

10   The correct answer is: An unmodified audit opinion

The maximum damages of $150,000 is not material to the financial statements at 2.3% of profit before tax and 0.2% of revenue. Therefore no modification to the audit opinion is required.

11   In relation to the composition of the current audit team, the fundamental principle of **professional competence** is at risk.

An appropriate safeguard to deal with this risk would be to **provide industry training for team members**.

The fundamental principle at risk is professional competence, as many of the audit team are new and do not have relevant experience in relation to the specialised industry in which Fir Co operates. It is not appropriate to reinstate the previous partner as, in line with the ACCA *Code of Ethics and Conduct*, the previous partner has been rotated after seven years to prevent a familiarity threat. The audit firm should offer appropriate training for the audit team to ensure they have the necessary knowledge to carry out the work.

12   The correct answer is: A familiarity threat; a different audit manager should be appointed

As the previous audit manager has taken up employment with the client as the finance director, there is a familiarity threat due to the ongoing relationship between the old and new audit manager. The familiarity threat is not so severe that the firm would need to resign but a new audit manager should be appointed.

13   The correct answer is:

Non-audit service	Threat to independence
	Payroll
	Recruitment
	Tax

As per the ACCA *Code of Ethics and Conduct*, the following threats would be created from carrying out the non-audit services requested by Fir Co:

Payroll – Self-review as the auditor will also be involved in auditing the figures included in the financial statements in relation to wages and salaries.

Recruitment – Self-interest as the auditor would be involved in selecting an officer of the company who has significant influence over the financial statements.

Tax – Advocacy as the auditor may be perceived to be representing and promoting Fir Co's interest in liaising with the tax authority.

14   The correct answer is: The use of separate teams to provide the audit and non-audit services

Using separate teams will not address the self-interest threat from the fee levels, as separating the teams will not alleviate the firm's potential financial dependence on Fir Co and therefore the risk that work is not carried out independently for fear of losing the client.

15   The correct answer is: If there is a legal requirement to report money laundering, this overrides the principle of confidentiality.

As per the ACCA *Code of Ethics and Conduct* – Confidential information may be disclosed when such disclosure is required by law.

Section B

Question 16

Marking scheme

		Marks

(a) Methods for documenting the sales system
- Narrative notes — 3
- Questionnaires — 3
- Flowcharts — 3

Restricted to — **6**

(b) Control deficiencies and recommendations (only 7 issues required)
- New customers' creditworthiness assessed by sales staff — 2
- Sales staff have discretion to grant discounts up to 10% — 2
- Access to master file data — 2
- Inventory not checked by salespeople prior to order being placed — 2
- No copy of order with the sales ordering department, unable to identify unfulfilled orders — 2
- Orders not sequentially numbered — 2
- Warehouse dispatch team do not receive a copy of the sales order — 2
- Goods dispatch notes filed by warehouse dispatch team — 2
- Salesperson responsible for chasing invoices over 90 days old — 2

Max 7 issues, 2 marks each — **14**

(c) Controls to reduce risk of payroll fraud
- Proof of identity checks undertaken for all new joiners — 2
- Review of the number of employees per department to the payroll system — 2
- Human resources department initiates request for new joiners — 2
- Authorisation of all new joiners by payroll director — 2

	Marks
• Relatives not permitted to undertake interrelated processes	2
• Payroll system reviews same bank account name and number	2
• Bank transfer requests authorised by senior responsible official, independent	<u>2</u>
Restricted to	6

(d) **Substantive procedures for revenue**

• Analytical review over revenue compared to budget and prior year	1
• Analytical review of main product categories of sales compared to prior year	1
• Gross margin review	1
• Agree sales prices for customers to price list or master file data	1
• Review credit notes	1
• Follow orders to goods dispatched note, to sales invoice and to sales ledger	1
• Sales cut-off	<u>1</u>
Restricted to	<u>4</u>
Total marks	<u>30</u>

(a) **Documenting the sales system**

There are several methods which can be used to document the sales system.

Narrative notes

Narrative notes consist of a written description of the system; they would detail what occurs in the system at each stage and would include any controls which operate at each stage.

Advantages of this method include:

- They are simple to record; after discussion with staff members, these discussions are easily written up as notes.

- They can facilitate understanding by all members of the audit team, especially more junior members who might find alternative methods too complex.

Disadvantages of this method include:

- Narrative notes may prove to be too cumbersome, especially if the system is complex or heavily automated.

- This method can make it more difficult to identify missing internal controls as the notes record the detail but do not identify control exceptions clearly.

Questionnaires

Internal control questionnaires (ICQs) or internal control evaluation questionnaires (ICEQs) contain a list of questions; ICQs are used to assess whether controls exist whereas ICEQs assess the effectiveness of the controls in place.

Advantages of this method include:

- Questionnaires are quick to prepare, which means they are a timely method for recording the system.

- They ensure that all controls present within the system are considered and recorded; hence missing controls or deficiencies are clearly highlighted by the audit team.

Disadvantages of this method include:

- It can be easy for the staff members to overstate the level of the controls present as they are asked a series of questions relating to potential controls.

- A standard list of questions may miss out unusual or more bespoke controls used by the company.

Flowcharts

Flowcharts are a graphic illustration of the internal control system for the sales system. Lines usually demonstrate the sequence of events and standard symbols are used to signify controls or documents.

Advantages of this method include:

- It is easy to view the system in its entirety as it is all presented together in one diagram.

- Due to the use of standard symbols for controls, it can be effective in identifying missing controls.

Disadvantages of this method include:

- They can sometimes be difficult to amend, as any amendments may require the whole flowchart to be redrawn.

- There is still the need for narrative notes to accompany the flowchart and hence it can be a time-consuming method.

Note. Full marks will be awarded for describing **two** methods for documenting the sales system and explaining **one** advantage and **one** disadvantage for each method.

(b) **Deficiencies and controls over the sales system**

Control deficiency	Control recommendation
New customers' creditworthiness is assessed by a salesperson who sets the credit limit, which is authorised by the sales director. The sales staff have sales targets, and hence may suggest that new customers are creditworthy simply to meet their targets. This could result in sales being made to poor credit risks.	New customers should complete a credit application which should be checked through a credit agency with a credit limit set. Once authorised by the sales director, the limit should be entered into the system by a credit controller.
Sales staff have discretion to grant sales discounts to customers of up to 10%. This could result in a loss of revenue as they may award unrealistic discounts simply to meet sales targets. The discounts granted by sales staff are not being reviewed and could result in unauthorised discounts allowed.	All discounts to be granted to customers should be authorised in advance by a responsible official, such as the sales director. If not practical, then the supervisor of the sales staff should undertake this role.

Control deficiency	Control recommendation
Sales staff are able to make changes to the customer master data file, in order to record discounts allowed and these changes are not reviewed. There is a risk that these amendments could be made incorrectly resulting in a loss of sales revenue or overcharging of customers. In addition, the sales staff are not senior enough to be given access to changing master file data as this could increase the risk of fraud.	Sales staff should not be able to access the master data file to make amendments. Any such amendments to master file data should be restricted so that only supervisors and above can make changes. An exception report of changes made should be generated and reviewed by a responsible official.
Inventory availability does not appear to be checked by the salesperson at the time the order is placed. In addition, Heraklion Co markets itself on being able to dispatch all orders within three working days. There is a risk that where goods are not available, the customer would not be made aware of this prior to placing their order, leading to unfulfilled orders and customer dissatisfaction, which would impact the company's reputation.	Prior to the salesperson finalising the order, the inventory system should be checked in order for an accurate assessment of the availability of goods to be notified to customers.
Customer orders are recorded on a two-part pre-printed form; one copy is left with the customer and one with the salesperson. The sales department of Heraklion Co does not hold these orders centrally and hence would not be able to monitor if orders are being fulfilled on a timely basis. This could result in a loss of revenue and customer goodwill.	The order form should be amended to be at least four-part. The third part of the order should be sent to the warehouse department and the fourth part sent to the finance department. The copy the salesperson has should be stored centrally in the sales department. Upon dispatch, the goods dispatch note should be matched to the order; a regular review of unmatched orders should be undertaken by the sales department to identify any unfulfilled orders.
Customer orders are given a number based on the salesperson's own identification (ID) number. These numbers are not sequential. Without sequential numbers, it is difficult for Heraklion Co to identify missing orders and to monitor if all orders are being dispatched in a timely manner, leading to a loss of customer goodwill.	Sales orders should be sequentially numbered. On a regular basis, a sequence check of orders should be undertaken to identify any missing orders.
The salesperson emails the warehouse dispatch team with the customer ID and the sales order details, rather than a copy of the sales order itself, and a pick list is generated from this. There is a risk that incorrect or insufficient details may be recorded by the salesperson and this could result in incorrect orders being dispatched, orders being dispatched late or orders failing to be dispatched at all, resulting in a loss of customer goodwill and revenue.	The third part of the sales order as mentioned previously should be forwarded directly to the warehouse department. The pick list should be generated from the original order form and the warehouse team should check correct quantities and product descriptions are being dispatched, as well as checking the quality of goods being dispatched to ensure they are not damaged.

Control deficiency	Control recommendation
Sequentially numbered goods dispatched notes (GDNs) are completed and filed by the warehouse department. If the finance department does not receive a copy of these GDNs, they will not know when to raise the related sales invoices. This could result in goods being dispatched but not being invoiced, leading to a loss of revenue.	Upon dispatch of goods, a four-part GDN should be completed, with copies to the customer, warehouse department, sales department (to confirm dispatch of goods) and finance department. Upon receipt of the GDN, once matched to the fourth part of the sales order form, a clerk should raise the sales invoices in a timely manner, confirming all details to the GDN and order.
The salesperson is given responsibility to chase customers directly for payment once an invoice is outstanding for 90 days. This is considerably in excess of the company's credit terms of 30 days which will lead to poor cash flow. Further, as the salespeople have sales targets, they are more likely to focus on generating sales orders rather than chasing payments. This could result in an increase in bad debts and reduced profit and cash flows.	A credit controller should be appointed and it should be their role, rather than that of the salesperson, to chase any outstanding sales invoices which are more than 30 days old.

(c) Controls to reduce risk of payroll fraud

Control	Mitigate risk
Proof of identity checks should be undertaken by the human resources (HR) department and recorded on individuals' personnel files for all new employees set up on the payroll system.	This should reduce the risk of fictitious employees being set up, as in order to be set up on the system a fictitious set of identification would be required which would be an onerous process.
A count should be undertaken of the number of employees in each department of Heraklion Co; this should be reconciled to the number of employees on the payroll system.	This would identify if there are extra employees on the payroll system, which could then be investigated further.
The HR department should initiate the process for setting up new joiners by asking new employees to complete a joiner's form which will be approved by the relevant manager and HR. This request should then be forwarded to the payroll department, who should set up the employee.	This control introduces segregation of duties as in order to set up employees both the HR and payroll departments are involved. Without collusion with an HR employee, the payroll supervisor would be unable to set up fictitious employees.
All new joiners should only be set up by payroll on receipt of a joiner's form and any additions to the system should be authorised by the payroll director. An edit report should be generated and reviewed by HR.	As all new joiners would be authorised by the payroll director, it is unlikely that payroll employees would risk establishing fictitious joiners. A further review by the HR department would also detect any employees without an authorised joiner form.
Where possible, employees who are related should not be allowed to undertake processes which are interrelated whereby they can breach segregation of duty controls for key transaction cycles. A regular review of job descriptions of related employees should be carried out by HR.	This should reduce the risk of related staff colluding and being able to commit a fraud.

Control	Mitigate risk
The payroll system should be amended to run an exception report which identifies any employees with the same bank account name or number and this should be reviewed by HR.	Identifying the same bank account name or number will prevent multiple fraudulent payments being made to the same employee.
All bank transfer requests should be authorised by a senior responsible official, who is independent of the processing of payments; they should undertake spot checks of payments to supporting documentation, including employee identification cards/records.	This would introduce an additional layer of segregation of duties, which would reduce the risk of fraud occurring. In addition, the spot checks to employee identification cards/records would confirm the validity of payments.

(d)   Revenue substantive procedures

   (i)   Compare the overall level of revenue against prior years and budgets and investigate any significant fluctuations.

   (ii)   Obtain a schedule of sales for the year broken down into the main product categories and compare this to the prior year breakdown and for any unusual movements discuss with management.

   (iii)   Calculate the gross profit margin for Heraklion Co and compare this to the prior year and investigate any significant fluctuations.

   (iv)   Select a sample of sales invoices for customers and agree the sales prices back to the price list or customer master data information to ensure the accuracy of invoices.

   (v)   Select a sample of credit notes raised, trace through to the original invoice and ensure the invoice has been correctly removed from sales.

   (vi)   Select a sample of customer orders and agree these to the dispatch notes and sales invoices through to inclusion in the sales ledger and revenue general ledger accounts to ensure completeness of revenue.

   (vii)   Select a sample of dispatch notes both pre and post year end and follow these through to sales invoices in the correct accounting period to ensure that cut-off has been correctly applied.

Question 17

Workbook references. Chapters 12, 13, 17 and 19.

Top tips. This is a 20-mark audit evidence and going concern question. In part (a) the key is to note that you are being asked for substantive procedures relating to specific aspects eg **revaluation** of PPE, not all aspects of PPE. The examining team's report noted that in relation to inventory a significant proportion of candidates focused on inventory counts rather than **valuation** as required by the question. Make sure you read the information carefully noting important details like these.

You also need to ensure that you tailor your answer to the scenario rather than simply listing out standard audit procedures.

For part (b) make sure you understand the requirement. The question is asking for procedures, not going concern indicators.

Easy marks. Overall this is a demanding question due to the care required in reading the information and the need to tailor the answer specifically. However, you should have been able to pick up good marks for substantive procedures relating to the bank loan.

Marks

(a) (i) Substantive procedures for revaluation of property, plant and equipment (PPE)
- Cast schedule of PPE revalued this year and agree to TB/FS — 1
- Consider reasonableness of the valuer's qualifications, membership of professional body and experience — 1
- Discuss with management if the valuer has financial interests in the company which along with family relationship may impact his independence — 1
- Agree the revalued amounts to the valuation statement provided by the valuer — 1
- Consider if all items in the same class of assets have been revalued — 1
- Agree the revalued amounts included correctly in the non-current assets register — 1
- Recalculate the total revaluation adjustment and agree recorded in the revaluation surplus — 1
- Recalculate the depreciation charge for the year — 1
- Review the financial statements disclosures for compliance with IAS 16 *Property, Plant and Equipment* — <u>1</u>

Restricted to — 5

(ii) Substantive procedures for inventory valuation
- Cast a schedule of all raw materials, finished goods and work in progress (WIP) inventory and agree to TB/FS — 1
- Obtain breakdown and agree sample of WIP from the count to the WIP schedule, agree percentage completion — 1
- For a sample, obtain relevant cost sheets and confirm raw material costs to recent purchase invoices, labour costs to time sheets or wage records and overheads allocated are of a production nature — 1
- For a sample of inventory items, review the calculation for equivalent units and associated equivalent unit cost and recalculate the inventory valuation — 1
- Select a sample of year-end finished goods and review post year end sales invoices to ascertain if net realisable value (NRV) is above cost or if an adjustment is required — 1
- Select a sample of items included in WIP at the year end and ascertain the final unit cost price, verifying to relevant supporting documentation, and compare to the unit sales price included in sales invoices post year end to assess NRV — 1
- Review aged inventory reports, identify slow-moving goods, discuss with management — 1
- Compound E243, discuss with management plans for disposing of goods, why NRV is $400,000 — 1
- If any of defective goods have been sold post year end, agree to the sales invoice to assess NRV — 1
- Agree the cost of $720,000 for compound E243 to supporting documentation — 1

- Confirm the final adjustment for compound E243, discuss with management if adjustment made, if so, follow through the write down to confirm   1
- Review the financial statements disclosures for compliance with IAS 2 *Inventories*   1

Restricted to   6

(iii) Substantive procedures for bank loan
- Agree the opening balance to the prior year audit file and FS   1
- For loan payments made, agree to cash book and bank statements   1
- Review the bank correspondence for late payment penalties, agree to statement of profit or loss   1
- Obtain direct confirmation of year-end balance from bank, agree to the loan schedule   1
- Review loan agreement for details of covenants and recalculate to identify any breaches   1
- Agree closing balance to the trial balance and draft financial statements and review the disclosure of the current liability bank loan in the draft financial statements   1

Restricted to   4

(b) **Going concern procedures**
- Review cash flow forecasts
- Review bank loan agreements, breach of key ratios or covenants
- Review post year end sales and order book
- Review supplier's correspondence
- Enquire of lawyers for any litigation
- Subsequent events
- Board minutes
- Management accounts
- Consider additional disclosures under IAS 1 *Presentation of Financial Statements*
- Written representation   1

Restricted to   5

Total marks   20

(a) (i) **Substantive procedures for revaluation of property, plant and equipment (PPE)**

- Obtain a schedule of all PPE revalued during the year and cast to confirm completeness and accuracy of the revaluation adjustment and agree to trial balance and financial statements.

- Consider the competence and capability of the valuer, Martin Dullman, by assessing through enquiry his qualification, membership of a professional body and experience in valuing these types of assets.

- Consider whether the valuation undertaken provides sufficiently objective audit evidence. Discuss with management whether Martin Dullman has any financial interest in Elounda Co which along with the family relationship could have had an impact on his independence.

- Agree the revalued amounts to the valuation statement provided by the valuer.

- Review the valuation report and consider if all assets in the same category have been revalued in line with IAS 16 *Property, Plant and Equipment*.

- Agree the revalued amounts for these assets are included correctly in the non-current assets register.

- Recalculate the total revaluation adjustment and agree correctly recorded in the revaluation surplus.

- Recalculate the depreciation charge for the year to ensure that, for the assets revalued during the year, the depreciation was based on the correct valuation and was for 12 months.

- Review the financial statements disclosures relating to the revaluation to ensure they comply with IAS 16.

(ii) **Substantive procedures for inventory valuation**

- Obtain a schedule of all raw materials, finished goods and work in progress (WIP) inventory and cast to confirm completeness and accuracy of the balance and agree to trial balance and financial statements.

- Obtain the breakdown of WIP and agree a sample of WIP assessed during the count to the WIP schedule, agreeing the percentage completion as recorded at the inventory count.

- For a sample of inventory items (finished goods and WIP), obtain the relevant cost sheets and confirm raw material costs to recent purchase invoices, labour costs to time sheets or wage records and overheads allocated are of a production nature.

- For a sample of inventory items, review the calculation for equivalent units and associated equivalent unit cost and recalculate the inventory valuation.

- Select a sample of year-end finished goods and review post year end sales invoices to ascertain if net realisable value (NRV) is above cost or if an adjustment is required.

- Select a sample of items included in WIP at the year end and ascertain the final unit cost price, verifying to relevant supporting documentation, and compare to the unit sales price included in sales invoices post year end to assess NRV.

- Review aged inventory reports and identify any slow-moving goods, discuss with management why these items have not been written down or if an allowance is required.

- For the defective chemical compound E243, discuss with management their plans for disposing of these goods, and why they believe these goods have an NRV of $400,000.

- If any E243 has been sold post year end, agree to the sales invoice to assess NRV.

- Agree the cost of $720,000 for compound E243 to supporting documentation to confirm the raw material cost, labour cost and any overheads attributed to the cost.

- Confirm if the final adjustment for compound E243 is $320,000 (720 – 400) and discuss with management if this adjustment has been made; if so follow through the write down to confirm.

- Review the financial statements disclosures relating to inventory and WIP to ensure they comply with IAS 2 *Inventories*.

(iii)   Substantive procedures for bank loan

- Agree the opening balance of the bank loan to the prior year audit file and financial statements.

- For any loan payments made during the year, agree the cash outflow to the cash book and bank statements.

- Review bank correspondence to identify whether any late payment penalties have been levied and agree these have been charged to profit or loss account as a finance charge.

- Obtain direct confirmation at the year end from the loan provider of the outstanding balance and any security provided; agree confirmed amounts to the loan schedule and financial statements.

- Review the loan agreement for details of covenants and recalculate to identify any breaches in these.

- Agree closing balance of the loan to the trial balance and draft financial statements and that the disclosure is adequate, including any security provided, that the loan is disclosed as a current liability and that disclosure is in accordance with accounting standards and local legislation.

(b)   **Going concern procedures**

- Obtain Elounda's cash flow forecast and review the cash in- and outflows. Assess the assumptions for reasonableness and discuss the findings with management to understand if the company will have sufficient cash flows to meet liabilities as they fall due.

- Discuss with management their ability to settle the next instalment due for repayment to the bank and the lump sum payment of $800k in October 20X5 and ensure these have been included in the cash flow forecast.

- Review current agreements with the bank to determine whether any key ratios or covenants have been breached with regards to the bank loan or any overdraft.

- Review the company's post year end sales and order book to assess the levels of trade and if the revenue figures in the cash flow forecast are reasonable.

- Review post year end correspondence with suppliers to identify whether any restrictions in credit have arisen and, if so, ensure that the cash flow forecast reflects the current credit terms or where necessary an immediate payment for trade payables.

- Enquire of the lawyers of Elounda Co as to the existence of litigation and claims; if any exist, then consider their materiality and impact on the going concern basis.

- Perform audit tests in relation to subsequent events to identify any items which might indicate or mitigate the risk of going concern not being appropriate.

- Review the post year end board minutes to identify any other issues which might indicate financial difficulties for the company.

- Review post year end management accounts to assess if in line with cash flow forecast and to identify any issues which may be relevant to the going concern assessment.

- Consider whether any additional disclosures as required by IAS 1 *Presentation of Financial Statements* in relation to material uncertainties over going concern should be made in the financial statements.

- Obtain a written representation confirming the directors' view that Elounda Co is a going concern.

Question 18

Marking scheme

		Marks

(a) **Benefits of audit planning**
- Important areas of the audit
- Potential problems
- Effective and efficient audit
- Selection of engagement team members and assignment of work
- Direction, supervision and review
- Co-ordination of work

Restricted to   **4**

(b) **Audit risks and responses** (only 6 risks required)
- Goods in transit from Africa   2
- Research and development expenditure   2

- Capitalisation of costs of plant and machinery   2
- Senior management bonus scheme   2

- Allowance for receivables   2
- Introduction of new general ledger system   2

- April 20X5 control account reconciliations not undertaken   2
- Purchase ledger closed down on 8 May   2

Max 6 issues, 2 marks each   **12**

(c) **Supervising and reviewing audit assistants' work**
- Monitor the progress of the audit engagement to ensure the audit timetable was met   1
- Consider the competence and capabilities of team members re sufficient available time, understanding of instructions and if work in accordance with planned approach   1
- Address any significant matters arising, consider their significance and modifying the approach   1

- Responsible for identifying matters for consultation/consideration by senior team members — 1

- Work performed in line with professional standards and other requirements — 1

- Work supports conclusions reached and properly documented — 1

- Significant matters raised for partner attention or further consideration — 1

- Appropriate consultations have taken place with conclusions documented — 1

Restricted to — 4

Total marks — 20

(a) **Benefits of audit planning**

Audit planning is addressed by ISA 300 *Planning an Audit of Financial Statements*. It states that adequate planning benefits the audit of financial statements in several ways:

- Helping the auditor to devote appropriate attention to important areas of the audit

- Helping the auditor to identify and resolve potential problems on a timely basis

- Helping the auditor to properly organise and manage the audit engagement so that it is performed in an effective and efficient manner

- Assisting in the selection of engagement team members with appropriate levels of capabilities and competence to respond to anticipated risks and the proper assignment of work to them

- Facilitating the direction and supervision of engagement team members and the review of their work

- Assisting, where applicable, in co-ordination of work done by experts

(b) **Audit risk and auditor's responses**

Audit risk	Auditor's response
Sitia Sparkle Co purchases its goods from suppliers in Africa and the goods are in transit for up to three weeks. At the year end, there is a risk that the cut-off of inventory, purchases and payables may not be accurate and may be under/overstated.	The audit team should undertake detailed cut-off testing of purchases of goods at the year end and the sample of GRNs from before and after the year end relating to goods from suppliers in Africa should be increased to ensure that cut-off is complete and accurate.
Sitia Sparkle Co has incurred expenditure of $1.3 million in developing a new range of cleaning products. This expenditure is classed as research and development under IAS 38 *Intangible Assets*. The standard requires research costs to be expensed to profit or loss and development costs to be capitalised as an intangible asset. If the company has incorrectly classified research costs as development expenditure, there is a risk the intangible asset could be overstated and expenses understated. In addition, as the senior management bonus is based on year-end asset values, this	Obtain a breakdown of the expenditure and verify that it relates to the development of the new products. Undertake testing to determine whether the costs relate to the research or development stage. Discuss the accounting treatment with the finance director and ensure it is in accordance with IAS 38.

Audit risk	Auditor's response
increases this risk further as management may have a reason to overstate assets at the year end.	
In June 20X4, the company invested $0.9 million in a complex piece of plant and machinery. The costs include purchase price, installation and training costs. As per IAS 16 *Property, Plant and Equipment*, the cost of an asset includes its purchase price and directly attributable costs only. Training costs are not permitted under IAS 16 to be capitalised as part of the cost and therefore plant and machinery and profits are overstated.	Obtain a breakdown of the $0.9 million expenditure and undertake testing to confirm the level of training costs which have been included within non-current assets. Discuss the accounting treatment with the finance director and the level of any necessary adjustment to ensure treatment is in accordance with IAS 16.
The bonus scheme for senior management and directors of Sitia Sparkle Co has been changed; it is now based on the value of year-end total assets.	Throughout the audit, the team will need to be alert to this risk and maintain professional scepticism.
There is a risk that management might be motivated to overstate the value of assets through the judgements taken or through the use of releasing provisions or capitalisation policy.	Detailed review and testing on judgemental decisions, including treatment of provisions, and compare treatment against prior years. Any manual journal adjustments affecting assets should be tested in detail. In addition, a written representation should be obtained from management confirming the basis of any significant judgements.
The finance director of Sitia Sparkle Co believes that an allowance for receivables is excessive and unnecessary and therefore has not provided for it at the year end and has credited the opening balance to profit or loss.	Review and test the controls surrounding how Sitia Sparkle Co identifies receivables balances which may require a provision to ensure that they are operating effectively in the current year.
There is a risk that receivables will be overvalued; some balances may be irrecoverable and so will be overstated if not provided for.	Discuss with the finance director the rationale for not maintaining an allowance for receivables and releasing the opening provision.
In addition, releasing the allowance for receivables will increase asset values and hence the senior management bonus which increases the risk further.	Extended post year end cash receipts testing and a review of the aged receivables ledger to be performed to assess valuation and the need for an allowance for receivables.
A new general ledger system was introduced in February 20X5 and the old and new systems were run in parallel until May 20X5.	The auditor should undertake detailed testing to confirm that all of the balances at the transfer date have been correctly recorded in the new general ledger system.
There is a risk of the balances in May being misstated and loss of data if they have not been transferred from the old system completely and accurately. If this is not done, this could result in the auditor not identifying a significant control risk. In addition, the new general ledger system will require documenting and the controls over this will need to be tested.	The auditor should document and test the new system. They should review any management reports run comparing the old and new system during the parallel run to identify any issues with the processing of accounting information.

Audit risk	Auditor's response
A number of reconciliations, including the bank reconciliation, were not performed at the year end; however, they were undertaken in June and August. Control account reconciliations provide comfort that accounting records are being maintained completely and accurately. At the year end, it is important to confirm that balances including bank balances are not under- or overstated. This is an example of a control procedure being overridden by management and raises concerns over the overall emphasis placed on internal control.	Discuss this issue with the finance director and request that the July control account reconciliations are undertaken. All reconciling items should be tested in detail and agreed to supporting documentation.
The purchase ledger of Sitia Sparkle Co was closed down on 8 May, rather than at the year end of 30 April. There is a risk that the cut-off may be incorrect with purchases and payables over- or understated.	The audit team should undertake testing of transactions posted to the purchase ledger between 1 and 8 May to identify whether any transactions relating to the 20X6 year end have been included or any 20X5 balances removed.

(c)   Supervision and reviewing of the assistants' work

Supervision

During the audit of Sitia Sparkle Co, the supervisor should keep track of the progress of the audit engagement to ensure that the audit timetable is met and should ensure that the audit manager and partner are kept updated of progress.

The competence and capabilities of individual members of the engagement team should be considered, including whether they have sufficient time to carry out their work, whether they understand their instructions and whether the work is being carried out in accordance with the planned approach to the audit.

In addition, part of the supervision process should involve addressing any significant matters arising during the audit of Sitia Sparkle Co, considering their significance and modifying the planned approach appropriately.

The supervisor would also be responsible for identifying matters for consultation or consideration by the audit manager or engagement partner of Sitia Sparkle Co.

Review

The supervisor would be required to review the work completed by the assistants and consider whether this work has been performed in accordance with professional standards and other regulatory requirements and if the work performed supports the conclusions reached and has been properly documented.

The supervisor should also consider whether all significant matters have been raised for partner attention or for further consideration and, where appropriate consultations have taken place, whether appropriate conclusions have been documented.

ACCA

Applied Skills

Audit and Assurance

Mock Examination 2

Specimen exam CBE

Time allowed: 3 hours

This mock exam is divided into two sections:

Section A – ALL 15 questions are compulsory and MUST be attempted

Section B – ALL 3 questions are compulsory and MUST be attempted

BPP
LEARNING
MEDIA

Section A – ALL FIFTEEN questions are compulsory and MUST be attempted

Each question is worth 2 marks.

The following scenario relates to questions 1–5.

You are an audit manager of Buffon & Co, responsible for the audit of Maldini Co, and you have become aware of the following information.

Audit engagement partner

The audit engagement partner for Maldini Co, a listed company, has been in place for approximately eight years and her son has just been offered a role with Maldini Co as a sales manager. This role would entitle him to shares in Maldini Co as part of his remuneration package.

Internal audit function

Maldini Co's board of directors are considering establishing an internal audit function, and the finance director has asked the audit firm, Buffon & Co, about the differences in the role of internal audit and external audit. If the internal audit function is established, the directors have suggested that they may wish to outsource this to Buffon & Co.

Auditor characteristics

Following management's request for information regarding the different roles of internal and external auditors, the audit assistant has collated a list of key characteristics:

(1)   Appointed by audit committee
(2)   Reports are publicly available to shareholders
(3)   Review effectiveness of internal controls to improve operations
(4)   Express an opinion on the truth and fairness of the financial statements

Fees

The finance director has suggested to the board that if Buffon & Co are appointed as internal as well as external auditors, then fees should be renegotiated with at least 20% of all internal and external audit fees being based on the profit after tax of the company, as this will align the interests of Buffon & Co and Maldini Co. This fee income would be significant to Buffon & Co.

1   Your audit assistant has highlighted a number of potential threats to independence in respect of the audit of Maldini Co.

      Identify which of the following represent valid threats to independence, matching each threat to the appropriate category.

Facts	Category of threat
Length of time the audit engagement partner has been in position	Self-interest
Maldini Co's request for advice regarding internal audit	Self-interest
Potential holding of shares by audit partner's son	Familiarity
Possible provision of internal audit services	Self-review
Basis of fee	

2   In relation to the audit engagement partner holding the role for eight years, and her son's offer of employment with Maldini Co:

Which of the following safeguards should be implemented in order to comply with ACCA's *Code of Ethics and Conduct*?

☐ The audit partner should be removed from the audit team.

☐ An independent quality control reviewer should be appointed.

☐ A third party such as a professional body should be consulted on key audit judgments.

☐ Buffon & Co should resign from the audit.

3   In line with ACCA's *Code of Ethics and Conduct*, which TWO of the following factors must be considered before the internal audit engagement should be accepted?

☐ Whether the external audit team have the expertise to carry out the internal audit work.

☐ If the assignments will relate to the internal controls over financial reporting.

☐ If management will accept responsibility for implementing appropriate recommendations.

☐ The probable timescale for the outsourcing of the internal audit function.

4   Following management's request for information regarding the different roles of internal and external audit, you have collated a list of key characteristics.

Match the following characteristics to the appropriate auditor.

Characteristic	Type of auditor
1	Internal auditor
2	Internal auditor
3	External auditor
4	External auditor

5   If the internal and external audit assignments are accepted, what safeguards, if any, are needed in relation to the basis for the fee?

☐   As long as the total fee received from Maldini Co is less than 15% of the firm's total fee income, no safeguards are needed.

☐   The client should be informed that only the internal audit fee can be based on profit after tax.

☐   The fees should be based on Maldini Co's profit before tax.

☐   No safeguards can be applied and this basis for fee determination should be rejected.

The following scenario relates to Questions 6–10.

It is 1 July 20X5. Balotelli Co operates a number of hotels providing accommodation, leisure facilities and restaurants. You are an audit senior of Mario & Co and are currently conducting the audit of Balotelli Co for the year ended 31 December 20X4. During the course of the audit a number of events and issues have been brought to your attention:

Non-current assets

Balotelli Co incurred significant capital expenditure during the year updating the leisure facilities at several of the company's hotels. Depreciation is charged monthly on all assets on a straight line (SL) basis and it is company policy to charge a full month's depreciation in the month of acquisition and none in the month of disposal. The audit team has obtained the following extract of the non-current assets register detailing some of the new leisure equipment acquired during the year:

Date	Description	Original cost	Depreciation policy	Accumulated depreciation	Charge for the year	Carrying value
		$		$	$	$
01/05/X4	15 treadmills	18,000	36 months SL	0	4,000	14,000
15/05/X4	20 exercise bikes	17,000	3 years SL	0	5,667	11,333
17/08/X4	15 rowing machines	9,750	36 months SL	0	2,167	7,583
19/08/X4	10 cross trainers	11,000	36 months SL	0	1,528	9,472
		55,750		0	13,362	42,388

In order to verify the depreciation charge for the year the audit team has been asked to recalculate a sample of the depreciation charges. The audit team has also been asked to carry out detailed testing on the valuation of non-current assets.

Food poisoning – litigation

Balotelli Co's directors received correspondence in November 20X4 from a group of customers who attended a wedding at one of the company's hotels. They have alleged that they suffered severe food poisoning from food eaten at the hotel and are claiming substantial damages. Management has stated that, based on discussions with their lawyers, the claim is unlikely to be successful.

Trade receivables circularisation

The audit team has obtained the following results from the receivables circularisation:

Customer	Balance per sales ledger $	Balance per customer confirmation $	Comment
Willow Co	42,500	42,500	
Cedar Co	35,000	25,000	Invoice raised 28 December 20X4
Maple Co	60,000	45,000	Payment made 30 December 20X4
Laurel Co	55,000	55,000	A balance of $20,000 is currently being disputed by Laurel Co

Trade receivables

Balotelli Co's trade receivables have historically been low as most customers are required to pay in advance or at the time of visiting the hotel. However, during the year a number of companies opened corporate accounts which are payable monthly in arrears. As such, the trade receivables balance has risen significantly and is now a material balance.

6   Which of the following correctly calculates the depreciation expense for the new assets for the year ended 31 December 20X4 and explains the resultant impact on non-current assets?

☐   Depreciation should be $10,660, assets are understated

☐   Depreciation should be $18,583, assets are understated

☐   Depreciation should be $9,111, assets are overstated

☐   Depreciation should be $12,549, assets are overstated

---

7   Which **FOUR** of the following audit procedures are appropriate to test the **VALUATION** assertion for non-current assets?

☐   Review board minutes for evidence of disposals during the year and verify that these are appropriately reflected in the non-current assets register

☐   Agree a sample of additions included in the non-current asset register to purchase invoice and cash book

☐   Review the repairs and maintenance expense account for evidence of items of a capital nature

☐   Recalculate the depreciation charge for a sample of assets ensuring that it is being applied consistently and in accordance with IAS 16 *Property, Plant and Equipment*

☐   Review physical condition of non-current assets for any signs of damage

☐   Ensure disposals are correctly accounted for and recalculate gain/loss on disposal

---

8   Which of the following audit procedures would provide the auditor with the **MOST** reliable audit evidence regarding the likely outcome of the litigation?

☐   Request a written representation from management supporting their assertion that the claim will not be successful

☐   Send an enquiry letter to the lawyers of Balotelli to obtain their view as to the probability of the claim being successful

☐   Review the correspondence from the customers claiming food poisoning to assess whether Balotelli has a present obligation as a result of a past event

☐   Review board minutes to understand why the directors believe that the claim will not be successful

9   Which **TWO** of the following are benefits of carrying out a trade receivables circularisation?

☐   It provides evidence from an independent external source.

☐   It provides sufficient appropriate audit evidence over all relevant balance assertions.

☐   It improves audit efficiency as all customers are required to respond.

☐   It improves the reliability of audit evidence as the process is under the control of the auditor.

10   The audit team has been asked to assess whether any additional audit work is required.

Based on the results of the circularisation, match each customer to the appropriate audit procedure.

Customer	Audit procedure
Willow Co	Agree to post-year end cash book and bank statement
Cedar Co	Discuss with management and consider whether amount should be included in allowance for receivables
Maple Co	No further audit procedures required
Laurel Co	Agree to pre year end invoice

The following scenario relates to Questions 11–15.

It is 1 July 20X5. Cannavaro.com is a website design company whose year end was 31 December 20X4. The audit is almost complete and the financial statements are due to be signed shortly. Profit before tax for the year is $3.8 million and revenue is $11.2 million.

Form and content of auditor's report

The company has only required an audit for the last two years and the board of directors has asked your firm to provide more detail in relation to the form and content of the auditor's report. In particular they have queried why the following elements are included:

(1)   Date of report

(2)   Addressee

(3)   Auditor's responsibilities

(4)   Opinion paragraph

Balance due from Pirlo Co

During the audit it has come to light that a key customer, Pirlo Co, with a receivables balance at the year end of $285,000, has just notified Cannavaro.com that it is experiencing cash flow difficulties and is unable to make any payments for the foreseeable future. The finance director of Cannavaro.com has notified the audit team that he will write this balance off as an irrecoverable debt in the 20X5 financial statements.

Audit work

The audit partner has asked you to perform the following work in respect of the receivables balance due from Pirlo Co:

(1)   Make an initial assessment of the materiality of the issue and consider the overall impact on the financial statements

(2)   Perform additional procedures in order to conclude on whether the financial statements require adjustment

11   Match the following elements of the unmodified auditor's report, to the correct explanation for its inclusion.

Element of auditor's report	Reason for inclusion
1	Explains that the financial statements are presented fairly
2	Demonstrates the point at which sufficient appropriate evidence has been obtained
3	Clarifies who may rely on the opinion included in the report
4	Explains the role and remit of the audit

12   The audit assistant assigned to the audit of Cannavaro.com wants a better understanding of the effect subsequent events have on the audit and has made the following statements.

Identify, by clicking on the relevant box in the table below, whether each of the following statements is true or false.

All material subsequent events require the numbers in the financial statements to be adjusted.	TRUE	FALSE
A non-adjusting event is a subsequent event for which **no** amendments to the current year financial statements are required.	TRUE	FALSE
The auditor's responsibilities for subsequent events which occur prior to the audit report being signed are different from their responsibilities after the auditor's report has been issued.	TRUE	FALSE
The auditor should request a written representation confirming that all relevant subsequent events have been disclosed.	TRUE	FALSE

13   Which of the following correctly summarises the effect of the outstanding balance with Pirlo Co?

Option	Material	Impact on accounts
A	No	Revenue is overstated
B	No	Gross profit is understated
C	Yes	Profit is overstated
D	Yes	The going concern basis is in doubt

☐   Option A

☐   Option B

☐   Option C

☐   Option D

---

14   Which **TWO** of the following audit procedures should be performed to form a conclusion as to whether the financial statements require amendment?

☐   Discuss with management the reasons for not amending the financial statements

☐   Review the cash book post year end for receipts from Pirlo Co

☐   Send a request to Pirlo Co to confirm the outstanding balance

☐   Agree the outstanding balance to invoices and sales orders

---

15   The finance director has asked you to outline the appropriate audit opinions which will be provided depending on whether the company decides to amend or not amend the 20X5 financial statements for the issue identified regarding the recoverability of the balance with Pirlo Co.

Complete the following sentences by dragging and dropping the appropriate audit opinions.

If the 20X4 financial statements are not amended, our opinion will be [   ]

If the appropriate adjustment is made to the financial statements, our opinion will be [   ].

Audit opinion	
Adverse	Disclaimer
Unmodified with emphasis of matter paragraph	Qualified 'except for'
Unmodified	

(Total = 30 marks)

Section B – ALL THREE questions are compulsory and MUST be attempted

Question 16

Milla Cola Co (Milla) manufactures fizzy drinks such as cola and lemonade as well as other soft drinks and its year end is 30 September 20X5. It is 1 July 20X5. You are an audit manager of Totti & Co and are currently planning the audit of Milla. You attended the planning meeting with the audit engagement partner and finance director last week and the minutes from the meeting are shown below. You are reviewing these as part of the process of preparing the audit strategy document.

Minutes of planning meeting for Milla

Milla's trading results have been strong this year and the company is forecasting revenue of $85 million, which is an increase from the previous year. The company has invested significantly in the cola and fizzy drinks production process at the factory. This resulted in expenditure of $5 million on updating, repairing and replacing a significant amount of the machinery used in the production process.

As the level of production has increased, the company has expanded the number of warehouses it uses to store inventory. It now utilises 15 warehouses; some are owned by Milla and some are rented from third parties. There will be inventory counts taking place at all 15 of these sites at the year end.

A new accounting general ledger has been introduced at the beginning of the year, with the old and new systems being run in parallel for a period of two months. In addition, Milla has incurred expenditure of $4.5 million on developing a new brand of fizzy soft drinks. The company started this process in July 20X4 and is close to launching its new product into the marketplace.

As a result of the increase in revenue, Milla has recently recruited a new credit controller to chase outstanding receivables. The finance director thinks it is not necessary to continue to maintain an allowance for receivables and so has released the opening allowance of $1.5 million.

The finance director stated that there was a problem in April in the mixing of raw materials within the production process which resulted in a large batch of cola products tasting different. A number of these products were sold; however, due to complaints by customers about the flavour, no further sales of these goods have been made. No adjustment has been made to the valuation of the damaged inventory, which will still be held at cost of $1 million at the year end.

As in previous years, the management of Milla is due to be paid a significant annual bonus based on the value of year-end total assets.

Required

(a)   Explain audit risk and the components of audit risk.   **(5 marks)**

(b)   Using the minutes provided, identify and describe **SEVEN** audit risks, and explain the auditor's response to each risk, in planning the audit of Milla.

        Note. Prepare your answer using two columns headed Audit risk and Auditor's response respectively.   **(14 marks)**

(c)   Identify the main areas, other than audit risks, which should be included within the audit strategy document for Milla; and for each area provide an example relevant to the audit.
                                                                                                                         (4 marks)

The finance director has requested that the deadline for the 20X6 audit be shortened by a month and has asked the audit engagement partner to consider if this will be possible. The partner has suggested that in order to meet this new tighter deadline the firm may carry out both an interim and a final audit for the audit of Milla to 30 September 20X6.

Required

(d)   Explain the difference between an interim and a final audit.   (3 marks)

(e)   Explain the procedures which are likely to be performed during an interim audit of Milla and the impact which it would have on the final audit.   (4 marks)

(Total = 30 marks)

Question 17

It is 1 July 20X5. Baggio International Co (Baggio) is a manufacturer of electrical equipment. It has factories across the country and its customer base includes retailers as well as individuals, to whom direct sales are made through its website. The company's year-end is 30 September 20X5. You are an audit supervisor of Suarez & Co and are currently reviewing documentation of Baggio's internal control in preparation for the interim audit.

Baggio's website allows individuals to order goods directly, and full payment is taken in advance. Currently the website is not integrated into the inventory system and inventory levels are not checked at the time when orders are placed.

Inventory is valued at the lower of cost and net realisable value.

Goods are dispatched via local couriers; however, they do not always record customer signatures as proof that the customer has received the goods. Over the past 12 months there have been customer complaints about the delay between sales orders and receipt of goods. Baggio has investigated these and found that, in each case, the sales order had been entered into the sales system correctly but was not forwarded to the dispatch department for fulfilling.

Baggio's retail customers undergo credit checks prior to being accepted and credit limits are set accordingly by sales ledger clerks. These customers place their orders through one of the sales team, who decides on sales discount levels.

Raw materials used in the manufacturing process are purchased from a wide range of suppliers. As a result of staff changes in the purchase ledger department, supplier statement reconciliations are no longer performed. Additionally, changes to supplier details in the purchase ledger master file can be undertaken by purchase ledger clerks as well as supervisors.

In the past six months, Baggio has changed part of its manufacturing process and as a result some new equipment has been purchased; however, there are considerable levels of plant and equipment which are now surplus to requirement. Purchase requisitions for all new equipment have been authorised by production supervisors and little has been done to reduce the surplus of old equipment.

Required

(a)   In respect of the internal control of Baggio International Co:

   (i)   Identify and explain **SIX** deficiencies;

   (ii)   Recommend a control to address each of these deficiencies; and

   (iii) Describe a test of control Suarez & Co would perform to assess whether each of these controls, if implemented, is operating effectively.

   Note. Prepare your answer using three columns headed Control deficiency, Control recommendation and Test of control respectively. The total marks will be split equally between each part.   (18 marks)

(b)   Describe substantive procedures Suarez & Co should perform at the year end to confirm plant and equipment additions.   (2 marks)

(Total = 20 marks)

Question 18

It is 1 July 20X5. Vieri Motor Cars Co (Vieri) manufactures a range of motor cars and its year end is 31 March 20X5. You are the audit supervisor of Rossi & Co and are currently preparing the audit programmes for the year-end audit of Vieri. You have had a meeting with your audit manager and he has notified you of the following issues identified during the audit risk assessment process:

Land and buildings

Vieri has a policy of revaluing land and buildings; this is undertaken on a rolling basis over a five-year period. During the year Vieri requested an external independent valuer to revalue a number of properties, including a warehouse purchased in October 20X4. Depreciation is charged on a pro rata basis.

Work in progress

Vieri undertakes continuous production of cars, 24 hours a day, 7 days a week. An inventory count is to be undertaken at the year end and Rossi & Co will attend. You are responsible for the audit of work in progress (WIP) and will be part of the team attending the count as well as the final audit. WIP constitutes the partly assembled cars at the year end and this balance is likely to be material. Vieri values WIP according to percentage of completion, and standard costs are then applied to these percentages.

Required

(a) Explain the factors Rossi & Co should consider when placing reliance on the work of the independent valuer.
(5 marks)

(b) Describe the substantive procedures the auditor should perform to obtain sufficient and appropriate audit evidence in relation to the revaluation of land and buildings and the recently purchased warehouse.
(6 marks)

(c) Describe the substantive procedures the auditor should perform to obtain sufficient and appropriate audit evidence in relation to the valuation of work in progress.
(4 marks)

During the audit, the team has identified an error in the valuation of work in progress, as a number of the assumptions contain out of date information. The directors of Vieri have indicated that they do not wish to amend the financial statements.

Required

(d) Explain the steps Rossi & Co should now take and the impact on the auditor's report in relation to the directors' refusal to amend the financial statements.
(5 marks)

(Total = 20 marks)

Answers

DO NOT TURN THIS PAGE UNTIL YOU HAVE
COMPLETED THE MOCK EXAM

Plan of attack

If this were the real Audit and Assurance exam and you had been told to turn over and begin, what would be going through your mind?

An important thing to say (while there is still time) is that it is vital to have a good breadth of knowledge of the syllabus because all the questions are compulsory. However, don't panic. Below we provide guidance on how to approach the exam.

Looking through the exam

Section A has three objective test cases, each with five questions. This is the section of the exam where the examining team can test knowledge across the breadth of the syllabus. Make sure you read these cases and questions carefully. The distractors are designed to present plausible, but incorrect, answers. Don't let them mislead you. If you really have no idea – guess. You may even be right.

Section B has three longer questions:

- **Question 16** is a 30-mark question focused on the planning stage, covering audit risk and the audit strategy document, with an unrelated coda on interim audits. Don't panic – take your time to read the scenario and what you are asked to do.

- **Question 17** is a 20-mark internal controls question. In part (a) it is crucial that you relate your answer to the scenario.

- **Question 18** is a 20-mark question dealing with a number of issues: an independent valuer, revaluations, work in progress, and auditor reporting.

Allocating your time

BPP's advice is to always allocate your time **according to the marks for the question**. However, **use common sense**. If you're doing a question but haven't a clue how to do part (b), you might be better off reallocating your time and getting more marks on another question, where you can add something you didn't have time for earlier on. Make sure you leave time to recheck the OTs and make sure you have answered them all.

Forget about it

And don't worry if you found the exam difficult. More than likely other candidates will too. If this were the real thing you would need to forget the exam the minute you left the exam hall and think about the next one. Or, if it is the last one, celebrate!

Section A

1 The correct answer is:

Facts	Category of threat
Length of time the audit engagement partner has been in position	Familiarity
Maldini Co's request for advice regarding internal audit	No threat
Potential holding of shares by audit partner's son	Self-interest
Possible provision of internal audit services	Self-review
Basis of fee	Self-interest

Fact 1 – Partner has been in role for eight years, this contravenes the Code and represents a familiarity threat.

Fact 2 – Providing information on internal audit is not a threat to independence.

Fact 3 – Partner's son holding shares represents a self-interest threat as a close family member of the partner holds a financial interest.

Fact 4 – Providing internal audit services raises a self-review threat as it is likely that the audit team will be looking to place reliance on the internal control system reviewed by internal audit.

Fact 5 – This represents fees on a contingent basis and raises a self-interest threat as the audit firm's fee will rise if the company's profit after tax increases.

2 The correct answer is: The audit partner should be removed from the audit team.

If the engagement partner's son accepts the role and obtains shares in the company it would constitute a self-interest threat but, as the partner has already exceeded the seven year relationship rule, in line with ACCA's *Code of Ethics and Conduct*, the partner should be rotated off the audit irrespective of the decision made by her son.

As Maldini Co is a listed company an engagement quality control reviewer should already be in place in line with ISA 220.

Consulting a third party on key audit judgments would be a potential safeguard in respect of overdependence on fees but would not be adequate in the circumstances described.

It is unlikely that the firm needs to resign from the audit (due to the stated circumstances) as the threat to objectivity can be mitigated.

3 The correct answer is:

If the assignments will relate to the internal controls over financial reporting.

If management will accept responsibility for implementing appropriate recommendations.

Statement 1 is inappropriate as the external and internal audit team should be separate and therefore consideration of the skills of the external audit team is not appropriate in the circumstances.

Statement 4 does not apply because the timescale of the work is not relevant to the consideration of the threats to objectivity.

Statements 2 and 3 are valid considerations – as per ACCA's *Code of Ethics and Conduct*, providing internal audit services can result in the audit firm assuming a management role. To mitigate this, it is appropriate for the firm to assess whether management will take responsibility for implementing recommendations (ACCA *Code of Ethics and Conduct*: para. 605.4). Further, for a listed company the Code prohibits the provision of internal audit services which review a significant proportion of the internal controls over financial reporting as these may be relied upon by the external audit team and the self-review threat is too great (ACCA *Code of Ethics and Conduct*: para. R605.5).

4   The correct answer is:

Characteristic		Type of auditor
(1)	Appointed by audit committee	Internal auditor
(2)	Reports are publicly available to shareholders	External auditor
(3)	Review effectiveness of internal controls to improve operations	Internal auditor
(4)	Express an opinion on the truth and fairness of the financial statements	External auditor

Internal audit is appointed by the audit committee (external audit usually by the shareholders) and it is the role of internal audit to review the effectiveness and efficiency of internal controls to improve operations. External audit looks at the operating effectiveness of internal controls on which they may rely for audit evidence and a by-product may be to comment on any deficiencies they have found but this is not a key function of the role.

Therefore statements 1 and 3 relate to internal audit.

The external auditor's report is publicly available to the shareholders of the company (internal audit reports are addressed to management/those charged with governance) and the external auditor provides an opinion on the truth and fairness of the financial statements.

Therefore statements 2 and 4 relate to external audit.

5   The correct answer is: No safeguards can be applied and this basis for fee determination should be rejected.

The proposal in relation to the fees is a contingent fee basis which is expressly prohibited by ACCA's *Code of Ethics and Conduct* and therefore the only viable option here is to reject the fee basis (ACCA *Code of Ethics and Conduct*: para. R410.10-11).

6   The correct answer is: Depreciation should be $10,660, assets are understated

Depreciation should be calculated as:

Treadmills/exercise bikes = (18,000 + 17,000)/36 × 8 months =	7,778
Rowing machines/cross trainers = (9,750 + 11,000)/36 × 5 months =	2,882
Total	10,660

Therefore depreciation should be $10,660 and assets are currently understated as too much depreciation has currently been charged.

The second option is based on depreciation being applied for a full year instead of for the relevant months.

The third option is based on depreciation not being charged in the month of acquisition (ie seven and four months).

The fourth option is based on depreciation for the exercise bikes being divided by the three years instead of allocated on a monthly basis.

7   The correct answer is:

Agree a sample of additions included in the non-current asset register to purchase invoice and cash book

Recalculate the depreciation charge for a sample of assets ensuring that it is being applied consistently and in accordance with IAS 16 *Property, Plant and Equipment*

Review physical condition of non-current assets for any signs of damage

Ensure disposals are correctly accounted for and recalculate gain/loss on disposal

The review of board minutes for evidence of disposals during the year and verify that these are appropriately reflected in the non-current assets register is a test for existence and reviewing the repairs and maintenance expense account for evidence of items of a capital nature is a test for completeness.

All other tests are relevant for valuation.

8   The correct answer is: Send an enquiry letter to the lawyers of Balotelli to obtain their view as to the probability of the claim being successful

While all procedures would be valid in the circumstances, only the written confirmation from the company's lawyers would allow the auditor to obtain an expert, third-party confirmation on the likelihood of the case being successful. This would provide the auditor with the most reliable evidence in the circumstances.

9   The correct answer is:

It provides evidence from an independent external source.

It improves the reliability of audit evidence as the process is under the control of the auditor.

As per ISA 505 *External Confirmations*, the evidence obtained from the trade receivables circularisation should be reliable as it is from an external source and the risk of management bias and influence is restricted due to the process being under the control of the auditor (ISA 505).

Customers are not obliged to answer and often circularisations have a very low response rate. A circularisation will not provide evidence over the valuation assertion for receivables and therefore the second and third statements are drawbacks of a circularisation.

10   The correct answer is:

Customer	Audit procedure
Willow Co	No further audit procedures required
Cedar Co	Agree to pre year end invoice
Maple Co	Agree to post-year end cash book and bank statement
Laurel Co	Discuss with management and consider whether amount should be included in allowance for receivables

Willow Co – The external confirmation has confirmed the balance and no further work is required.

Cedar Co – The difference represents an invoice in transit and therefore should be confirmed to a pre year end invoice to verify that it is a legitimate timing difference.

Maple Co – The difference represents a payment in transit and should be agreed to post year end payment to confirm that it is a legitimate timing difference.

Laurel Co – The customer is disputing the balance and therefore the need for an allowance against the balance should be assessed.

11   The correct answer is:

Element of auditor's report	Reason for inclusion
Date of report	Demonstrates the point at which sufficient appropriate evidence has been obtained
Addressee	Clarifies who may rely on the opinion included in the report
Auditor's responsibilities	Explains the role and remit of the audit
Opinion paragraph	Explains that the financial statements are presented fairly

Date of report – The auditor's report shall be dated no earlier than the date on which the auditor has obtained sufficient appropriate audit evidence on which to base the auditor's opinion on the financial statements. The date of the audit report is important in the case of subsequent events which impact the financial statements.

Addressee – Sets out who the report is addressed to (usually the shareholders) and is there to clarify who can place reliance on the audit opinion.

Auditor's responsibilities – This paragraph sets out that the auditor is required to express an opinion on the financial statements and seeks to explain the difference between the role of the auditor and those charged with governance. Thus this paragraph sets out the role and remit of the auditor.

Opinion paragraph – This paragraph sets out the auditor's conclusion on the financial statements. In an unmodified report this takes the form of the auditor confirming that the financial statements present a true and fair view or are presented fairly.

12   The correct answer is:

All material subsequent events require the numbers in the financial statements to be adjusted.		False
A non-adjusting event is a subsequent event for which **no** amendments to the current year financial statements are required.		False
The auditor's responsibilities for subsequent events which occur prior to the audit report being signed are different from their responsibilities after the auditor's report has been issued.	True	
The auditor should request a written representation confirming that all relevant subsequent events have been disclosed.	True	

Statement 1 is false as not all subsequent events will require an adjustment to the numbers within the financial statements. IAS 10 *Events After the Reporting Period* makes a distinction between an adjusting and non-adjusting event. Only material adjusting events would require an amendment to the figures within the financial statements (IAS 10).

Statement 2 is false as, while a non-adjusting event would not require a change to the numbers within the financial statements, IAS 10 may require a disclosure to be made. If the non-adjusting event is material, non-disclosure could still result in a modification to the audit report.

Statement 3 is true as the auditor is required to carry out procedures up to the date of the audit report to gain sufficient appropriate audit evidence that all relevant subsequent events have been identified and dealt with appropriately. After the auditor's report is issued, the auditor does not need to actively look for subsequent events but is only required to respond to subsequent events which they become aware of.

Statement 4 is true as ISA 560 *Subsequent Events* requires the auditor to obtain written confirmation from management/those charged with governance that all subsequent events have been identified and dealt with in accordance with the appropriate reporting framework (ISA 560).

13   The correct answer is:

Option	Material	Impact on accounts
C	Yes	Profit is overstated

The outstanding balance with Pirlo Co is likely to be irrecoverable as the customer is experiencing financial difficulties.

The balance is material at 7.4% of profit before tax and 2.5% of revenue.

Currently profit and assets are overstated by $285,000. Therefore the correct option is C.

14   The correct answer is:

Discuss with management the reasons for not amending the financial statements

Review the cash book post year end for receipts from Pirlo Co

Writing to the customer/agreeing to invoices, while valid procedures during the audit to verify the existence of an outstanding balance, would not allow the auditor to assess the recoverability of the balance which is the key issue in determining whether an adjustment is required.

Post year end cash testing is the best way for the auditor to assess if the balance is recoverable wholly or in part and therefore the cash book should be reviewed for any receipts which will change the assessment of the debt after the year end. The issue should also be discussed with management to understand their reasons for not wanting to amend the financial statements as this may be due to a change in circumstances.

15   The correct answer is: If the 20X4 financial statements are not amended, our opinion will be **qualified on the grounds of material misstatement.**

If the appropriate adjustment is made to the financial statements, our opinion will be **unmodified.**

The debt with Pirlo Co should be provided for and is material to the financial statements at 7.4% of profit before tax and 2.5% of revenue. This represents a material misstatement which is material but not pervasive. As such, if no adjustment is made the auditor will be required to provide a qualified 'except for' opinion. If the required change is made, then no material misstatement exists and therefore the auditor will be able to issue an unmodified opinion.

Section B

Question 16

		Marks
(a)	**Component of audit risk**	
	Explanation of audit risk	2
	Explanation of components of audit risk: Inherent, control and detection risk	<u>3</u>
		5
(b)	**Audit risk and auditor's response** (only 7 risks required)	
	$5 million expenditure on production process	2
	Inventory counts at 15 warehouses at year end	2
	Treatment of owned v third-party warehouses	2
	New general ledger system introduced at the beginning of the year	2
	Release of opening provision for allowance for receivables	2
	Research and development expenditure	2
	Damaged inventory	2
	Sales returns	2
	Management bonus based on asset values	<u>2</u>
	Max 7 issues, 2 marks each	14
(c)	**Audit strategy document**	
	Main characteristics of the audit	1
	Reporting objectives of the audit and nature of communications required	1
	Factors which are significant in directing the audit team's efforts	1
	Results of preliminary engagement activities and whether knowledge gained on other engagements is relevant	1
	Nature, timing and extent of resources necessary to perform the audit	<u>1</u>
	Restricted to	4
(d)	**Difference between interim and final audit**	
	Interim audit	2
	Final audit	<u>2</u>
	Restricted to	3
(e)	**Procedures/impact of interim audit on final audit**	
	Example procedures	3
	Impact on final audit	<u>3</u>
	Restricted to	<u>4</u>
Total marks		<u>30</u>

(a)   **Audit risk and its components**

Audit risk is the risk that the auditor expresses an inappropriate audit opinion when the financial statements are materially misstated. Audit risk is a function of two main components being the risks of material misstatement and detection risk (ISA 200). Risk of material misstatement is made up of two components, inherent risk and control risk.

Inherent risk is the susceptibility of an assertion about a class of transaction, account balance or disclosure to a misstatement which could be material, either individually or when aggregated with other misstatements, before consideration of any related controls (ISA 200).

Control risk is the risk that a misstatement which could occur in an assertion about a class of transaction, account balance or disclosure and which could be material, either individually or when aggregated with other misstatements, will not be prevented, or detected and corrected, on a timely basis by the entity's internal control (ISA 200).

Detection risk is the risk that the procedures performed by the auditor to reduce audit risk to an acceptably low level will not detect a misstatement which exists and which could be material, either individually or when aggregated with other misstatements. Detection risk is affected by sampling and non-sampling risk (ISA 200).

(b) **Audit risk and auditor's response**

Audit risk	Auditor's response
Milla has incurred $5m on updating, repairing and replacing a significant amount of the production process machinery. If this expenditure is of a capital nature, it should be capitalised as part of property, plant and equipment (PPE) in line with IAS 16 *Property, Plant and Equipment*. However, if it relates more to repairs, then it should be expensed to the statement of profit or loss If the expenditure is not correctly classified, profit and PPE could be under- or overstated.	The auditor should review a breakdown of these costs to ascertain the split of capital and revenue expenditure, and further testing should be undertaken to ensure that the classification in the financial statements is correct.
At the year end there will be inventory counts undertaken in all 15 warehouses. It is unlikely that the auditor will be able to attend all 15 inventory counts and therefore they need to ensure that they obtain sufficient appropriate audit evidence over the inventory counting controls, and completeness and existence of inventory for any warehouses not visited.	The auditor should assess which of the inventory sites they will attend the counts for. This will be any with material inventory or which have a history of significant errors. For those not visited, the auditor will need to review the level of exceptions noted during the count and discuss with management any issues which arose during the count.
Inventory is stored within 15 warehouses; some are owned by Milla and some rented from third parties. Only warehouses owned by Milla should be included within PPE. There is a risk of overstatement of PPE and understatement of rental expenses if Milla has capitalised all 15 warehouses.	The auditor should review supporting documentation for all warehouses included within PPE to confirm ownership by Milla and to ensure non-current assets are not overstated.
A new accounting general ledger system has been introduced at the beginning of the year and the old system was run in parallel for two months. There is a risk of opening balances being misstated and loss of data if they have not been transferred from the old system correctly. In addition, the new accounting general ledger system will require documenting and the controls over this will need to be tested.	The auditor should undertake detailed testing to confirm that all opening balances have been correctly recorded in the new accounting general ledger system. They should document and test the new system. They should review any management reports run comparing the old and new system during the parallel run to identify any issues with the processing of accounting information.

Audit risk	Auditor's response
Milla has incurred expenditure of $4.5 million on developing a new brand of fizzy drink. This expenditure is research and development under IAS 38 *Intangible Assets*. The standard requires research costs to be expensed and development costs to be capitalised as an intangible asset (IAS 38). If Milla has incorrectly classified research costs as development expenditure, there is a risk the intangible asset could be overstated and expenses understated.	Obtain a breakdown of the expenditure and undertake testing to determine whether the costs relate to the research or development stage. Discuss the accounting treatment with the finance director and ensure it is in accordance with IAS 38.
The finance director of Milla has decided to release the opening balance of $1.5 million for allowance for receivables as he feels it is unnecessary. There is a risk that receivables will be overvalued, as despite having a credit controller, some balances will be irrecoverable and so will be overstated if not provided against. In addition, due to the damaged inventory there is an increased risk of customers refusing to make payments in full.	Extended post year end cash receipts testing and a review of the aged receivables ledger to be performed to assess valuation and the need for an allowance for receivables. Discuss with the director the rationale for releasing the $1.5m opening allowance for receivables.
A large batch of cola products has been damaged in the production process and will be in inventory at the year end. No adjustment has been made by management. The valuation of inventory as per IAS 2 *Inventories* should be at the lower of cost and net realisable value (IAS 2). Hence it is likely that this inventory is overvalued.	Detailed cost and net realisable value testing to be performed to assess how much the inventory requires writing down by.
Due to the damaged cola products, a number of customers have complained. It is likely that for any of the damaged goods sold, Milla will need to refund these customers. Revenue is possibly overstated if the sales returns are not completely and accurately recorded.	Review the breakdown of sales of damaged goods, and ensure that they have been accurately removed from revenue.
The management of Milla receives a significant annual bonus based on the value of year-end total assets. There is a risk that management might feel under pressure to overstate the value of assets through the judgements taken or through the use of releasing provisions.	Throughout the audit, the team will need to be alert to this risk. They will need to maintain professional scepticism and carefully review judgemental decisions and compare treatment against prior years.

(c)   **Audit strategy document**

The audit strategy sets out the scope, timing and direction of the audit and helps the development of the audit plan (ISA 300). It should consider the following main areas:

It should identify the main characteristics of the engagement which define its scope. For Milla it should consider the following:

- Whether the financial information to be audited has been prepared in accordance with IFRS

- To what extent audit evidence obtained in previous audits for Milla will be utilised

- Whether computer-assisted audit techniques will be used and the effect of IT on audit procedures

- The availability of key personnel at Milla

It should ascertain the reporting objectives of the engagement to plan the timing of the audit and the nature of the communications required, such as (ISA 300):

- The audit timetable for reporting and whether there will be an interim as well as final audit

- Organisation of meetings with Milla's management to discuss any audit issues arising

- Location of the 15 inventory counts

- Any discussions with management regarding the reports to be issued

- The timings of the audit team meetings and review of work performed

- If there are any expected communications with third parties

The strategy should consider the factors which, in the auditor's professional judgement, are significant in directing Milla's audit team's efforts, such as:

- The determination of materiality for the audit

- The need to maintain a questioning mind and to exercise professional scepticism in gathering and evaluating audit evidence

It should consider the results of preliminary audit planning activities and, where applicable, whether knowledge gained on other engagements for Milla is relevant, such as:

- Results of previous audits and the results of any tests over the effectiveness of internal controls

- Evidence of management's commitment to the design, implementation and maintenance of sound internal control

- Volume of transactions, which may determine whether it is more efficient for the audit team to rely on internal control

- Significant business developments affecting Milla, such as the change in the accounting system and the significant expenditure on an overhaul of the factory

The audit strategy should ascertain the nature, timing and extent of resources necessary to perform the audit, such as:

- The selection of the audit team with experience of this type of industry

- Assignment of audit work to the team members

- Setting the audit budget

Note. The answer is longer than required for four marks but represents a teaching aid.

(d) **Differences between an interim and a final audit**

Interim audit

The interim audit is that part of the audit which takes place before the year end. The auditor uses the interim audit to carry out procedures which would be difficult to perform at the year end because of time pressure. There is no requirement to undertake an interim audit; factors to consider when deciding upon whether to have one include the size and complexity of the company along with the effectiveness of internal controls.

Final audit

The final audit will take place after the year end and concludes with the auditor forming and expressing an opinion on the financial statements for the whole year subject to audit. It is important to note that the final opinion takes account of conclusions formed at both the interim and final audit.

(e)   Procedures which could be undertaken during the interim audit include:

- Review and updating of the documentation of accounting systems at Milla

- Discussions with management on the recent growth and any other changes within the business which have occurred during the year to date at Milla to update the auditor's understanding of the company

- Assessment of risks which will impact the final audit of Milla

- Undertake tests of controls on Milla's key transaction cycles of sales, purchases and inventory, and credit control

- Perform substantive procedures on profit and loss transactions for the year to date and any other completed material transactions

Impact of interim audit on final audit

If an interim audit is undertaken at Milla, then it will have an impact on the final audit and the extent of work undertaken after the year end. First, as some testing has already been undertaken, there will be less work to be performed at the final audit, which may result in a shorter audit and audited financial statements possibly being available earlier. The outcome of the controls testing undertaken during the interim audit will impact the level of substantive testing to be undertaken. If the controls tested have proven to be operating effectively, then the auditor may be able to reduce the level of detailed substantive testing required as they will be able to place reliance on the controls. In addition, if substantive procedures were undertaken at the interim audit, then only the period from the interim audit to the year end will require testing.

Question 17

Marking scheme

		Marks
(a)	**Control deficiencies, recommendations and tests of controls**	
	Website not integrated into inventory system	3
	Customer signatures	3
	Unfulfilled sales orders	3
	Customer credit limits	3
	Sales discounts	3
	Supplier statement reconciliations	3
	Purchase ledger master file	3
	Surplus plant and equipment	3
	Authorisation of capital expenditure	3
	Max 6 issues, 3 marks each	18

(b)   **Substantive procedures for PPE**

Cast list of additions and agree to non-current asset register	1
Vouch cost to recent supplier invoice	1
Agree addition to a supplier invoice in the name of Baggio to confirm rights and obligations	1
Review additions and confirm capital expenditure items rather than repairs and maintenance	1
Review board minutes to ensure authorised by the board	1
Physically verify them on the factory floor to confirm existence	1
Other	
Restricted to	—
Total marks	2 / 20

(a)   Baggio International's (Baggio) internal control

Deficiency (i)	Control recommendations (ii)	Test of control (iii)
Currently the website is not integrated into the inventory system. This can result in Baggio accepting customer orders when they do not have the goods in inventory. This can cause them to lose sales and customer goodwill. For goods dispatched by local couriers, customer signatures are not always obtained. This can lead to customers falsely claiming that they have not received their goods. Baggio would not be able to prove that they had in fact dispatched the goods and may result in goods being dispatched twice.	The website should be updated to include an interface into the inventory system; this should check inventory levels and only process orders if adequate inventory is held. If inventory is out of stock, this should appear on the website with an approximate waiting time. Baggio should remind all local couriers that customer signatures must be obtained as proof of delivery and payment will not be made for any dispatches with missing signatures.	Test data could be used to attempt to process orders via the website for items which are not currently held in inventory. The orders should be flagged as being out of stock and indicate an approximate waiting time. Select a sample of dispatches by couriers and ask Baggio for proof of delivery by viewing customer signatures.
There have been a number of situations where the sales orders have not been fulfilled in a timely manner. This can lead to a loss of customer goodwill and if it persists will damage the reputation of Baggio as a reliable supplier.	Once goods are dispatched, they should be matched to sales orders and flagged as fulfilled. The system should automatically flag any outstanding sales orders past a predetermined period, such as five days. This report should be reviewed by a responsible official.	Review the report of outstanding sales orders. If significant, discuss with a responsible official to understand why there is still a significant time period between sales order and dispatch date. Select a sample of sales orders and compare the date of order to the goods dispatch date to ascertain whether this is within the acceptable predetermined period.

Deficiency (i)	Control recommendations (ii)	Test of control (iii)
Customer credit limits are set by sales ledger clerks. Sales ledger clerks are not sufficiently senior and so may set limits too high, leading to irrecoverable debts, or too low, leading to a loss of revenue.	Credit limits should be set by a senior member of the sales ledger department and not by sales ledger clerks. These limits should be regularly reviewed by a responsible official.	For a sample of new customers accepted in the year, review the authorisation of the credit limit, and ensure that this was performed by a responsible official. Enquire of sales ledger clerks as to who can set credit limits.
Sales discounts are set by Baggio's sales team. In order to boost their sales, members of the sales team may set the discounts too high, leading to a loss of revenue.	All members of the sales team should be given authority to grant sales discounts up to a set limit. Any sales discounts above these limits should be authorised by sales area managers or the sales director. Regular review of sales discount levels should be undertaken by the sales director, and this review should be evidenced.	Discuss with members of the sales team the process for setting sales discounts. Review the sales discount report for evidence of review by the sales director.
Supplier statement reconciliations are no longer performed. This may result in errors in the recording of purchases and payables not being identified in a timely manner.	Supplier statement reconciliations should be performed on a monthly basis for all suppliers and these should be reviewed by a responsible official.	Review the file of reconciliations to ensure that they are being performed on a regular basis and that they have been reviewed by a responsible official.
Changes to supplier details in the purchase ledger master file can be undertaken by purchase ledger clerks. This could lead to key supplier data being accidentally amended or fictitious suppliers being set up, which can increase the risk of fraud.	Only purchase ledger supervisors should have the authority to make changes to master file data. This should be controlled via passwords. Regular review of any changes to master file data by a responsible official and this review should be evidenced.	Request a purchase ledger clerk to attempt to access the master file and to make an amendment; the system should not allow this. Review a report of master data changes and review the authority of those making amendments.
Baggio has considerable levels of surplus plant and equipment. Surplus unused plant is at risk of theft. In addition, if the surplus plant is not disposed of, then the company could lose sundry income.	Regular review of the plant and equipment on the factory floor by senior factory personnel to identify any old or surplus equipment. As part of the capital expenditure process, there should be a requirement to confirm the treatment of the equipment being replaced.	Observe the review process by senior factory personnel, identifying the treatment of any old equipment. Review processed capital expenditure forms to ascertain if the treatment of replaced equipment is as stated.

BPP
LEARNING
MEDIA

Deficiency (i)	Control recommendations (ii)	Test of control (iii)
Purchase requisitions are authorised by production supervisors. Production supervisors are not sufficiently independent or senior to authorise capital expenditure.	Capital expenditure authorisation levels to be established. Production supervisors should only be able to authorise low value items; any high value items should be authorised by the board.	Review a sample of authorised capital expenditure forms and identify if the correct signatory has authorised them.

(b)   Substantive procedures – additions

- Obtain a breakdown of additions, cast the list and agree to the non-current asset register to confirm completeness of plant and equipment (P&E).

- Select a sample of additions and agree cost to supplier invoice to confirm valuation.

- Verify rights and obligations by agreeing the addition of P&E to a supplier invoice in the name of Baggio.

- Review the list of additions and confirm that they relate to capital expenditure items rather than repairs and maintenance.

- Review board minutes to ensure that significant capital expenditure purchases have been authorised by the board.

- For a sample of additions recorded in P&E, physically verify them on the factory floor to confirm existence.

Question 18

Marking scheme

		Marks
(a)	**Reliance on independent valuer**	
	ISA 500 requires consideration of competence and capabilities of expert	1
	Consider if member of professional body or industry association	1
	Assess independence	1
	Assess whether relevant expertise of type of properties as Vieri Motor Cars	1
	Evaluate assumptions	1
		5
(b)	**Substantive procedures for revaluation of land and buildings**	
	Cast schedule of land and buildings revalued this year	1
	Agree the revalued amounts to the valuation statement provided by the valuer	1
	Agree the revalued amounts included correctly in the non-current assets regist	1
	Recalculate the total revaluation adjustment and agree recorded in the revaluation surplus	1
	Agree the initial cost for the warehouse to invoices to confirm cost	1
	Confirm through title deeds that the warehouse is owned by Vieri	1
	Recalculate the depreciation charge for the year	1
	Review the financial statements disclosures for compliance with	

IAS 16 *Property, Plant and Equipment*   1

Other   —

Restricted to   6

(c) **Substantive procedures for work in progress (WIP)**

Discuss with management how the percentage completions are attributed to WIP   1

Observe the procedures carried out in the count in assessing the level of WIP; consider reasonableness of the assumptions used   1

During the count, agree a sample of percentage completions are in accordance with Vieri's policies   1

Discuss with management the basis of the standard costs   1

Review the level of variances between standard and actual costs   1

Obtain a breakdown of the standard costs and agree a sample of these costs to actual invoices   1

Cast the schedule of total WIP and agree to the trial balance and financial statements   1

Agree sample of WIP assessed during the count to the WIP schedule, agree percentage completion is correct and recalculate the inventory valuation   1

Other   —

Restricted to   4

(d) **Impact on audit report**

Discuss with management reasons for non-amendment   1

Assess materiality   1

Immaterial – schedule of uncorrected adjustments   1

Material not pervasive – qualified opinion   1

Basis for qualified opinion paragraph   1

Opinion paragraph – qualified 'except for'   1

Restricted to   5

Total marks   20

(a) **Reliance on the work of an independent valuer**

ISA 500 *Audit Evidence* requires auditors to evaluate the competence, capabilities including expertise and objectivity of a management expert. This would include consideration of the qualifications of the valuer and assessment of whether they were members of any professional body or industry association (ISA 500).

The expert's independence should be ascertained, with potential threats such as undue reliance on Vieri Motor Cars Co (Vieri) or a self-interest threat such as share ownership considered.

In addition, Rossi & Co should meet with the expert and discuss with them its relevant expertise, in particular whether it has valued similar land and buildings to those of Vieri in the past. Rossi & Co should also consider whether the valuer understands the accounting requirements of IAS 16 *Property, Plant and Equipment* in relation to valuations.

The valuation should then be evaluated. The assumptions used should be carefully reviewed and compared to previous revaluations at Vieri. These assumptions should be discussed with both management and the valuer to understand the basis of any valuations.

(b) **Substantive procedures for land and buildings**

(1) Obtain a schedule of land and buildings revalued this year and cast to confirm completeness and accuracy of the revaluation adjustment.

(2) On a sample basis, agree the revalued amounts to the valuation statement provided by the valuer.

(3)   Agree the revalued amounts for these assets are included correctly in the non-current assets register.

(4)   Recalculate the total revaluation adjustment and agree correctly recorded in the revaluation surplus.

(5)   Agree the initial cost for the warehouse addition to supporting documentation such as invoices to confirm cost.

(6)   Confirm through a review of the title deeds that the warehouse is owned by Vieri.

(7)   Recalculate the depreciation charge for the year to ensure that, for assets revalued during the year, the depreciation was based on the correct valuation and for the warehouse addition that the charge was for six months only.

(8)   Review the financial statements disclosures of the revaluation to ensure they comply with IAS 16.

(c)   **Substantive procedures for work in progress (WIP)**

(1)   Prior to attending the inventory count, discuss with management how the percentage completions are attributed to the WIP. For example, is this based on motor cars passing certain points in the production process?

(2)   During the count, observe the procedures carried out by Vieri staff in assessing the level of WIP and consider the reasonableness of the assumptions used.

(3)   Agree for a sample that the percentage completions assessed during the count are in accordance with Vieri's policies communicated prior to the count.

(4)   Discuss with management the basis of the standard costs applied to the percentage completion of WIP, and how often these are reviewed and updated.

(5)   Review the level of variances between standard and actual costs and discuss with management how these are treated.

(6)   Obtain a breakdown of the standard costs and agree a sample of these costs to actual invoices or payroll records to assess their reasonableness.

(7)   Cast the schedule of total WIP and agree to the trial balance and financial statements.

(8)   Agree sample of WIP assessed during the count to the WIP schedule, agree percentage completion is correct and recalculate the inventory valuation.

(d)   **Auditor's report**

Discuss with the management of Vieri why they are refusing to make the amendment to WIP.

Assess the materiality of the error; if immaterial, it should be added to the schedule of unadjusted differences. The auditor should then assess whether this error results in the total of unadjusted differences becoming material; if so, this should be discussed with management; if not, there would be no impact on the audit report.

If the error is material and management refuses to amend the financial statements, then the auditor's report will need to be modified. It is unlikely that any error would be pervasive as, although WIP in total is material, it would not have a pervasive effect on the financial statements as a whole. As management has not complied with IAS 2 *Inventories* and if the error is material but not pervasive, then a qualified opinion would be necessary.

A basis for qualified opinion paragraph would need to be included after the opinion paragraph. This would explain the material misstatement in relation to the valuation of WIP and the effect on the financial statements. The opinion paragraph would be qualified 'except for'.

ACCA

Applied Skills

Audit and Assurance

Mock Examination 3

December 2016 CBE

Time allowed: 3 hours

This mock exam is divided into two sections:

Section A – ALL 15 questions are compulsory and MUST be attempted

Section B – ALL 3 questions are compulsory and MUST be attempted

Section A – ALL 15 questions are compulsory and MUST be attempted

Each question is worth 2 marks.

The following scenario relates to questions 1–5.

It is 1 July 20X5. The board of directors of Sistar Co is concerned that they are not currently applying best practice in terms of corporate governance and are seeking to make improvements.

The company currently has three non-executive directors (NEDs) on the board, who are paid a fee which changes annually depending on company performance. The NEDs all sit on the audit, nomination and remuneration committees. There are currently no formal documents setting out the responsibilities of these committees.

At present, Sistar Co does not have an internal audit function but the directors are establishing a team which will be responsible for a range of internal audit assignments.

The following is the current proposed structure for the internal audit (IA) department.

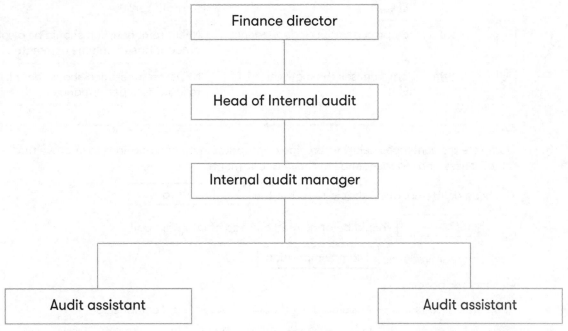

The only role still to be filled is the Head of internal audit. There are two potential candidates: Paul Belling, a consultant who helped design and implement the company's current control system, and Maria Marquez, who is currently an audit manager at Rossi & Bell, an audit firm which has never been used by Sistar Co.

Out of the other three members of the proposed IA department, two of them have moved from other departments in Sistar Co and one of the audit assistants has audit experience.

1   Which of the following should be included in the document setting out the responsibilities of the audit committee?

(1)   To monitor and review the effectiveness of the newly established internal audit function

(2)   To evaluate the balance of skills, experience and independence of board members

(3)   To take responsibility for the appointment and removal of the external auditors

(4)   To monitor and review the effectiveness of internal financial controls established by the company

☐ 1 and 2

☐ 1 and 4

☐ 2 and 3

☐ 3 and 4

2   Indicate which of the following options correctly describes the deficiency relating to NEDs' remuneration and makes a valid recommendation for improvement.

Option		Deficiency	Recommendation
☐	(1)	Compromises NED independence	NEDs should be remunerated on the same basis as the executive team
☐	(2)	Compromises the motivation of NEDs	NEDs' remuneration should be tied to profit targets
☐	(3)	Compromises NED independence	NEDs' remuneration should be a set amount based on time committed
☐	(4)	Compromises the motivation of NEDs	NEDs' remuneration should be linked to individual performance

3   Complete the sentences below to provide appropriate recommendations to improve the effectiveness and independence of the IA department.

The head of internal audit should report to the [Report to]

[Head of IA] should be appointed as head of internal audit.

The audit team requires [Team composition]

Picklists for boxes:

Head of IA reports to	Appointed head of IA	Audit team composition
Finance director	Maria Marquez	More senior staff with audit experience
Audit committee	Paul Belling	No change to its current composition
Chief executive		More external staff to be appointed

4   The board has started to compile a list of tasks for the IA department to carry out once it is up and running. It has been agreed that the first assignment to be completed will be for IA to review Sistar Co's processes over capital expenditure to verify if the right items are purchased at an appropriate time and competitive price.

What type of internal audit assignment does this represent?

☐ A value for money audit

☐ A management audit

☐ A financial audit

☐ An IT audit

5   When deciding on the role of the IA department in undertaking operational audits, which of the following should the team **NOT** be involved in?

☐   Observing procedures carried out by Sistar Co's staff

☐   Reperforming procedures documented in procedures manuals

☐   Designing and implementing internal control procedures to address deficiencies

☐   Reporting findings directly to the board of directors

The following scenario relates to questions 6–10.

You are an audit manager of Elm & Co and are finalising the audit of the financial statements of Oak Co for the year ended 31 December 20X4. It is 1 July 20X5. You are reviewing the results of the final analytical procedures and other outstanding points on the audit file, prior to recommending the final audit opinion, which is due to be signed on 12 July 20X5.

The following ratio analysis has been completed as part of the final analytical procedures:

	20X4 final	20X4 planning	20X3 final
Gross profit margin	9%	11%	12%
Quick ratio	0.2	0.6	0.8
Payables payment period	45	40	37
Inventory holding period	50	40	42

Discussions with the finance director have also revealed the following:

(1)   Oak Co lost a major customer, Beech Co, in December 20X4, but new business has been won post year end which has mitigated the impact of the loss of Beech Co.

(2)   Oak Co is due to repay a substantial loan on 31 August 20X5. Oak Co is currently negotiating revised terms with the bank but it is unlikely that negotiations will be concluded before the auditor's report is signed. This will be disclosed in the financial statements.

The financial statements for the year ended 31 December 20X4 have been prepared on a going concern basis.

6   As part of the going concern assessment, the following additional issues have been noted on the audit file.

Which **TWO** of the following issues could individually cast doubt over the going concern assumption for
Oak Co?

☐   A number of personnel in the purchasing department left during the year and have not been replaced.

☐   A major supplier to Oak Co has just gone out of business with a number of unfulfilled orders.

☐   A new product which was due to account for 30% of revenue has proved to be unsuccessful.

☐   A litigation claim has been raised against Oak Co after the year end with potential damages totalling 3% of this year's profit.

---

7   As part of your review of the final analytical procedures, you compare the results to the following comments on the audit file:

(1)   The company has increased the sales prices charged to customers while maintaining costs at a level comparable to 20X3.

(2)   The company has become more reliant on its overdraft facility during the year.

(3)   Due to cash restrictions, the company has encountered delays in paying suppliers.

(4)   At the year-end inventory count, a lower level of slow-moving inventory was noted compared to the prior year.

Which of the above comments are **INCONSISTENT** with the results of the final analytical procedures?

☐   1 and 2

☐   1 and 4

☐   2 and 3

☐   3 and 4

---

8   Which of the following procedures would provide the **MOST** reliable evidence in relation to the new business won post year end?

☐   Review of post-year end sales orders from the new customer

☐   Inspect email correspondence between the sales director of Oak Co and the new customer

☐   Obtain a written representation confirming the level of business agreed with the new customer

☐   Review of board minutes discussing the contract with the new customer

---

9   The initial going concern assessment conducted by the management of Oak Co covers the period to
30 June 20X5.

Which of the following is an appropriate course of action in the circumstances described above?

☐   Request management extend the assessment to the date of the auditor's report

☐   Design and carry out procedures to only assess going concern in the period from 31 December 20X4 to the date of the auditor's report

☐   Request management extend the assessment to cover at least until 31 December 20X5

☐   Accept the time frame used by management as the going concern review is their responsibility

10   The audit engagement partner has concluded that the disclosure included in the financial statements in relation to the loan negotiations is adequate. Additionally, the audit partner has commented that this disclosure is fundamental to the users' understanding of the financial statements.

Complete the following sentence, identifying what form of auditor's report should be issued.

The audit engagement partner has concluded that the disclosure included in the financial statements in relation to the loan negotiations is adequate. Additionally, the audit partner has commented that this disclosure is fundamental to the users' understanding of the financial statements.

An auditor's report with [Opinion] Opinion and [Paragraph] paragraph should be issued.

Picklists for boxes:

Opinion	Paragraph
a modified	an other matter
an unmodified	a material uncertainty relating to going concern

---

The following scenario relates to questions 11–15.

You are an audit senior at Jones & Co and are currently performing the final audit of Walker Co for the year ended 30 April 20X5. It is 1 July 20X5. The company is a manufacturer and retailer of shoes and boots. The current audit senior is ill and you have been asked to complete the audit of payroll in their absence.

On arrival at the head office of Walker Co, you determine the following data from a review of the current year and prior year audit files:

(1)   As at 30 April 20X4, Walker Co had 500 employees.

(2)   On 1 May 20X4, 10% of staff were made redundant, effective immediately, due to discontinuation of a product line.

(3)   On 1 July 20X4, all remaining staff received a 6% pay rise.

(4)   Over the course of the year, sales levels met performance targets which resulted in a fixed bonus of $1,500 being paid to each employee on 30 April 20X5.

11   Which of the following statements explains the **CUT-OFF** assertion for wages and salaries?

☐   Wages and salaries have been fairly allocated within the statement of profit or loss.

☐   Wages and salaries have been appropriately calculated taking into account all relevant taxation costs and adjustments.

☐   Wages and salaries which have been incurred during the period have been accounted for in respect of all personnel employed by Walker Co.

☐   Wages and salaries accounted for relate to the current year ended 30 April 20X5.

---

12   Order the evidence, in terms of its reliability, starting with the **MOST RELIABLE**.

Audit evidence	Order of reliability
Proof in total calculation performed by an audit team member	1 – Most
Written representation from the directors of Walker Co confirming the accuracy of wages and salaries	2
Verbal confirmation from the finance director of Walker Co confirming the accuracy of wages and salaries	3
Recalculation of the gross and net pay for a sample of employees by an internal audit team member of Walker Co	4 – Least

13   The prior year financial statements for Walker Co included $17m for wages and salaries in the statement of profit or loss.

What would be the estimated current year wages and salaries expense, ignoring redundancy costs, based upon the data gathered from the review of the audit files?

☐ $16,740,000

☐ $16,893,000

☐ $16,815,000

☐ $18,600,000

14   Which **TWO** of the following are substantive **ANALYTICAL PROCEDURES** for wages and salaries?

☐   Trace and agree the total wages and salaries expense per the payroll system to the draft financial statements

☐   Recalculate the gross and net pay for a sample of employees, agree to payroll records and investigate discrepancies

☐   Compare the current year total payroll expense to the prior year and investigate any significant differences

☐   Perform a proof in total calculation and compare expected expense to actual expense within the draft financial statements

15   You have been given a list of procedures to carry out on revenue and you have decided to prioritise those which deal with the key assertion of occurrence.

Which of the following substantive procedures provide evidence over the **OCCURRENCE** assertion for revenue?

(1)   Compare the reported revenue figure to the budget and to the previous year, investigating any significant differences

(2)   Select a sample of goods dispatched notes (GDNs) and agree to invoices in the sales day book

(3)   Select a sample of invoices from the sales day book and agree to GDNs

(4)   Select a sample of invoices and recalculate the invoiced amount agreeing to price list

☐   1 and 2

☐   1 and 3

☐   2 and 4

☐   3 and 4

(Total = 30 marks)

Section B – ALL THREE questions are compulsory and MUST be attempted

Question 16

You are an audit supervisor of Ant & Co and are planning the final audit of Centipede Co, which is a listed company, for the year ended 31 March 20X5. It is 1 July 20X5. The company purchases consumer packaged goods and sells these through its website and to wholesalers. This is a new client for your firm and your audit manager has already had a planning meeting with the finance director and has provided you with the following notes along with financial statement extracts.

Client background and notes from planning meeting

Rather than undertaking a full year-end inventory count, the company undertakes monthly perpetual inventory counts, covering one-twelfth of all lines monthly. As part of the interim audit which was completed earlier in the year, an audit assistant attended a perpetual inventory count in September and noted that there were a large number of exceptions where the inventory records were consistently higher than the physical inventory in the warehouse. When discussing these exceptions with the finance director, the assistant was informed that this had been a recurring issue all year. In addition, the audit assistant noted that there were some lines of inventory which, according to the records, were at least 90 days old.

Centipede Co has a head office where the audit team will be based to conduct the final audit fieldwork. However, there are four additional sites where some accounting records are maintained and these sites were not visited during the interim audit. The records for these sites are incorporated monthly through an interface to the general ledger. A fifth site was closed down in the year ending 20X4; however, the building was only sold in 20X5 at a loss of $825,000.

One of Centipede Co's wholesale customers is alleging that the company has consistently failed to deliver goods in a saleable condition and on time, hence it has commenced legal action against Centipede Co for a loss of profits claim.

The directors have disclosed their remuneration details in the financial statements in line with IFRS, which does not require a separate list of directors' names and payments. However, in the country in which Centipede Co is based, local legislation requires disclosure of the names of the directors and the amount of remuneration payable to each director.

FINANCIAL STATEMENT EXTRACTS FOR THE YEAR ENDED 31 MARCH

	Draft 20X5 $'000	Final 20X4 $'000
Revenue	25,230	21,180
Cost of sales	(15,840)	(14,015)
Gross profit	9,390	7,165
Operating expenses	(4,903)	(3,245)
	4,487	3,920
Inventory	2,360	1,800
Trade receivables	1,590	1,250
Cash	–	480
Trade payables	3,500	2,800
Overdraft	580	–

Required

(a) Describe the matters which Ant & Co should have considered prior to accepting the audit of Centipede Co. (5 marks)

(b) Calculate **SIX** ratios, for **BOTH** years, which would assist you in planning the audit of Centipede Co. (6 marks)

(c) From a review of the above information and the ratios calculated, describe **SEVEN** audit risks and explain the auditor's response to each risk in planning the audit of Centipede Co.

   Note. Prepare your answer using two columns headed Audit risk and Auditor's response respectively. (14 marks)

The finance director of Centipede Co informed Ant & Co that one of the reasons it was appointed as auditors was because of its knowledge of the industry. Ant & Co audits a number of other consumer packaged goods companies, including Centipede Co's main rival. The finance director has enquired into how Ant & Co will keep information obtained during the audit confidential.

Required

(d) Explain the safeguards which Ant & Co should implement to ensure that this conflict of interest is properly managed. (5 marks)

(Total = 30 marks)

Question 17 (amended)

Caterpillar Co is a clothing retailer which operates 45 stores throughout the country. The company's year end is 31 March 20X5. It is 1 July 20X5. Caterpillar Co has an internal audit department which has undertaken a number of internal control reviews specifically focusing on cash controls at stores during the year. The reviews have taken place in the largest 20 stores as this is where most issues arise. You are an audit supervisor of Woodlouse & Co and are reviewing the internal controls documentation in relation to the cash receipts system in preparation for the interim audit which will involve visiting a number of stores and the head office.

Each of Caterpillar Co's stores has on average three or four cash tills to take customer payments. All employees based at the store are able to use each till and individuals do not have their own log-on codes, although employees tend to use the same till each day. Customers can pay using either cash or a credit card and for any transaction either the credit card payment slips or cash are placed in the till by the cashier. Where employees' friends or family members purchase clothes in store, the employee is able to serve them at the till point.

At the end of each day, the tills are closed down with daily readings of sales taken from each till; these are reconciled to the total of the cash in the tills and the credit card payment slips and any discrepancies are noted. To save time, this reconciliation is done by the store's assistant manager in aggregate for all of the store tills together. Once this reconciliation has taken place, the cash is stored in the shop's small safe overnight and in the morning it is transferred to the bank via collection by a security company. If the store is low on change for cash payments, a junior sales clerk is sent by a till operator to the bank with money from the till and asked to change it into smaller denominations.

The daily sales readings from the tills along with the cash data and credit card payment data are transferred daily to head office through an interface with the sales and cash receipts records. A clerk oversees that this transfer has occurred for all stores. On a daily basis, he also agrees the cash transferred by the security company has been banked in full by agreeing the cash deposit slips to the bank statements, and that the credit card receipts have been received from the credit card company. On a monthly basis, the same clerk reconciles the bank statements to the cash book. The reconciliations are reviewed by the financial controller if there are any unreconciled amounts.

Required

(a)   State **TWO** control objectives of Caterpillar Co's cash receipts system. **(2 marks)**

(b)   Identify and explain **THREE KEY CONTROLS** which the auditor may seek to place reliance on in Caterpillar Co's cash receipts system; and describe a **TEST OF CONTROL** the auditor should perform to assess if each of these key controls is operating effectively.

Note. Prepare your answer using two columns headed Key controls and Test of control respectively. **(6 marks)**

(c)   Identify and explain **SIX DEFICIENCIES** in Caterpillar Co's cash receipts system and provide a recommendation to address each of these deficiencies.

Note. Prepare your answer using two columns headed Control deficiency and Control recommendation respectively. **(12 marks)**

(Total = 20 marks)

Question 18

You are an audit manager of Snail & Co and you are in charge of two audits which are due to commence shortly. Insects4U Co is a registered charity which promotes insect conservation and has been an audit client for several years. Spider Spirals Co, also an existing audit client, manufactures stationery products and its draft total liabilities are $8.1 million. Both clients' financial years ended on 30 April 20X5. It is 1 July 20X5. The following matters have been brought to your attention for each company.

Insects4U Co

(i)   **Completeness of income**

Insects4U Co is a not-for-profit organisation which generates income in a number of ways. It receives monthly donations from its many subscribers and these are paid by bank transfer to the charity. In addition, a large number of donations are sent through the post to the charity. Insects4U Co also sells tickets for its three charity events held annually. During the audit planning, completeness of income was flagged as a key risk.

Note. Assume that the charity adopts IFRSs. **(4 marks)**

Spider Spirals Co

(ii)   **Trade payables**

The finance director of Spider Spirals Co has informed you that at the year end the purchase ledger was kept open for one week longer than normal as a large bank transfer and cheque payment run was made on 3 May 20X5. Some purchase invoices were received in this week and were recorded in the 20X5 purchase ledger as well as the payment run made on 3 May. **(6 marks)**

(iii)   **Trade receivables**

Spider Spirals Co has a large number of small customers; the normal credit terms offered to them is 30 days. However, the finance director has informed you that the average trade receivables collection period has increased quite significantly this year from 34 days to 55 days. This is partly due to difficult trading conditions and also because for six months of the year the role of credit controller was vacant. The company has historically maintained on average an allowance for trade receivables of 1.5% of gross trade receivables. **(5 marks)**

Required

(a)   Describe substantive procedures the auditor should perform to obtain sufficient and appropriate audit evidence in relation to the above three matters.

   Note. The mark allocation is shown against each of the three matters above.

(b)   The finance director of Spider Spirals Co has informed you that he is not proposing to make an adjustment for the trade payables payment run made on 3 May, as the total payment of $490,000 would only require a change to trade payables and the bank overdraft, both of which are current liabilities.

   Required

   Discuss the issue and describe the impact on the auditor's report, if any, should this issue remain unresolved.   (5 marks)

                                                                                        (Total = 20 marks)

Answers

DO NOT TURN THIS PAGE UNTIL YOU HAVE
COMPLETED THE MOCK EXAM

Plan of attack

If this were the real Audit and Assurance exam and you had been told to turn over and begin, what would be going through your mind?

An important thing to say (whilst there is still time) is that it is vital to have a good breadth of knowledge of the syllabus because all the questions are compulsory. However, don't panic. Below we provide guidance on how to approach the exam.

Looking through the exam

Section A has three objective test cases, each with five questions. This is the section of the exam where the examining team can test knowledge across the breadth of the syllabus. Make sure you read these cases and questions carefully. The distractors are designed to present plausible, but incorrect, answers. Don't let them mislead you. If you really have no idea – guess. You may even be right.

Section B has three longer questions:

*   **Question 16** is a 30-mark question focused on the planning stage, covering analytical procedures, audit risk, acceptance procedures and ethics. Read the requirements carefully, taking note in particular of the number of ratios that you have been asked to calculate and that they must be calculated for both years.

*   **Question 17** is a 20-mark internal controls question. Here you need to consider strengths in the system as well as identifying weaknesses.

*   **Question 18** is a 20-mark question dealing with substantive procedures relating to income, trade payables and trade receivables. You are also asked to consider the impact on the auditor's report of any unresolved issues.

Allocating your time

BPP's advice is to always allocate your time **according to the marks for the question**. However, **use common sense**. If you're doing a question but haven't a clue how to do part (b), you might be better off reallocating your time and getting more marks on another question, where you can add something you didn't have time for earlier on. Make sure you leave time to recheck the OTs and make sure you have answered them all.

Forget about it

And don't worry if you found the exam difficult. More than likely other candidates will too. If this were the real thing you would need to forget the exam the minute you left the exam hall and think about the next one. Or, if it is the last one, celebrate!

Section A

1   The correct answer is: 1 and 4

The audit committee should be responsible for monitoring the effectiveness of the internal audit function and the company's internal control system. Therefore statements 1 and 4 should be included.

2   The correct answer is:

Compromises NED independence, NEDs' remuneration should be a set amount based on time committed

NEDs remuneration should not be tied to the performance of Sistar Co as this can compromise their independence. NEDs remuneration should be based on the time committed to carry out the role.

3   The correct answers are: Audit committee; Maria Marquez; More senior staff with audit experience.

To improve the effectiveness and independence of the internal audit function, the head of internal audit should report to the audit committee. Maria Marquez should be appointed as the head of internal audit as she is completely independent of Sistar Co and the audit team needs more senior staff with relevant experience.

4   The correct answer is: A value for money audit.

The assignment described represents a value for money audit as it is focused on assessing the economy, efficiency and effectiveness of Sistar Co's capital expenditure.

5   The correct answer is: Designing and implementing internal control procedures to address deficiencies

Internal audit should not be involved in designing and then implementing internal control procedures as this would result in a self-review threat to independence.

6   The correct answers are: A major supplier to Oak Co has just gone out of business with a number of unfulfilled orders; A new product which was due to account for 30% of revenue has proved to be unsuccessful.

The loss of a major supplier could have a serious impact on Oak Co if no alternative can be found and poor results in a product line expected to account for 30% of revenue could also have a significant impact on the company going forward

7   The correct answer is: 1 and 4.

Gross margin has dropped which implies that the company is not gaining as good a return as in the prior year - this would most likely be due to an increase in C.O.S or drop in sales price. Therefore the comment regarding increasing sales price contradicts the results of the AR.

The inventory holding period has increased significantly implying that items are taking longer to sell, given the comment regarding the observation made at the inventory count this would warrant further investigation given the increase in the inventory holding period.

Therefore comment 1 and 4 should be investigated and are inconsistent with the final AR.

8   The correct answer is: Review of post-year end sales orders from the new customer

The review of post year-end sales would provide the best evidence that the new customer is genuine and is ordering goods. This to some extent will then allow the auditor to assess the level of sales being made to the new customer and to determine whether this does therefore mitigate for the loss of Beech Co.

9   The correct answer is: Request management extend the assessment to cover at least until 31 December 20X5

As per ISA 570 *Going Concern*, the period of assessment should be at least 12 months from the date of the financial statements.

10   The correct answers are: a modified; a material uncertainty relating to going concern.

As per ISA 570 *Going Concern*, where there is a matter of fundamental importance to the users' understanding regarding an uncertainty over going concern, as long as this is adequately disclosed the auditor should include a material uncertainty paragraph related to going concern. The audit opinion is unmodified in this regard.

11   The correct answer is: Wages and salaries accounted for relate to the current year ended 30 April 20X5.

The cut-off assertion relates to ensuring that transaction are recorded in the correct accounting period, and therefore that wages and salaries accounted for relate to the year ended 30 April 20X5.

12

Audit evidence	Order of reliability
Proof in total calculation performed by an audit team member	1 – Most
Written representation from the directors of Walker Co confirming the accuracy of wages and salaries	3
Verbal confirmation from the finance director of Walker Co confirming the accuracy of wages and salaries	4 – Least
Recalculation of the gross and net pay for a sample of employees by an internal audit team member of Walker Co	2

13   The correct answer is: $16,740,000

Working:

17,000,000 × 90% × 2/12 = 2,550,000

(17,000,000 × 106%) × 90% × 10/12 = 13,515,000

450 × 1,500 = 675,000

2,550,000 + 13,515,000 + 675,000 = 16,740,000

14   The correct answers are:

Compare the current year total payroll expense to the prior year and investigate any significant differences

Perform a proof in total calculation and compare expected expense to actual expense within the draft financial statements.

Comparisons with prior years and proof in total calculations are examples of substantive analytical procedures.

15   The correct answer is: 1 and 3

(2) provides evidence that goods dispatched have been invoiced

(4) provides evidence of accuracy

Section B

Question 16

Marking scheme

		Marks
(a)	**Matters to be considered prior to accepting the audit of Centipede Co**	
	• Compliance with ACCA's *Code of Ethics and Conduct*	1
	• Competent	1
	• Reputation and integrity of directors	1
	• Level of risk of Centipede Co audit	1
	• Fee adequate to compensate for risk	1
	• Write to outgoing auditor after obtaining permission to contact	1
	• Previous auditor permission to respond	1
	• Review response for any issues	1
	Restricted to	**5**
(b)	**Ratio calculations** (½ mark for each year)	
	• Gross margin	1
	• Operating margin	1
	• Inventory holding period/Inventory turnover	1
	• Receivables collection period	1
	• Payables payment period	1
	• Current ratio	1
	• Quick ratio	1
	Restricted to	**6**
(c)	**Audit risks and responses** (only 7 risks required)	
	• New client, increased detection risk	2
	• Perpetual inventory count adjustments	2
	• Valuation of inventory	2
	• Branch records	2
	• Disposal of building	2
	• Legal case	2
	• Directors' remuneration disclosure	2
	• Revenue growth	2

		Marks
•	Misclassification of costs between cost of sales and operating	2
•	Going concern	2
	Max 7 issues, 2 marks each	14

(d) **Safeguards to deal with conflict of interest**

		Marks
•	Notify Centipede Co and its competitor	1
•	Advise seek independent advice	1
•	Separate engagement teams	1
•	Procedures prevent access to information	1
•	Clear guidelines on security and confidentiality	1
•	Confidentiality agreements	1
•	Monitoring of safeguards	1
	Restricted to	5
Total marks		**30**

(a) **Matters to be considered prior to accepting the audit of Centipede Co**

ISA 220 *Quality Control for an Audit of Financial Statements* provides guidance to Ant & Co on the steps they should have taken in accepting the new audit client, Centipede Co. It sets out a number of processes which the auditor should perform prior to accepting a new engagement.

Ant & Co should have considered any issues which might arise which could threaten compliance with ACCA's *Code of Ethics and Conduct* or any local legislation, such as the level of fees from Centipede Co, to ensure they are not unduly reliant on these fees, as well as considering whether any conflicts of interest arise with existing clients. If issues arise, then their significance must be considered.

In addition, they should have considered whether they were competent to perform the work and whether they would have appropriate resources available, as well as any specialist skills or knowledge required for the audit of Centipede Co.

Ant & Co should have considered what it already knows about the directors of Centipede Co; it needed to consider the reputation and integrity of the directors. If necessary, the firm may have wanted to obtain references if it does not formally know the directors.

Additionally, Ant & Co should have considered the level of risk attached to the audit of Centipede Co and whether this was acceptable to the firm. As part of this, it should have considered whether the expected audit fee was adequate in relation to the risk of auditing Centipede Co.

Ant & Co should have communicated with the outgoing auditor of Centipede Co to assess if there were any ethical or professional reasons why they should not have accepted appointment. They should have obtained permission from Centipede Co's management to contact the previous auditor; if this was not given, then the engagement should have been refused. Once received, the response from the previous auditor should have been carefully reviewed for any issues which could affect acceptance.

(b) **Ratios**

Ratios to assist the audit supervisor in planning the audit:

	20X5	20X4
Gross margin	9,390/25,230 = 37.2%	7,165/21,180 = 33.8%
Operating margin	4,487/25,230 = 17.8%	3,920/21,180 = 18.5%
Inventory holding period or	2,360/15,840 × 365 = 54 days	1,800/14,015 × 365 = 47 days
Inventory turnover	15,840/2,360 = 6.7	14,015/1,800 = 7.8
Receivables collection period	1,590/25,230 × 365 = 23 days	1,250/21,180 × 365 = 22 days
Payables payment period	3,500/15,840 × 365 = 81 days	2,800/14,015 × 365 = 73 days
Current ratio	3,950/4,080 = 0.97	3,530/2,800 = 1.26
Quick ratio	(3,950 – 2,360)/4,080 = 0.39	(3,530 – 1,800)/2,800 = 0.62

(c) **Audit risks and auditor's responses**

Audit risk	Auditor's response
Centipede Co is a new client for Ant & Co and is a listed company. As the team is not familiar with the accounting policies, transactions and balances of the company, there will be an increased detection risk on the audit.	Ant & Co should ensure it has a suitably experienced team. Also, adequate time should be allocated for team members to obtain an understanding of the company and the risks of material misstatement, including attendance at an audit team briefing.
The company utilises a perpetual inventory system at its warehouse rather than a full year-end count. Under such a system, all inventory must be counted at least once a year, with adjustments made to the inventory records on a timely basis. Inventory could be under- or overstated if the perpetual inventory counts are not complete. During the interim audit, it was noted that there were significant exceptions with the inventory records being higher than the inventory in the warehouse. As the year-end quantities will be based on the records, this is likely to result in overstated inventory.	The completeness of the perpetual inventory counts should be reviewed and the controls over the counts and adjustments to records should be tested. In addition, the level of adjustments made to inventory should be considered to assess their significance. This should be discussed with management as soon as possible as it may not be possible to place reliance on the inventory records at the year end, which could result in the requirement for a full year-end inventory count.
During the interim audit, it was noted that there were some lines of inventory which according to the records were at least 90 days old. In addition, the inventory holding period has increased from 47 to 54 days. It would appear that there may be an increase in slow-moving inventory. The valuation of inventory as per IAS 2 *Inventories* should be at the lower of cost and net realisable value. Hence there is a risk that obsolete inventory has not been appropriately written down and inventory is overvalued.	The aged inventory report should be reviewed and discussed with management to assess if certain lines of products are slow moving. Detailed cost and net realisable value testing to be performed to assess whether an allowance or write down of inventory is required.

Audit risk	Auditor's response
Centipede Co maintains accounting records at four additional sites which were not visited during the interim audit, and the records from these sites are incorporated monthly into the general ledger.	Discuss with management the significance and materiality of the records maintained at the four sites. The team may then need to visit some of these sites during the final audit to undertake testing of the records held there.
Ant & Co needs to ensure that it has obtained sufficient appropriate audit evidence over all the accounting records of the company, not just for those at head office. There is a detection risk if the team does not visit or undertake testing of the records at these sites. Further, if the interface does not occur appropriately, there is a risk that accounting records are incomplete.	In addition, computer-assisted audit techniques could be utilised by the team to sample test the monthly interface of data from each site to head office to identify any errors.
During 20X5 a building was disposed of with a loss on disposal of $825,000. There is a risk that the disposal has not been removed appropriately from the accounting records or that the loss on disposal calculation is incorrect. In addition, significant profits or losses on disposal are an indication that the depreciation policy for land and buildings may not be appropriate. Therefore depreciation may be understated and consequently assets overstated.	Agree that the asset has been removed from the non-current assets register, recalculate the loss on disposal calculation and agree all items to supporting documentation. Discuss the depreciation policy for land and buildings with the finance director to assess its reasonableness. Review the level of losses on disposal generated from other asset sales to ascertain if this is a more widespread issue.
A customer of Centipede Co has commenced legal action against Centipede Co for a loss of profits claim. If it is probable that the company will make payment to the customer, a legal provision is required. If the payment is possible rather than probable, a contingent liability disclosure would be necessary. If Centipede Co has not done this, there is a risk over the completeness of any provisions and the necessary disclosure of contingent liabilities.	Ant & Co should write to the company's lawyers to enquire of the existence and likelihood of success of any claim from the wholesale customer. The results of this should be used to assess the level of provision or disclosure included in the financial statements.
The directors have not disclosed the individual names and payments for each of the directors' remuneration. This is in line with IFRS but disclosure of this is required by local legislation. In cases where the local legislation is more comprehensive than IFRS, it is likely the company must comply with the local legislation. The directors' remuneration disclosure will not be complete and accurate if the names and individual payments are not disclosed in accordance with the relevant local legislation and hence the financial statements will be misstated as a result of the non-compliance.	Discuss this matter with management and review the requirements of the local legislation to determine if the disclosure in the financial statements is appropriate.

Audit risk	Auditor's response
Revenue has grown by 19% in the year; however, cost of sales has only increased by 13%. This is a significant increase in revenue and along with the increase in gross margin may be due to an overstatement of revenue.	During the audit a detailed breakdown of sales will be obtained, discussed with management and tested in order to understand the sales increase. Increased cut-off testing should also be undertaken to verify that revenue is recorded in the right period and is not overstated.
Gross margin has increased from 33.8% to 37.2%. Operating margin has decreased from 18.5% to 17.8%. This movement in gross margin is significant and there is a risk that costs may have been omitted or included in operating expenses rather than cost of sales.	The classification of costs between cost of sales and operating expenses will be compared with the prior year to ensure consistency. Also increased cut-off testing should be performed at the year end to ensure that costs are complete.
The overall liquidity of the company is in decline, with the current and quick ratios decreasing from 1.26 to 0.97 and 0.62 to 0.39 respectively. In addition, the cash balances have decreased significantly over the year, and the company now has an overdraft of $580,000 at the end of the year. Further, the trade payables payment period has increased from 73 to 81 days, implying the company is struggling to meet its liabilities as they fall due. All of these changes in key ratios could signal going concern difficulties.	Detailed going concern testing to be performed during the audit as there may be a doubt over going concern and the basis of accounting should be discussed with management to ensure that the going concern basis is reasonable.

(d) **Safeguards to deal with conflict of interest**

- Both Centipede Co and its rival competitor should be notified that Ant & Co would be acting as auditors for each company and, if necessary, consent obtained.

- Advising one or both clients to seek additional independent advice.

- The use of separate engagement teams, with different engagement partners and team members; once an employee has worked on one audit, such as Centipede Co, then they should be prevented from being on the audit of the competitor for a period of time.

- Procedures to prevent access to information, for example, strict physical separation of both teams, confidential and secure data filing.

- Clear guidelines for members of each engagement team on issues of security and confidentiality. These guidelines could be included within the audit engagement letters.

- Potentially the use of confidentiality agreements signed by employees and partners of the firm.

- Regular monitoring of the application of the above safeguards by a senior individual in Ant & Co not involved in either audit.

Question 17

Workbook reference. Chapters 9 and 10.

Top tips. This is a 20-mark question on controls and tests of controls in the cash system. Part (b) of the question asks you to identify key controls in the system and tests of controls. Make sure you can distinguish between tests of controls and substantive procedures. Tests of controls aim to provide evidence that controls are operating effectively.

Part (c) should be a familiar requirement asking for the identification of weaknesses and recommendations to address each weakness. This type of requirement is typically well answered but take care when making your recommendations. Examining team comments have often referred to the fact that recommendations are often phrased in vague terms. Make sure you explain clearly the procedure which needs to be performed, and if possible who should perform it.

Easy marks. These are available in part (a).

Marking scheme

		Marks	
(a)	**Control objectives – cash receipts system**		
	• To ensure that all valid cash receipts are received and deposited promptly in the bank	1	
	• To ensure all cash receipts are recorded in the cash book	1	
	• To ensure that all receipts are recorded at the correct amounts in the cash books	1	
	• To ensure that cash receipts are correctly posted to the general ledger	1	
	• To ensure that cash receipts are recorded in the correct accounting period	1	
	• To ensure that cash is safeguarded to prevent theft	1	
	• To ensure that management has accurate and timely information regarding the cash position	<u>1</u>	
	Restricted to		2
(b)	**Key controls and tests of control** (3 strengths required)		
	• Internal audit department which undertakes cash control reviews at stores	2	
	• Daily sales readings taken from tills and reconciled to cash and credit card payment slips, exceptions noted	2	
	• Cash collected daily and taken to the bank by security company	2	
	• Daily interface to head office for sales, cash and credit card data into sales and cash receipts books	2	
	• Daily agreement of cash banked by security company and cash received from credit card company into bank statements	2	
	• Monthly bank reconciliations undertaken	<u>2</u>	
	Max 3 issues, 2 marks each		6
(c)	**Control deficiencies and recommendations** (only 6 issues required)		
	• Internal audit only visits 20 largest stores rather than all 45	2	
	• All employees able to use tills and no individual log-on codes	2	
	• Employees can serve friends and family members at the till points	2	
	• Daily till reading reconciliations performed in aggregate for all tills in store rather than individually	2	
	• Cashing up of tills undertaken by just one individual	2	
	• Cash stored on site overnight	2	

	Marks
• Junior sales clerks given cash and sent to the bank to change notes into smaller denominations	2
• Lack of segregation of duties in head office for recording and reconciling of cash	2
• Bank reconciliations not always reviewed by the financial controller	2
Max 6 issues, 2 marks each	12
Total marks	20

(a) **Control objectives – cash receipts system**

- To ensure that all valid cash receipts are received and deposited promptly in the bank

- To ensure all cash receipts are recorded in the cash book

- To ensure that all receipts are recorded at the correct amounts in the cash book

- To ensure that cash receipts are correctly posted to the general ledger

- To ensure that cash receipts are recorded in the correct accounting period

- To ensure that cash is safeguarded to prevent theft

- To ensure that management has accurate and timely information regarding the cash position

(b) **Caterpillar Co's cash cycle strengths and tests of control**

Key controls	Test of control
Caterpillar Co has an internal audit (IA) department which has undertaken a number of internal control reviews, which specifically focused on cash controls at stores during the year. This is a strong monitoring control as stores will aim to ensure that company procedures are maintained as they would not wish IA to report any exceptions at their store.	Discuss with IA the programme of their visits to stores and the areas addressed on these visits. This will assess the strength of this monitoring control. In particular, enquire of IA whether over a rolling period all stores will be visited. Review the IA department files for the results of the store visits, to confirm that the 20 stores programmed to be visited did all actually take place and for exceptions noted and actions taken.
At the end of each day, the tills are closed down with daily readings of sales taken; these are reconciled to the total of the cash in the tills and the credit card payment slips and any discrepancies are noted. Daily cashing up procedures should ensure that the cash is controlled and reduces the risk of fraud as employees are aware that the assistant manager will be looking for cash discrepancies.	For a sample of stores visited, the auditor should review the file of daily reconciliations to ascertain if end of day till reconciliations have taken place on a daily basis. For reconciliations with discrepancies, discuss with the store manager what actions were taken and how these differences were resolved.

Key controls	Test of control
Cash received from customers is taken to the bank daily via collection by a security company. This ensures that cash is safeguarded and that the risk of theft when transferring to the bank is minimised.	During the store visits, enquire of staff how the cash is transferred to the bank. A sample of invoices from the collection company should be reviewed and confirmed that they are charging Centipede Co on a daily basis. In addition, during these visits observe the cash collection process carried out by the security company.
The daily sales readings from the tills along with the cash and credit card data are transferred to head office through a daily interface into the sales and cash receipts records. This should ensure that sales and cash records are updated on a prompt basis and are complete and accurate.	During the interim audit at head office, compare the daily sales readings from individual stores, including some visited by the audit team, to the sales and cash receipt records within the general ledger. Review the date on which the sales and cash receipt records were updated to ensure this occurred promptly. Any discrepancies should be discussed with the clerk responsible for overseeing this process.
On a daily basis the clerk agrees that the cash banked and the credit card receipts from the credit card company have been credited to the bank statements in full. This should ensure the completeness of cash receipts, as they are transferred in from two sources, being the security company and the credit card operator.	Discuss with the clerk responsible for reconciling the cash and credit card receipts the process he undertakes. Review the daily reconciliations he has completed to confirm the process has been undertaken as described.
Bank reconciliations are undertaken on a monthly basis. This should ensure that any discrepancies between the cash book and the bank statements are identified promptly.	Review the file of bank reconciliations to ascertain if there is one for each month and that they are either fully reconciled, or the financial controller has evidenced their review of any unreconciled amounts.

(c)   Caterpillar Co's cash system deficiencies and controls

Control deficiency	Control recommendation
The IA department only undertakes cash control visits to the 20 largest stores as they feel this is where most issues arise. However, Caterpillar Co has 45 stores in total which means over half of the stores are not being checked. This increases the likelihood of control errors, as these stores may not comply with company procedures and with it being a cash business heightens the chance of frauds occurring.	Caterpillar Co's IA department should have a rolling programme of visits to all 45 stores. This programme can have a bias to large and high risk stores, but it should ensure that all stores are visited on a cyclical basis.
All store employees are able to use each till and none have an individual log-on code when using the tills. Allowing all employees access to the till points increases the risk of fraud and error arising. Also in the event of cash discrepancies arising in the tills, it would be difficult to ascertain which employees may be responsible as there is no way of tracking who used which till.	Only employees for whom criminal record/credit checks have been undertaken should be able to use the tills to take customer payments. Each employee should have a designated till and a log-on code, which is required for each payment transaction.

BPP
LEARNING
MEDIA

Control deficiency	Control recommendation
Where employees' friends or family members purchase clothes in store, the employee is able to serve them at the till point. There is a significant fraud risk as employees could fail to put the goods through the till, but retain the cash paid by the friend/family members. Additionally, they could give the goods away for free or undercharge for goods sold, thereby granting unauthorised discounts.	Caterpillar Co should instigate a policy whereby employees are unable to serve friends or family members at the till points. They should be required to request that a manager or supervisor put these goods through the till. In addition, CCTV cameras could be placed in the shops, near to the till points to record the daily till transactions. This would act as a deterrent to employees as well as provide evidence in the case of fraudulent transactions occurring. Caterpillar Co should also carry out regular inventory counts to identify if goods in the stores are below the levels in the inventory records, as this could identify goods being given away for free.
The daily reading of sales and reconciliations to the tills is performed in aggregate rather than for each till. This means if exceptions arise, it will be difficult to identify which till caused the difference and therefore which employees may require further till training or have undertaken fraudulent transactions.	The reconciliations should be undertaken on an individual till by till basis rather than in aggregate.
The cashing up of tills along with the recording of any cash discrepancies is undertaken by just one individual, the assistant store manager. There is a fraud risk as the store manager could remove some of the cash and then simply record that there was an exception on this till.	The cashing up process should be undertaken by two individuals together, ideally the assistant and the store manager. One should count the cash and the other record it. Any exceptions to the till reading should be double checked to confirm that they are not simply addition errors.
The cash is kept at the store overnight in a small safe. Although in a safe, this is not secure as it is likely that the cash sales for one day would be a significant sum. This cash is at risk of being stolen overnight.	The cash should continue to be collected daily by the security company, but rather than in the morning it should be collected as the store closes in the evening so that cash does not have to be stored overnight.
If a store needs change, a junior sales clerk is sent to the bank by a till operator to change it into smaller denominations. There is a risk of the cash being misplaced or stolen on the way to the bank or collusion between the junior clerk and till operator as no record appears to be kept of the money removed from the till in these instances and no confirmation of how much cash is returned is carried out.	Caterpillar Co's head office should stipulate a float amount per till and how the note denominations should be comprised. When assigning the cash float in the morning, the store manager should ensure that this policy is adhered to. If, during the day, further smaller denomination notes are required, the store manager should authorise a member of staff to obtain cash from the bank and should fully record movements in and out of the till.

Control deficiency	Control recommendation
One clerk is responsible for several elements of the cash receipts system. He oversees the daily interface from stores, agrees that cash has cleared into the bank statements and undertakes the bank reconciliations. There is a lack of segregation of duties and errors will not be identified on a timely basis as well as increasing the risk of fraud.	These key roles should be split between a few individuals, with ideally the bank reconciliations being undertaken by another member of the finance team.
The bank reconciliations are only reviewed by the financial controller if there are any unreconciled amounts. The bank reconciliation could reconcile but still contain significant errors as there could be compensating errors which cancel each other out. In addition, for a cash based business, the bank reconciliation is a key control which reduces the risk of fraud. If it is not reviewed, then this reduces its effectiveness.	The bank reconciliations should be reviewed by the financial controller on a monthly basis, even if there are no exceptions, and he should evidence his review by way of signature on the bank reconciliation.

Question 18

Workbook references. Chapters 14, 16 and 20.

Top tips. This is a 20-mark question which tests substantive procedures relating to income, trade payables and trade receivables, together with auditors' reports. In part (a) you must read the scenario carefully and tailor your substantive procedures. In the past the examining team has commented that candidates often provide lists of standard audit work without consideration of the facts in the question. Also note that in relation to income the question considers the assertion of completeness specifically. Again you must ensure you address this in your answer.

In part (b) the key is to note that you need to discuss the issues as well as commenting on the impact on the auditor's report. Your discussion should support the conclusion you have come to.

Easy marks. No specific part of this question is straightforward but there are some easier marks available in part (b).

Marks

(a) (i) Substantive procedures for completeness of Insects4U Co income
- Cast schedule of all of the company's income
- Compare individual categories of income to prior year
- Trace monthly donations from bank statements to cash book
- New subscribers agree subscription forms to donations received account, cash book and bank statements
- For donations, review correspondence from donors, agree to donations account, cash book and bank statements
- Perform proof in total of tickets sold multiplied by ticket price, compare to actual and investigate significant difference

Restricted to   4

(ii) Substantive procedures for Spider Spirals Co trade payables
- Calculate trade payables payment period 1
- Compare total trade payables and list of accruals against prior year 1
- Discuss with management process to quantify misstatement of payables 1
- Sample invoices received between 1 and 7 May, if post year end, then agree excluded from ledger 1
- Review after-date payments 1
- Review supplier statements reconciliations 1
- Perform a trade payables circularisation 1
- Cut-off testing pre and post year end GRN 1

Restricted to 6

(iii) Substantive procedures for Spider Spirals Co trade receivables
- Aged receivables report to identify any slow-moving balances 1
- Review customer correspondence to assess whether there are any invoices in dispute 1
- Review the after-date cash receipts 1
- Review board minutes 1
- Calculate level of irrecoverable receivables, assess if material and discuss with management 1
- Recalculate allowance for receivables 1
- Post year end sales returns/credit notes 1

Restricted to 5

(b) Effect of uncorrected misstatement and impact on auditor's report
- Discussion of issue 1
- Calculation of materiality 1
- Type of auditor's report modification required 2
- Impact on auditor's report 1

Restricted to 5

Total marks 20

(a) (i) Substantive procedures for Insects4U Co income

- Obtain a schedule of all Insects4U Co's income and cast to confirm completeness and accuracy of the balance.

- Compare the individual categories of income against prior year and investigate any significant differences.

- For monthly donations, trace a sample of donations received in the bank statements to the cash book to ensure that they are recorded completely and accurately.

- For a sample of new subscribers in the year, agree from their completed subscription form the monthly sum and start date, trace to the monthly donations received account and agree to the cash book and bank statements.

- For donations received in the post, review correspondence from donors, agree to the donations account and trace sums received to the cash book and bank statements to ensure all completely recorded.

- For the charity events, undertake a proof in total calculation of the number of tickets sold multiplied by the ticket price, compare this to the income recorded and discuss any significant differences with management.

(ii) **Substantive procedures for Spider Spirals Co trade payables**

- Calculate the trade payables collection period for Spider Spirals Co, compare with prior years and investigate any significant difference, in particular any decrease for this year due to the payment run on 3 May.

- Compare the total trade payables and list of accruals against prior year and investigate any significant differences.

- Discuss with management the process they have undertaken to quantify the misstatement of trade payables due to the late payment run and cut-off error of purchase invoices and consider the materiality of the error in isolation as well as with other misstatements found.

- Select a sample of purchase invoices received between the period of 1 and 7 May, ascertain through reviewing goods received notes (GRNs) if the goods were received pre or post year end; if post year end, then confirm that they have been excluded from the ledger or follow through to the correcting journal entry.

- Review after-date payments; if they relate to the current year, then follow through to the purchase ledger or accrual listing to ensure they are recorded in the correct period.

- Obtain supplier statements and reconcile these to the purchase ledger balances, and investigate any reconciling items.

- Select a sample of payables balances and perform a trade payables circularisation, follow up any non-replies and any reconciling items between the balance confirmed and the trade payables balance.

- Select a sample of GRNs before the year end and after the year end and follow through to inclusion in the correct period's payables balance, to ensure correct cut-off.

(iii) **Substantive procedures for Spider Spirals Co trade receivables**

- Review the aged receivables listing to identify any slow-moving or old receivables balances; discuss the status of these balances with the finance director to assess whether they are likely to pay.

- Review customer correspondence to identify any balances which are in dispute or unlikely to be paid.

- Review whether there are any after-date cash receipts for slow-moving/old receivables balances.

- Review board minutes to identify whether there are any significant concerns in relation to payments by customers.

- Calculate the potential level of receivables which are not recoverable and assess whether this is material or not and discuss with management.

- Recalculate the allowance for receivables and compare to the potentially irrecoverable balances to assess if the allowance is adequate.

- Inspect post year end sales returns/credit notes and consider whether an additional allowance against receivables is required.

BPP LEARNING MEDIA

(b) **Impact on auditor's report**

The company made a payment run of $490,000 for payables on 3 May, which is post year end. The trade payables which were outstanding at the year end have been understated as they have been recorded as being paid. In addition, the bank overdraft is overstated as the payments are recorded as coming out of the year-end bank balance. This is evidence of window dressing, as the company has attempted to record a lower level of payable obligations at the year end. The finance director's argument that no adjustment is necessary because the balances affected are both current liabilities is irrelevant as, although both balances are liabilities, they should each still be materially correct.

The amount of the payment run is $490,000 which represents 6.0% of total liabilities (490/8,100) and hence is a material matter.

If management refuses to adjust for the post year end payment run, the auditor's report will need to be modified. As trade payables are understated and the bank overdraft is overstated and there is a material misstatement which is not pervasive, a qualified opinion would be necessary. A basis for qualified opinion paragraph would need to be included subsequent to the opinion paragraph. This would explain the material misstatement in relation to the treatment of the trade payables and bank overdraft and the effect on the financial statements. The opinion paragraph would be qualified 'except for'.

ACCA

Applied Skills

Audit and Assurance

Mock Examination 4

March/June 2019 Hybrid Exam CBE

Time allowed: 3 hours

This mock exam is divided into two sections:

Section A – ALL 15 questions are compulsory and MUST be attempted

Section B – ALL 3 questions are compulsory and MUST be attempted

Section A – ALL 15 questions are compulsory and MUST be attempted

Each question is worth 2 marks.

The following scenario relates to questions 1–5.

You are an audit manager at Horti & Co and you are considering a number of ethical issues which have arisen on some of the firm's long-standing audit clients. It is 1 July 20X5.

Tree Co

Horti & Co is planning its external audit of Tree Co. Yesterday, the audit engagement partner, Charlie Thrower, discovered that a significant fee for information security services, which were provided to Tree Co by Horti & Co, is overdue. Charlie hopes to be able to resolve the dispute amicably and has confirmed that he will discuss the matter with the finance director, Percy Marsh, at the weekend, as they are both attending a party to celebrate the engagement of Charlie's daughter and Percy's son.

Bush Co

Horti & Co is the external auditor of Bush Co and also provides other non-audit services to the company. While performing the audit for the year ended 30 November 20X4, the audit engagement partner was taken ill and took an indefinite leave of absence from the firm. The ethics partner has identified the following potential replacements and is keen that independence is maintained to the highest level:

Brian Smith	who is also the partner in charge of the tax services provided to Bush Co
Monty Nod	who was the audit engagement partner for the ten years ended 30 November 20X3
Cassie Dixon	who introduced Bush Co as a client when she joined the firm as an audit partner five years ago
Pete Russo	who is also the partner in charge of the payroll services provided to Bush Co

Plant Co

Plant Co is a large private company, with a financial year to 31 March, and has been an audit client of Horti & Co for several years. Alan Marshlow, a partner of Horti & Co, has acted as the Engagement Quality Control Reviewer (EQCR) on the last two audits to the year ended 31 March 20X5. At a recent meeting, he advised that he can no longer be EQCR on the engagement as he is considering accepting appointment as a non-executive director and will sit on the audit committee of Plant Co.

The board of directors has also asked Horti & Co if they would be able to provide internal audit services to the company.

Weed Co

Weed Co, a listed company, is one of Horti & Co's largest clients. Last year the fee for audit and other services was $1.2m and this year it is expected to be $1.3m which represents 16.6% and 18.1% of Horti & Co's total income respectively.

1   Which of the following statements correctly explains the possible threats to Horti & Co's independence and recommends an appropriate safeguard in relation to their audit of Tree Co?

(1)   An intimidation threat exists due to the overdue fee and Tree Co should be advised that all fees must be paid prior to the auditor's report being signed

(2)   A self-review threat exists due to the nature of the non-audit work which has been performed and an engagement quality control review should be carried out

(3)   A self-interest threat exists due to the relationship between Charlie and Percy and Charlie should be removed as audit partner

☐ 1, 2 and 3

☐ 1 and 2 only

☐ 2 only

☐ 3 only

2   Taking into account the concern of the ethics partner, which of the partners identified as potential replacements should take over the audit of Bush Co for the year ended 30 November 20X4?

☐ Brian Smith

☐ Monty Nod

☐ Cassie Dixon

☐ Pete Russo

3   Which of the following options correctly identifies the threats to Horti & Co's independence and proposes an appropriate course of action for the firm if Alan Marshlow accepts appointment as a non-executive director of Plant Co?

	Threats	Course of action
Option 1	Self-interest and familiarity	Can continue with appropriate safeguards
Option 2	Self-interest and self-review	Must resign as auditor
Option 3	Self-interest and familiarity	Must resign as auditor
Option 4	Familiarity only	Can continue with appropriate safeguards

☐ Option 1

☐ Option 2

☐ Option 3

☐ Option 4

---

4   You are separately considering Plant Co's request to provide internal audit services and the remit of these services if they are accepted.

Which of the following would result in Horti & Co assuming a management responsibility in relation to the internal audit services?

(1)   Taking responsibility for designing and maintaining internal control systems

(2)   Determining which recommendations should take priority and be implemented

(3)   Determining the reliance which can be placed on the work of internal audit for the external audit

(4)   Setting the scope of the internal audit work to be carried out

☐ 1 and 3

☐ 2, 3, and 4

☐ 1, 2 and 4

☐ 3 and 4 only

---

5   **Which of the following actions should Horti & Co take to maintain their objectivity in relation to the level of fee income from Weed Co?**

(1)   The level of fee income should be communicated to those charged with governance

(2)   Separate teams should be used for the audit and non-audit work

(3)   Request payment of the current year's audit fee in advance of any work being performed

(4)   Request a pre-issuance review be conducted by an external accountant

☐ 1 and 4 only

☐ 3 and 4 only

☐ 2 and 3 only

☐ 1, 2, 3 and 4

The following scenario relates to questions 6–10.

Chester Co manufactures and sells pet toys to the wholesale market. It has prepared its financial statements to 28 February 20X5. It is 1 July 20X5. You are an audit assistant with Durham & Co and you have been assigned the current liabilities balances in the audit work plan.

You have calculated the payables payment period to be 66 days in 20X5 (45 days in 20X4) and have asked the directors of Chester Co to provide an explanation as to the increase in days.

Chester Co receives monthly statements from its main suppliers and performs regular supplier statement reconciliations. There were inconsistencies noted in respect of the following at 28 February 20X5:

Supplier	Balance per purchase ledger ($)	Balance per supplier statement ($)
Oxford Co	151,480	296,120
Poole Co	(72,168)	84,235
Bath Co	82,348	92,340

Oxford Co

Chester Co has a credit agreement with Oxford Co under which it receives goods 14 days before the supplier raises the invoice. Chester Co received goods worth $144,640 on 18 February 20X5 for which the invoice was received shortly after the year end in accordance with the agreement. Chester Co entered the transaction into its accounting records at the date of invoice.

Poole Co

The difference on this balance has still to be investigated.

Bath Co

Chester Co's finance director has informed you that there was an error in closing the purchase ledger and it was closed three days early. Invoices received 26, 27 and 28 February 20X5 were posted to the 20X6 ledger. The directors of Chester Co have confirmed that following discovery of this error, a manual adjustment was made using the journal book.

6   Which of the following supplier balances would indicate a high risk in relation to the COMPLETENESS of the liability recorded at the year end?

☐ A supplier with a high balance at the year end and with a low volume of transactions during the year

☐ A supplier with a low balance at the year end and with a high volume of transactions during the year

☐ A supplier with a low balance at the year end and with a low volume of transactions during the year

☐ A supplier with a high balance at the year end and with a high volume of transactions during the year

7   Which of the following would correctly explain why the payables payment period has increased from 45 days in 20X4 to 66 days in 20X5?

☐ Chester Co received a prompt payment discount from one of its suppliers for the first time in 20X5

☐ Chester Co obtained a trade discount from one of its biggest suppliers which has reduced the amount owed to that supplier by 10% in the year

☐ Chester Co purchased an unusually high level of goods in February 20X5 to satisfy a large order and had not paid for those goods by the year end

☐ Chester Co took advantage of extended credit terms offered by a new supplier in respect of a large order which it had fully settled by the year end

8   Which of the following is an appropriate action in respect of the inconsistency in the balance with Oxford Co?

☐ The auditor should take no further action as this is a timing difference which was resolved upon receipt and posting of the invoice

☐ The auditor should request that the purchase ledger balance is amended at the reporting date to reflect the recent invoice

☐ The auditor should contact the supplier and request a supplier statement as at the current date

☐ The auditor should request that an accrual is created in respect of the goods received but not yet invoiced

9   Which of the following would be a valid explanation for the difference in respect of Poole Co?

(1)   An invoice for $156,403 has been paid twice

(2)   An invoice for $156,403 has been posted as a debit note

(3)   An invoice for $156,403 has been received and processed prior to receipt of the goods

☐ 1 only

☐ 1 and 2 only

☐ 2 and 3 only

☐ 1, 2 and 3

10   Which of the following would NOT provide sufficient and appropriate audit evidence over the COMPLETENESS of the purchase ledger balance in respect of Bath Co?

☐ Obtain the journal book and confirm that all invoices recorded as received from Bath Co dated 26–28 February have been manually adjusted for

☐ Review the accruals listing to ensure goods received from Bath Co post year end for which an invoice has not been received have been recorded in the correct period

☐ For post year-end cash book payments to Bath Co, confirm date of matching invoice and if pre year end agree to liability

☐ Review a sample of invoices received from Bath Co recorded post year end and match to GRN to determine if they should have been recorded at the year end

---

The following scenario relates to questions 11–15.

Viola Co is a manufacturer of shoes. You are an audit manager with Cello & Co and you are performing an overall review of the financial statements for the year ended 31 December 20X4 prior to the issue of the auditor's report. It is 1 July 20X5. Profit before tax for the year was $131.4m (20X3: $120.9m).

Analytical procedures

As part of your overall review, you have performed analytical procedures over the draft financial statements and have noted that the trade receivables collection period is lower than it was during the interim audit performed in October 20X4. You are aware that the credit controller of Viola Co left the company in November 20X4 and that the directors have said that, as a result, the company is experiencing difficulties in debt collection.

Disclosures

During the year, Viola Co revalued its head office and as part of your review, you are considering the detail which is disclosed in the property, plant and equipment note in the draft financial statements.

Uncorrected misstatements

Your review also includes an assessment of uncorrected misstatements. These have been recorded by the audit team as follows:

		$000
(1)	Interest payable omitted in error	1,942
(2)	Additional allowance for receivables required	9,198
(3)	Error in sales invoice processing resulting in understatement of sales	8,541
(4)	Write off in respect of faulty goods	2,900

Faulty goods

The adjustment for faulty goods listed as an uncorrected misstatement above, relates to an entire batch of shoes, which was produced on 12 December 20X4. The audit work concluded that the cost of this inventory exceeded its net realisable value by $2.9m. The directors dispute the audit team's figures and believe that the realisable value of the inventory still exceeds its cost.

11   Which of the following would form part of the auditor's overall review of the financial
      statements?

      (1)   Establishing whether the pre-conditions for an audit are present

      (2)   Assessing whether the information and explanations obtained during the audit are
             adequately reflected

      (3)   Performing a detailed review of the audit working papers to ensure the work has
             been properly performed

      (4)   Reviewing the adequacy of the disclosure of accounting policies

      ☐   1 and 2

      ☐   3 and 4

      ☐   1 and 3

      ☐   2 and 4

---

12   Which of the following is a valid explanation for the INCONSISTENCY between the
      results of the analytical procedures on trade receivables and the directors' statement
      regarding debt collection problems?

      ☐   A change in sales mix towards high value products

      ☐   An increase in the proportion of cash sales since November 20X4

      ☐   An increase in the rate of sales tax in December 20X4

      ☐   Sales growth of 1% per month over the year

---

13   Which of the following details should be disclosed in respect of the revaluation of the
      head office if the auditor is to conclude that the disclosures are adequate?

      (1)   Effective date of the revaluation

      (2)   Name of the valuer

      (3)   The amount of the revaluation increase

      (4)   Carrying amount of the head office under the cost model

      ☐   1, 2 and 3 only

      ☐   1, 3 and 4 only

      ☐   2, 3 and 4 only

      ☐   1, 2, 3 and 4

14　Which of the uncorrected misstatements numbered (1), (2) and (3) by the audit team MUST be adjusted for if the auditor is to issue an unmodified audit opinion?

☐ Misstatements 2 and 3 only

☐ Misstatements 1 and 3 only

☐ Misstatements 1, 2 and 3

☐ Misstatement 2 only

15　All adjustments required by the auditors have been made to the financial statements with the exception of adjustment (4) relating to the faulty goods.

Which of the following correctly describes the effect of this matter on the auditor's report?

☐ Unmodified opinion with no further disclosure

☐ Unmodified opinion with disclosure in an emphasis of matter paragraph

☐ Qualified opinion due to material misstatement

☐ Qualified opinion due to inability to obtain sufficient appropriate audit evidence

(Total = 30 marks)

Section B – ALL THREE questions are compulsory and MUST be attempted

Question 16

(a) Auditors are required to document a company's accounting and internal control systems as part of their audit process. Two methods available for documenting internal control systems are narrative notes and questionnaires.

Required

For each of the two methods, NARRATIVE NOTES and QUESTIONNAIRES:

(i)   Describe the method for documenting internal control systems; and
(ii) Explain an ADVANTAGE of using this method.

Note: The total marks will be split equally between each part.   **(4 marks)**

Freesia Co is a company listed on a stock exchange. It manufactures furniture which it supplies to a wide range of retailers across the region. The company has an internal audit (IA) department and the company's year end is 31 January 20X5. It is 1 July 20X5. You are an audit supervisor with Zinnia & Co, preparing the draft audit programmes and reviewing extracts from the internal controls documentation in preparation for the interim audit.

Sales

Freesia Co generates revenue through visits by its sales staff to customers' premises. Sales ledger clerks, who work at head office, carry out credit checks on new customers prior to being accepted and then set their credit limits. Sales staff visit retail customers' sites personally and orders are completed using a four-part pre-printed order form. One copy is left with the customer, a second copy is returned to the sales ordering department, the third is sent to the warehouse and the fourth to the finance department at head office. Each sales order number is based on the sales person's own identification number in order to facilitate monitoring of sales staff performance.

Retail customers are given payment terms of 30 days and most customers choose to pay their invoices by bank transfer. Each day Lily Shah, a finance clerk, posts the bank transfer receipts from the bank statements to the cash book and updates the sales ledger. On a monthly basis, she performs the bank reconciliation.

Purchases and inventory

Receipts of raw materials and goods from suppliers are processed by the warehouse team at head office, who agree the delivery to the purchase order, check the quantity and quality of goods and complete a sequentially numbered goods received note (GRN). The GRNs are sent to the finance department daily. On receipt of the purchase invoice from the supplier, Camilla Brown, the purchase ledger clerk, matches it to the GRN and order and the three documents are sent for authorisation by the appropriate individual. Once authorised, the purchase invoices are logged into the purchase ledger by Camilla, who utilises document count controls to ensure the correct number of invoices has been input.

The company values its inventory using standard costs, both for internal management reporting and for inclusion in the year-end financial statements. The basis of the standard costs was reviewed approximately 18 months ago.

Payroll

Freesia Co employs a mixture of factory staff, who work a standard shift of eight hours a day, and administration and sales staff who are salaried. All staff are paid monthly by bank transfer. Occasionally, overtime is required of factory staff. Where this occurs, details of overtime worked per employee is collated and submitted to the payroll department by a production clerk. The payroll department pays this overtime in the month it occurs. At the end of each quarter, the company's payroll department sends overtime reports which detail the amount of overtime worked to the production director for their review.

 BPP LEARNING MEDIA

Freesia Co's payroll package produces a list of payments per employee which links into the bank system to produce a list of automatic bank transfer payments. The finance director reviews the total to be paid on the list of automatic payments and compares this to the total payroll amount to be paid for the month per the payroll records. If any issues arise, then the automatic bank transfer can be manually changed by the finance director.

Required

(b)   In respect of the internal controls of Freesia Co:

    (i)   Identify and explain SIX deficiencies;

    (ii)   Recommend a control to address each of these deficiencies; and

    (iii)   Describe a TEST OF CONTROL the external auditors should perform to assess if each of these controls, if implemented, is operating effectively to reduce the identified deficiency.

Note: Prepare your answer using three columns headed Control deficiency, Control recommendation and Test of control respectively. The total marks will be split equally between each part.   **(18 marks)**

Freesia Co deducts employment taxes from its employees' wages and salaries on a monthly basis and pays these to the local taxation authorities in the following month. At the year end, the financial statements will contain an accrual for employment tax payable.

Required

(c)   Describe the substantive procedures the auditor should perform to obtain sufficient and appropriate audit evidence in respect of Freesia Co's year-end accrual for employment tax payable.   **(4 marks)**

The listing rules of the stock exchange require compliance with corporate governance principles and the directors of Freesia Co are confident that they are following best practice in relation to this. However, the chairman recently received correspondence from a shareholder, who is concerned that the company is not fully compliant. The company's finance director has therefore requested a review of the company's compliance with corporate governance principles.

Freesia Co has been listed for over eight years and its board comprises four executive and four independent non-executive directors (NEDs), excluding the chairman. An audit committee comprised of the NEDs and the finance director meets each quarter to review the company's internal controls.

The directors' remuneration is set by the finance director. NEDs are paid a fixed fee for their services and executive directors are paid an annual salary as well as a significant annual bonus based on Freesia Co's profits. The company's chairman does not have an executive role and so she has sole responsibility for liaising with the shareholders and answering any of their questions.

Required

(d)   Describe TWO corporate governance weaknesses faced by Freesia Co and provide a recommendation to address each weakness to ensure compliance with corporate governance principles.

Note: Prepare your answer using two columns headed Weakness and Recommendation respectively.   **(4 marks)**

(Total = 30 marks)

Question 17

(a) Define and explain materiality and performance materiality. **(4 marks)**

You are an audit supervisor of Daffodil & Co and are planning the audit of Peony Co for the year ending 31 May 20X5. It is 1 July 20X5. The company is a food retailer with a large network of stores across the country and four warehouses. The company has been a client of your firm for several years and the forecast profit before tax is $28·9m. The audit manager has attended a planning meeting with the finance director and has provided you with the following notes of the meeting.

Planning meeting notes

Peony Co has an internal audit (IA) department which undertakes controls testing across the network of stores. Each store is visited at least once every 18 months. The audit manager has discussed with the finance director that the external audit team may rely on the controls testing which is undertaken by IA.

During the meeting, the finance director provided some forecast financial information. Revenue for the year is expected to increase by 3% as compared to 20X4; the gross margin is expected to increase from 56% to 60%; and the operating margin is predicted to decrease from 21% to 18%.

Peony Co values inventory in line with industry practice, which is to use selling price less average profit margin. The directors consider this to be a close approximation to cost.

The company does not undertake a full year-end inventory count and instead undertakes monthly perpetual inventory counts, each of which covers one-twelfth of all lines in stores and the warehouses. As part of the interim audit which was completed in January, an audit junior attended a perpetual inventory count at one of the warehouses and noted that there were a large number of exceptions where the inventory records showed a higher quantity than the physical inventory which was present in the warehouse. When discussing these exceptions with the financial controller, the audit junior was informed that this had been a recurring issue.

During the year, IA performed a review of the non-current assets physically present in around one-third of the company's stores. A number of assets which had not been fully depreciated were identified as obsolete by this review.

The company launched a significant TV advertising campaign in January 20X5 in order to increase revenue. The directors have indicated that at the year end a current asset of $0·7m will be recognised, as they believe that the advertisements will help to boost future sales in the next 12 months. The last advertisement will be shown on TV in early May 20X5.

Peony Co decided to outsource its payroll function to an external service organisation. This service organisation handles all elements of the payroll cycle and sends monthly reports to Peony Co which detail wages and salaries and statutory obligations. Peony Co maintained its own payroll records until 31 December 20X4, at which point the records were transferred to the service organisation. Peony Co is planning to expand the company by opening three new stores during July 20X5 and in order to finance this, in March 20X5 the company obtained a $3m bank loan. This is repayable in arrears over five years in quarterly instalments. In preparation for the expansion, the company is looking to streamline operations in the warehouses and is planning to make approximately 60 employees redundant after the year end. No decision has been made as to when this will be announced, but it is likely to be in May 20X5.

Required

(b) Describe EIGHT audit risks and explain the auditor's response to each risk in planning the audit of Peony Co.

Note: Prepare your answer using two columns headed Audit risk and Auditor's response respectively. **(16 marks)**

(Total = 20 marks)

Question 18

Hyacinth Co develops and manufactures computer components and its year end was 31 March 20X5. It is 1 July 20X5. The company has a large factory, and two warehouses, one of which is off-site. You are an audit supervisor of Tulip & Co and the final audit is due to commence shortly. Draft financial statements show total assets of $23·2m and profit before tax of $6·4m. The following three matters have been brought to your attention:

Inventory valuation

Your firm attended the year-end inventory count for Hyacinth Co and confirmed that the controls and processes for recording work in progress (WIP) and finished goods were acceptable. WIP and finished goods are both material to the financial statements and the audit team was able to confirm both the quantity and stage of completion of WIP.

Before goods are dispatched, they are inspected by the company's quality control department. Just prior to the inventory count, it was noted that a batch of product line 'Crocus', which had been produced to meet a customer's specific technical requirements, did not meet that customer's quality and technical standards. This inventory had a production cost of $450,000. Upon discussions with the production supervisor, the finance director believes that the inventory can still be sold to alternative customers at a discounted price of $90,000.

Research and development

Hyacinth Co includes expenditure incurred in developing new products within intangible assets once the recognition criteria under IAS 38 *Intangible Assets* have been met. Intangible assets are amortised on a straight line basis over four years once production commences. The amortisation policy is based on past experience of the likely useful lives of the products. The opening balance of intangible assets is $1·9m.

In the current year, Hyacinth Co spent $0·8m developing three new products which are all at different stages of development.

Sales tax liability

Hyacinth Co is required by the relevant tax authority in the country in which it operates to charge sales tax at 15% on all products which it sells. This sales tax is payable to the tax authority. When purchasing raw materials and incurring expenses in the manufacturing process, the company pays 15% sales tax on any items purchased and this can be reclaimed from the tax authority. The company is required to report the taxes charged and incurred by completing a tax return on a quarterly basis, and the net amount owing to the tax authority must be remitted within four weeks of the quarter end. The draft financial statements contain a $1·1m liability for sales tax for the quarter ended 31 March 20X5.

Required

(a) Describe substantive procedures the auditor should perform to obtain sufficient and appropriate audit evidence in relation to the VALUATION of Hyacinth Co's inventory.
(6 marks)

(b) Describe substantive procedures the auditor should perform to obtain sufficient and appropriate audit evidence in relation to Hyacinth Co's research and development expenditure.
(4 marks)

(c) Describe substantive procedures the auditor should perform to obtain sufficient and appropriate audit evidence in relation to Hyacinth Co's year-end sales tax liability.
(4 marks)

The audit is now almost complete and the auditor's report is due to be signed shortly. The following matter has been brought to your attention:

On 3 May 20X5, a flood occurred at the off-site warehouse. This resulted in some damage to inventory and property, plant and equipment. However, there have been no significant delays to customer deliveries or complaints from customers. Hyacinth Co's management has investigated the cause of the flooding and believes that the company is unlikely to be able to claim on its insurance. The finance director of Hyacinth Co has estimated that the value of damaged inventory and property, plant and equipment was $0·7m and that it now has no scrap value.

Required

(d)   (i)   Explain whether the 20X5 financial statements of Hyacinth Co require amendment in relation to the flood; and

(ii)   Describe audit procedures which should be performed in order to form a conclusion on any required amendment.

Note: The total marks will be split equally between each part.   (6 marks)

(Total = 20 marks)

Answers

DO NOT TURN THIS PAGE UNTIL YOU HAVE
COMPLETED THE MOCK EXAM

Plan of attack

If this were the real Audit and Assurance exam and you had been told to turn over and begin, what would be going through your mind?

An important thing to say (whilst there is still time) is that it is vital to have a good breadth of knowledge of the syllabus because all the questions are compulsory. However, don't panic. Below we provide guidance on how to approach the exam.

Looking through the exam

Section A has three objective test cases, each with five questions. This is the section of the exam where the examining team can test knowledge across the breadth of the syllabus. Make sure you read these cases and questions carefully. The distractors are designed to present plausible, but incorrect, answers. Don't let them mislead you. If you really have no idea – guess. You may even be right.

Section B has three longer questions:

- **Question 16** is a 30-mark question covering internal control deficiencies, substantive procedures on one area and then corporate governance. Read the requirements carefully, and try to relate your answers to the specific scenario as much as you can .

- **Question 17** is a 20-mark question set at the planning stage of an audit. Part (a) tests your knowledge of materiality, while part (b) asks for eight audit risks and auditor responses. The scenario is full of potential points, so if you work through it methodically then you can produce a good answer.

- **Question 18** is a 20-mark question dealing with substantive procedures, inventory, development costs and the sales tax liability, with the requirement relating to inventory focusing just on one assertion. The final part then tests your assessment of a subsequent event.

Allocating your time

BPP's advice is to always allocate your time **according to the marks for the question**. However, **use common sense**. If you're doing a question but haven't a clue how to do part (b), you might be better off reallocating your time and getting more marks on another question, where you can add something you didn't have time for earlier on. Make sure you leave time to recheck the OTs and make sure you have answered them all.

Forget about it

And don't worry if you found the exam difficult. More than likely other candidates will too. If this were the real thing you would need to forget the exam the minute you left the exam hall and think about the next one. Or, if it is the last one, celebrate!

Section A

1   The correct answer is: 3 only

In line with ACCA's *Code of Ethics and Conduct*, a self-interest threat would arise due to the personal relationship between the audit engagement partner and finance director. A self-interest threat, not intimidation threat, would arise as a result of the overdue fee and due to the nature of the non-audit work, it is unlikely that a self-review threat would arise.

2   The correct answer is: Cassie Dixon

In order to maintain independence, Cassie Dixon would be the most appropriate replacement as audit engagement partner as she has no ongoing relationship with Bush Co. Appointing any of the other potential replacements would give rise to self-review or familiarity threats to independence.

3   The correct answer is: Option 2

If Alan Marshlow accepts the position as a non-executive director for Plant Co, self-interest and self-review threats are created which are so significant that no safeguards can be implemented. Further as per ACCA's *Code of Ethics and Conduct*, no partner of the firm should serve as a director of an audit client and as such, Horti & Co would need to resign as auditor.

4   The correct answer is: 1, 2 and 4

Assuming a management responsibility is when the auditor is involved in leading or directing the company or making decisions which are the remit of management. Designing and maintaining internal controls, determining which recommendations to implement and setting the scope of work are all decisions which should be taken by management.

5   The correct answer is: 1 and 4 only

Weed Co is a listed company and the fees received by Horti & Co from the company have exceeded 15% of the firm's total fees for two years. As per ACCA's *Code of Ethics and Conduct*, this should be disclosed to those charged with governance and an appropriate safeguard should be implemented. In this case, it would be appropriate to have a pre-issuance review carried out prior to issuing the audit opinion for the current year.

6   The correct answer is: A supplier with a low balance at the year-end but with a high volume of transactions during the year.

This may indicate that not all liabilities have been recorded at the year-end date.

7   The correct answer is: Chester Co purchased an unusually high level of goods in February 20X5 to satisfy a large order and had not paid for those goods by the year end

A purchase of a large volume of goods close to the year-end would increase the payables payment period. The prompt payment and trade discounts would both decrease the payables payment period, and the extended credit terms in this instance would have no impact as there is no closing balance with the new supplier.

8   The correct answer is: The auditor should request that an accrual is created in respect of the goods received but not yet invoiced

The difference of $144,640 with Oxford Co relates to goods which were received by Chester Co prior to the year-end but were not recorded in the accounting records until after the year-end date. As Chester Co had a liability to pay for the goods at the date of receipt, an accrual should be created for the goods received not yet invoiced.

9   The correct answer is: 1 only

The difference in respect of Poole Co may have arisen if the invoice had been paid twice in error as an additional $156,403 will have been debited to the supplier account.

10   The correct answer is: Review the accruals listing to ensure goods received from Bath Co post year end for which an invoice has not been received have been recorded in the correct period

      Reviewing the accruals listing would not help the auditor confirm the purchase ledger balance with Bath Co as accruals are recorded separately from the purchase ledger balance.

11   The correct answer is: 2 and 4

      As part of the overall review of the financial statements, the auditor should assess whether the information and explanations gathered during the audit and accounting policies are adequately reflected and disclosed. Pre-conditions should be considered as part of the auditor's acceptance procedures and a detailed review of the audit working papers is conducted as part of the firm's quality control procedures.

12   The correct answer is: An increase in the proportion of cash sales since November 20X4

      An increase in the proportion of cash sales since the interim audit would increase sales but not trade receivables resulting in a decreased trade receivables collection period.

13   The correct answer is: 1, 3 and 4 only

      The effective date of the revaluation, the amount of the revaluation increase and the carrying amount of the head office under the cost model are disclosures required by IAS 16 *Property, Plant and Equipment*.

14   The correct answer is: Misstatements 2 and 3 only

      Misstatements (2) and (3) are individually material and would require adjustment for an unmodified opinion to be issued. Misstatement (1) is immaterial and if Viola Co did not make this adjustment, an unmodified opinion could still be issued.

15   The correct answer is: Unmodified opinion with no further disclosure

      Misstatement (4) is immaterial at 2.2% of profit before tax ($2.9m/$131.4m) and would not require further disclosure. Therefore as all other adjustments have been made, no material misstatement exists and an unmodified opinion can be issued.

BPP
LEARNING
MEDIA

Section B

Question 16

Workbook references. Chapters 3, 10 and 16.

Top tips. Part (a) was the knowledge-based part, and as such you should be aiming for full marks here. It is important that you stick to the requirement precisely, eg you should only give an advantage of each method – one advantage, with no marks available for disadvantages. The marks for describing each method were among the easiest in the exam.

Part (b) was the core of this question, and asked for six deficiencies for which you needed to develop controls and then tests of control. Your response should therefore be connected across all three columns. As ever, the requirement is to 'identify and explain' each deficiency, which suggests that your answer could be structured as two sentences / paragraphs within the left column, the first of which says what is happening (identifying the problem), and the second of which says why this is a problem (or why it is wrong). Your control and test of control must then be explained in enough detail to get a full mark each. It is a good idea to think of these two columns together – try to suggest a control for which you can easily suggest a test.

Part (c) asked for substantive procedures in relation to the employment tax accrual; quite a lot of the points here should not be difficult to think of, so this requirement is a good opportunity to score marks.

Part (d) covered corporate governance. This requirement is not actually asking a great deal here, particularly given the length of the related scenario, so again this should not have been overly taxing.

Easy marks. Part (a) was knowledge-based and should have been within your reach.

Examination team comments. Internal control questions remain a highly examinable area and performance in June 2019 was mixed. The scenarios included in exam questions contain more issues than are required to be discussed. It was pleasing in this session that candidates were generally able to identify (for ½ mark each) the required number of issues from the scenarios. However some candidates were unable to correctly identify the deficiency from the scenario. They were able to pick the relevant fact from the scenario but failed to spot what the actual deficiency was. For example, from the scenario candidates identified 'invoices have a unique number' but the actual issue was that the unique numbers were not sequential. Additionally, this session there was an increase in the number of answers with irrelevant deficiencies being given. This seems to stem from a lack of understanding of the scenario and possibly due to a lack of question practice.

In common with previous sittings many candidates did not clearly explain the implication of the deficiencies. It is important that the explanation fully details the impact to the company. As an example, for a deficiency of 'purchase invoices are not sequentially numbered' a suitable, well-explained implication would be 'this could result in the recording of purchases and payables being incomplete and suppliers being paid late'. Many candidates did not go on to explain the impact on the company in sufficient detail, for example just stating, 'this could result in invoices being missed'.

Most candidates were able to provide good recommendations to address the deficiencies they identified. However, some of the recommendations were either poorly described, did not clearly address the specific control deficiency identified or were impractical suggestions. Many candidates just repeated the converse of the deficiency and to obtain the one mark for the recommendation more detail is needed. For example, for the deficiency 'a lack of segregation of duties around inventory management' some candidates stated a recommendation of 'segregation should be introduced'. However, to obtain the full mark this recommendation needed to cover what elements of the role should be separated. Additionally, as with ethics and corporate governance questions, recommendations must be actions rather than just objectives.

		Marks
(a)	Methods of documenting internal control systems	
	Narrative notes	2
	Questionnaires	2
		4
(b)	Control deficiencies, recommendations and tests of control (only 6 required)	
	Credit limits	3
	No sequential numbering of orders	3
	Segregation of duties – cash receipts	3
	Insufficient copies of GRN	3
	Controls over inputting of invoices	3
	Out-of-date standard costs	3
	Overtime not authorised	3
	Authorisation of bank transfer	3
	Max 6 issues, 3 marks each	18
(c)	Substantive procedures – accrual for employment tax	
	Compare to prior year and investigate differences	1
	Agree accrual to year-end payroll records	1
	Recalculate accrual and consider reasonableness	1
	Perform proof in total and investigate variances	1
	Confirm post year-end payment	1
	Review correspondence with tax authorities for any additional liabilities	1
	Review disclosure and confirm in line with accounting standards	1
	Restricted to	4
(d)	Corporate governance weakness and recommendations (2 issues required)	
	Composition of audit committee	2
	Finance director sets remuneration	2
	Executive directors' remuneration	2
	Only chairman liaises with shareholders	2
	Max 2 issues, 2 marks each	4
Total marks		30

ANSWERS

(a)   Documenting systems

	Description	Advantage
Narrative notes	Narrative notes consist of a written description of the system. They detail what occurs in the system at each stage and include any controls which operate at each stage.	They are simple to record; after discussion with staff members, these discussions are easily written up as notes. They can facilitate understanding by all members of the audit team, especially more junior members who might find alternative methods too complex.
Questionnaires	Internal control questionnaires (ICQs) or internal control evaluation questionnaires (ICEQs) contain a list of questions for each major transaction cycle; ICQs are used to assess whether controls exist whereas ICEQs assess the effectiveness of the controls in place.	Questionnaires are quick to prepare, which means they are a timely method for recording the system. They ensure that all controls present within the system are considered and recorded, hence missing controls or deficiencies are clearly highlighted to the audit team.

(b)   Deficiencies, controls and test of controls

Control deficiency	Control recommendation	Test of control
Customer credit limits are set by sales ledger clerks. Sales ledger clerks are not sufficiently senior and so may set limits too high, leading to irrecoverable debts, or too low, leading to a loss of sales.	Credit limits should be set by a senior member of the sales department and not by sales ledger clerks. These limits should be regularly reviewed by a responsible official.	For a sample of new customers accepted in the year, review the authorisation of the credit limit, and ensure that this was performed by a responsible official. Enquire of sales ledger clerks as to who can set credit limits.
Customer orders are given a number based on the sales person's own identification number. These numbers are not sequential. Without sequential numbers, it is difficult for Freesia Co to identify missing orders and to monitor if all orders are being dispatched in a timely manner. If they are not, this could lead to a loss of customer goodwill.	Sales orders should be sequentially numbered. On a regular basis, a sequence check of orders should be undertaken to identify any missing orders.	Re-perform the control by undertaking a sequence check of sales orders. Discuss any gaps in the sequence with sales ordering staff.

Control deficiency	Control recommendation	Test of control
Lily Shah, a finance clerk, is responsible for several elements of the cash receipts system as she posts the bank transfer receipts from the bank statements to the cash book, updates the sales ledger and performs the bank reconciliations. There is a lack of segregation of duties and errors will not be identified on a timely basis. There is also an increased risk of fraud.	The key roles of posting bank receipts, updating the sales ledger and performing bank reconciliations should be split between different individuals. If this is not practical, then as a minimum, the bank reconciliations should be undertaken by another member of the finance team.	Review the file of completed bank reconciliations to identify who prepared them. Review the log of IDs of individuals who have posted bank receipts and updated the sales ledger to assess whether these are different individuals. Discuss with the financial controller which members of staff undertake the roles of processing of bank receipts and updating of the cash book and sales ledger.
GRNs are only sent to the finance department. Failing to send a copy to the purchase ordering department means that it is not possible to monitor the level of unfulfilled orders. This could result in a significant level of unfulfilled orders leading to stock-outs and a consequent loss of sales. In addition, if the GRN is lost, then it will not be possible for the finance department to match the invoice to proof of goods being received. This could result in a delay to the invoice being paid and a loss of supplier goodwill.	The GRN should be created in three parts with one copy of the GRN being sent to the ordering department. The second copy should be held at the warehouse and the third sent to the finance department. A purchase ordering clerk should agree their copy of the GRN to the purchase order and change the order status to complete. On a regular basis, a review should be undertaken for all unfulfilled orders and these should be followed up with the relevant supplier.	Review the file of copy GRNs held by the purchase ordering department and review for evidence that these are matched to orders and flagged as complete. Review the file of unfulfilled purchase orders for any overdue items and discuss their status with an ordering clerk.

ANSWERS

Control deficiency	Control recommendation	Test of control
Camilla Brown, the purchase ledger clerk, only utilises document count controls when inputting invoices into the purchase ledger. Document count controls can confirm the completeness of input. However, they do not verify the accuracy or validity of input. If the invoices are not input correctly, suppliers may not be paid on time, or paid incorrect amounts leading to an overpayment or loss of supplier goodwill who may withdraw credit facilities.	The purchase ledger clerk should instead input the invoices in batches and apply application controls, such as control totals, rather than just completeness checks to ensure both completeness and accuracy over the input of purchase invoices. In addition, sequence checks should be built into the system to ensure completeness of input.	The audit team should utilise test data procedures to assess whether data can be entered without the use of batch control totals and also whether sequence checks are built into the system. Observe the inputting of purchase invoices and identify what application controls are utilised by the clerk.
The company values its inventory using standard costs, which are not being kept up-to-date. If the standard costs were reviewed 18 months ago, there is the risk that the costs are misstated as changes in raw materials and wages inflation may not have been adjusted for. This could result in inventory being under or overvalued and profits being misstated. In addition for year-end reporting, IAS 2 *Inventories* only allows standard costs to be used for valuation purposes if they are a close approximation to actual costs, which is unlikely if the standard costs remain unchanged for a long period of time. Therefore the valuation may not be in line with IAS 2.	A review of all standard costs currently in use should be undertaken by a senior manager in the production department. Actual costs for materials, labour and overheads should be ascertained and compared to the proposed standard costs to ensure they are a close approximation. The revised standard costs should be reviewed by the production director who should evidence this review. At least annually, a review of the standard costs should be undertaken to ensure they are up-to-date.	Obtain a copy of the standard costs used for inventory valuation, assess when the review was last undertaken and inspect for evidence of review by the production director.

Control deficiency	Control recommendation	Test of control
Overtime worked is not authorised prior to being paid. The information per employee is collated and submitted to payroll by a production clerk, but not authorised. The production director is only informed about overtime levels via quarterly reports. These reports are reviewed sometime after the payments have been made which could result in unauthorised overtime or amounts being paid incorrectly and Freesia Co's payroll cost increasing.	All overtime should be authorised by a responsible official prior to the payment being processed by the payroll department. This authorisation should be evidenced in writing.	Review the overtime report for evidence of authorisation and note the date this occurred to ensure that this was undertaken prior to the payment of the overtime.
The finance director compares the total of the list of bank transfers with the total to be paid per the payroll records. There could be employees omitted or fictitious employees added to the payment listing so that, although the total payments list agrees to payroll totals, there could be fraudulent or erroneous payments being made.	The finance director, when authorising the payments, should on a sample basis perform checks from the human resource department's staff records to payment list and vice versa to confirm that payments are complete and only made to *bona fide* employees. The finance director should sign the payments list as evidence that these checks have been undertaken.	Obtain a sample of payments lists and review for signature by the finance director as evidence that the control is operating correctly.

(c) Accrual for employment tax payable

Substantive procedures the auditor should adopt in respect of auditing this accrual include:

- Compare the accrual for employment tax payable to the prior year, investigate any significant differences.

- Agree the year-end employment tax payable accrual to the payroll records to confirm accuracy.

- Re-perform the calculation of the accrual for a sample of employees to confirm the accuracy.

- Undertake a proof in total test for the employment tax accrual by multiplying the payroll cost for January 20X5 with the appropriate tax rate. Compare this expectation to the actual accrual and investigate any significant differences.

- Agree the subsequent payment to the post year-end cash book and bank statements to confirm completeness.

BPP
LEARNING
MEDIA

- Review any correspondence with tax authorities to assess whether there are any additional outstanding payments due. If so, confirm they are included in the year-end accrual.

- Review any disclosures made of the employment tax accrual and assess whether these are in compliance with accounting standards and legislation.

(d) Corporate governance weaknesses and recommendations

Weakness	Recommendation
The finance director is a member of the audit committee. The audit committee should be made up entirely of independent NEDs. The role of the committee is to maintain objectivity with regards to financial reporting; this is difficult if the finance director is a member of the committee as the finance director will be responsible for the preparation of the financial statements.	The audit committee must be comprised of independent NEDs only; therefore the finance director should resign from the committee.
The remuneration for directors is set by the finance director. However, no director should be involved in setting their own remuneration as this may result in excessive levels of pay being set.	There should be a fair and transparent policy in place for setting remuneration levels. The NEDs should form a remuneration committee to decide on the remuneration of the executives. The board as a whole should decide on the pay of the NEDs.
Executive remuneration includes a significant annual profit related bonus. Remuneration should motivate the directors to focus on the long-term growth of the business, however, annual targets can encourage short-term strategies rather than maximising shareholder wealth.	The remuneration of executives should be restructured to include a significant proportion based on long-term company performance. For example, executives could be granted share options, as this would encourage focus on the longer term position.
The chairman has sole responsibility for liaising with the shareholders and answering any of their questions. However, this is a role which the board as a whole should undertake.	All members of the board should be involved in ensuring that satisfactory dialogue takes place with shareholders, for example, all should attend meetings with shareholders such as the annual general meeting. The board should state in the annual report the steps they have taken to ensure that the members of the board, and in particular the non-executive directors, develop an understanding of the views of major shareholders about the company.

Question 17

Workbook references. Chapter 6.

Top tips. Part (a), on materiality and performance materiality, involved an element of recall. The more difficult marks were for the explanation, particularly of performance materiality, but you should be aiming to score at least three marks on a requirement like this.

Part (b) was an application-based requirement. It is essential that you only include eight audit risks in your solution; the 16 marks available divide themselves into one each for describing the audit risk and then for the auditor's response to it. Your description of the audit risk should say what is happening and then, crucially, why this poses an audit risk. This statement of why could address a problem that could be encountered during the audit (eg due to lack of available information), or simply which balances could be over or understated. The auditor's response is then focused on reducing the audit risks.

Easy marks. There are marks in (b) for giving a simple description of each audit risk from the scenario (the marks for identification), and these are easy to get.

Examining team's comments. As noted in previous Examining team's Reports a fundamental factor in planning and assessing the risks of an audit of an entity is an assessment of audit risk, and this remains a highly examinable area. Audit risk questions typically require a number of audit risks to be identified (½ marks each), explained (½ marks each) and an auditor's response to each risk (1 mark each). Typically candidates can be required to identify and explain in the region of six to eight risks and responses.

A significant minority of candidates stated the risk was 'under/over stated' when it was clearly one or the other. They were not awarded credit and this scattergun approach is not recommended. Additionally, candidates must state the specific area of the financial statements impacted, as opposed to a general statement. As an example, a significant loss on disposal is indicative of an inappropriate depreciation policy resulting in 'property, plant and equipment being overstated or depreciation being understated'. No credit would be awarded just for stating 'assets are overstated' or 'profit is overstated'.

An auditor's response does not have to be a detailed audit procedure, rather an approach the audit team will take to address the identified risk. In common with previous sessions, auditor responses were sometimes too weak e.g. 'discuss with management' or 'obtain a breakdown and confirm it is reasonable'. In addition, it was noted that some candidates focussed on what management should do rather than the auditor, and/or, gave responses that were inappropriate to the scenario. For example, in this session a company had encountered significant fraud in its warehouse, some candidates recommended that 'the company install CCTV cameras'. This is an inappropriate auditor response and so would have gained no marks as it addresses the issue from the perspective of the company and not the audit. 'Peony Co' from the 'Sample March/June 2019 Questions' is a good scenario based question on audit risks and responses to practise.

Marking scheme

		Marks
(a)	Materiality and performance materiality	
	Materiality definition	1
	Material due to size or nature	1
	Materiality benchmarks	1
	Depends on judgement and risk	1
	Performance materiality definition	1
	Used for testing individual balances	1
	Set at lower level than materiality	1
	Restricted to	4

(b)   Audit risks and responses (only 8 required)

Reliance on internal audit – increased detection risk	2
Unusual movement in margins	2
Inventory valuation policy	2
Perpetual inventory system	2
Obsolete PPE	2
Advertising expenditure	2
Use of payroll service organisation	2
Transfer of data to service organisation	2
Bank loan	2
Redundancy plan	2
Max 8 issues, 2 marks each	16
Total marks	**20**

(a)   **Materiality and performance materiality**

Materiality and performance materiality are dealt with under ISA 320 *Materiality in Planning and Performing an Audit*. Auditors need to establish the materiality level for the financial statements as a whole, as well as assess performance materiality levels, which are lower than the overall materiality for the financial statements as a whole.

Materiality

Materiality is defined in ISA 320 as follows: 'Misstatements, including omissions, are considered to be material if they, individually or in the aggregate, could reasonably be expected to influence the economic decisions of users taken on the basis of the financial statements.'

If the financial statements include a material misstatement, then they will not present fairly (give a true and fair view) the position, performance and cash flows of the entity.

A misstatement may be considered material due to its size (quantitative) and/or due to its nature (qualitative) or a combination of both. The quantitative nature of a misstatement refers to its relative size. A misstatement which is material due to its nature refers to an amount which might be low in value but due to its prominence and relevance could influence the user's decision, for example, directors' transactions.

As per ISA 320, materiality is often calculated using benchmarks such as 5% of profit before tax or 1% of total revenue or total assets. These values are useful as a starting point for assessing materiality, however, the assessment of what is material is ultimately a matter of the auditor's professional judgement. It is affected by the auditor's perception of the financial information, the needs of the users of the financial statements and the perceived level of risk; the higher the risk, the lower the level of overall materiality.

In assessing materiality, the auditor must consider that a number of errors each with a low value may, when aggregated, amount to a material misstatement.

Performance materiality

Performance materiality is defined in ISA 320 as follows: 'The amount set by the auditor at less than materiality for the financial statements as a whole to reduce to an appropriately low level the probability that the aggregate of uncorrected and undetected misstatements exceeds materiality for the financial statements as a whole.'

Hence performance materiality is set at a level lower than overall materiality for the financial statements as a whole. It is used for testing individual transactions, account balances and disclosures. The aim of performance materiality is to reduce the risk that the total of all of the errors in balances, transactions and disclosures exceeds overall materiality.

(b)   Audit risks and auditor's response

Audit risk	Auditor's response
The external audit team may place reliance on the controls testing work undertaken by the IA department. If reliance is placed on irrelevant or poorly performed testing, then the external audit team may form an incorrect conclusion on the strength of the internal controls at Peony Co. This could result in them performing insufficient levels of substantive testing, thereby increasing detection risk.	The external audit team should meet with IA staff, read their reports and review their files relating to store visits to ascertain the nature of the work undertaken. Before using the work of IA, the audit team will need to evaluate and perform audit procedures on the entirety of the work which they plan to use, in order to determine its adequacy for the purposes of the audit. In addition, the team will need to re-perform some of the testing carried out by IA to assess its adequacy.
Forecast ratios from the finance director show that the gross margin is expected to increase from 56% to 60% and the operating margin is expected to decrease from 21% to 18%. This movement in gross margin is significant and inconsistent with the fall in operating margin. There is a risk that costs may have been omitted or included in operating expenses rather than cost of sales. Misclassification of expenses would result in understatement of cost of sales and overstatement of operating expenses.	The classification of costs between cost of sales and operating expenses should be reviewed in comparison to the prior year and any inconsistencies investigated.
Peony Co's inventory valuation policy is selling price less average profit margin, as this is industry practice. Inventory should be valued at the lower of cost and net realisable value (NRV). IAS 2 Inventories allows this as a cost calculation method as long as it is a close approximation to cost. If this is not the case, then inventory could be under or overvalued.	Testing should be undertaken to confirm cost and NRV of inventory and that on a line-by-line basis the goods are valued correctly. In addition, valuation testing should focus on comparing the cost of inventory to the selling price less margin for a sample of items to confirm whether this method is actually a close approximation to cost.

Audit risk	Auditor's response
The company utilises a perpetual inventory system at its warehouse rather than a full year-end count. Under such a system, all inventory must be counted at least once a year with adjustments made to the inventory records on a timely basis. Inventory could be under or overstated if the perpetual inventory counts are not all completed, such that some inventory lines are not counted in the year. During the interim audit, it was noted that there were significant exceptions with the inventory records being higher than the inventory in the warehouse. As the year-end quantities will be based on the records, this is likely to result in overstated inventory.	The timetable of the perpetual inventory counts should be reviewed and the controls over the counts and adjustments to records should be tested. In addition, the level of adjustments made to inventory should be considered to assess their significance. This should be discussed with management as soon as possible as it may not be possible to place reliance on the inventory records at the year end, which could result in the requirement for a full year-end inventory count.
A number of assets which had not been fully depreciated were identified as being obsolete. This is an indication that the company's depreciation policy of non-current assets may not be appropriate, as depreciation in the past appears to have been understated. If an asset is obsolete, it should be written off to the statement of profit or loss. Therefore depreciation may be understated and profit and assets overstated.	Discuss the depreciation policy for non-current assets with the finance director and assess its reasonableness. Enquire of the finance director if the obsolete assets have been written off. If so, review the adjustment for completeness.
Peony Co is planning to include a current asset of $0·7m, which relates to advertising costs incurred and adverts shown on TV before the year end. The costs were incurred and adverts shown in the year ending 20X5 and there is no basis for including them as a current asset at the year end. The costs should be recognised in operating expenses in the current year financial statements. If these costs are not expensed, current assets and profits will be overstated.	Discuss with management the rationale for including the advertising as a current asset. Request evidence to support the assessment of probable future cash flows, and review for reasonableness. Review supporting documentation for the advertisements to confirm that all were shown before the 20X5 year end. Request that management remove the current asset and record the amount as an expense in the statement of profit or loss.
During the year, Peony Co outsourced its payroll function to an external service organisation. A detection risk arises as to whether sufficient and appropriate evidence is available at Peony Co to confirm the completeness and accuracy of controls over the payroll cycle and liabilities at the year end.	Discuss with management the extent of records maintained at Peony Co for the period since January 20X5 and any monitoring of controls which has been undertaken by management over payroll. Consideration should be given to contacting the service organisation's auditor to confirm the level of controls in place, a type 1 or type 2 report could be requested.

Audit risk	Auditor's response
The payroll function was transferred to the service organisation from 1 January 20X5, which is five months prior to the year end. If any errors occurred during the transfer process, these could result in wages and salaries being under/overstated.	Discuss with management the transfer process undertaken and any controls which were put in place to ensure the completeness and accuracy of the data. Where possible, undertake tests of controls to confirm the effectiveness of the transfer controls. In addition, perform substantive testing on the transfer of information from the old to the new system.
A $3m loan was obtained in March 20X5. This finance needs to be accounted for correctly, with adequate disclosure made. The loan needs to be allocated between non-current and current liabilities. Failure to classify the loan correctly could result in misclassified liabilities.	Re-perform the company's calculations to confirm that the split of the loan note is correct between non-current and current liabilities and that total financing proceeds of $3m were received. In addition, the disclosures for this loan note should be reviewed in detail to ensure compliance with relevant accounting standards.
Peony Co is planning to make approximately 60 employees redundant after the year end. The timing of this announcement has not been confirmed; if it is announced to the staff before the year end, then under IAS 37 *Provisions, Contingent Liabilities and Contingent Assets*, a redundancy provision will be required at the year end as a constructive obligation will have been created. Failure to provide or to provide an appropriate amount will result in an understatement of provisions and expenses.	Discuss with management the status of the redundancy announcement; if before the year end, review supporting documentation to confirm the timing. In addition, review the basis of and recalculate the redundancy provision.

Question 18

Workbook references. Chapters 12, 13, 16 and 19.

Top tips. Part (a) of this question covered substantive procedures in relation to inventory, this time focusing only on the valuation assertion. It should be obvious, but this means that there are no marks for procedures that relate to any other assertions.

Parts (b) and (c) also cover substantive procedures – in relation to research and development expenditure and the sales tax liability respectively – but here no assertion is specified. This makes these requirements easier. With all of the parts (a) to (c), you can approach the question by reading the scenario with the requirements in mind, allowing the issues in the situation to trigger your knowledge of procedures, which you can then tailor to this specific question.

Part (d) featured a subsequent non-adjusting event. As long as you knew the material here then part (i) should have been a nice source of marks, with part (ii) asking for yet more procedures.

Easy marks. Part (d) was likely to have been the easiest part of the question.

BPP
LEARNING
MEDIA

ANSWERS

ANSWERS

BPP
LEARNING
MEDIA

Answers **453**

Marking scheme

		Marks
(a)	Substantive procedures – valuation of inventory	
	Agree percentage completion recorded at inventory count to final inventory records	1
	Confirm costs to invoice/timesheets	1
	Inspect post year-end sales invoices for finished goods to assess NRV	1
	Discuss basis of WIP valuation with management	1
	Inspect WIP valuation with sales prices less costs to complete	1
	Review aged inventory reports and discuss allowance	1
	Discuss with management basis of valuation for Crocus products	1
	Inspect post year-end sales value of Crocus products	1
	Confirm adjustment regarding Crocus products	_1_
	Restricted to	_6_
(b)	Substantive procedures – R&D expenditure	
	Obtain schedule, cast and agree to trial balance	1
	Review reasonableness of useful lives	1
	Recalculate amortisation and confirm in line with policy	1
	Discuss with management treatment of costs for new products	1
	Agree research costs expensed	1
	For capitalised costs, confirm IAS 38 criteria met	1
	Inspect budgets to confirm adequate resources to complete	1
	Review disclosure and confirm in line with accounting standards	_1_

Restricted to $\underline{\underline{4}}$

(c) Substantive procedures – accrual for sales tax liability

Obtain schedule/return, cast and agree to trial balance | 1

Recalculate sales tax in relation to sales and agree to return | 1

Recalculate sales tax in relation to purchases and agree to return | 1

Recalculate overall amount due to tax authority | 1

Compare liability to prior year end, investigate differences | 1

Confirm payment to post year-end cashbook and bank statements | 1

Review correspondence with the tax authority for evidence of additional liability | 1

Review disclosure and confirm in line with IAS 37 | $\underline{1}$

Restricted to | $\underline{4}$

(d) Subsequent event

Discussion of amendment | 3

Audit procedures | $\underline{3}$

Total marks | $\underline{\underline{6}}$

(a) **Inventory valuation**

- Obtain the breakdown of WIP and agree a sample of WIP assessed during the inventory count to the WIP schedule, agreeing the percentage completion to that recorded at the inventory count.

- For a sample of inventory items (finished goods and WIP), obtain the relevant cost sheets and agree raw material costs to recent purchase invoices, labour costs to time sheets or payroll records and confirm overheads allocated are of a production related nature.

- Examine post year-end credit notes to determine whether there have been returns which could signify that a write down is required.

- Select a sample of year-end finished goods and compare cost with post year-end sales invoices to ascertain if net realisable value (NRV) is above cost or if an adjustment is required.

- Discuss the basis of WIP valuation with management and assess its reasonableness.

- Select a sample of items included in WIP at the year end and ascertain the final unit cost price by verifying costs to be incurred to completion to relevant supporting documentation. Compare to the unit sales price included in sales invoices post year-end to assess NRV

- Review aged inventory reports and identify any slow moving goods, discuss with management why these items have not been written down or if an allowance is required.

- For the defective batch of product Crocus, review board minutes and discuss with management their plans for selling these goods, and why they believe these goods have a NRV of $90,000.

BPP
LEARNING
MEDIA

- If any Crocus products have been sold post year end, review the sales invoice to assess NRV.

- Agree the cost of $450,000 for product Crocus to supporting documentation to confirm the raw material cost, labour cost and any overheads attributed to the cost.

- Confirm if the final adjustment for the damaged product is $360,000 ($450,000 – $90,000) and discuss with management if this adjustment has been made. If so, follow through the write down to confirm.

(b) Research and development

- Obtain and cast a schedule of intangible assets, agree the closing balances to the general ledger, trial balance and draft financial statements.

- Discuss with the finance director the rationale for the four-year useful life and consider its reasonableness.

- Recalculate the amortisation charge for a sample of intangible assets which have commenced production and confirm that it is in line with the amortisation policy of straight line over four years and that amortisation only commenced from the point of production.

- For the three new computing software projects, discuss with management the details of each project along with the stage of development and whether it has been capitalised or expensed.

- For those expensed as research, agree the costs incurred to invoices and supporting documentation and to inclusion in profit or loss.

- For those capitalised as development, agree costs incurred to invoices.

- Confirm technically feasible and intention to complete the project by discussion with development managers or review of feasibility reports.

- Review market research reports to confirm Hyacinth Co has the ability to sell the product once complete and probable future economic benefits will arise.

- Review the costs, projected revenue and cash flow budgets for the each of the three projects to confirm Hyacinth Co has adequate resources to complete the development stage and that probable future economic benefits exist. Agree the budgets to supporting documentation.

- Review the disclosures for intangible assets in the draft financial statements to verify that they are in accordance with IAS 38 *Intangible Assets*.

(c) Sales tax liability

- Agree the year-end sales tax liability in the trial balance to the tax return/reconciliation submitted to the tax authority and cast the return/reconciliation.

- Agree the quarterly sales tax charged equates to 15% of the last quarter's sales as per the sales day book.

- Recalculate the sales tax incurred as per the reconciliation is equal to 15% of the final quarter's purchases and expenses as per the purchase day book.

- Recalculate the amount payable to the tax authority as being sales tax charged less sales tax incurred.

- Compare the year-end sales tax liability to the prior year balance or budget and investigate any significant differences.

- Agree the subsequent payment to the post year-end cash book and bank statements to confirm completeness and that it has been paid in line with the terms of the tax authority.

- Review any current and post year-end correspondence with the tax authority to assess whether there are any additional outstanding payments due. If so, confirm they are included in the year-end liability.

- Review any disclosures made of the sales tax liability to ensure that it is shown as a current liability and assess whether disclosures are in compliance with accounting standards and legislation.

(d) **Subsequent event**

A flood has occurred at the off-site warehouse and property, plant and equipment and inventory valued at $0.7 million have been damaged and now have no scrap value. The directors do not believe they are likely to be able to claim on the company's insurance for the damaged assets. This event occurred after the reporting period and is not an event which provides evidence of a condition at the year end and so this is a non-adjusting event.

The damaged assets of $0.7 million are material as they represent 10.9% ($0.7m/$6·4m) of profit before tax and 3.0% ($0.7m/$23.2m) of total assets. As a material non-adjusting event, the assets do not need to be written down to zero in this financial year. However, the directors should consider including a disclosure note detailing the flood and the value of assets impacted.

The following audit procedures should be applied to form a conclusion on any amendment:

- Obtain a schedule showing the damaged property, plant and equipment and agree the net book value to the non-current assets register to confirm the total value of affected assets.

- Obtain a schedule of the water damaged inventory, visit the off-site warehouse and physically inspect the impacted inventory. Confirm the quantity of goods present in the warehouse to the schedule; agree the original cost to pre year-end production costs.

- Review the condition of other PPE and inventory to confirm all damaged assets identified.

- Review the damaged property, plant and equipment and inventory and discuss with management the basis for the zero scrap value assessment.

- Discuss with management why they do not believe that they are able to claim on their insurance; if a claim were to be made, then only uninsured losses would require disclosure, and this may be an immaterial amount.

- Discuss with management whether they will disclose the effect of the flood, as a non-adjusting event, in the year-end financial statements.

Notes

BPP
LEARNING
MEDIA

Notes

Review Form – Audit and Assurance (02/20)

Name: _____ Address: _____

_____

_____

How have you used this Kit?
(Tick one box only)

☐ On its own (book only)

☐ On a BPP in-centre course_____

☐ On a BPP online course

☐ On a course with another college

☐ Other _____

Why did you decide to purchase this Kit?
(Tick one box only)

☐ Have used the Workbook

☐ Have used other BPP products in the past

☐ Recommendation by friend/colleague

☐ Recommendation by a lecturer at college

☐ Saw advertising

☐ Other _____

During the past six months do you recall seeing/receiving any of the following?
(Tick as many boxes as are relevant)

☐ Our advertisement in *Student Accountant*

☐ Our advertisement in *Pass*

☐ Our advertisement in *PQ*

☐ Our brochure with a letter through the post

☐ Our website www.bpp.com

Which (if any) aspects of our advertising do you find useful?
(Tick as many boxes as are relevant)

☐ Prices and publication dates of new editions

☐ Information on product content

☐ Facility to order books

☐ None of the above

Which BPP products have you used?

Workbook ☐		*Other* ☐
Practice & Revision Kit ☑		

Your ratings, comments and suggestions would be appreciated on the following areas.

	Very useful	Useful	Not useful
Passing AA			
Questions			
Top Tips etc in answers			
Content and structure of answers			
Mock exam answers			

Overall opinion of this Practice & Revision Kit   Excellent ☐   Good ☐   Adequate ☐   Poor ☐

Do you intend to continue using BPP products?   Yes ☐   No ☐

The BPP author of this edition can be emailed at: learningmedia@bpp.com

Review Form (continued)

TELL US WHAT YOU THINK

Please note any further comments and suggestions/errors below.